THE MYSTICAL ELEMENT IN THE METAPHYSICAL POETS OF THE SEVENTEENTH CENTURY

THE MYSTICAL ELEMENT IN THE
METAPHYSICAL POETS
OF THE SEVENTEENTH CENTURY

By

ITRAT-HUSAIN, M.A., Ph.D. (Edinburgh)

SOMETIME SENIOR CARNEGIE RESEARCH SCHOLAR IN ENGLISH,
EDINBURGH UNIVERSITY
FELLOW OF THE CALCUTTA UNIVERSITY
PROFESSOR OF ENGLISH AND PRINCIPAL, ISLAMIA COLLEGE, CALCUTTA

BIBLO and TANNEN
NEW YORK
1 9 6 6

Originally published, 1948
Reprinted by
BIBLO and TANNEN
BOOKSELLERS and PUBLISHERS, Inc.
63 Fourth Avenue   New York, N.Y. 10003

Library of Congress Catalog Card Number: 66-23522

Printed in U.S.A. by
NOBLE OFFSET PRINTERS, INC.
NEW YORK 3, N. Y.

FOREWORD

By Evelyn Underhill

This long and elaborate treatise consists of an introductory chapter on mysticism in general, followed by detailed studies of Donne, Herbert, Crashaw, Henry and Thomas Vaughan and Traherne. The author's general purpose appears to be to establish the amount of personal spiritual experience which lies behind the work of these poets. The whole of the relevant literature seems to have been examined, and the treatise as a whole is a monument of industry and research; and on several points original conclusions of real value have been arrived at.

In the first chapter, on the general characteristics of mysticism, Mr. Husain's use of his authorities is painstaking, and the last four pages on the relation between mysticism and poetry are excellent. In the discussion of the poets the writer is equally at home in poetry or mystical theology and the doctrines and experiences of the medieval contemplatives. The chapter on Donne is a really interesting and constructive piece of criticism, based on very wide reading, and successfully demonstrates, over against Miss Ramsay and other critics, Donne's emancipation from the scholasticism in which he had been reared, his mystical and anti-intellectual religious outlook, and the width, suppleness and originality of his mind.

The study of Vaughan is equally good and brings out the peculiar qualities of his spirituality and the degree of experience which appears to be implied in his poems; whilst escaping the temptation to prove too much by assuming that every apparently personal passage describes a personal experience. His conclusion that Vaughan's greatest poems celebrate the "state of illumination," but that there is no evidence that he attained to the "Unitive life" during his literary period, seems to me to be sound.

The chapter on Herbert also reaches a high level; with real skill he has traced Herbert's spiritual evolution in his writings. I think that he is right, over against Palmer, in his view of the real nature of the crisis revealed in the Bemerton poems; and his analysis, well supported by reference to the mystics, has real value.

In his chapter on Crashaw, Mr. Husain has tried to describe the peculiar brand of Catholic piety and estimate the sublimated eroticism which plays so large a part in these poems. He has successfully shown over against Crashaw's critics like Gosse, Courthope, and Canon Beeching that there is nothing exotic in the erotic imagery which plays so large a part in his poems. It is based on the symbolism derived from the Spanish mysticism especially of St. Teresa. He has rightly pointed out that "ecstasy" and "abandonment" and the "rapture" or "flight of the spirit" in Crashaw's poems are not really *literary devices* or religious moods of exalted sensibility, but expressions of rare *mystical states*. Mr. Husain has given parallel quotations from St. Teresa to illustrate the truth of this observation. It is not the concept of a particular literary form that determines the experience of Crashaw, but, as in the case of the saints, it is the nature of his mystical experience that predetermines the matter to a particular form. I agree with him in regarding Crashaw as a devotee rather than a mystic; but the other view, strongly put by Mr. E. I. Watkin, deserves consideration. The chapter on Traherne as a Christian Platonist is well and carefully done.

Mr. Husain's scholarly work on Donne [1] has already won recognition by eminent critics like Sir Herbert Grierson and the Rev. Dr. James Moffatt, and by this distinctly meritorious work he is sure to establish his reputation as a sound and scholarly critic of the poets of the seventeenth century.

[1] This refers to *The Dogmatic and Mystical Theology of John Donne* (S.P.C.K., London, 1938) by Itrat-Husain.

CONTENTS

INTRODUCTION

In this study of the metaphysical poets of the seventeenth century I carry a step further the method I employed in the interpretation of *The Dogmatic and Mystical Theology of John Donne* (S.P.C.K., London, 1938). It was gratifying to note that my elucidation and exposition of Donne's theology gained the approval of such eminent critics as Sir Herbert Grierson and Dr. James Moffatt.[1] I had tried to place Donne, the Anglican, in the main tradition of the Reformed Church which was based on the *via media* of the Elizabethan establishment by comparing his thought with that of Hooker, Bishop Andrewes, Laud and others. I have now attempted to estimate the nature and character of the mystical element in the metaphysical poets by comparing them with the Christian mystics of the Medieval and Renaissance times.

I did not hazard the study of the metaphysical poets in a hurry, but tried to understand the complex content of their poetic and religious thought over a period of ten years; and the full understanding came only when I had grasped the significance of the cross-currents of the religio-social, political and theological thought of the Elizabethan and Jacobean ages. It was by no means an easy process, for the seventeenth century was a complex and troubled age; the spirit of the Renaissance which had flowered in the knightly and chivalrous poetry of Sidney and Spenser had soon to face the religious and political passions aroused by the Reformation; and later on the ardour and exaltation of the Counter-Reformation deeply influenced the minds of such diverse men as Nicholas Ferrar, Richard Crashaw and Lancelot Andrewes, who valued the continuity of the tradition of the Catholic Church (following Donne, I

---

[1] Sir Herbert Grierson said in his Preface, "My impression is that Mr. Husain has established his main contention, viz. that Donne was in all his explicit statements on dogmas and practice an orthodox Anglican, completely."

Dr. James Moffatt (*The Hibbert Journal*, July 1938), "The Indian scholar, with striking thoroughness, exhibits two qualities in Donne's religious writings; one is the homogeneity of his mind, and the other is its honesty—meaning that Donne did not defend his creed as a mere advocate but with genuine conviction."

will not call it Roman).[1]   I had to study not only the political
and the religious background of the age, which together make
its historical consciousness, but also the theological thought,
controversial and otherwise, of the Reformed and Roman
churches, some understanding and knowledge of which I had
utilized in my study of Donne's theology.   I believe that these
poets cannot be criticized on purely literary grounds; one has
to take into consideration their theological beliefs and the
mystical traditions which have roots in the rich and diverse
lives of the saints of the Catholic Church.[2]   Criticism which
does not take into account the vital and real element of
theological dogma in the spiritual life of the sixteenth and
seventeenth centuries is likely to lead to facile generalizations.
Speaking of the Renaissance, John Masefield has remarked
that the imagination of man "overflowed the moulds of the
worlds of mind.   Those moulds, both of Church and State,
were broken.   Both by knowledge and imagination, the
world's mind had grown bigger; it needed a larger scheme in
which it could believe." [3]   The mind of man had not in fact
grown so big that the sublimity of the spacious Catholic Church
could not satisfy it, it had really grown so narrow, as in our
own times, through sin and over-estimation of individual
wisdom, that it failed to realize the largeness of the Church;
it found its spiritual home in the life of sects, or the narrow
doctrines of Calvinism.

Donne had realized the "littleness" of man; in one of his
sermons he declared that considered apart from God "Man
is so much less than a worm" [4]; it is in God alone that Man
discovers the fullness of his personality, for "to this man
comes this God, God that is infinitely more than all, to man
that is infinitely less than nothing." [4]

The proud and haughty intellectual independence of the
Renaissance as exemplified in Marlowe's *Tamburlaine* and
Faust and Webster's *Bosola* was over; men such as these

[1] To Donne the Church "Where all things necessary for salvation are
administered to thee, and where no erroneous doctrine is affirmed and held—
that is the Catholic Church."—*LXXX Sermons*, No. 76.
[2] The metaphysical poets provide a fine illustration of T. S. Eliot's dictum that
"Literary criticism should be completed by criticism from a definite and theological
standpoint."—*Essays, Ancient and Modern*, p. 93.
[3] *Shakespeare and Spiritual Life*, by John Masefield (Oxford, 1924).
[4] *LXXX Sermons*, No. 7.

metaphysical poets had again to discover through prayer, meditation and the agony of purgation that Man's life, when divorced from God, becomes barren, and in such a waste-land only scepticism, self-torture and bitterness grow and thrive. It is not easy for us to-day, particularly for a person belonging to an alien tradition, to enter fully into the national life of the past ages, especially that of the Elizabethan and Jacobean times, for the contradictions and complexities of the age baffle us at every step.   Lytton Strachey has truly observed, "Human beings, no doubt, would cease to be human beings unless they were inconsistent, but the inconsistency of the Elizabethans exceeds the limits permitted to man.   Their elements fly off one another wildly; we seize them; we struggle hard to shake them together into a single compound, and the retort bursts. How is it possible to give a coherent account of their subtlety and their naïveté, their delicacy and their brutality, their piety and their lust?   Wherever we look, it is the same.   By what perverse magic were intellectual ingenuity and theo-logical ingenuousness intertwined in John Donne?   Who has ever explained Bacon?" [1]

Apart from the difficulty of recovering the sensibility of a great epoch, there is also the problem of "belief."   There can be "no complete severance," as I. A. Richards holds,[2] between the "beliefs" of a poet and the product of his creative imagina-tion, poetry; for "belief" [3] on the plane of devotional life also requires imaginative comprehension.   Coleridge, discuss-ing George Herbert as the poet of the Anglican Church, remarked, "To appreciate this volume [*The Temple*], it is not enough that the reader possess a cultivated judgement, classical taste, or even poetic sensibility, unless he be likewise a Christian, and both a zealous and an orthodox, both a devout and devotional, Christian.   But even this will not suffice.   He must be an affectionate and dutiful child of the Church."   I can say from my own personal experience that Coleridge has exaggerated the *difficulty* of appreciating devotional poetry such as that of Herbert, which is based on the intense and

[1] *Elizabeth and Essex*, p. 9.
[2] *Science and Poetry*, by I. A. Richards, p. 76.
[3] For example, the belief in the Incarnation and the Crucifixion is, to a mystic, an act of creative understanding and imagination, and not merely a matter of intellectual assent or doctrinal acceptance.

living faith in the doctrine, tradition and life of the Anglican Church. One need not belong to the faith or share "the belief" of Herbert to appreciate *The Temple*, but the reader must possess the capacity of sympathetic entrance into the minds of great devotional poets and be willing to judge them by *their* own ethical and theological standards. Herbert cannot be judged from the standpoint of Buddhist or Islamic theology, nor can he be appreciated on the basis of Marxist socialism; so what is required is an "identification of self"; by which I mean that the reader should identify himself with the "poetic self" of Herbert, or Crashaw, or any other poet; the "poetic self" here includes all those "beliefs" which have become a *part* of the *imagination* of the poet, as the philosophy of St. Thomas Aquinas had become an integral part of the creative imagination of Dante.

T. S. Eliot has remarked, "I deny that the reader must share the beliefs of the poet in order to enjoy the poetry fully. I have also asserted that we can distinguish between Dante's beliefs as a man and his belief as a poet. . . . If you deny the theory that full poetic appreciation is possible without belief in what the poet believed, you deny the existence of 'poetry' as well as 'criticism'; and if you push this denial to its conclusion, you will be forced to admit that there is very little poetry that you can appreciate and that your appreciation of it will be a function of your Philosophy or Theology or something else." [1] I do not know what exactly Mr. Eliot means by "share"; but I hold that the reader need not *accept* the beliefs of the poet (we need not have "belief" in witches or ghosts to enjoy *Macbeth* or *Hamlet*), but he must *share imaginatively* Herbert's *belief* in the Incarnation or Dante's *belief* in the Thomist philosophy. But this "sharing" need not last after you have closed *The Temple* or *The Divine Comedy*. This process may negatively be called, in the words of Coleridge, "suspension of disbelief"; but it is much more, for it is a *positive sharing* through our imagination of the *beliefs* which

---

[1] T. S. Eliot's essay on *Dante* (Note to Section II), "The Purgatorio and The Paradiso." By sharing, I mean imaginative assent. For me "poetic self" is an indivisible entity, and all that becomes a *part* of the poetic imagination, whether a belief in the Philosophy of St. Thomas Aquinas or Hermes Trismegistus, or even witches (as in Shakespeare), or belief in the reality of the Incarnation and Crucifixion, constitutes the poetic self, and requires the "identification" of the reader with this self.

have become a *part* of the poetic self of Herbert or Dante.[1]
I have described briefly and crudely the *process* of my own
understanding of these devotional poets; this may not be valid
for others more gifted than myself.

The reading of John Donne was a revelation to me, and it
was the intellectual discipline which is necessary to understand his poetry, and the origins of his poetic and theological
ideas, that enabled me to study with comparative ease the
other metaphysical poets who belong to the Donnean tradition.

I have tried to estimate the *content* [2] of the religious thought
of these poets in order to determine the nature and significance
of the mystical element in their poetry, and have compared
their mystical life as revealed in their poetry with that of such
great Christian mystics as St. Augustine, St. Bernard, St. John
of the Cross, St. Teresa and others, for they constitute the
classical and authentic tradition of Christian mysticism.

These metaphysical poets, unlike Wordsworth or Shelley,
were *Christian* mystics, for they were either priests like Donne,
Herbert or Crashaw, or like Vaughan declared their allegiance
in no uncertain terms to their Mother Church. They con-
sciously or unconsciously shared the life of the Catholic Church
(either Roman or Anglican) and they have many points of
contact with the saints of the Middle Ages and Renaissance;
moreover, as Evelyn Underhill has pointed out,[3] *Christ* alone
is the fountainhead of all mystical life and thought and
He dieth not, as He is *reborn* in the soul of every Christian
mystic. The mystical experience of such great saints as St.
Bernard or St. John of the Cross can alone serve as a safe and
orthodox standard by which we may measure the success
achieved by these poets on the Mystic Way; it is in fact the
mystical experience of the saints which alone can help us in
understanding the nature of the mystical life of these poets
as unfolded in their poetry and not *vice versa*.

In these troubled times, when society is in the melting-pot

[1] We need not inquire whether such "beliefs" are "artistic," as was perhaps
Shakespeare's "belief" in ghosts, witches, and fairies, or whether they are
"religious *beliefs*" like those of Herbert and Dante.

[2] When, in order to understand Donne, I read the *Summa Theologica* and *Summa
Contra Gentiles* of St. Thomas Aquinas, I soon realized that I had come in contact
with an intellect of the utmost keenness and force, alive at every point with a
buoyant and intense vitality the like of which was nowhere to be found.

[3] In *The Mystic Way*.

and England's leaders declare that she had waged war for the preservation of European civilization, let the essentially Christian life of these English poets of the seventeenth century remind their fellow-countrymen to-day that European civilization can only be rebuilt on the rock of the Catholic Church as Donne understood it.   The *Summa* of human effort has again to be dedicated to God.   Donne declared: "The Church loves the name of catholique, and wherein she is harmonious, that is those universal and fundamental doctrines which in all Christian ages, in all Christian churches have been agreed by all to be necessary to salvation, and then thou art a true Catholique.   Otherwise, that is, without relation to this Catholique and universal doctrine, to call a particular Church catholique (that is, universal in dominion, but not in doctrine) is such a solecisme, as to speak of 'a white blacknesse, or a great littlenesse.   A particular Church to be universal, implies such a contradiction." [1]

T. S. Eliot also urges the necessity of a Christian society organized under the fold of the Catholic Church, which does not exclude the existence of national churches, "However bigoted the announcement may sound, the Christian can be satisfied with nothing less than a Christian organization of society, which is not the same thing as a society consisting exclusively of devout Christians." [2]

The Christian society which consists both of the clergy and laity should be organized into a visible church, but this national church must stand in a vital relation to the universal Catholic Church.   "It must be kept in mind that even in a Christian society as well organized as we can conceive possible in this world, the limit would be that our temporal and spiritual life should be harmonized; the temporal and the spiritual world would never be identified.   There would always remain a dual allegiance to the State and to the Church, to one's countrymen and to one's fellow-Christians everywhere, and the latter would always have the primacy." [3]

Donne urged the necessity of the visible Church not only on the ground of ordered living, and of establishing a just relation between the spiritual life as represented by the Church

[1] *LXXX Sermons*, No. 71.
[2] *The Idea of a Christian Society*, by T. S. Eliot, p. 34 (4th edition).   [3] *Ibid.*

and the temporal world as constituted by the State (there is, however, no such *conscious* dualism in his thought), but because *Christ is always with the Church*, while His presence in the individual soul is not felt as a permanent possession due to the sinfulness of man. He also justifies the union of the Church and State on the plea that it would minimize the growth of schism and dissension.

"The principal fraternity and brotherhood that God respects is spiritual; brethren in the profession of the same true religion, . . . and that God loves; that a natural, a secular, a civil fraternity, and a spiritual fraternity should be joined together. . . . God saw a better likelihood of avoiding schism and dissension, when those whom he called to a new spiritual brotherhood in one Religion, were natural brothers too; and tied in civil bonds as well as spiritual." [1]

But the organization of the Church was essentially a spiritual necessity, for, as Donne has said, the "grace" of Christ in the individual soul could never become a lasting possession, "he comes and he knocks, and he enters, and he stayes and he sups and yet for their [men's] unworthinesse goes away again," but he is ever present with His Church:

"He keeps us not in fear of *Resumption*; for ever taking himself from the Church again; nay he hath left himself no power of Revocation; I am *with you*, says he, to the end of the world." [2]

Donne and Eliot both conceive an essentially Christian society organized within the fold of a visible national Church, joined in a "spiritual fraternity" with the State, and having

[1] *LXXX Sermons*, No. 71.

[2] *L Sermons*. I have read with much instruction and pleasure Mr. Middleton Murry's lucid and thoughtful chapter on Rousseau (in *Heaven and Earth*); but Rousseau's conception, or rather vision, of society was not in any sense Christian, in spite of his emphasis (like Plato) on ethical will in society. Even a Rousseauist like Mr. Murry confesses that Rousseau believed in such a profound improvement in society that it was enough "to relieve men of the need or the necessity of looking exclusively to another order of existence to have their hearts' desire fulfilled" (p. 188). Mr. Murry is obviously unjust to the Catholic Church when he says that it believed in a different order of existence (supernatural as distinguished from temporal) because it held that things were "pretty bad" and there was no chance of "radical improvement" in the present order of society. Mr. Murry seems to have imperfectly understood the Catholic doctrine of "grace," which teaches us that without Christ's grace, and without his rebirth in the human soul, man cannot achieve "newness" in life; the social improvement was therefore a problem of the reorientation of human personality, and not only a problem, as Rousseau held, of how to secure that "the general will" should be truly expressed and obeyed, because the Christian holds that the "general will," unless it is informed and aided by the divine grace, cannot really express its desire for good.

a larger vision of Christendom by ever striving to unite all the Christian churches under one Universal Catholic Church. It is such a conception of society which should quicken the vision of those who have been called upon to build on the débris of a Europe which is trying to discover the inner unity of her life again.

I do not agree with thinkers like Sir Radha Krishnan that we should strive for a synthesis of the great religions of the world on the ground that the *germ* of such a unity is already present in the universality of mystical experiences, for each religion, like Christianity and Islam, has grown within its distinctive traditions, and has a distinguishing climate of thought. If civilization in Europe is to survive and rest on a secure foundation it can only be as a *Christian* civilization, and Europe can truly subsist as Christendom within the fold of a traditional Catholic Church alone, that is, in conscious relation to a spiritual order of being; and Man as well as State shall have to give up the Renaissance conception of the sovereign autonomy of self which was developed under the false lure of the Liberal and Naturalistic philosophy of Rousseau and the other heretics of the French Revolution.

The life and experience of these seventeenth-century devotional poets can at least be of *some* help to their fellow-countrymen, for theirs was an age similar to our own in its agony of civil war and confusion and chaos in the life of the State and Church.[1] It is only through the re-entering of Christ into the consciousness of Europe that men will realize again the fullness of their life. As St. Augustine declared in his *Confessions*, "When I shall cleave to thee [Christ] with all my being, then shall I in nothing have pain and labour, and my life shall be a real life, being wholly full of Thee."

It was a rare privilege for me to have worked under Sir Herbert Grierson, for there is no scholar in England or on the Continent who has a better understanding of the life, poetry, and thought of seventeenth-century English literature. I am

---

[1] Henry Vaughan also expresses the tortured agony of the present generation when he says, "Arise, O God, and let thine enemies be scattered, and let those that hate thee flee before thee. Behold the robbers are come into thy sanctuary, and the persecuters are within thy walls, our necks are under persecution, we labour and have no rest. Yea, thine own inheritance is given to strangers and thine own portion unto aliens."—*Man in Darkness*, L.C. Martin, vol. i, p. 170.

also indebted to Professor A. E. Taylor for helping me to enter into the *spirit* of medieval theology and philosophy, and without his critical guidance it would have been difficult for me to trace the *ideas* of Donne to their scholastic sources. It is needless to say that, like other men of my generation, I have lived and worked under the spell of Mr. T. S. Eliot's poetry and criticism, for he has not only *deepened* our understanding of the metaphysical poets by his criticism, but has also revealed in his own poetry the richness and significant vitality of the Donnean tradition.

Like other students of seventeenth-century poetry, I have found Professor L. C. Martin's great editions of Richard Crashaw and Henry Vaughan of invaluable help in unravelling the complexities of their thought. Mr. John Sparrow's edition of Donne's *Devotions* and Mr. Geoffrey Keynes' *Bibliography* were also of great help to me. The mystical treatises of Dean Inge and Miss Evelyn Underhill made it easier for me to understand the nature of Christian as distinguished from Islamic or Buddhist mysticism. Miss Evelyn Underhill was kind enough to read the manuscript of this book a few years ago and readily acceded to my request for a short preface. In her we lost a profound critic and interpreter of mysticism and a fine devotional poet. The Trustees of the Carnegie Trust (Scotland) not only awarded me a scholarship to continue the research work embodied in these pages, but have also financed the publication of this book. My debt, therefore, to their generosity is more than can ever be expressed. I am grateful to Dr. Kitchin for making various suggestions and reading the proofs, which must have been an arduous task, and to Mr. Manuj Kumar Chatterjee for preparing the index. I must also thank my wife, Saida, for helping me to revise the text and checking the quotations.

CHAPTER I

THE GENERAL CHARACTERISTICS OF MYSTICISM

(i)

DURING the last forty-five years, since Dean Inge delivered his Bampton Lectures on Christian Mysticism at Oxford in 1899, the various aspects of mysticism have received an ever-increasing attention from literary critics, philosophers and psychologists. The works of scholars like Dean Inge, Baron Von Hügel, Evelyn Underhill, Rufus M. Jones, A. B. Sharp, Dom C. Butler, W. K. Fleming and H. Delacroix, to name only a few, have dealt with nearly every aspect of mystical philosophy and psychology. Dean Inge and Miss Underhill have studied the medieval and modern mystics such as Plotinus, the Blessed Angela of Foligno, Juliana of Norwich, Walter Hylton, William Law, Wordsworth, Robert Browning, and the German mystics like Eckhart, Tauler and Ruysbroeck; but so far no attempt has been made to study the mystical poets of the seventeenth century in a systematic way; the critics and scholars like Sir H. J. C. Grierson, Dr. Jessopp, Sir Edmund Gosse, T. S. Eliot, Mario Praz, George Williamson and Basil Willey [1] have discussed the cross-currents of the philosophical and religious thought of the seventeenth century in relation to the sacred as well as the secular poets of the age, and their learned treatises have proved invaluable to me in understanding the mind and art of the poets as well as the religious, philosophical and social background of this complex period in the history of English literature. I have not studied these poets primarily from the point of view of either mystical philosophy or psychology, though psychology and philosophy have been used to illustrate their thought, and I have also avoided the discussion of the theories of poetic creation of

---

[1] Hodgson in her book *English Mystics* has briefly dealt with these poets, and Rufus M. Jones has included Traherne in his *Spiritual Reformers in the Sixteenth and Seventeenth Centuries*.

scholars like Henri Bremond, [1] who have tried to describe the affinities between mystical experience and poetical inspiration; my aim has been to trace only the mystical element in the metaphysical poets.   In order to determine the nature of the mystical experience of these poets I have compared them with typical Christian mystics like St. Augustine, St. Bernard, St. John of the Cross and others.

It is a significant fact in the history of mysticism, that great epochs of mystical activity have followed the great periods of artistic and intellectual civilization; in the thirteenth century the medieval culture had reached its perfection in religion, philosophy and art; it had already built the Gothic cathedrals, idealized the code of chivalry, and produced the great scholastic philosophers like St. Bonaventura (1221–1274) and St. Thomas Aquinas (1226–1274); while the fourteenth century produced such great mystics as Dante (1265–1321), Meister Eckhart (1260–1329), John Ruysbroeck (1293–1381), Thomas à Kempis (1380–1471), Richard Rolle of Hampole (1300–1349), and Juliana of Norwich (1345—died after 1413).   It is also an important fact that when the Renaissance and Humanism had opened a new epoch in the history of human thought, the great mystics appeared again in the sixteenth and seventeenth centuries; it seems as if at the end and perfection of every great period the mystic "snatches the torch, and carries it on." [2]   The sixteenth and the seventeenth centuries produced such great mystics as St. Ignatius Loyola (1491–1556), St. Teresa (1515–1582), St. John of the Cross (1542–1591), Jacob Boehme (1573–1624).   In the seventeenth century the religious ferment and the ardour of the devotional life in England produced great mystics like George Fox (1524–1690), Gertrude More (1606–1633), Augustine Baker (1575–1641); and the religious life of the century flowered into the devotional and philosophical mysticism of poets like John Donne, George Herbert, Richard Crashaw, Henry Vaughan, Thomas Traherne and Henry More, who belongs to the group of the Cambridge Platonists.   This latter cult includes such men as John Smith, Benjamin Whichcote and John Norris, in whom the mystical tendencies are harmoniously blended with the humanism and

---

[1] *Prayer and Poetry*, by Henri Bremond.   London, 1927.
[2] *Mysticism*, by E. Underhill (London, 1927), p. 50.

piety of the Anglican Church. Though the metaphysical poets and the Cambridge Platonists represent two compact groups, as far as the main religious and philosophical principles and tendencies are concerned, nearly every poet tries to approach mysticism from a different and individual point of view. The definition of mysticism which perhaps applies to all these poets more correctly than any other is that of Rufus M. Jones, who has called it "religion in its most acute, intense and living stage" [1]; but it is a religion in which, as Dr. Moberly says, God "ceases to be an object and becomes an experience." [2]

I have shown that John Donne not only outlived the scepticism of his youth, but also the rationalistic element in the philosophy of St. Thomas, and became a mystic. He tried to approach God through an agonized sense of sin and the realization of the need of purgation and passionate faith in Christ, as the Saviour. Donne's mysticism, in spite of his interest in philosophy and "controverted divinity," is independent of his philosophy; he is mainly interested in the practical, devotional and empirical side of mysticism, the attainment of Illumination, through personal holiness, and the adoration of Christ, His Passion and Crucifixion. Like St. Bernard he tried to "recall devout and loving contemplation to the Image of the crucified Christ." [3] This was, according to Dean Inge, the great achievement of St. Bernard, and this aspect of mysticism greatly influenced Donne. A careful study of George Herbert's poetry shows that the two sides of his religious genius, the institutional and the mystical, were complementary to each other; while his devotion to his Mother Church found satisfaction in the doctrine and ritual of the Church, his mystical temperament was not satisfied with mere ethical discipline or outward conformity, but led him to seek a direct communion with God. He himself has described his poetry as "a picture of the many spiritual conflicts that have passed betwixt God and my soul." [4] His individual experience of God is the matter and theme of his religious poetry; Richard Baxter truly said of him, "He speaks

[1] *Studies in Mystical Religion*, by Rufus M. Jones, 1909.
[2] *Atonement and Personality*, by Dr. Moberly, 1899.
[3] Inge, *Christian Mysticism* (7th edition, 1899), p. 145.
[4] *The English Works of George Herbert*, edited by G. H. Palmer (3rd edition, 1905), p. 171.

of God like a man that really believeth in God." [1] In Crashaw's poetry we find a tone of mystical exaltation and joy in a perfect communion with Christ and His saints, there is however little evidence of his ever having attained a direct vision of God in illumination. I have studied Henry Vaughan as a mystic of the Anglican Church and tried to trace the purgative, illuminative, and unitive stages of mystical life in his poetry, and have also traced the influence of Thomas Vaughan's conception of God and Nature in the poetry of Henry Vaughan. I have studied Thomas Traherne primarily as a philosophical mystic who gave to *love* a peculiar and significant place in his mystical speculations. I have attempted to trace the influence of Plato and Plotinus on Traherne, and shown how, like Goethe, he believed in the unconscious or "child-like" (as Traherne calls it) integration with Nature and then conscious separation from Nature, so that one may concentrate on wisdom, which to him was inseparable from love. Traherne is a philosopher in the ancient sense of being the seeker after "life-wisdom," which he discovered was nothing else but love, for like St. Paul he knew that "though I have the gift of prophecy, and understand all mysteries, and all knowledge, and though I have all faith so that I could remove mountains, and have not love, I am nothing." I have also shown Traherne's affinities with the Cambridge Platonists.

These poets are more concerned with describing the first two stages of the mystical life, Purgation and Illumination. It is only seldom that they tell us anything about the direct vision or experience of God which is the essence of mysticism; and when Henry Vaughan has told us "I saw eternity the other night" what else is there to be communicated, for the supreme vision of Reality is not often repeated, and it is difficult to convey the richness of this unique experience through language at all? Mystical experience in the language of St. John of the Cross is an "obscure contemplation," and its supreme expression in the words of Pseudo-Dionysius is a "ray of Divine Darkness,"

---

[1] *The English Works of George Herbert*, edited by G. H. Palmer, vol. i, p. 109. All quotations are from this edition; the admirable definitive edition of George Herbert by the Rev. F. E. Hutchinson in the Oxford Text Series appeared too late for my purpose.

"O quanto è corto il dire, è come fioco
    Al mio concetto!"

Dante, *Paradiso*, xxxiii, 121–122.

(How scant the speech, and how faint, for my conception!)

The eyes of the mystic, like those of Dante in the *Paradiso*, cannot behold the radiance of God, which often appears to him as an "endless light."

"Within its depths I saw ingathered, bound by love in one mass, the scattered leaves of the universe. Substance and accidents and their relations, as though together fused, so that what I speak of is one simple flame. The universal form of this complex I think I saw, because, as I say thus, more largely I feel myself rejoice. One single moment to me is more lethargy than twenty-five centuries upon the enterprise which made Neptune wonder at the shade of the Argo (passing over him)."—T. S. Eliot's translation.

The imagery of light is here used to convey the form of mystical experience, the images are not poetic devices but, as T. S. Eliot has aptly observed, "serious and practical means of making the spiritual visible." I have attempted to discuss the various elements and characteristics of these poets in order to *isolate* the mystical elements in their religious experience and thought, and to determine its quality by comparing it to that of the typical Christian mystics. Dean Inge has admirably defined the scope and nature of religious mysticism as "the attempt to realize the presence of the living God in the soul and in nature, or more generally, as *the attempt to realize, in thought and feeling, the immanence of the temporal in the eternal, and of the eternal in the temporal.*" [1] The mystical quest of these poets is at best *an attempt* to apprehend God in a direct mystical experience, and to determine the measure of their success is the main purpose of this inadequate study.

(ii)

No word in our times has been more misused than mysticism. It has been applied to theosophy, to spiritualism, to occult philosophy, to the attempt of man to disclaim the necessity of the doctrine and ritual and discipline of the Church, and

[1] Inge, *op. cit.*, p. 5.

even to the state of the human mind under the effect of intoxicants. "The drunken consciousness," says William James, "is a bit of Mystic consciousness." Some modern writers on mysticism [1] have called the love of God and the extreme form of monastic piety and asceticism the sum and substance of mysticism.[2]

Mysticism is not the word used by such great mystics as St. Augustine and St. Bernard: "contemplation" is the word they employ to denote their unique experience of God. Mysticism historically has associations with the mystery cults of the Greeks—one who had had the privilege of having been initiated into the secrets of Divine knowledge was called a gnostic. In the early history of European mysticism we find that mystical knowledge was regarded as worthy of being imparted to the inner circle of the devotees alone; it was revealed rather than acquired, through a long process of purgation and moral discipline, which we have now come to associate with mysticism. Clement of Alexandria holds that the divine secrets of the faith could be revealed or taught only to those who have already been initiated into the mystery of Divine knowledge [3]; thus mystical knowledge became the privilege of the gnostics alone and was denied to the general body of believers.

Pseudo-Dionysius was the first to apply the word mysticism to Christian experience of God in his great treatise *Mystical Theology*, but mystical experience, the attempt of the individual soul to realize the presence of God, is much older than Christianity itself. Some of the most profound forms of mystical thought are to be found in the "Upanishads," while the freshness of the joy of the human soul in its apprehension of God can be seen earlier in the Vedic hymns. The whole philosophy of the "Upanishads," which was the result of the reaction against the increasing formalism of the Vedic ritual, tends to bring into the foreground the central doctrine of mysticism, the union of the soul with God. The "Upanishads" taught the significant fact that in the higher stages of mystical life the distinction between the subject and the object, the worshipper and the worshipped, disappears. "If a man

---

[1] *The Varieties of Religious Experience*, by William James, 1902.
[2] Harnack, cited by Dean Inge, *op. cit.*
[3] See *Clement of Alexandria*, by J. B. Mayer, cap. iii.

worships another divinity with the idea that he and the God are different, he does not know." [1]   And in almost a Christian way the "Upanishads" assert that freedom from the bondage of the self cannot be had through any amount of repentance and purification; it is an act of the grace of God, which is called "Devaprasda."

"This Atman cannot be attained through study or intelligence or much learning—when he wishes to attain by him it can be attained. To him the Atman reveals its true nature." [2] Mysticism is the keynote of the great hymn of Krishna, the *Bhagvat Gita*, and then later we find that Buddha taught some of the highest forms of mystical discipline to attain *Nirvana*, the final absorption of the self in Godhead. And about the same time Lao Tzu summed up the mystical traditions of his ancient race in *Tao Tehking*, and then two centuries later we find in Plato's *Dialogues* some of the most sublime thoughts about the relation of the human soul with God, and later on Plotinus carried Plato's philosophy to its mystical conclusion. Between Plato and Plotinus had come the new revelation of Christ, which was to give to Europe some of its greatest mystics.

And from the first century of the Christian era begins the history of mystical experience which has enriched both life and literature alike, mysticism in the Epistles of St. John and St. Paul reaches the highest flights which Christian mysticism was ever destined to achieve. Till the seventh century before the rise of Islam in the Near East, Christianity had already produced such great mystics as St. Augustine, Dionysius the Areopagite, and St. Gregory the Great.

In Islam the great poets have also been great mystics: Rumi, Hafiz, Jami, Saadi are recognized as great religious teachers and mystics. The twelfth and thirteenth and four-teenth centuries are perhaps the most important centuries in the history of mysticism, in the West and East alike, while this human search for the eternal truth through mysticism is carried on till the seventeenth century, with different emphasis but essential unity, among the different nations of Europe.

In this imposing array of mystical genius stretched over two thousand years, with all the diversity of language and culture, race and religion, one central fact looms large—the essential

---

[1] *Brab. I. U.*, 10.　　　　　　　[2] *I Mundaka*, iii, 2, 3.

unity of the Mystic Experience throughout the ages, in spite of the difference which obviously exists between Western and Eastern forms of mysticism. The *Gita* says:

"I am the pure fragrance in the earth, I am the light of fire, the life in all creation, and I am the austerity of those who are ascetics. Know, O son of Pritha, I am the eternal seed of all creation. I am the Budhi [intellect] of the intelligent, and I am the glory of those that possess glory."

And we find St. Augustine describing the same experience of the Vision of God:

"What is that which gleams through me and strikes my heart without hurting it; and I shudder and I kindle? I shudder inasmuch as I am unlike it; I kindle inasmuch as I am like it. It is Wisdom, Wisdom's self, which gleameth through me." [1]

Jalaluddin Rumi, the great mystic and poet of Persia, finds freedom from the duality of self in his union with God:

> "My place is the Placeless, my trace is the traceless.
> 'Tis neither body nor soul, for I belong to the soul of the Beloved.
> I have put duality away, I have seen that the two worlds are one.
> One I seek, one I know, one I see, one I call." [2]

The supreme quest of the spirit of man in different countries and ages has been the search for God, and a yearning of the human soul for the union with God. Miss Underhill thinks that there are certain characteristics which are possessed by the great mystics of all countries: "There are certain characteristics which seem common to all such adventures. Their point of departure is the same, the desire of spirit for the spiritual, the soul's hunger for its home. Their object is the same, the attainment of that home, the achievement of Reality, union with God."

This is the central fact of mysticism which distinguishes it from mystical philosophy and mystical theology and all other forms which the soul of man has tried to achieve in order to transcend the limitations of "Self." Mysticism can be studied as a form of religious philosophy or theology, and it can also be used as a storehouse for the study of the psychology of the mystics, but our purpose here is to describe the characteristics of Christian mysticism as the supreme attempt of the human soul to be united with God.

---

[1] Evelyn Underhill, *Mysticism*.   [2] R. A. Nicholson's translation.

The two essential features of the "mystic-consciousness" which the study of the life of the great mystics reveal are the acute consciousness of God and the belief in the capacity of the human soul to realize the living presence of God within it. The mystic realizes that his soul, unless it is purified, can never be granted the Vision of the Supreme Reality, God.   He who tries to find the *one* behind the complexities of *many* believes that for him the real content of things is still hidden, that he lacks the true knowledge of "the self," and his faculty of perception is therefore incomplete, perhaps incorrect.

To have a clear vision and see "into the life of things" is one of the passions of the mystic, but this knowledge, for the true religious mystic, comes only through the knowledge of God and from no other source—such as pantheism, theosophy or philosophy.   The recognition of the fact that there is a Reality higher than the one manifested *here* constitutes one of the fundamental beliefs of the mystic.

"The strongest power," says Eucken, "within the world constitutes in reality the conviction of an overworld." [1]

With the purification of the self begins the process which is called the Purgative Way.   The vision of the Lord is promised in the Sermon on the Mount to the pure in heart alone: "Blessed are the pure in heart, for they shall see God."   Thus the soul is recognized as the dwelling-place of God and its purification the first stage of the mystical life.

St. Augustine realizes the immanence and transcendence of God when he says, "Thou wert more inward to me than my most inward part, and higher than my highest." [2]   It is the paradox of mysticism that the beyond is within, but before this truth could be realized the soul must become purified, and it must learn the virtues of humility, obedience and surrender to the Will of God and thus become humble in His sight. Humility, self-surrender and self-control are the virtues which the mystic cultivates in the Purgative Way.   St. Bernard in a thoughtful passage has described his conception of purgation which he holds is essential for a life of "contemplation": "The taste for contemplation is not due except to obedience to God's commandments. . . . 'What then would you have me do?'

---

[1] *The Truth of Religion.*   London and New York, 1911, London, 1913.
[2] *Confessions*, III, ii.

In the first place I would have you cleanse your conscience from every defilement of anger and murmuring and envy and dispute. . . . In the next place I would wish you to adorn yourself with flowers of good works and laudable studies of every kind, and seek the sweet perfumes of virtues . . . that your conscience may everywhere be fragrant with the perfumes of piety, of peace, of gentleness, of justice, of obedience, of cheerfulness, of humility." [1]

St. Augustine has elaborately described the purgative process, and for this purpose he has divided the different faculties of the soul into seven grades; he holds that the soul is the basis of life, of sensation, of intelligence, of morality, and the other three stages correspond to the three familiar stages of the mystical life: purgation, illumination and union, which St. Augustine respectively calls "tranquillitas," the calming of passions; the "ingressio," the approach to contemplation, and the last is the contemplation itself. [2]

Asceticism as an expression of disciplined spiritual life is an essential part of mysticism. "This mortifying process is necessary not because the legitimate exercise of the senses is opposed to Divine Reality, but because those senses have usurped a place beyond their station; become the forces of energy, steadily drained the vitality of the self." [3]

While Dean Inge recognizes the necessity of asceticism, he is opposed to the orthodox forms of monkish asceticism of the Middle Ages: "Monkish asceticism (so far as it goes beyond the struggle to live unstained) under unnatural conditions rests on a dualistic view of the world which does not belong to the essence of mysticism." [4]

The Christian mystic recognizes the divine necessity of suffering and pain in this process of "becoming" and points to the Passion of Christ as proof that the inner process of spiritual perfection involves suffering, the Way of the Cross.

The mystic, like the artist and lover in their intense moods, is unsocial, and Plotinus has given reasons for the mystic's desire for seclusion and detachment: "Just as someone waiting to hear a voice that he loves should separate himself

[1] Canticle, xlv, 5, 7. *Western Mysticism*, by Dom C. Butler.
[2] *Western Mysticism*, by Dom C. Butler.
[3] *Mysticism*, by E. Underhill, p. 220.
[4] Inge, *Christian Mysticism*, pp. 11, 12.

from other voices and prepare his ear for the hearing of the more excellent sound when it comes near; so here it is necessary to neglect sensible sounds, so far as we can keep the Soul's powers of attention pure and ready for the reception of Supernal Sounds."

When the soul of the mystic has been cleansed and purified it begins to have a glimpse of God. A very wide range of mystical experience is perceptible in the illuminative stage, but we must remember that the mystic has not yet attained the union with God which the Christian mystics call the "spiritual marriage," or what Plotinus called the "flight of the Alone to the Alone." Ruysbroeck distinguishes the "contemplative life" from the "unitive life," and points out that in the first one simply passes "into the presence of God," while in the second "we are swallowed up" in the immensity and the "deep quiet of Godhead." [1]

It is a common experience of the mystics that before the soul comes into direct communion with God a strange quiet and peace pervades their spirit. They call it "introversion," in which the sense impressions and images are obliterated from the mind to enable the soul to concentrate primarily on God. St. Augustine has expressed this sense of the quiet and peace in a passage of rare beauty: "We said then: If the tumult of the flesh were hushed, hushed the sense impressions of earth, sea, sky; hushed also the heavens yea the very soul be hushed to herself . . . hushed all dreams and revelations which come by imagery; if every tongue, every symbol, and all things subject to transiency were wholly hushed . . . so that we may hear His word, not through any tongue of flesh nor angels, voice nor sound of thunder nor any similitude, but His voice when we live in these His creatures—may hear His very self without an intermediary."[2]

The main characteristic of illumination is the certitude of the Divine Presence and the consequent mystical joy of the lover who has won the love of the Beloved, but in all the great Christian mystics the centre of interest is not the mystic's *own soul which is thus exalted but God who exalts the soul*. St. John of the Cross says:

---

[1] *Mysticism*, by E. Underhill, cap. iv.   [2] *Confessions*, ix, 25.

"O burn that burns to heal!
O more than pleasant wound!
And O soft hand, O touch most delicate
That dost new life reveal,
That dost in grace abound
And, staying, dost from death to life translate." [1]

The characteristic of the illuminated mystic's love for God is a passionate joy combined with Christian humility.

But illumination is not a reward, it is a gift from God to man, and depends not so much on good works as Divine grace, which is granted to the mystic in response to his vehement desire for the love of God. "The grace of contemplation," says St. Bernard, "is granted only in response to a longing and importunate desire. Nevertheless He will not present Himself, even in passing, to every soul, but to the soul only which is shown by great devotion, vehement desire, and tender affection, to be His Bride and to be worthy that the word in all His beauty should visit her as a Bridegroom." [2]

St. Bernard has called "Illumination" the Kiss of Christ's hand, the "Purgation" being the Kiss of His Feet, and the unitive life the Kiss of His Mouth. [3]

The Dark Night of the Soul is a stage which intervenes between the illuminative and the unitive stages, and in which God seems to withdraw Himself from the soul of the mystic. To the mystic God is an object of love and adoration, and there can be no greater source of dejection and suffering for him than to realize the fact that He has deserted him.

To some mystics like St. John of the Cross this is a state of "Passive Purification" in which the soul lies like clay in Divine Hands; while mystics like Suso and some mystics of the German school have felt it as a period of intense activity and moral conflict, an actual preparation for the unitive life.

St. Teresa describing her own experience says: "It is impossible to describe the suffering of the Soul in this state. It goes about in quest of relief, and God suffers it to find none. The light of reason in the freedom of its will remains, but it is not clear, it seems to me as if its eyes were covered with a veil." [4]

The classical account, however, of the Dark Night of the

[1] St. John of the Cross, *Flama de Amor Viva* (translated by Arthur Symons).
[2] Canticles ix. 7.
[3] Canticles iii and iv.
[4] *Mysticism*, by E. Underhill, p. 393.

Soul, is given by St. John of the Cross in his treatise called *The Dark Night of the Soul*. According to him, the soul begins to enter the dark night when God withdraws it out of "the state of beginners" [1] into "that of proficients," so that having endured its suffering "they may arrive at the state of the perfect, which is that of the divine union with God." [1]

He has divided the Dark Night into two stages, the Purgation of the senses, and the Purgation of the spirit. [2] Speaking of the second and the higher kind of Purgation, St. John of the Cross says, "Therefore in this night ensuing both parts of the soul are purified together: this is the end for which it was necessary to have passed through the re-formation of the first night." [3]   He calls the Dark Night an "infused contemplation," which is a passive state of receptivity when "God secretly teaches the soul and instructs it in the perfection of love, without effort on its own part beyond a loving attention to God." [4]   The sense of alienation from God, of the consequent pain and suffering are the characteristics of the Dark Night of the Soul which is often called the Mystical Death. Eckhart says, "He acts as if there were a wall erected between Him and us." [5]

In his travail of suffering and privation the soul learns the lesson of complete self-surrender to the will of God, it is in reality the extinction of "selfhood," and the final acquiescence in the purpose of God.

Having been thus trained and perfected, the soul now embarks on the last stage of mystical life, the unitive stage, in which the mystic comes face to face with God. This state is not an illusion because it becomes the permanent possession of the mystic, and transforms his whole attitude towards life; it is not a mere dream for the mystic is wide awake and conscious of it as a unique experience. It is not a sudden acquirement of spiritual energy but the last stage of the arduous process of self-purification and the strenuous training of the soul. St. Augustine truly says: "In this kind of vision is seen the brightness of God, not by some corporeally or spiritually figured signification as through a glass in an enigma, but face

[1] *The Dark Night of the Soul*, by St. John of the Cross, translated by David Lewis, p. 5.
[2] *Ibid.*, p. 27.   [3] *Ibid.*, p. 65.   [4] *Ibid.*, p. 68.
[5] *Mysticism*, by E. Underhill, p. 389.

to face, or as Moses, mouth to mouth; that is by the species by which God is what He is, how little so ever the mind, even when cleansed from all earthly stain and alienated and carried out of all body and image of body, is able to grasp him!"

This union is essentially a union of oneness in which all sense of duality is obliterated. Ruysbroeck says: "This fruition of God is a still and glorious and essential oneness beyond the differentiation of the Persons." [1] Through an arduous process of spiritual regeneration knowledge becomes vision, vision revelation, revelation contemplation and contemplation existence itself.

All great mystics have found the *unitive stage* to be a transformation and energization of life; the life of the mystic who has attained this highest stage of the mystic way is the only real life known to us; life has been raised to the highest levels of reality and power, and the promise "where the Spirit of the Lord is there is liberty" has thus been fulfilled. Baron Von Hügel has remarked: "The mystics are amongst the great benefactors of our race; for it is especially this presence of the Infinite in Man, and man's universal subjection to an operative consciousness of it, which are the deepest cause and the constant object of the adoring awe of all truly spiritual mystics, in all times and places." [2]

The question that now arises is whether there is any affinity between the experience of mystics like St. Bernard or St. John of the Cross and a "mystic-poet" like Herbert or Richard Crashaw.

It has been often said that the mystic is not bound to reveal his secret, his vision of Reality has been described by Plotinus as the "flight of the alone to the Alone"; but the important fact is that, in spite of the difficulties inherent in describing such a unique experience as theirs, mystics have tried through suggestion, symbolism and negative phraseology to convey to us some idea of the richness of their exalted vision.

There is a great disparity not only between the mystic's own experience and the language he employs to express it, but also between his mind and the minds of his audience, which must be raised to higher levels of emotion and feelings to understand

[1] *Mysticism*, by E. Underhill, cap. x.
[2] *The Mystical Element of Religion*, by Baron Von Hügel (1908), vol. ii, p. 340.

the significance of his experience. It is here that poetry comes to the aid of the mystic; and this is why artistic language charged with high imaginative power is employed in the Bible, especially in the New Testament, the Apocalypse, the Prophetic Books and the Psalms, while in the Song of Songs the poet and the mystic have become one. Underhill says: "Thus when Clement of Alexandria compares the Logos to a 'New Song,' when Suso calls the Eternal Wisdom a 'sweet and beautiful wild flower,' when Dionysius the Areopagite speaks of the Divine Dark which is the Inaccessible Light, and Ruysbroeck of 'the unwalled world,' we recognize a sudden flash of the creative imagination; evoking for us a truth greater, deeper and more fruitful than the merely external parallel which it suggests." [1]

It is not only in the use of the poetic language that the mystic comes nearer to the poet; their affinity lies deep in their experience. "There are certainly striking resemblances between the flashes of inspiration which the poet experiences and the mysterious working of the Divine Presence granted to the mystics."

Critics like Henri Bremond have tried to understand the mystery of the poetic experience by the aid of mystical experience. Bremond says: "It is not Shelley's experience that helps me to know better the experience of St. John of the Cross, but conversely it is the experience of the Saint which makes a little less obscure the mystery of the experience of the poet." [2] But this process of understanding the complexity of the poetic experience presupposes a close resemblance between the experience of the poet and that of the mystic.

But what we as readers demand from the mystic we do not expect of the poet; the greatness of the mystic rests on the genuineness of his experience, its truth, reality and intensity. He *is* a mystic because of his supreme experience of God, he may convey that experience to us or not, it does not alter the fact of his being a mystic, though we shall not be able to share his experience if it is not communicated to us. But the poet is a poet because he conveys his experience to us and he is at liberty to alter, modify and transform his experience in

[1] *The Essentials of Mysticism*, by E. Underhill.
[2] *Prayer and Poetry*, by Henri Bremond, p. 84.

conveying it to us, while we expect the mystic to give us his experience in all its richness and complexity unaltered by any
other considerations, even those of the means of conveying
his experience.

But in its essence the mystical experience is incommunicable,
for, like St. Catherine of Genoa, the mystic claims "my Being
is God not by simple participation but by a true transformation
of my Being." [1]

If the purpose of art is to unveil Reality, the mystic and the
poet can both claim an identity of purpose. In Blake's words,
the purpose of art is to "cleanse the doors of perception, so
that everything may appear as it is—Infinite," and it is the
Infinite Himself, God, on whom the gaze of the mystic is fixed.

The poet, however, cannot say with St. Bernard, "My Secret
to myself"; the poet is bound to sing, otherwise he would no
longer be a poet. "He is the mediator," says Underhill,
"between his brethren and the Divine, for art is the link
between appearance and reality."

The religious mystic and the "mystic-poet" have many
things in common, their search for Reality, and their method
of communicating the richness of their experience through
artistic and highly imaginative language, for we must remember
that the mystics have given to the poet a large number of poetic
similes and metaphors, such as the Desert of Godhead, the Kiss
of Christ, the Cloud of Unknowing, the Marriage of the Soul,
the Divine Dark, and the Beatific Vision—to name only a few.

But when the poet happens to be a mystic, like Donne,
Vaughan, Traherne and Crashaw, he comes very close indeed
to the great religious mystics like St. Augustine or St. Bernard,
the difference being then of the degree, and not of the quality
of mystical experience, for we must remember that such great
mystics as St. John of the Cross, St. Francis of Assisi and
Richard Rolle were also poets.

St. John of the Cross says:

> "O living flame of love
> How painless is the smart
> Thy tender wounds create
> Within my very heart;
> O, end at last the weary strife
> And break the web of this, my life." [2]

---

[1] *Mysticism*, by E. Underhill, p. 179.   [2] David Lewis's translation.

Almost in a similar strain Henry Vaughan declared:

> "O what high joys
> The turtle voice
> And songs I hear!   O quickening showers
> Of my Lord's belov'd
> You make rocks bud
> And crown dry hills with wells and flowers!" [1]

The "mystic-poets" like Blake have thought that their mission was to bring their illumination within the range of comprehension of their fellow-men: ". . . I rest not upon my great task, to open the Eternal Worlds, to open the Immortal Eyes of Man inwards into the Worlds of thought, into Eternity Ever Expanding in the Bosom of God, the Human Imagination." [2]

Miss Underhill maintains that the apprehension of the Infinite life immanent in all living things by poets like Keats, Shelley, Wordsworth, Tennyson, Browning and Whitman is a form of mysticism, but when this power is raised to its "highest denomination" and "faith has vanished into sight," [3] then "we reach the point at which the mystic swallows up the poet." [3] And the poet becomes the mystic.

Jacques Maritain, however, holds that all Christian art contains the elements which we find in the life of saints and mystics:

"I do not mean that in order to do Christian work the artist must be a saint who might be canonized or a mystic who has attained to transforming union.   I mean that, strictly speaking, mystic contemplation and sanctity in the artist are the goal to which the formal exigencies of a Christian work as such spontaneously tend, and I say that a work is in fact Christian so far as some element derived from the life which makes saints and contemplatives is transmitted—howsoever and with whatsoever deficiencies—through the soul of the artist." [4]

The work of a Christian poet may thus contain the elements which are peculiar to the mystics and the contemplatives; but when poetry and the contemplative life are combined in a way, as they are in Donne, Herbert, Crashaw, Vaughan and

[1] *The Works of Henry Vaughan*, edited by L. C. Martin, ii, p. 535.
[2] *Jerusalem*.
[3] *Mysticism*, by E. Underhill, p. 235.
[4] *Art and Scholasticism*, by J. Maritain.

Traherne, the mystical element in their poetry bears close resemblance to the mystical experience of such great saints as St. Augustine, St. Bernard, and St. John of the Cross; and it is from this point of view that I have studied them in the following pages.

> " . . . and put off
> In self-annihilation all that is not of God alone.
> To put off self and all I have, for ever and ever.   Amen."
>
> Blake's *Milton.*

CHAPTER II

THE SCEPTICAL, SCHOLASTIC AND MYSTICAL ELEMENTS IN JOHN DONNE'S THOUGHT

JOHN DONNE's relation to the different schools of philosophy is one of the most difficult problems in the criticism of his poetry and thought. We know that his knowledge of the schoolmen was extensive and profound and that he recognized the value of their intellectual discipline and the peculiar rôle which Thomist Philosophy had played in the history of medieval thought.

Donne was profoundly impressed by the encyclopædic learning and the keen penetrating and subtle intellect of St. Thomas Aquinas, whom he called "another instrument and engine of Thine whom Thou hadst so enabled that nothing was too mineral nor centric for the search and reach of his wit." [1] Donne was conversant with the whole field of scholastic philosophy and theology and knew such contemporary schoolmen as Dominicans Victoria, Soto, and Bannes, the last surviving as late as 1604. But it is also true that Donne in no period of his life owed complete allegiance to the Thomist School, and that he had widely read its opponents, the Nominalists, especially Duns Scotus, and like other Renaissance thinkers he had also come for a short time under the spell of sceptic philosophers, especially Sextus Empiricus.

Donne's learning had attracted wide attention and won recognition and respect even in an age of such learned theologians and divines as Parker, Hooker, and Andrewes; but his contemporaries like Ben Jonson, Walton, Carew, and Bishop King, themselves men of learning and taste, did not characterize his thought as essentially medieval or scholastic; his asceticism and saintliness of later years reminded his contemporaries of the piety of the early Fathers of the Church, but his learning or philosophy did not appear to them as medieval; in fact

---

[1] *Essays in Divinity*, edited by Dr. Jessopp (1855), p. 37.

what impressed them was the originality and freshness of his wit, his freedom from the traditional moulds of thought.

It is the many-sidedness of Donne's thought that has led his modern critics astray; some critics, like Mr. T. S. Eliot, have called his erudition "incoherent," and remarked that his poetry expresses no settled belief in anything,[1] while others, like Miss Ramsay, have tried to reduce the richness and multiplicity of his philosophical interest to the simplicity of the unquestioning faith of a medievalist. In order to place his thought in its true perspective it is necessary to trace its development and growth at the various stages of his life.

The legend of Donne's medievalism arose because of his immense learning, which embraced the whole field of scholastic philosophy, medieval theology, the Hermetic physics, the new science of Copernicus, Galileo and Bacon; and in the words of Donne this "immoderate desire of human learning and languages" took him to the untrodden and unfamiliar by-paths of medieval learning. But though Donne was one of the greatest scholars of his age, the extent of his learning has no doubt been exaggerated by his modern critics, Miss Ramsay, Mrs. Simpson and others. There is no reason to suppose that his learning was greater or more medieval than that of his contemporaries Hooker or Bishop Andrewes. But Donne does express his varied philosophical interests in his poetry and prose.

In Donne's poetry and philosophy alike many strands of thought meet and illuminate one another. Philosophy in the seventeenth century had lost the simple outlines of Platonic abstractions such as we find in the poetry of Spenser; the Renaissance thought had been crossed with the boundless passion of the Reformation for a purer life and religion, with the result that poetic emotion and philosophical speculation both became more complex, daring and audacious. Donne became the curious explorer of the human soul; the adventures of the spirit became more exciting than Raleigh's voyages of discovery; men became more introspective, intent on self-examination and reform. Donne wrote in one of his letters: "Whilst I have been talking of others, methinks I have opened

---

[1] "Donne in our Time," in *A Garland for John Donne*, edited by Theodore Spencer (Cambridge, Harvard University Press, 1931).

a casement to gaze upon passengers which I love not much, though it might seem a recreation to such as who have their houses, that is themselves, so narrow and ill furnished, yet I can be content to look inward upon myself." [1]

Donne's contemporaries did not characterize either his poetic conceits or thought as essentially scholastic or medieval. Carew wrote his *Elegy* in 1633, and in 1640 appeared Walton's *Life of Donne*, that piece of vivid portraiture and delicate etching which was largely based on the personal observation of Walton, and on those facts which Donne might have from time to time related to his friend in his later years.

Though Walton compared Donne's life to St. Augustine: "Now the English Church has gained a second St. Austin, for, I think none was so like him before his conversion; none so like St. Ambrose after it" [2]; and his preaching to St. Paul,[2] he did not label his thought as medieval; in fact Walton, like his other contemporaries, has laid emphasis not on the medieval cast of Donne's mind, but on "his sharp wit and high fancy" and "choice metaphors," in which both Nature and all the arts joined to assist him with their utmost skill.[3] While discussing Donne's learning ("for he left the resultance of 1400 authors, most of them abridged and analysed with his own hand"), Walton is careful to stress the universality of Donne's interests in literature and philosophy. He was not only a great scholar of the civil and canon law but also of "many other studies and arguments, as enter into the consideration of many, that labour to be thought great clerks and pretend to know all things." [4] Sir Herbert Grierson in his instructive chapter on Donne's learning has shown to what uncommon and obscure corners did his "immoderate desire of human learning and languages" lead him.[5]

Thomas Fuller in his *Worthies* (1662) and John Aubrey in his *Lives* (1669–1696) did not display any critical acumen in treating Donne's poetry and philosophy; they praised him as "one of excellent wit" and as one of the greatest preachers of his day; in fact Edward Phillips, in his *Theatrum Poetarum*

---

[1] *The Life and Letters of John Donne*, by E. Gosse (1899), vol. ii, p. 16.
[2] *Walton's Lives*, edited by T. Zouch (1817), pp. 90, 91. All quotations are from this edition.
[3] *Ibid.*, p. 120.   [4] *Ibid.*, p. 134.
[5] *Donne's Poetical Works*, Grierson, vol. ii.

Anglicanorum (1675), characterized his learning as of the "Politer Kind," and thus not essentially theological. He says: "John Donne . . . accomplished himself with the politer kind of learning . . . ; and frequented good company, to which the sharpness of his wit, and the gaiety of fancy, rendered him not a little grateful." [1]

William Winstanley's *Life of Donne* [2] (1687) and his *England's Worthies* (1689) were largely based on Walton's and Phillips' *Lives*, but he declared: "This pleasant poet, painful preacher, and pious person" being "an eminent poet, he became a much more eminent preacher."

It was not the scholastic element but the poetic quality of Donne's "thought" which attracted Winstanley, for he asserts that he improved rather than "relinquished his poetical fancy, only converting it from *humane* and worldly to divine and heavenly subjects." [2]

Anthony à Wood in his *Athenae Oxonienses* (1691–1692) also noted the wide learning of Donne, "a person sometimes noted for his divinity, knowledge in several languages and other learning." Thus it is obvious that neither Donne's contemporaries nor his immediate successors characterized his thought as medieval, metaphysical, or scholastic. John Dryden was the first critic to call Donne and his followers "metaphysical," in his famous dedication of *A Discourse concerning the Origin and Progress of Satire* to the Earl of Dorset in 1693, but evidently Dryden had only Donne's conceits and not his philosophy in mind when he wrote this essay. But this is not the first reference to Donne in the critical canon which he was trying to establish. Dryden had already (*An Essay on Dramatic Poesy*, 1668) defined the style of a poet whom he does not name (perhaps John Cleveland):

"'Tis easy to guess whom you intend, said Lisideius; and without naming them I ask you, if one of them does not perpetually pay us with clenches upon words, and a certain clownish kind of raillery? if now and then he does not offer at a catachresis or clevelandism, wrestling and torturing a word into another meaning?" [3]

[1] E. Phillips, *Theatrum Poetarum Anglicanorum* (Geneva, 1824), vol. ii, pp. 2–3.
[2] W. Winstanley, *The Lives of the Most Famous Poets* (1687), pp. 117, 119, 120.
[3] *An Essay on Dramatic Poesy* (*Essays of John Dryden*), edited by W. P. Ker, vol. i, p. 31.

Dryden, who himself had "affected the metaphysical" in his *Heroic Stanzas on the Lord Protector*, had now become the herald of the age of Reason and Correctness. He disapproved of the metaphysical conceits which tortured an idea until the whole content of feeling was made available to poetic imagery. One year before writing his dedication to the Earl of Dorset, Dryden had already (in his dedication of *Eleanore*) distinguished the two inseparable elements of Donne's style—his wit and his poetic form. He styled Donne "the greatest wit, tho' not the greatest poet of our nation," and in 1668 he had said in his criticism of Cleveland's satires, ". . . so that there is this difference betwixt his satire and doctor Donne's; that the one gives us deep thoughts in common language, though rough cadence; the other gives us common thoughts in abstruse words."

Dryden's reaction to Donne's poetry varied as he advanced in years and as the concepts of Reason and Correctness became more pronounced in his criticism and poetry alike. In 1668 Dryden had admired Donne for giving "deep thoughts in common language," and in 1692 he still thought Donne to be "the greatest wit" though not "the greatest poet," but in 1693 he wrote to the Earl of Dorset: "Donne alone of all your countrymen had your talent; but was not happy enough to arrive at your versification; and were he translated into numbers, and English, he would yet be wanting in the dignity of expression," which he declared was "the prime virtue and chief ornament of Virgil." Donne fell short of these classical standards, and so could not be compared to the Earl of Dorset, who excelled him "in the manner and words."

It is significant that throughout this important passage Dryden has been discoursing mainly on the quality of Donne's conceits, his "manners and words"; he thus applied the term "metaphysical" not to the philosophy of Donne but to his conceits—"concetti metaphysici ed ideali"—a term which the Italian poet Testi (1593-1646) had used earlier in the century.[1]

Dryden said of Donne's love poetry: "He affects the metaphysics, not only in his satires, but in his amorous verses, where nature only should reign; and perplexes the minds of the fair sex with nice speculations of philosophy, when he

---

[1] Also see Grierson, *Donne*, vol. ii, p. 2.

should engage their hearts and entertain them with the softness of love." [1]

Dryden, with his new ideals of correctness and reason, could not appreciate the naked realism, the harsh tone of Donne's passion, and the mere display of learning more sportive than serious in his "Songs" and "Sonnets" and satires and elegies. He points out that Donne "perplexes" the minds of women with his subtle scholastic distinctions while he should delight them with sweet compliments expressing "the softness of love." [1]

Donne was anything but "soft" in love; to express the woes of love in poetry according to the Petrarchan tradition was to him unmanly:

> "Let me not know that others know
> That she knowes my paines, lest that so
> A tender shame make me mine owne new woe."
>
> *Love's Exchange.*

And in the same poem he declared:

> "Such in love's warfare is my case,
> I may not article for grace,
> Having put Love at last to shew this face."

That Dryden is referring to Donne's conceits in love poems and not to his philosophy is evident from the few succeeding lines of the same passage. Dryden in comparing Cowley with Donne says: "In this (if I may be pardoned for so bold a truth) Mr. Cowley copied him to a fault so great a one, in my opinion, that it throwes his Mistress infinitely below his Pindarics . . . which are undoubtedly the best of his poems and the most correct.

As long as "wit" and "conceit" meant "intellect" and "imagination" the metaphysical poets were held in high esteem, but in the age of Reason new theories of wit, style and form became popular in England, and wit and conceit were reduced to the position of "fancy" and "ingenuity," and consequently metaphysical poets were censured for the exercise of their wit, which was declared to be unnatural, far-fetched and divorced from poetic emotion.

John Oldmixon, in his *Arts of Logic and Rhetorick* (1728), realized the true significance of Dryden's remarks when he

---

[1] Dryden's *Essays*, edited by W. P. Ker, p. 19.

wrote: "Dryden tells us, in his preface to Juvenal, that Cowley copied Dr. Donne to a Fault in his Metaphysicks, which his love verses abound with. . . ."

It is thus evident that, till the age of Dryden, Donne's philosophy was hardly commented upon, it was his poetic conceits, and their metaphysical character, which were made the subject of criticism, while his learning was recognized to be unusual even in the age of encyclopædic learning, but even in this respect the universality of his knowledge was emphasized, and the medieval and scholastic aspect of his thought was not yet discovered.

It is significant that the reaction against the metaphysical poets was accompanied with a pronounced reaction against Petrarch, in whose love poetry also "concetti metafisici" abound. Mario Praz has traced the metaphysical cast of some of the lyrics of Spenser, Wyatt and Donne to Petrarch. He says: "As we survey Donne's poetry after such a distance of time, we can hardly fail to notice how much this poet, who in a sense led the reaction against Petrarchism in England, was himself a Petrarchist, thanks to his medievally trained mind." [1] It is curious that in the reaction against Donne and his followers Petrarch also fell from the high position he had occupied in the love poetry of the Elizabethans. Joseph Warton in his *Essay on the Writings and Genius of Pope* (1756) made a significant remark about Petrarch which shows the tendency of the age. He says: "Indeed to speak the truth, there appears to be little valuable in Petrarch, except the purity of his diction. His sentiments, even of love, are metaphysical and far-fetched." [2] And these were the qualities of metaphysical poetry, its far-fetched conceits drawn from the storehouse of medieval learning and modern science, which Dr. Johnson singled out for censure and condemnation. Dryden compared Donne to Virgil, while Johnson connected Donne with the metaphysical poetry of Dante and his circle, and traced his conceits to Marino and his school:

"This kind of writing, which was, I believe, borrowed from Marino and his followers, had been recommended by the

---

[1] "Donne's relation to the Poetry of his Time," *A Garland for John Donne*, pp. 65–66.

[2] Joseph Warton's *Essay on the Writings and Genius of Pope* (1756), p. 66.

example of Donne, a man of very extensive and various
knowledge." [1]   It was really in Italy, in the "*dolce stil nuovo*"
of Guido Guinicelli and Dante, that the "metaphysical"
conceits first became an important element in the love poetry
of Europe, and erudition was also the distinctive feature of
this school of poetry.[2]   Johnson thus placed Donne and his
school in its true perspective, but he was mainly concerned
with the wit, the conceits and the sources of Donne's imagery;
he had little to say about the scholastic and medieval element
in Donne's thought.

Johnson, however, was shrewd enough to distinguish between
the subtlety of Donne as applied to "scholastic speculation"
and as exercised on "common subjects."   He pointed out:
"It must be however confessed of these writers, that if they are
upon common subjects often unnecessarily and unpoetically
subtle, yet where scholastic speculation can be properly
admitted their copiousness and acuteness may justly be
admired." [3]

Johnson's celebrated discourse on the Metaphysical Poets in
his *Life of Cowley* is largely based on his judgment of their wit,
and the incorporation of learning in their poetic sensibility.
He however did not characterize their thought or philosophy
as essentially medieval or scholastic.   He is silent on this point,
for he had confined himself to "a general representation of the
style and sentiments of the Metaphysical Poets." [4]

The other element which Johnson condemned in these poets
was the analytical quality of their style.   The subtle, argumentative and analytical method of developing a single
poetic idea as in "The Dream," so that erudition and intellect
are fused into an original pattern of thought, could not appeal
to Johnson.   He therefore condemned the analytical quality
of "Metaphysical Wit and Conceit":

"Their attempts were always analytical, they broke every
image into fragments, and could no more represent by their
slender conceits and laboured particularities, the prospects of
nature or the scenes of life than he who dissects a sunbeam

[1] Samuel Johnson's "Life of Cowley": *Lives of the Most Eminent English Poets*,
by Samuel Johnson, edited by W. E. Henley, 1896, vol. i, p. 15.
[2] *The First Half of the Seventeenth Century*, H. J. C. Grierson (1906), p. 157.
[3] Johnson, *op. cit.*, pp. 27–29.
[4] *Ibid.*, p. 29.

with a prism can exhibit the wide effulgence of a summer noon."

Though Johnson recognized that "Metaphysical Poets were men of learning," he was evidently wrong when he declared that "to show their learning was their whole endeavour," for Donne drew his imagery from the province of learning not because he wanted to "show off" his scholarship, but because it enabled him to avoid traditional mythological imagery and worn-out Elizabethan diction, and sometimes he can be transparently simple where his thinking is most impassioned.[1]

Johnson knew that "to write on their plan, it was at least necessary to read and think," though he did not realize that Donne's thinking modified his poetic sensibility. As T. S. Eliot has aptly remarked: "A thought to Donne was an experience, it modified his sensibility."[2]

It was thus clear that Dryden and Johnson both condemned Donne's conceits and the application of metaphysical wit and learning to poetic imagery and they separated wit from poetic thought. Dryden called him "The greatest wit, though not the greatest poet of our nation," though wit and the poetic emotion are inseparable in Donne; and Johnson even condemned the argumentative and analytical quality of his wit. The rough and rugged satires of Donne, the harsh quality of his lyric thought, could not be reduced to the Neo-Classical ideal of reason and correctness. This opinion was transmitted through Johnson to the nineteenth century, when attempts were made by Coleridge and De Quincey to revive interest in Donne.

Coleridge also held that Donne misapplied his learning, for he refers to "the utmost boundless stores of capacious memory, and exercised on subjects where we had no right to expect it."

---

[1] Sometimes Donne's impassioned poetic language is so simple that the words fall in natural prose order:

(a) For Godsake hold your tongue and let me love. (*The Canonization.*)
(b) All day the same our postures were,
    And we said nothing, all the day. (*The Extasie.*)
(c) Why should we rise, because 'tis light?
    Did we lie down, because 'twas night? (*The Breake of Day.*)

Here no "heterogeneous ideas are yoked by violence together" as Dr. Johnson held.

[2] *Selected Essays*, by T. S. Eliot, p. 287.

He expressed the same opinion in his notes on Donne's *Sermons*, where he traced the origin of his conceits to scholastic and medieval philosophy. This tradition of exploring and estimating the element of "learning" has passed on to those critics who have helped in the remarkable revival of interest in Donne during the last two decades.

Miss M. P. Ramsay [1] and Mrs. Simpson [2] have both declared Donne to be a schoolman in theology and philosophy with some modern faculty of self-analysis and tolerance in religion. They have neglected the strain of scepticism in his philosophy, nor have they tried to assign to the scholastic and mystical elements in his thought their proper significance, and Sir Herbert Grierson alone has emphasized the importance of scepticism in Donne's poetry:

"A Spirit of Scepticism and Paradox plays through and disturbs everything he wrote, except at moments when an intense mood of feeling, whether love or devotion, begets faith, and silences the sceptical and destructive wit by power of vision rather than of intellectual conviction." [3]

I, however, do not agree that this is true of "everything he wrote," for intellectual conviction through "controverted divinity" preceded his faith and power of vision as revealed in his *Sermons*.

Donne's scepticism should be studied in relation to the rise of Pyrrhonism in Renaissance literature, for it influenced him as it had done other Elizabethans, like Bacon, Nash, and Shakespeare; even the Cambridge Platonists of the seventeenth century like Chillingworth did not escape the influence of Sextus Empiricus.

The publication of the *Hypotyposes* of Sextus Empiricus in 1559, with a Latin translation by Henri Estienne, was an important event in the history of Renaissance thought, for the writings of this ancient sceptical philosopher deeply influenced Montaigne, whose wide influence sent abroad a wave of scepticism and doubt.

Montaigne and Donne as Sceptics.—Montaigne's essays were published by John Florio in 1603, and by 1632 two editions

---

[1] *Les Doctrines Médiévales chez Donne* (Oxford, 1917).
[2] *Study of the Prose Works of John Donne*, chapter v (Oxford).
[3] *Donne's Poetical Works*, Sir Herbert Grierson, vol. ii, p. x.

had already appeared; that Donne had read Montaigne we know by a letter he wrote to Sir George More. He is saying that "no other kind of conveyance is better for knowledge or love than letters" and points out that: "The Italians, which are most discursive, and think the world owes them all wisdom, abound so much in this kind of expressing, that Michel Montaigne says, he hath seen (as I remember) 400 volumes of Italian letters. But it is the other capacity which must make mine acceptable, that they are also the best conveyers of love." [1]

Montaigne was a "sceptic" in the original sense of the word, for in his *Apology of Raymond Sebond* he brought all his power of learning and intellect to bear on his main purpose, which was to discredit *reason* and shake all *certainty*. Pascal defined the essential character of Montaigne's philosophy when he censured him for "putting all things in doubt."

"Montaigne," according to J. Robertson, "at this stage was full of Pyrrhonism he had drawn from Sextus Empiricus and will allow no virtue to reason save as a means of discrediting reason."

Sextus Empiricus was also translated into English, for Nash refers to a translation now lost. R. B. McKerrow in his notes on Nash's (*Summer's Last Will*) remarks: "The whole of this (lines 670–735) comes ultimately from the *Pyrrhoniae Hypotyposes* of Sextus Empiricus, though not of course directly from the Greek, nor even, I believe, from the Latin translation of Henri Estienne." In 1591 Nash spoke of the works of Sextus having been "latelie translated into English for the benefit of unlearned writers" (iii, 332, 31–34), and in i, 174, 4, and 185, 8, where, quoting from him, he wrongly substitutes "ashes" for "asses" and "bones" for "beans," we seem to have evidence that he was himself using an incorrect copy of such a translation. I have, however, failed to discover any early Englishing of the work.[2] McKerrow has pointed out that S. Rowland, in his tract entitled *Brieve's Ghost Haunting Conycatchers*, borrowed the whole of his discourse from Sextus on "A notable scholar-like discourse upon the nature of Dogges." [3]

[1] *The Life and Letters of John Donne*, Gosse, vol. i, p. 122.
[2] *Works of Thomas Nash*, edited by R. B. McKerrow, vol. iv, pp. 428–431.
[3] *Ibid.*

It is significant that Donne also knew the *Hypotyposes* of Sextus as well as the account of the famous Greek sceptic Pyrrho (in Diogenes Laertius), about whom Sextus says: "In the definition of the sceptic system there is also implicitly included that of the Pyrrhonean Philosopher: he is the man who participates in this 'ability.'" [1]

Donne refers to Sextus in his *Essays in Divinity*; he is discussing the "boldness" which the casuists, sceptics and schoolmen have taken with the "words," and he refers to Sextus:

"But therefore we may spare Divine authority and ease our Faith too, because it is present to our reason. For omitting the quarrelsome contending of Sextus Empiricus, the Pyrrhonian (of the author of which sect Laertius says, that he handled Philosophy bravely, having invented a way by which a man should determine nothing of everything), who with his ordinary weapon, a two-edged sword, thinks he cuts off all arguments against production of nothing, by this *Non sit quod jam est, nec quod non est; nam non patitur mutationem quod non est*; and omitting those idolaters of nature, the Epicureans, who pretending a mannerly lothness to trouble God, because *Nec bene pro meritis capitur, nec tangitur ira*, indeed out of their pride are loth to be beholden to God, say that we are sick of the fear of God, *Quo morbo mentem concussa, Timore Deorum?*"

It is significant that Donne just before he became a priest remembered the sceptical philosophers in his study of the Holy Scriptures only to discredit them. Donne brought the accumulated learning of centuries to bear upon his reading of the Holy Scriptures, and nothing reveals to us the mind of Donne the theologian better than these curious, learned, but sincere *Essays in Divinity*. [2]

In one of his sermons preached at Whitehall, April 21, 1618, Donne again referred to the sceptical philosophers who undermined all certainty and doubted the truth of all things: "Those Sceptic Philosophers that doubted of all, though they affirmed nothing, yet they denied nothing neither, but they saw no reason in the opinion of others" [3]; and here it is important to remember that the central problem in faith to Donne was

---

[1] *Outlines of Pyrrhonism*, translated by the Rev. R. G. Bury, 1933, p. 9.
[2] *Essays in Divinity*, edited by Dr. Jessopp (1855), pp. 70–71.
[3] Donne's *Sermons*, vol. v, p. 562, edited by Henry Alford.

the "certainty" of salvation; it is a theme which he has treated with a wealth of learning and imagination in his poems as well as in his sermons.

That Donne was attracted by the Renaissance scepticism which has left its mark on his early writings is beyond doubt. The spirit of scepticism is present in his "Paradoxes and Problems" as well as in his "Sonnets" and "Satires"; and this is significant, for Donne's early training was in the hands of the Jesuits, his uncle himself being a well-known Jesuit, Father Jasper Haywood, who succeeded Father Parsons as head of the English Jesuit Mission, and Donne was thus familiar from his early youth [1] with the different schools of medieval philosophy and learning. He has himself told us (in *Pseudo-Martyr*) that he "surveyed and digested the whole body of divinity controverted between ours and the Roman Church." The cardinal principle of the scholastic system is that it affords "certainty" in belief, as Pope Leo XIII has said of St. Thomas that by his method "of Philosophysing, not only in teaching the truth but also in refuting error, he has gained this prerogative for himself," [2] and it is the note of restless intellectual curiosity rather than that of serene certainty which we find in Donne's early poetry and prose.

It is thus evident that Donne, like other poets, such as Nash and Shakespeare, was also interested in scepticism. Bacon made it fashionable in his *Essays*. Montaigne, the great sceptic of the Renaissance, was very popular in Elizabethan England; Ben Jonson (in his *Volpone*, Act III, Sc. 11) declared that "all our English Writers . . . will deign to steal . . . from Montaigne," and J. M. Robertson [3] has shown the curious borrowings of Shakespeare from Montaigne. Donne, it seems, had read Sextus Empiricus and the other ancient Greek sceptics in Latin, and though Montaigne's subtle and discursive intellect might have fascinated him, his search for truth is far more serious and philosophical than that of Montaigne. Montaigne doubted even the immortality of the

---

[1] Walton tells us that "about the nineteenth year" Donne began to study the works of Cardinal Bellarmine, but Dr. Jessopp has pointed out that Walton was wrong, for the Cardinal's *Disputations* were not published till 1593.

[2] *Summa Theologica of St. Thomas Aquinas* (Dominican Fathers' Translation), vol. i, No. 1, p. xxiv.

[3] *Montaigne and Shakespeare*, by J. M. Robertson (1897).

soul; but Donne is a more serious inquirer about truth than Montaigne; even his third satire, written as early as 1594, becomes a sermon; it opens with a serious inquiring note:

> "Is not our Mistresse faire Religion,
>   As worthy of all our Soules devotion,
>   As virtue was to the first blinded age?"

Montaigne's retreat from Paris into the quiet of his magnificent library in the village of his birth presents a strange contrast to Donne's conception of life as a continual warfare in which all the energies of man's soul and intellect should be cast on the side of goodness. Montaigne wrote in his essay on "Solitude":

"We should reserve a storehouse for ourselves . . . altogether ours, and wholly free, wherein we may hoard up and establish our true liberty, the principal retreat and solitariness, wherein we must go alone to ourselves. . . . We have lived long enough for others; let us live for ourselves at least this latter end of our life; let us bring our thoughts and our purposes home to ourselves, and for our full content."

A resolution of quite another kind breathes through Donne's early writings; even in his Paradox 9, where scepticism and cynicism cross and illumine each other, he declares: "Truly this *life* is a *Tempest* and a *Warfare*, and he which *dares dye*, to escape the *Anguish* of it, seems to me but so *valiant*, as he which *dares hang* himself, lest he bee *prest* to the *wars*"; and in his last sermon he again declared: "*Militia Vita*, our whole life is a warfare, God would not chuse *cowards*." [1]

Donne could not retire into "the insipid country" and devote himself to the culture of his soul and rejoice like Montaigne in "his liberty and tranquillity and leisure"; he had a horror of inactivity and idle leisure, as is evident from his letters written from his "dungeon of Mitcham." [2] His inactivity was the cause of his "melancholy" during his residence at Mitcham, "for to this hour I am nothing, or so little, that I am scarce subject and argument good enough for one of mine own letters": he did not believe in a life of leisure, and benevolent, passive "goodness": "But if I ask myself what I have done in the last watch, or would do in the next,

---

[1] *Sermons*, p. 436.
[2] Donne's letter to Sir Henry Goodyer—Gosse, vol. i, p. 194.

I can say nothing; if I say that I have passed without hurting any, so may the spider in my window." [1] The resolve to do something worthy of his high intellectual capacities is ever with him in the darkest hour of gloom; "yet I would live, and be some such thing as you might not be ashamed to love," [2] he wrote to Goodyer.

Nothing illustrates the difference between the minds of Donne and Montaigne better than their attitude towards their own death. Montaigne declared that "among the number of several other offices which the general and principal character of knowing how to live includes, is this article of knowing how to die, and it is amongst the lightest, if our fears did not give weight to it." [3] And in another essay he declared in a personal tone that "in judging another's life I observe always how its close has borne itself, and my chief endeavour regarding mine own end is that it may carry itself well, that is to say, quietly and insensibly." [4] Donne's elaborate preparation to meet his death is too well known to be related here; the intellectual quality of Donne's mind, and the sombre majesty of his imagination, is nowhere so vividly revealed as in his meditations on death in his divine poems, sermons and devotions. His idea about his manner of dying written as early as 1608 provides us with an interesting contrast with Montaigne's desire to die "quietly and insensibly": "I would not that death should take me asleep, I would not have him merely seize me, and only declare me to be dead, but win me and overcome me." [5]

Montaigne considered the day of death to be the Day of Judgement, while to Donne every day of life is a Day of Judgement, for it helps or retards the growth of man in goodness and sanctification. Montaigne said: "It is thus that all the other days of our lives must be put to the touch and tested by this last stroke. It is the master-day, it is the day that is the judge

[1] Donne's letter to Sir Henry Goodyer—Gosse, vol. i, p. 194.　[2] *Ibid.*, p. 190.
[3] See Montaigne's essay "Of Physiognomy," Book III, chapter 12, *The Essays of Montaigne*, translated by G. B. Ives (1925). Pascal criticized Montaigne's conception of death, and said that "his wholly pagan feeling about death cannot be excused, for one must relinquish all piety, if one does not desire to die, at least, in a Christian Manner; now throughout his book he has in mind only to die weakly and gently."
[4] *Montaigne's Essays*, Ives, p. 104.
[5] Donne's letter to Sir Henry Goodyer—Gosse, vol. i, p. 191.

of all other days.   It is the day, says one of the ancients, which
is to pass judgement on all my past years." [1]

Donne in his last sermon passionately declared: "Our
criticall day is *not* the *very day* of our *death*; but the whole course
of our life.   I thank him that *prayes* for me when my *Bell* tolles,
but I thank him much more that *catechises mee*, or *preaches* to
mee, or *instructs mee how to live*." [2]

Donne's humanism is made of a richer texture than that of
Montaigne; it was enriched by the passionate ardour of his
soul's attempt to apprehend God, an attempt which Montaigne
ruled out of his scheme of life.   Though Donne was interested
in the Renaissance scepticism, in fact he is not a sceptic in the
literal sense of the word.   The main weapon in the hands of
the Renaissance sceptics like Montaigne, and the ancient
sceptics like Sextus Empiricus, was to discredit reason, suspend
judgement, and undermine all certainty; and this approach
is foreign to Donne's mind.

That Donne played with these ideas, which have left their
impression on his early writings, is beyond doubt, but that he
seriously believed in them at any stage of his life is improbable.
It must be remembered that in the third satire, before he
counsels us to "doubt wisely," he has proved the futility of
the various Christian Churches, which do not embody the
spirit of Christ.   Religion was no longer to be found at Rome,
where ". . . shee was a thousand years agoe"; nor could he
love the Calvinistic Church—

> ". . . who at Geneva is called
> Religion, plaine, simple, sullen, yong,
> Contemptuous, yet unhansome."

Nor did the Anglican Church nearer home appeal to him;
for he was in search of the one Universal Catholic Church,
the one True Church of Christ, which like the idealists in every
age he was not destined to find.   In his characteristic manner
Donne declared:

> ". . . though truth and falsehood bee
> Neare twins, yet truth a little elder is;
> Be busie to seeke her, believe me this,
> Hee's not of none, nor worst, that seekes the best."

---

[1] *Montaigne's Essays*, Ives, p. 103.

[2] Kafka also said: "Only our concept of time makes it possible for us to speak
of the Day of Judgement by that name; in reality it is a summary court in
perpetual session."

This is not the language of scepticism but of an earnest inquirer after truth, who has embarked on that odyssey of the spirit, the search for a "true religion."

Donne could not say with Montaigne "Que sais je?" (What do I know?)—he was intent on finding truth for himself; and instead of adoration or scorn ("To adore, or scorn an image, or protest, may all be bad") he discovered another way of search;

> ". . . doubt wisely; in strange way
> To stand inquiring right, is not to stray;
> To sleepe, or runne wrong, is." [1]

To inquire in a wise manner and the right spirit was to Donne a better course than to neglect truth or to be afraid of facing it; and that he proceeded in this search not with any cynical disregard of the opposite points of view, or with the essential purpose of searching all things with the eye of a sceptic, he tells us in his preface to *Pseudo-Martyr* [2]: "In which search and disquisition, that God which awakened me then, and hath never forsaken me in that industry, as He is the author of that purpose, so is He a witness of this protestation, that I behaved myself, and proceeded therein with humility and diffidence in myself, and by that which by His grace I took to be the ordinary means, which is frequent prayer and indifferent affections." It was Donne's earnest desire to "use no inordinate haste nor precipitation in binding my conscience to any real religion" that led him to "doubt wisely" and "inquire rightly." In this satire an important element has often been neglected: Donne definitely expresses himself against accepting any interpretation of religious truth on the authority of temporal power, and it implies his distrust at this stage of his life of the principles on which he thought the Roman Catholic as well as the Reformed Churches were based—Donne says:

> "Foole and wretch, wilt thou let they Soul be tyed
> To mans lawes, by which she shall not be tryed

---

[1] *The Poetical Works of J. Donne*, edited by Professor Grierson, vol. i, p. 157.

[2] Bacon was the first to use this term when he was prosecuting Campion. In reply to Campion's protestation that he did not meddle in the high politics of the State, Bacon retorted "whereby may appear what trust is to be given to the words of such *Pseudo-Martyrs*": *Execution of Justice in England for Maintenance of Public and Christian Peace against certain Stirrers of Sedition.* December 1583.

At the last Day?   or will it then boot thee
To say a Philip or a Gregory,
A Harry or a Martin taught thee this?
Is not this excuse for mere contraries
Equally strong? can not both sides say so?
That thou mayest rightly obey power, her bounds know." [1]

It is interesting to compare Montaigne's view in such matters, who advised complete obedience to the ecclesiastical authority: "We must either submit altogether to the authority of our ecclesiastical governments or dispense with it altogether: it is not for us to fix how much obedience we owe it." [2]

It is thus evident that when Montaigne declared "what do I know?" and when Donne advised us to "doubt wisely" they were expressing two different types of mind, one that of the sceptic and the other that of an earnest seeker after truth, who at the same time was fully alive in his age and interested in its philosophical speculations and scientific discoveries. It is true Donne was attracted by the scepticism of Sextus and Montaigne, and we should recognize the importance of this element in Donne's thought, for it marks a point of departure in his spiritual development. It was his reading of the "sceptical philosophers" which revealed to him the dangers of their negative knowledge and taught him to distrust reason in the interest of what Donne called "spiritual reason," which is a faculty of vision given to the "regenerate Christian" and which "natural man" does not possess.

The Rev. R. G. Bury [3] has defined scepticism thus: "A 'sceptic,' in the original sense of the Greek term, is simply an inquirer or investigator. But inquiry often leads to an impasse and ends in credulity or despair of solution; so that the 'inquirer' becomes a 'doubter' or a disbeliever." Donne was never a sceptic in this sense.

Donne inquired and sometimes perhaps doubted, but he never disbelieved; he was not a sceptic in the philosophical sense of the word. Sextus Empiricus declared that "scepticism is an ability or mental attitude, which opposes appearance to judgments in any way whatsoever, with the result that, owing to the equipollence of the objects and reasons thus opposed, we are brought forcibly to a state of mental suspense

[1] *The Poetical Works of J. Donne*, edited by Professor Grierson, vol. i. p. 157.
[2] *Montaigne's Essays*, Ives, p. 242.
[3] Sextus Empiricus, vol. i, p. xxix.

and next to a state of 'unperturbedness' or 'quietude,'" and he further defined "Suspense" and "quietude" ingeniously: "Suspense is a state of mental rest owing to which we neither deny nor affirm anything; quietude is an untroubled and tranquil condition of soul." [1]

It was in this spirit of scepticism that Montaigne inscribed on the walls of his library: "I determine nothing: I do not comprehend things; I suspend judgement; I examine." This attitude of mind, to examine in order to determine nothing, is foreign to Donne's mind. T. S. Eliot has declared that Donne "was more interested in *ideas* themselves as objects than he was in the *truth* of ideas." [2] But the whole endeavour of Donne's learning and devotion seems to be to apprehend the "truth of ideas" as objective realities, his distrust of rationalism being based on the inadequacy of ideas as such; "controverted divinity" failed to satisfy his intellect and soul alike, and "for the agony and exercise of our sense and spirit" [3]—as Donne himself describes his search—he had to go, as he tells us, to "prayer and meditation." [3] Donne was fascinated by the different categories of ideas which he came across in his "immoderate desire of human learning and languages," and he played with them dialectically, "catlike," as T. S. Eliot puts it; but ideas in themselves never satisfied the eager curiosity of his intellect or the hunger of his soul. His agile mind was attracted by the scepticism of Sextus Empiricus and Montaigne's negative attitude towards philosophical truth also fascinated him, for he once said:

> "There's nothing simply good, nor ill alone,
> Of every quality comparison,
> The onely measure is, and judge, opinion." [4]

---

[1] *Outlines of Pyrrhonism*, trans. by Bury, p. 9.

[2] *A Garland for John Donne*, 2 p. 11.

[3] See Gosse, vol. i, p. 190.

[4] *The Progress of the Soul* was composed in 1601; Donne must have read Montaigne in the original as Florio's translation did not appear till 1603; the letter to his father-in-law, Sir George More, where Donne refers to Montaigne, Gosse assigns to 1603. Donne's interest in scepticism soon waned, and curiously it coincided with his loss of sympathy with the Roman Church. This must have been well known to Donne's friends and admirers, otherwise how could he have been commissioned to help Thomas Morton? Donne's sympathies for the Roman Catholic Church should be considered to have definitely ended by 1604, for by 1605 he was openly helping Morton against his brilliant Catholic and Jesuit opponents.

Montaigne had also said that "the taste of Good and Evil depends, for a good part, upon the opinion we have of them." These ideas were in the air, and the Elizabethan poets were "playing" with them as Donne had done in his early writings. Hamlet had said "there is nothing good or bad, but thinking makes it so," and Marston (in *What you Will*) had also declared:

"... all that exists
Takes valuation from opinion."

Donne was interested in scepticism as he was interested in the scientific discoveries and concepts of his age, but we cannot agree with Brevold when he says, "yet his youthful scepticism profoundly influenced him." [1]   His scepticism was a passing phase in the development of his religious life and he used it in the body of his poetry as he did the dialectics of the schoolmen and the astronomical concepts of Kepler.

The scientific discoveries of his age, like those of Kepler, Copernicus and Galileo, not only altered his medieval conception of the physical universe, but also undermined "certainty" in philosophy and helped him to assume a sceptical attitude towards philosophical truth in his early years. In his *Bia-thanatos*, written in 1608, he refers to Kepler's *De Stella Nova in Pede Serpentarii*, published in 1606, and in his *Conclave Ignatii* he tells us of his study of Copernicus and Galileo, "who of late both summoned the other worlds, the stars to come nearer to him and to give him an account of themselves," and again in the following well-known lines he described the disintegrating influence of the New Astronomy on his mind:

"And New Philosophy calls all in doubt
The Element of fire is quite put out;
The Sun is lost, and Th'Earth, and no mans wit
Can well direct him where to looke for it."

An Anatomie of the World.

And he realized that

"'Tis all in pieces, all coherence gone:
All just supply, and all Relation."

Professor Grierson has admirably treated the effect of the New Astronomy on Donne's poetic sensibility,[2] for his imagina-

[1] "The Naturalism of Donne in relation to some Renaissance Traditions," *The Journal of English and Germanic Philology*, 1923, 471–502.
[2] Grierson, vol. ii, Introduction, p. xxviii.   Professor Grierson has here pointed out the disintegrating effect on "accepted beliefs" exercised by the new astronomy;

tion never lost the impress of the new astronomical thought of Kepler and Galileo. "Copernicism in the mathematics," wrote Donne in a letter (1615), "hath carried earth farther up, from the stupid centre and yet not honoured it, nor advantaged it, because for the necessity of appearance it hath carried heaven so much higher from it." [1] Donne even remembered the new philosophy in his devotions: "I am up, and I seem to *stand*, and I go *round*, and I am a new *Argument* of the *new Philosophie*, That the *Earth* moves round, why may I not believe, that the *whole earth* moves in *round motion*, though that seems to mee to *stand*, when as I seem to *stand* to my *company*, and yet am carried, in a giddy and *circular motion* as I *stand*?" [2]

But this "New Philosophy" did not give rise to scepticism in the original sense of the word, for Donne ever fervently believed in God and recognized the need of religion and the Church; while the sceptics had adopted a negative attitude even in their theory of the existence of God. Sextus Empiricus asks: "How shall we be able to reach a conception of God when we have no agreement about his substance or his form, or his place of abode? . . . consequently, the existence of God cannot be proved from any other fact. But if God's existence is neither automatically pre-evident nor proved from another fact it will be inapprehensible." [3]

This negative attitude of mind could not satisfy Donne's intellect, which was essentially positive. Donne is perhaps referring to the sceptical philosophers when in one of his sermons he said: "One philosopher thinks he is dived to the bottome when he says, he knowes nothing, but this, that he knowes nothing."

It has become a commonplace of the criticism of Donne to

Joan Bennett (*Four Metaphysical Poets*) has, however, made a curious remark about Donne's attitude to astronomy. She says: "He expressed no opinion as to the facts. . . . The poetry tells us nothing about Donne's intellectual attitude to astronomy, except that he was aware both of obsolete and of recent theories." But surely Donne was aware of the disintegrating influence of the new astronomy, for he knew that it had called in doubt the accepted and settled view of the universe, and this was an intellectual attitude towards the new astronomy. Donne could of course no more pronounce an authoritative opinion about the scientific merits of Kepler's *De Stella Nova* than could Tennyson on Robert Chambers' *Vestiges of the Natural History of Creation* (1844) or Darwin's *Origin of Species* (1859).

[1] Gosse, ii, 78-79.
[2] *Donne's Devotions*, edited by John Sparrow, p. 128.
[3] *Sextus Empiricus: Outlines of Pyrrhonism*, 3, Rev. R. G. Bury, pp. 330-331.

quote the following lines from his third satire, to prove his scepticism in his early years:

> "Doubt wisely; in strange way,
>   To stand inquiring right, is not to stray;
>   To sleepe, or runne wrong, is."

But it has not yet been noticed that Donne was echoing St. Thomas Aquinas, who has expressed almost the same view in his commentary on Aristotle's *Metaphysics*:

"Any one who seeks after truth must begin by doubting stoutly, because the finding of truth is nothing else but the solving of doubt. . . . It is clear that anyone who does not know where he is going, cannot go straight except by chance. Hence no one can keep on the right path in the search for truth unless he knows beforehand the doubt of the question . . . just as in the courts no one can act as judge who has not heard all sides, so that the hearer of philosophy is better able to act as umpire if he has been told all that the doubting adversaries have to say for themselves. . . . Those whose aim is to discuss truth and truth only must not take up an attitude of hostility to any of the disputants on whose claims they are to sit in judgement. Their proper attitude towards all parties is that of impartial investigation." [1]

And Aquinas quotes Aristotle: "To those who wish to investigate truth it belongs to doubt rightly."

Donne seems to have literally followed the advice of the Angelic Doctor in his search for truth, for he doubted wisely and inquired rightly and with strict impartiality surveyed the whole body of "controverted divinity." Donne was not alone in adopting this attitude; Chapman had also realized, though not in such an acute form, the disturbing influence of the new astronomy on the settled view of the universe:

> "Heaven moves so far off that men say it stands;
>   And Earth is turn'd the true and moving Heaven;
>   And so, 'tis left; and so all truth is driven
>   From her false bosom; all is left alone,
>   Till all be ordered with confusion." [2]

The disintegrating influence of the new philosophy and

---

[1] In Metaphysical Lecture, I. Also see *The Catholic Church and Philosophy*, by V. MacNabb, pp. 64, 65.
[2] "The Tears of Peace," Chapman's *Poems*, edited by Shepherd, p. 114.

astronomy resulted in changing Donne's "world view," which was no longer consistent with the scholastic view of the universe.[1] The "climate" of Donne's thought in his early writings is peculiarly that of the Renaissance. Miss Ramsay has neglected the Renaissance elements in his thought, such as scepticism, the influence of the new philosophy, and the peculiar inquiring and questioning spirit which animated such diverse men as Erasmus, Bacon and Hooker. She has depicted Donne essentially as a Neo-Platonist, undisturbed by any philosophical doubt.[2] Professor Picavet[3] has emphasized the Neo-Platonic element in medieval philosophy, and following him Miss Ramsay resolved the complex and rich texture of Donne's thought into the simplicity of medieval doctrines of unquestioning faith. Donne's temperament, as Professor Grierson has pointed out, "was rather that of the Renaissance than that either of the Puritan England or of the Counter-Reformation, whether in Catholic countries or in the Anglican Church."

But it was the emptiness of scepticism and inadequacy of reason that led him to mysticism. Donne knew how the light of reason goes out, leaving a man helpless in matters of faith, and how God damps the understanding and darkens the intellect. He knew that the greatest affliction comes when "God worketh upon the spirit itself and damps that, that he casts a sooty cloud upon the understanding and darkens that."[4] Donne gained, as we shall see, the "modest assurance" of his salvation not through intellectual conviction and philosophical reasoning but through mystical faith.

Donne the Schoolman.—Miss Ramsay has exhaustively quoted from his works to prove that Donne's conception of God and Nature is essentially scholastic. Mrs. Simpson in summarizing Miss Ramsay's conclusions says:

[1] According to the scholastic conception the heavenly bodies are incorruptible and therefore fixed, for in all corruptible things the form does not penetrate the matter completely and so the object remains in a state of potentiality, and this enables it to move, but as in the stars "the form fills the whole potentiality of matter," they "consist of their entire matter" (*Contra Gentiles*, Book III). The circular movement was proper to heavenly bodies because they were without a "contrary," while the straight-line movements of all the other elements, fire, air, water and earth, showed that they had "contraries" away from which they had a tendency to move. This tendency the stars did not possess and were therefore fixed (*Summa Theologica*, Part II, ques. 85, art. 6).
[2] See *Les Doctrines Médiévales chez Donne* (1917), p. 18.
[3] In his book *Esquisse d'une histoire générale et comparée des philosophies médiévales.* Paris, 1907.   [4] Alford, v., p. 326.

"Miss M. P. Ramsay has shown that his thought belongs to the Middle Ages rather than to the Renaissance." She shows that Donne's thought is marked by three characteristics— it is fundamentally theological, its attitude towards science and the knowledge of the external world is in harmony with that of the Middle Ages, and it assigns to authority a place very similar to that given to it by medieval times. Though he often criticizes the super-subtlety of the schoolmen, he accepts their fundamental doctrines, their point of view, and their vocabulary. His philosophy starts from an unshakeable belief in the existence of God and he sees God everywhere in the universe.

"In his method of expounding this great reality he followed the schoolmen in their respect for the past, in the constant appeal to authority and in the frequent use of the allegorical system of interpretation." [1]

The platonic element in Donne's thought, which has been noticed by Professor Mario Praz,[2] came to him through scholasticism. Doctrines, the source of which may be traced to Plato or Aristotle, were familiar to Donne in the philosophy of St. Thomas Aquinas and the elaborate discussions of the scholastic theology, and they entered the scholastic philosophy through the system of Plotinus and his followers.

It was through St. Augustine, Boëthius and Pseudo-Dionysius that the Neo-Platonic philosophy became an important element in the theology of the schoolmen; but we are not concerned here with this problem; our limited purpose is to determine how far Donne, who was steeped in the philosophy of St. Thomas Aquinas, agreed with the scholastic conception of God, intellect, knowledge, faith and reason—to take only a few themes of Thomism.

Donne's acceptance of the scholastic doctrines of St. Thomas has been assumed to be an established fact; Mrs. Simpson has even asserted that "he accepts their fundamental doctrines, their point of view, and their vocabulary." [3]

He is in fact represented as still believing and preaching a philosophy which in the seventeenth century had fallen into

---

[1] *A Study of the Prose Works of John Donne*, by Evelyn M. Simpson, p. 94.
[2] "Donne and the Poetry of his Time," Mario Praz. *A Garland for John Donne*.
[3] *A Study of the Prose Works of John Donne*, by E. M. Simpson.

disrepute, and whose citadel had been stormed by the "New Philosophy of Bacon." [1] Donne really did not exclusively belong to one system of thought; his great passion for learning and languages, as well as his restless curiosity, led him to a large number of medieval philosophers of various schools and denominations, and he quoted them freely in his poems, devotions and sermons. It was really his acceptance of the Creed that gave shape and coherence to his immense learning.

The fact that Donne has been supposed to belong exclusively to the scholastic philosophy of St. Thomas has led to much confusion; and we are still far from having a clear and definite view of his philosophy and mysticism.

If we take for example the different views which Mrs. Simpson has expressed about the scholastic and mystical elements in Donne's thought we do not get any clear and definite idea about the philosophy of Donne and the school to which he belongs. She has no doubt whatsoever about his having been brought up in the scholastic system of thought: "Thus he was reared up in the philosophical and the theological system of St. Thomas Aquinas and his followers, so that he was in full sympathy with the scholastic method of argument"; then she observes: "His thought is medieval in character and most of his ideas can be traced back through Aquinas to St. Augustine and other early Christian writers who brought into the Catholic Church much of the Philosophy of Neo-Platonism." [2]

She further makes mysticism an integral part of Donne's thought. "Donne's mysticism cannot be isolated from the rest of his thought; for his whole philosophy is that of a Christian mystic reared in the Neo-Platonic tradition which the scholastic writers of the Middle Ages had inherited." [3] The fact is that Mrs. Simpson apparently equates scholasticism with Thomism and accepts Professor Picavet's exaggerated view about the influence of Plotinus.

It is strange that, while Mrs. Simpson calls Donne "a mystic reared in the Neo-Platonic tradition," Miss Ramsay asserts

[1] Professor Basil Willey has written an instructive chapter on "Bacon and the Rehabilitation of Nature" in *The Seventeenth-century Background*. Chatto and Windus, 1934.
[2] *A Study of the Prose Works of John Donne*, by E. M. Simpson, p. 88.
[3] *Ibid.*, p. 97.

that he lacked the completeness, certainty and serenity of the Neo-Platonic mystic: "Donne's work remains a collection of fragments, unified only by the ineluctable impression that one strange and fascinating mind produced them all. From the intellectual struggle there was indeed a way of escape of which Donne seems unconscious, or from which perhaps his own temperament excluded him"—meaning the Neo-Platonic thought.[1]

Scholasticism is not one continuous and compact system of philosophy in the Middle Ages. It dominated the imagination of the Christian philosophers from the ninth to the fourteenth centuries A.D., when its decay began; during these long five centuries of philosophical speculation many modifications and additions were made to scholastic philosophy. The scientific writings of Aristotle came into the hands of European philosophers only in the later half of the twelfth century, and so it was only in the thirteenth century, after the assimilation of the philosophy of Aristotle, that scholasticism in the hands of St. Thomas attained its perfection. This period can be divided as follows:

1. The eighth, ninth and tenth centuries form a period in which we find only the beginnings of those controversies and problems which were to occupy the minds of the schoolmen in the later ages.

2. It was in the eleventh and the twelfth centuries that schoolmen began to apply the conclusions of metaphysical logic to explain the theological dogma.

3. The thirteenth century is the great age of scholasticism, when St. Thomas tried to build a comprehensive system based on the fusion of philosophy with Christian theology and dogma.

The fourteenth and fifteenth centuries saw the decline of scholastic philosophy under the influence of Duns Scotus and Occam, who tried to separate philosophical speculation from theology.[2]

---

[1] "Donne's relation to Philosophy," *A Garland for John Donne*.
[2] The literature on the scholastic philosophy is very extensive, but the following books have a special bearing on the points discussed here:

(a) *The Scholastic Philosophy in its relation to Christian Theology*, by B. L. Hereford.
(b) *Scholasticism*, by J. Rickaby.
(c) *A History of Christian Doctrine*, by K. R. Hagenbach.
(d) *The Conception of God in the Philosophy of Aquinas*, by R. L. Patterson.
(e) *St. Thomas Aquinas*, by J. Maritain.

St. Thomas Aquinas' (1225–1274) great achievement was that he wove the philosophy of Aristotle into the fabric of the Christian dogma. In seventeen folio volumes he tried to systematize the teachings of Aristotle, St. Augustine and Pseudo-Dionysius, with the doctrine and teaching of the Church.[1] In the fertile mind of the Angelic Doctor the scholastic system assumed a universality and completeness seldom attained by any school of philosophy. He tried to synthesize many streams of thought, like that of Plato, Aristotle, Plotinus, and Dionysius the Areopagite, with the revelation of the Christian dogma as embodied in the teachings of the Church.

The aim of the encylopædic learning of the schoolmen was to obtain a unification of knowledge; a "summa" was the end to be achieved, and every branch of human thought was to have its relation to the whole defined, and this whole in turn to be related to God and His Church. But in Donne's age humanism and the new learning were aiming at secularizing human knowledge, to discover a beauty that was essentially of this earth, and a pagan strain runs through all the Renaissance literature in England.

Jusserand, speaking of the influence of the Renaissance on European literature and arts, says:

"Christian and Pagan ideas mingle, the notion of Sacrilege fades, men of culture call the mass 'sacra Deorum'; Pulci dedicates his second canto to the 'sovereign Jupiter crucified for us,' Michael Angelo paints in the Sistine Chapel a Christ who seems to be hurling thunderbolts." [2]

In his early poetry, his "Sonets" and "Elegies," Donne is a typical child of the Renaissance, eager for the adventures of the body and the mind alike. The naturalist and sceptical strain in his poetry reveals an attitude of mind towards life and religion which is far removed from that of the schoolmen even of his times; and the importance of this way of thinking is further enhanced when we remember that Donne had been educated by the Jesuits, who were trained in the system of St. Thomas Aquinas, and were themselves the product of the great movement of the Counter-Reformation started after the

[1] *The Philosophy of St. Thomas*, by A. E. Taylor.
[2] Jusserand, *A Literary History of the English People*, vol. i, p. 15.

Council of Trent, where the "summa" was placed on the altar along with the Bible. Pope Leo XIII said: "But we now come to the greatest glory of Thomas—a glory which is altogether his own, and shared with no other catholic Doctor. In the midst of the Council of Trent, the assembled Fathers so willing it, the *Summa* of Thomas Aquinas lay open on the altar, with the Holy Scriptures and the decrees of the supreme Pontiffs, that from it might be sought counsel and reasons and answers." [1]

Donne has himself related the story of his struggles and intellectual effort to free himself from "the Roman Religion," and his rejection of the Roman Catholic religion could not but affect his view of the scholastic philosophy which was still the main weapon of defence of the Roman Catholic faith.[2] Donne says:

"I had a longer work to do than many other men, for I was first to blot out certain impressions of the Roman religion, and to wrestle both against the examples and against the reasons by which some hold was taken and some anticipations early laid upon my conscience, both by persons who by nature had a power of superiority over my will, and others who by their learning and good life seemed to me justly to claim an interest for the guiding and rectifying of mine understanding in these matters." [3]

It is thus evident that Donne had to wrestle not only against the heroic examples of the Catholic martyrs of his own family and of his living Jesuit uncle, Jasper Haywood, men learned, honest, sincere, fearless and bold, but also against "the reasons by which some hold was taken" upon his "conscience"; and these reasons perhaps included the theology of the great schoolmen of the Middle Ages as expounded by his Jesuit teachers, who had defended the dogma of the Church with such learning and philosophical subtlety and ingenuity as could not but interest Donne.

Miss Ramsay has pointed out that amongst other things which the system of St. Thomas Aquinas offered to Christian believers was "certainty": "the second quality I would

[1] *Summa Theologica*, Dominican Fathers' Translation, p. xxvi.
[2] A. L. Moore, *History of the Reformation in England and on the Continent*, pp. 304–305.
[3] See Preface to *Pseudo-Martyr*.

emphasize is its certainty; it offers certainty, and indeed lays it on man as a duty to attain Certainty." [1]

But for Donne, as soon as he had succeeded in blotting out of his memory "certain impressions of the Roman Religion," at least for some time, there was no certainty.

> "'Tis all in peeces, all cohærence gone;
> All just supply, and all Relation!"

It was only after he had surveyed the whole field of controversial theology that he could give intellectual assent to the Anglican Church, but he soon realized that it was not reason but prayer and meditation that could lead to peace and serenity. This approach is already evident in his Mitcham period, and later expounded in his *Essays in Divinity*. In several letters addressed to Goodyer from Mitcham he counsels him to be firm in his allegiance to the Anglican Church, while he writes in *Pseudo-Martyr* as a confirmed Anglican. He had not only blotted out the impressions of Roman religion, but also discovered the essential reasonableness and soundness of the Anglican Church, and at the same time realized that the Anglican Church in matters of continuity of tradition, ordination, and the preaching and practice of the true doctrine was also Catholic.

Though Donne believed that religious toleration and intellectual conviction were necessary for the healthy growth of religious life, he was against showing any wavering when one has accepted a certain form of faith only to show one's tolerance and broadmindedness. In an interesting letter to Sir Henry Goodyer, Donne rebuked him for creating an impression on the Puritans and the Papists alike that he could be converted. Donne had the humanist's broad outlook on life and morals to recognize that "the channels of God's mercies run through both fields; and they are sister teats of His graces," [2] but he could not approve that tolerance should create an impression of weakness of faith. He observes: "Yet let me be bold to fear, that that sound true opinion, that in all

---

[1] "Donne's relation to Philosophy," *A Garland for John Donne*, p. 105. This is not a correct view of St. Thomas's views about the certainty of salvation; in fact he declared that it was not possible to be certain of salvation in this life. See *Summa*, 1a, 2a, c, ques. 112, art. 5.

[2] Gosse, vol. ii, p. 78.

Christian professions there is way to Salvation, (which I think you think), may have been so incommodiously or intempestively sometimes uttered by you; or else your having friends equally near you of all the impressions of religion, may have testified such an indifferency, as hath occasioned some to further such inclinations as they have mistaken to be in you. This I have feared, because heretofore the inobedient puritans and now over-obedient Papists, attempt you." [1]

Donne and St. Thomas's Conception of Intellect, Word and Reason.—Donne realized the need of intellectual conviction, but it was through faith and not reason that he found it. St. Thomas Aquinas has emphasized the power of intellect in the process of "Knowing," and has related it to the soul:

"In our intellect three things exist, viz: The power of the intellect; the idea (species of the thing understood, which is its form, related to the intellect itself as the colour is to the eye), and the act of understanding, which is the operation of the intellect. None of these is signified by the exterior word pronounced by the voice. . . . The word inwardly conceived proceeds outwardly, as is proved by the exterior word, which is its sign, proceeds vocally from the one who utters it inwardly. That therefore is properly called the interior word which the intelligent agent forms by the understanding."

St. Thomas then shows how the "intellect" works and how the operations of the "intellect" are related to the "exterior word":

"And the intellect forms two things, according to its two operations; for by its operation which is called the intelligence of invisible things it forms definition; and by the operation whereby it compares and divides it forms enunciation, or something similar; and therefore what is formed and expressed by the operation of the intellect, either defining or enunciating signifies something by the exterior word." [2]

St. Thomas Aquinas proceeds to relate intellect to the soul on one side and to the exterior word on the other: "What therefore is formed and expressed in the soul is called the interior word; and is therefore related to the intellect, not as that *which it* understands but as that *in which* it understands;

[1] Gosse, vol. ii, p. 78.
[2] *Summa Theologica*, Introduction, opuscle No. xiii.

because in what is thus expressed it sees the nature of what it understands. From these premises, therefore, we can see these two things concerning the word, viz., that the word always proceeds from the intellect and exists in the intellect; and that the word is the idea (ratio) and likeness of what is Understood." [1]

It is instructive to compare Donne's view about the certainty of the operations of intellect of which he thinks there is no criterion. In a letter to Sir Henry Goodyer, he says:

"We consist of three parts, a soul, a body, and mind: which I call those thoughts and affections, and passions, which neither soul nor body hath alone, but have been begotten by their communication, as music results out of our breath and a cornet."

Donne points out that the diseases of the soul which are sins, and the diseases of the bodies to which we fall a victim, can be known with certainty for "our knowledge thereof is also certain." [2]

But of the diseases of the mind, which are doubt and uncertainty, there is no knowing. Donne does not refer his doubts to be cleared and silenced by the dogmas of the Church, but when he goes to human reason and intellect to which, unlike St. Thomas, he does not assign absolute certainty, he discovers that they do not provide any dependable interior of truth:

"But of the diseases of the mind there is no criterion, no canon, no rule, for our own taste and apprehension; and interpretation should be the judge, and that is the disease itself." [3]

Donne realizes, as St. Thomas often says, that the interpretation of a "thing" varies according to the capacity of the individual mind, but what St. Thomas calls "the nature of what it understands" has to Donne no ultimate criterion of truth:

"And I still vex myself with this, because if I know it not, nobody can know it and I comfort myself because I see dispassioned men are subject to the like ignorance. For divers minds out of the same thing often draw contrary conclusions,

---

[1] *Summa Theologica*, Introduction, opuscle No. xiii.
[2] Gosse, vol. i, pp. 184, 185.   [3] *Ibid.*

as Augustine thought devout Anthony to be therefore full of the Holy Ghost, because not being able to-read, he could say the whole Bible, and interpret it; and Thyreus the Jesuit for the same reason doth think all the Anabaptists to be possessed. And as often out of contrary things men draw one conclusion. As to the Roman Church magnificence and splendour hath ever been an argument of God's favour, and poverty and affliction to the Greek." [1]

Donne gives to the knowledge of the soul and of the senses a certain amount of certainty, but to the apprehensions of intellect he assigns no certainty at all, and this assumption is quite different from that which underlies the whole majestic system of the *Summa*. Donne points out:

"Out of this variety of minds it proceeds that though our souls would go to one end, heaven, and all our bodies must go to one end, the earth; yet our third part, the mind, which is our natural guide here, chooses to every man a several way; scarce any man likes what another doth, nor advisedly that which himself."

Aquinas, following Aristotle, has laid great emphasis on exact definition and shown the relation of the word, "verbum," to the intellect, for he maintains that "the word always proceeds from the intellect and exists in the intellect." The metaphysical poets like Donne who were well versed in the philosophy of St. Thomas Aquinas also related the *word* to the intellect rather than to emotion, and this may explain the fusion of the poetic emotion with the intellect in Metaphysical Poetry. Though to Donne "word" was a significant and important thing, he could hardly give it the same authority which St. Thomas has given to it in his philosophy, for Donne thought that the "word" could not express "the nature of what it Understands." He says in one of his letters: "Yea, words which are our subtlest and delicatest outward creatures, being composed of thoughts, and breath, are so muddy, so thick, that our thoughts themselves are so, because (except at the first rising) they are ever leavened with passions and affections." [2]

---

[1] Donne's letter to Sir H. Goodyer. Gosse assigns this letter to the spring of 1608.

[2] Donne's letter to Sir Henry Goodyer—Gosse, vol. i, p. 228.

Donne could not conceive of words in an abstract sense, "pure words, separated from thoughts (which are ever leavened with human passions and affections)," subsisting in the realm of intelligence as St. Thomas did.[1]

Miss Ramsay has given a quotation from Donne's *Sermons* where his imagination plays on the four elements of the medieval physics to prove that "he continues to think in terms of the old system, his reason continues to work upon the old notions . . . he still lets himself, lets the discursive reason work on the notion of the four elements; fire plays its constant part. In the quotation above—water, earth, fire, air—he passes each in review in reference to the dead body. Water and earth and fire and air are the proper boxes in which God lays up our bodies for the resurrection."[2]

A criticism of Donne's philosophy which is based on referring his images back to their medieval sources is destined to lead us nowhere; for it reveals Donne's *method* and not his *thought*. Donne, for the illustration and citation of his views and arguments, drew from the medieval learning as well as from the New Philosophy; it can be easily shown that it was his method in poetry as well as in his *Sermons*. In the following passage Donne uses the New Astronomy to prove man's nearness to Heaven as he had used the medieval physics to show where God shall deposit our ashes after the dissolution of the body:

"And I think, that as Copernicism in the mathematics hath carried earth farther up, from the stupid centre; and yet not honoured it, nor advantaged it, because for the necessity of appearances, it hath carried heaven so much higher from it; so the Roman profession seems to exhale, and refine our wills from earthly drugs and lees, more than the Reformed, and so seems to bring us nearer heaven; but then that carries heaven farther from us, by making us pass so many courts, and offices of saints in this life, in all our petitions, and lying in a painful prison in the next, during the pleasure, not of Him to whom we go, and who must be our Judge, but of them from whom we come, we know not our case."[3]

[1] St. Thomas's use of his vocabulary is judicious and scientific. In the *Summa* alone there are one million and a half words.
[2] "Donne's relation to Philosophy," p. 115, *A Garland for John Donne*.
[3] Gosse—a letter to Sir Henry Goodyer.

This method of illustrating his arguments is common in Donne and has often misled his critics.

Aristotle and the Church.—Those critics of Donne who, like Miss Ramsay, have over-emphasized the presence of the Neo-Platonic element in his thought have neglected the influence of Aristotle on St. Thomas Aquinas; the Aristotelean element in Thomism should be kept in view in any discussion of Donne's relation to philosophy.

Mrs. Simpson has declared Donne to be a "Christian mystic reared in the Neo-Platonic tradition," and also characterized his thought as "medieval in character, most of his ideas can be traced back through Aquinas to St. Augustine, the Pseudo-Dionysius and other early Christian writers who brought into the Catholic Church much of the Philosophy of Neo-Platonism." [1]

If we accept the philosophy of Donne to be largely Neo-Platonic, we cannot easily trace back "most of his ideas" through St. Thomas Aquinas to such great Christian mystics as St. Augustine and Pseudo-Dionysius, because Aquinas himself differs in many respects (take the theory of Predestination) from St. Augustine and the Neo-Platonic philosophers.

The Neo-Platonic element in the system of St. Thomas Aquinas is not the one which Plotinus originally preached; it was considerably modified due to the predominant influence of Aristotle on the scholastic philosophy. Neo-Platonism and scholasticism are not interchangeable terms.

The great achievement of St. Thomas Aquinas consists in having Aristoteleanized the whole philosophy of the Church. [2] Wicksteed says: "The feat is the more interesting and instructive because on many points the Aristotelean philosophy appears to be alien alike to the history and genius of Christianity, whereas there is a natural affinity between Christian thought and Platonism." [3]

It was Neo-Platonism which had helped in the crystallization of Christian philosophy and theology in the formative period of the Church: it is significant that St. Augustine, who

[1] *A Study of the Prose Works of John Donne,* p. 88.
[2] See Professor A. E. Taylor's lecture on "St. Thomas Aquinas as a Philosopher." He has argued for an untraditional use of Aristotle by Aquinas.
[3] *The Reactions between Dogma and Philosophy,* by Philip H. Wicksteed, 1920, p. 7.

dominated the Church philosophy before Aquinas, was thoroughly imbued with Platonism. The rise of Aristotle in the philosophy of the Church was a slow process. Aristotle's philosophy was introduced to Europe through the translation of the Arabic commentaries of Avicenna; the physical books were translated from the Arabic version into Latin by M. G. Toledo. The Synod of Paris officially condemned, in 1216, the application of the logic of Aristotle to the theology of the Church: "Theologians ought to expound theology according to the approved tradition of the saints" (Gregory IX). The discovery of Aristotle, tinged as it was with the sceptical thought of Averroës, sent abroad a wave of scepticism which the Church could not but condemn. From the sixth to the early twelfth century Christianity had no rival philosophical thought to question the authority of the Scriptures or the Christian conception of the Soul, Mind and Intelligence. Wicksteed has pointed out that "It was not till times approaching those of Thomas himself that contact with the high culture of Islam again compelled the Christian thinkers explicitly to face the necessity not only of finding a base for their belief in any divine revelation at all but also of vindicating, by an appeal to the common ground of human reason, the credit of the actual revelation that they accepted, against the scepticism of believers in a rival." [1]

The intense philosophical activity which followed the discovery of Aristotle had a lasting influence on the philosophy of the Catholic Church. In the beginning the Church resisted the influence of Aristotle; the use of Aristotelean logic was declared to be as of "carnal weapons." In 1210 David of Dinan, who, following Averroës, had declared that "God, intelligence, and matter are a single thing, one and the same," was strongly condemned by the Church.

But it was left to the genius of St. Thomas to effect a synthesis between theology on the one hand and philosophy on the other.

The ages of medieval philosophy may be chronologically divided as follows:

---

[1] P. Wicksteed, *The Reactions between Dogma and Philosophy*, p. 41. See also *The Catholic Church and Theology*, by Fr. Vincent MacNabb, O.P., 1927, pp. 31–37; and *Arabic Thought and its Place in History*, by De Lacy O'Leary, p. 31.

1. The formative period of theology before the Council of Nice (A.D. 325)—Clement and the school of Alexandria.
2. The period of Platonic agnosticism, fourth century A.D. —Gregory of Nazianzus.
3. The age of Christian Neo-Platonic mysticism, fifth century A.D. to seventh century—Pseudo-Areopagite and Maximus (622).
4. The period of Platonic mystical philosophy and Christian theology—John of Damascus (eighth century), Erigena (ninth century) (who translated the Areopagite).
5. Vincent of Beauvais, Albert, and Thomas.

In the early centuries of the Christian era, Plato's influence in the philosophy of the Church was supreme. H. B. Workman has pointed out that "the Aristotle whom the East had neglected became in due course the great doctor of the Latin Church. At the same time, though for theologians this is a minor matter, the Church inverted the position which Plato and Aristotle had held in the development of Philosophy." [1]

This change in philosophical authorities had a deeper significance for the organization of the Church. Plato's theory of the immanence of God leads to mysticism, which at its best tries to break off the shackles of ecclesiastical authority in favour of the individual soul-life; Plato's conception of the soul and the Fall and the physical world found a sympathetic exponent in St. Paul. Dean Inge says that "the whole doctrine of the spirit in his [St. Paul's] epistles corresponds closely to the Platonic *Nous*," [1] and that St. Paul's well-known saying, "the things that are seen are temporal, but the things that are not seen are eternal," [2] is pure Platonism. Plato's dream of an Ideal Republic and the Perfect Man set men thinking about their own imperfections and the imperfections of the temporal and spiritual organizations under which they lived, and thus Plato's authority could not help in the consolidation of the ecclesiastical power of the Popes. Plato stands for soul-life, while to Aristotle reason is supreme; Aristotle is not concerned with the ultimate origin of things, he is interested in the examination and analysis of the existing Nature, and he does not recognize Plato's conception of the

---

[1] *Christian Thought to the Reformation*, by H. B. Workman.
[2] *Platonic Tradition in English Religious Thought*, W. R. Inge, pp. 9–10.

illusory character of the world of senses. To Aristotle the
world of abstractions is not a world of prototypes of which
the existing actual world is a reflection and shadow, but a
"conceptual world," not existing apart from things but in
them. But it was in his "Theory of the Soul," expounded in his
De Anima, that Aristotle came nearer to the Christian conception
of the soul and its life; and this was one of the aspects which
attracted the keen intellect of St. Thomas Aquinas.

*The relation of the Body and Soul according to Plato, Aristotle,
Aquinas and Donne.*—St. Thomas's objections to Plato's theory
of body and soul have a peculiar interest for the students of
Donne, for Donne, like Aquinas, realizes the oneness and the
interdependence of body and soul. St. Thomas observes:

"Plato therefore and his followers laid it down that the
intellectual soul is not united with the body as form with
matter, but only as the mover is with the moved, saying that
the soul is in the body, as a sailor in his boat: thus the union
of soul and body would be virtual contact only. But as such
contact does not produce absolute oneness, this statement
leads to the awkward consequences that man is not absolutely
one, nor absolutely a being at all, but is a being only accidentally. To escape this conclusion, Plato laid it down that man
is not a compound of soul and body, but that the soul using
the body is man." [1]

Plato gave to material substances in his conception of the
world a lower place, and did not like the soul to be bound up
with matter, to be degraded. Spirit was to rule matter, and
when in man it was united with matter, as the result of the
Fall, it should try to live a life apart from the pleasure of the
senses. St. Thomas Aquinas largely based his arguments on
Aristotle's (*De Anima*, ii), which he quotes; St. Thomas's
arguments against Platonic theory are ingenious, sound and
interesting:

"A body moved does not take its species according to the
Power that moves it. If therefore the soul is united to the
body as mover to moved the body and its parts do not take
their species from the soul: therefore when the soul departs,
the body and the parts thereof will remain of the same species.
But this is manifestly false: for flesh and bone and hands and

[1] *Of God and His Creatures*, trans. by J. Rickaby, p. 118.

such parts, after the departure of the soul, do not retain their own names except by a *façon de parler* [1]; since none of these parts retains its proper activity, and activity follows species. Therefore the union of soul and body is not that of mover, or of man with his dress.

"If the soul is united with the body only as mover with moved, it will be in the power of the soul to go out of the body when it wishes, and, when it wishes, to reunite itself with the body. That the soul is united with the body as the proper form of the same, is thus proved. That whereby a thing emerges from potential to actual being is its form and actuality: for the being of a living thing is its life: moveover the seed before animation is only potentially alive, and by the soul it is made actually alive, the soul therefore is the form of the animated body.

"Again, as part is to part, so is the whole sentient soul to the whole body. But sight is the form and actuality of the eye: therefore the soul is the form and actuality of the body." [2]

The interdependence of body and soul is the constant theme of Donne's poetry and prose alike. Professor Grierson, commenting on one of Donne's verse letters to the Countess of Bedford, says:

"Thus the deepest thought of Donne's poetry, his love poetry and his religious poetry, emerges here again. He will not accept the antithesis between soul and body. The dignity of the body is hardly less than that of the soul. . . . In the highest spiritual life, as in the fullest and most perfect love, body and soul are complementary, are merged in each other; and after death the life of the soul is in the same measure incomplete, the end for which it was created is not obtained until it is reunited to the body." This is a constant theme of his sermons.

Donne declared that God dignified and exalted the body when His Son assumed it:

"That God, all spirit, served with spirits, associated to spirits, should have such an affection, such a love to this body, this earthly body, this deserves wonder. The Father was pleased to breathe into this body, at first, in the Creation. The

[1] See Aristotle, *De Anima*, ii, 1, 8, 10; *Politica*, i, p. 1253, a 20.
[2] *Op. cit.*, pp. 119, 120.

Son was pleased to assume this body himself, after, in the Redemption; the Holy Ghost is pleased to consecrate this body and make it his Temple, by his sanctification . . . thou wilt not dishonour this body as it is Christ's body, nor deform it as it is thine owne, with intemperance, but thou wilt behave thyself towards it so, as towards one, whom it hath pleased the King to honour, with a resurrection." [1]

It was this conception of the dignity of the body which led him to justify the interdependence of the body and soul in the ecstasy of love:

> "Loves mysteries in soules doe grow,
> But yet the body is his booke."

Though Donne followed St. Thomas Aquinas in his conception of body and soul, he could not give to reason and intellect the supreme place Aquinas had given in his system of philosophy. St. Thomas held that God's existence could be proved by reason,[2] and that our knowledge about Him could be acquired through intellect and reason: St. Thomas says: "Nor is it necessary for something greater than God to be conceivable if His non-existence is conceivable. For the possibility of conceiving Him not to exist does not arise from the imperfection or uncertainty of His Being, since His Being is of itself manifest, but from the infirmity of our understanding, which cannot disccrn Him as He is of Himself, but only by the effects which He produces; and so it is brought by reasoning to the knowledge of Him."

Donne began his search for truth by giving *reason* a high place in his thoughts (it was "God's viceroy" in him), but he soon discovered that reason, and intellect, necessary as they are for the proper understanding of faith, could never lead a man to the higher realms of devotional life, leading to illumination. In a letter to the Countess of Bedford which belongs to his early years Donne gives a subordinate place to reason:

> "Reason is our soules left hand, Faith her right,
> By these we reach divinity."

Aristotle conceives the acts of God as those of a Pure Intelligence; God to him is Pure Thought, "Noesis," and "Thought," "thinks himself, and the thinking is a thinking of thought"

---

[1] *LXXX Sermons*, 20, 194-197.   [2] See J. Rickaby, *op. cit.*, p. 11.

(*Metaphysics*, chapter xii). But Plato insists on the nobility of great passions like love, that control our life and become a stepping-stone for the higher stages of spiritual life. It is here that Plato comes so near to the Christian mystic's idea of God as pure Love. In Plato from beauty of body and form we rise to the beauty of soul and spirit, and thence to the Highest Beauty, God Himself:

"He who under the influence of true love rising upward from these begins to see that beauty is not far from the end. And the true order of going or being led by another to the things of love is to use the beauties of earth as steps along which he mounts upwards for the sake of that other beauty going from one to two, and from two to all fair forms, and from fair forms to fair practices, and from fair practices to fair notions, until from fair notions he arrives at the notion of Absolute Beauty and at last knows what the essence of beauty is. This is that life above all others which man should live, in the contemplation of beauty absolute." [1]

St. Thomas Aquinas, following Aristotle, conceived God more as a Pure Intelligence than Love. "God's Intelligence," he declared, is "His substance," and to him even Beatitude "consists essentially in the action of the intellect; and only accidentally in the action of the will."

Rudolf Steiner summed up the scholastic conception of God when he declared:

"Thus what was for the ancients vision, and appeared as a reality of the spiritual world, became for scholasticism something to be decided by all that acuteness of thought, all that suppleness and nice logic of which I have spoken to you to-day. The problem which formerly was solved by vision is brought down into the sphere of thought and reason. That is the essence of Thomism, the essence of 'Albertinism,' the essence of scholasticism." [2]

Donne, like the mystics in all ages, believed that the problem of the knowledge of God could not be solved through reason, intellect and philosophy, and that the comprehension of reality could only be attained after a prolonged exercise of "sense and spirit" resulting in illumination. To him, as to all the

[1] *Symposium*, Jowett, pp. 211–212.
[2] *The Philosophy of Thomas Aquinas*, by Rudolf Steiner, 1932, p. 69.

great Christian mystics, God is Love: "That God, who is Almighty, Alpha and Omega, First and Last, that God is also Love itself; and therefore this Love is Alpha and Omega, First and Last too"; and he also declared that "Nor can this pureness of heart, though by these means attained to, be preserved, but by this noble and incorruptible affection of Love, that puts a true value upon it, and therefore prefers it above all other things." [1]

This conception of Infinite Love permeating the universe is absent from the philosophy of Aristotle, who, with the acceptance of the system of St. Thomas Aquinas, superseded Plato in the philosophy of the Church. There are no visions and dreams in Aristotle, which constantly warm and kindle the imagination of Plato.

To Aristotle, "the high priest of common sense," the problem of life is to adjust the life of the soul to the needs of a practical world. It was precisely his philosophy which St. Thomas incorporated in his *Summa* that the Church needed to complete its process of systematization of the Spiritual Kingdom in the image of Cæsar's Empire. St. Thomas's vast intellect effected the synthesis between Aristotle's philosophy and the dogmas of the Church. Pope Leo XIII has truly said, "Thomas gathered together their doctrines like the scattered limbs of a body and moulded them into a whole. He arranged them in so wonderful order, and increased them with such great additions, that rightly and deservedly he is reckoned a singular safeguard and glory of the Catholic Church." [2]

England and the Break-up of Scholasticism.—The break-up of scholasticism has a significance for the theology of the Church and Christian mysticism alike. Leaving the great controversy of Nominalism and Thomism aside, the real cause of the decay of scholasticism was its failure to adjust Christian ideals of life to the Aristotelean theories of natural man in the world.

Scholasticism under St. Thomas had tried to evolve a sublime and harmonious system out of such diverse elements as Neo-Platonism, the teachings of St. Augustine, and the philosophy of Aristotle; and in his conquest of the Church it appeared that he had succeeded; but, says Professor A. S. Pringle Pattison, "Indeed no sooner was the harmony apparently

[1] *XXVI Sermons*, No. 24.   [2] See the Encyclical of Leo XIII.

established by Aquinas than Duns Scotus began the negative criticism which is carried much farther by William Occam." But this is equivalent to confessing that scholasticism had failed in its task which was to rationalize the doctrines of the Church. The Aristotelean form refused to fit a matter for which it was never intended; the matter of Christian theology refused to be forced into an alien form.

"The end of the period was thus brought about by the internal decay of its method as by the variety of external causes which contributed to transfer men's interest to other objects." [1] England played an important part in the break-up of scholasticism.

Roger Bacon, a monk of the thirteenth century, tried to substitute a scientific method of observation and collection of facts for an appeal to authority. He said: "If we wish to have complete and thoroughly varified knowledge we must proceed by the method of experimental science." But philosophical speculation had for him a moral rather than a scientific interest. He has been called a "Progressive schoolman." [2] The first great critic of St. Thomas Aquinas was Duns Scotus, who held that God is not Absolute Intelligence but Absolute Will. In twelve volumes he criticized the system of Thomas Aquinas and his rational ground of faith. He thus hastened the separation of philosophy from theology. He asserted that reason should not be applied to theology and that his belief in the Gospels rested wholly on the authority of the Church. Occam further broadened the breach between faith and reason. He claimed that the truth of theology could not be proved by philosophy, and that the apprehension of God was to be achieved through faith and not through reason. He also asserted that knowledge is never abstract, but is based on experience, and maintained, like a true nominalist, that the universal could not be known through the individual; but his main interest in separating faith from reason is not so much to advocate the scientific method as to reform the Church. He is the last of the great schoolmen, for his destructive criticism marks the beginning of the end of scholastic phil-

[1] *Encyclopædia Britannica,* 11th edition, article on "Scholasticism."
[2] English philosophers like Erigena had played an important part in the philosophical speculations of the Middle Ages. John Hales is claimed to be the first scholar of Aristotelean logic who applied it to Christian theology.

osophy. These critics of scholasticism, though they under-mined its authority and weakened its influence, were still schoolmen. The continuity of the influence of scholasticism in England till the sixteenth century is a fact we must bear in mind when we study Donne as a schoolman; between 1580-1600 an acute controversy was being waged in England about the logic of Aristotle, whose influence, in spite of the "humanistic studies," was still strong at the Universities.

John Case, an Oxford graduate (*d.* 1600), issued between 1584-1599 a series of seven text-books dealing comprehensively with the logic, ethics, politics and economics of Aristotle. John Sanderson, a graduate of Trinity College, Cambridge, wrote his *Institutionum Dialecticarum Libri quatuor* in 1589.

While two younger men, Digby and William Temple, were carrying on the serious controversy about the respective claims of the Old and New Logic, Digby delivered a course of lectures on the logic of Aristotle, shortly after 1573, which might have been heard by Bacon, who was then an undergraduate at Trinity College. He held Aristotle to be supreme and authori-tative and conducted the controversy with fine scholastic skill.

It was Temple, once secretary to Sir Philip Sidney, who popularized the *Dialectics* of Ramus in England. Ramus was the greatest opponent of the schoolmen and the Aristoteleans in France, and his influence was felt at Cambridge as early as 1573, when the *Dialectics* of Ramus took the place of Aristotle's *Organon*. The old problem of the universal and particular was also a point of contention between Digby and Temple, and this was mainly a problem of scholastic philosophy.

Donne and Bacon's attitude towards Scholastic Philosophy.—It is with the scientific method of Bacon, and in the heat and dust of the theological controversies of the Reformation, that the inquiry into the nature of faith, knowledge and reason begins anew. Bacon's was perhaps the first intellect to conceive the reconstruction of knowledge on a scientific and experimental basis.

It is with him that we shall now compare Donne's attitude towards scholasticism.

Though Donne was eleven years younger than Bacon, their period of activity nearly coincided. When Donne was acting as secretary to Sir Thomas Egerton (1598-1602), Bacon was constantly employed by Elizabeth as a learned counsel; moreover we know that Bacon and Donne both composed poems on the same theme, "Which kind of life is best, that of Court, country or city?" [1] It was in 1596 that Egerton was made Lord Keeper, and soon after he tried to restrain the fees of the clerk of the Star Chamber; and Bacon in a long letter to Sir Thomas Egerton discussed the whole question of the claimed fees. Donne also makes a reference to this in his fifth satire. Donne as Egerton's secretary must have handled the correspondence, which was protracted for a long time, and in this way may have come into personal contact with Bacon. We know that Donne read Bacon's reasoned and well-balanced *Discourse on Ecclesiastical Matters* in 1603 or 1604. In a letter Christopher Brooke wrote to Donne:

"Sir Henry Goodyere is well, but no better than when you saw him. When I was at Pyrford, I left behind me Mr. Bacon's *Discourse of Matters Ecclesiastical*; I pray you return it by this bearer." [2]

Bacon was appointed Privy Councillor in 1616 by King James, and the King had also persuaded Donne in 1615 to take Orders. Bacon was created Viscount of St. Albans in 1621, Donne was appointed Dean of St. Paul's in the same year. When Bacon published his *Advancement of Learning* in 1605 Donne was helping Thomas Morton in his controversies with the Jesuits. Bacon published *Novum Organum* in 1620, *De Augmentis* in 1623, and *New Atlantis* in 1624, and these were the years when Donne made his mark as a great Anglican preacher and controversialist.

We know definitely from a contemporary record that Bacon heard Donne preaching at St. Paul's. On March 29, John Chamberlayne wrote to Sir Dudley Carleton; "I had almost forgotten, that on Monday the 27th (24th) of this month 1616–17 being the King's day, the Archbishop of Canterbury, the Lord Keeper (Bacon) Lord Privy seal . . . were at Paul's cross and heard Donne, who made a dainty sermon upon the 11th verse of the 22nd Proverbs and was exceedingly well liked." [3]

---

[1] *Donne's Poetical Works*, Grierson, vol. ii, p. 140.
[2] Gosse, vol. i, p. 126.
[3] *The Court and Times of James I*, vol. ii, p. 4.

And when we remember Donne's habit of reading, which lasted all his life, it is almost certain that he must have read the works of his great contemporary.

To Aristotle knowledge was an end in itself, it showed the reach of human intellect; but Bacon affirms that knowledge "is not like a lark which can mount and sing and please itself and nothing else. The real value of knowledge lies in the fact that it is 'fruit-bearing.'" Bacon differed from Aristotle not only in his view of knowledge but also in his method. He tried to substitute the inductive and experimental method for the deductive and speculative method of Aristotle.

"I am building," he says in *Novum Organum*, "in the human understanding a true model of the world, such as it is in fact, not such as man's own reason would have it." In his Preface to *De Augmentis* he defined his experimental attitude towards things: "Our method is continually to dwell among things soberly . . . to establish for ever a true and legitimate union between the experimental and rational faculty."

In his attempt to separate philosophy (science) from faith he insisted that Truth is twofold [1]: the truth of science is based on experiment and reason, the truth of religion, or faith, on the divine authority of the Church. In this respect Bacon was a nominalist like Duns Scotus and Occam, for like them he held that the particular or indivisional things only were real, and the universals or abstractions were mere *flatus Vocis*—only names. He however raised religion far above the reach of reason, which should concern itself with sensible things. He held that "sacred theology must be drawn from the word and oracles of God" and not from the light of nature, or dictates of reason.[2] Bacon called scholastic philosophy "degenerate learning," and he says:

"Schoolmen having strong and sharp wits, and abundance of leisure, and small variety of learning; but their wits being shut up in the cell of a few authors (chiefly Aristotle their dictator) as their persons were shut up in the cells of monasteries and colleges; and knowing little history, either of nature or time, did out of no great quantity of matter, and infinite

---

[1] He declared that "it is therefore most wise soberly to render unto faith the things that are faith's" (*Novum Organum*).
[2] *De Augmentis*, Book IX.

agitation of wit spin out unto us those laborious webs of learning which are extant in their books. For the wit and mind of
man, if it work upon matter, which is the contemplation of
the creatures of God, worketh according to the stuff and is
limited thereby; but if it work upon itself as the spider
worketh his web than it is endless, and brings forth indeed
cowebs of learning, admirable for the fairness of thread and
work but not of substance or profit." [1]

It is a remarkable coincidence that what strikes us first in
Donne's attitude towards scholastic philosophy is his revulsion
against the subtlety and minute distinctions of the schoolmen
about "indifferent things"—what Bacon calls the "cowebs"
of learning"—

> "O wrangling schooles, that search what fire
> Shall burn this world"   (A. Feaver).

—and in one of his earliest letters to the Countess of Bedford
Donne speaks of the labyrinths of schools—

> "As all which goe to Rome, doe not thereby
> Esteeme religions, and hold fast the best,
> But serve discourse, and curiosity,
> With that which doth religion but invest,
> And shunne th'entangling laborinths of Schooles,
> And make it wit, to thinke the wiser fooles." [2]

This note of disapproval of the scholastic method, of these
entangling cowebs of learning, is too persistent in Donne's
poetry and sermons alike to be lightly dismissed, for it is a
rejection of the scholastic method which is an integral part of
the philosophy of Aquinas. It was the substitution of the
experimental and scientific method for the scholastic that
ultimately led to the rejection of scholasticism in the seventeenth
century. In one of his sermons Donne ridiculed the infinite
subtlety of the schoolmen:

"Let the Schoole dispute infinitely, (for he will not content
himself with means of salvation, till all schoole points be reconciled, will come too late), let Scotus and his Heard think,
that Angels, and separate soules have a naturall power to
understand thoughts, though God for his particular glory
restrains the exercise of that power in them . . . and let

[1] Also see chapters i and ii of *The Seventeenth-century Background,* by Basil Willey.
[2] *Donne,* edited by H. J. C. Grierson, vol. i, p. 192.

Aquinas present his arguments to the contrary, that those spirits have no naturall power to know thoughts; we seek no farther, but that Christ Jesus himself thought it argument enough to convince the Scribes and Pharisees, and prove himself God, by knowing their Thoughts."

Donne, as we have seen, was closely following the scientific thought of his age and he could not but realize that the scholastic method had become obsolete: "Young men mend not their sight by using old men's Spectacles; and yet we look upon Nature but with *Aristotle's* spectacles, and upon the body of man with *Galen's*, and upon the world with Ptolomie's spectacles." [1] And yet Pearsall Smith thinks that Donne's "mind had its habitation in the smaller earth-centred Ptolemaic creation"! [2]

Donne's condemnation of the scholastic method of building an edifice of argument out of the strict analysis of minute details is significant for the determination of his relation to scholastic philosophy. Donne says:

> "We see in Authors, too stiffe to recant,
> A hundred controversaries of an Ant;
> And yet one watches, starves, freeses, and sweats,
> To know but Catechismes and Alphabets,
> Of unconcerning things, matters of fact."
>
> *The Second Anniversary.*

Speaking about the "schoole-divinity" of the Roman Catholic Church just before the Reformation, Donne remarked:

"When for the Art and science of Divinity itself, they had buried it in the darkness of the schoole, and wrapped up that, they should save our soules, in those perplexed and inextricable clouds of schoole-divinity, and their schoole-divinity subject to such changes as that a Jesuit professes, that in the compasse but of thirty years, since *Gregory de Valentia* writ . . . we may truly say, that we have a new art of Divinity risen amongst us." [3]

This clearly shows that Donne strongly disapproved of the scholastic method in theology as well as in philosophy.

Donne's Conception of Reason, Faith and Knowledge.—The

---

[1] *LXXX Sermons*, Alford, vol. i, p. 820. Preached at the funeral of Sir William Cokayne, Knight, Alderman of London, December 12, 1626; also see sermon xxix, vol. i, p. 287, preached at St. Paul's upon Whitsunday 1628.

[2] Pearsall Smith, *Introduction to Donne's Sermons—Selected Passages.*

[3] *LXXX Sermons*, No. 60, p. 605.

dispute between reason and faith has figured prominently in the history of medieval thought, especially in the great controversy between nominalism and the scholasticism of St. Thomas Aquinas. In the nominalism which Occam developed the distinction between reason and faith was given an important place; Occam denied that God could be known through intellect and thus denied the basis on which the *Summa* was based; the truth of theology was thus separated from the truth of philosophy and this phase of medieval thought was carried to its logical conclusions by Peter D'Ailly (1350–1425) and John Gerson (1363–1429). It is interesting to note here that Donne was deeply learned in the opponents of the Thomists, the Nominalists, as well as the Sceptics. Donne in *Biathanatos* calls Pomponatius (1462–1526) an "excellent Philosopher." He was the Professor of Philosophy at Bologna, and when he was accused of heresy for doubting the immortality of the soul, perhaps under the influence of the philosophy of Averroës, he declared: "I believe as a Christian what I cannot believe as a philosopher." The Lateran Council in 1512 condemned this ingenious statement of Pomponatius as heretical, and it was declared that as "what is true can never contradict what is true, we determine that every proportion which is contrary to the truth of the revealed faith is entirely false." [1]

The conception of the identity of the content of faith with that of knowledge (or reason and faith), which achieved its triumph in the philosophy of Aquinas, was thus attacked by nominalists and other independent philosophers alike.

Donne had started his search for truth with an implicit confidence in the power of knowledge to give satisfaction; and with this aim in view he had, as he tells us, "surveyed and digested the whole body of Divinity controverted between ours and the Roman Church." [2]

But Donne's study of the ancient and modern philosophers, as well as his realization of the significance of love in the higher stages of religious life, must have convinced him that, though religion does not contradict reason, the truth of religion can never be comprehended through reason and intellect alone; and therefore, long before he became a priest, he began to

[1] Punger, *History of the Christian Philosophy of Religion*, 1887, pp. 50–52.
[2] Gosse, vol. i, p. 250.

assign a subordinate place to reason. In one of his letters to the Countess of Bedford (1607–1608) he observed:

> "Reason is our Soules left hand, Faith her right,
> By these we reach divinity,"

A careful study of Donne's religious life bears out the fact that the "modest assurance" of salvation which he possessed in the later years of his saintly life grew not out of reason but faith.   He held that to search the mysteries of religion by the help of reason was to go astray: "So this *eternall*, and this *supernaturall* light, *Christ* and *faith*, enlightens, warmes, purges, and doth all the profitable offices of *fire*, and light if we keep it in the right spheare, in the proper place, (that is, if we consist in *points necessary* to Salvation, and *revealed* in the Scriptures) but when we bring this light to the common light of *reason*, to our inferences, and consequencies, it may be in danger to vanish itselfe, and perchance extinguish our reason too; we may search so far, and reason so long of *faith* and *grace*, as that we may lose not only them, but even our reason too, and sooner become mad than good." [1]

St. Thomas Aquinas has given to intelligence a marvellous power not only in what he calls "order and control" of the world but also in the comprehension of truth and the acquisition of the knowledge of God.

In defining "the Function of the Wise Man," St. Thomas says: "Now the last end of everything is that which is intended by the prime author or mover thereof.   The prime author and mover of the Universe is intelligence. . . . Therefore the last end of the Universe must be the good of intelligence, and that is truth" [2]; and it was with this confidence in the power of the intellect that St. Thomas proceeded to build up his philosophy, which to him was "the science of truth." [2]

St. Thomas further justified the use of reason in determining the truth of faith on the ground that his aim was also to convince the Gentiles, who did not believe in the revelation of the Scriptures:

"Secondly, because some of them, as Mohammedans and Pagans, do not agree with us in recognizing the authority of

---

[1] *L Sermons*, No. 36.

[2] St. Thomas Aquinas, ' 'Of God as He is in Himself," *Summa Contra Gentiles*, translated by J. Rickaby, p. 1.

any Scripture, available for their conviction, as we can argue against the Jews from the Old Testament, and against heretics from the New. But these receive neither, hence it is necessary to have recourse to natural reason, which all are obliged to assent to." [1]

It is instructive to quote a passage from Donne's *Sermons* where he is also discussing the problem of the application of reason to prove the truth of the Holy Scriptures. Donne compares them to a net:

"The Gospel of Christ Jesus is a net. . . . A net is *res nodosa*, a knotty thing; and so is the Scriptures, full of knots, of scruple, of perplexity, and anxiety and vexation if thou wilt go about to entangle thyself in those things, which appertain not to thy Salvation. . . . The Scriptures will be out of thy reach and out of thy use, if thou cast and scatter them upon reason, upon philosophy, upon morality, to try how the Scriptures will fit all them, and believe them but so far as they agree with thy reason; but draw the Scripture to thine own heart, and to thine own actions, and thou shalt find it made for that; all the promises of the Old Testament made, and all accomplished in the New Testament, for the Salvation of thy soul hereafter, and for thy consolation in the present application of them."

Donne did not advocate blind faith, reason could no doubt help us to a certain extent and that extent was to him a well-defined limit; but within this limit he recognized the value of reason. His mind was so agile and alert that he could not rest content in mere imitation and acceptance of the opinion of others. In one of his letters to Sir Henry Goodyer he complains that "we are patterns or copies, we inform or imitate" [2]: and to Sir T. Lucy he wrote: "But as sometimes we had rather believe a traveller's lie than go to disapprove him, so men rather cleave to these ways than seek new." [3] Reason was thus to him an affirmation of the singleness of his individuality.

Donne even speaks with reverence of the deep-searching but heretical wit of Averroës (whom he calls "a very subtle but very deep wit"), and in the same letter he said: "It is as imperfect which is taught by that religion which is most

---

[1] St. Thomas Aquinas, "Of God as He is in Himself," *Summa Contra Gentiles*, translated by S. J. Rickaby, p. 2.   [2] Gosse, i, p. 177.   [3] *Ibid*, p. 176.

accommodate to sense (I dare not say to reason, though it have appearance of that too), because none may doubt that religion is certainly best which is reasonablest." [1]

But Donne gave a subordinate place to reason, which in his latter years he grew to distrust altogether; in his elegy on Prince Henry (1612) he calls faith "a centre of Greatness" while reason is a centre of "Weight" only:

> "Look to mee, *Faith*; and looke to my *Faith*, God:
> For both my *Centres* feel this *Period*.
> Of *Waight*, one Centre; one of *Greatness* is;
> And Reason is That Centre; Faith is This."

St. Thomas has assigned an important place to sense in acquiring the knowledge of God, for reason and intelligence can only work with the help of the senses, though intelligence he claims does not subsist in matter. [2]

"In the reasoning whereby the existence of God is demonstrated it is not necessary to assume for a premise the essence or quiddity of God; but instead of the quiddity, the effect is taken for a premise, as is done in demonstration *a Posteriori* from effect to cause. All the names of God are imposed either on the principle of denying of God Himself certain effects of His power, or from some habitude of God towards those effects. Although God transcends sense and the objects of sense, nevertheless sensible effects are the basis of our demonstration of the existence of God. Thus the origin of our own knowledge is in sense, even of the things that transcend sense." [3]

Donne began early to doubt the ability of intellect to comprehend God, and this belief animated some of his finest divine poems and sermons. He argues that natural reason and the senses can comprehend only natural objects and things, as they work within a narrow circumference:

> "For into our *Reason* flow, and there do end,
> All, that this naturall world doth comprehend;
> *Quotidian* things, and Equi-distant hence,
> Shut in, for Men, in one *circumference*."

And Donne develops his favourite argument that human reason cannot comprehend the divine essence:

---

[1] Gosse, vol. ii, p. 8.   [2] *Contra Gentiles*, p. 117.
[3] *Of God and His Creatures*, translated by J. Rickaby, p. ii.

> "But for th'enormous *Greatnesses,* which are
> So disproportion'd and so angulare,
> As is God's *Essence, Place* and *Providence,*
> *Where, How, When, What Soules* do, departed hence:
> These *Things* (*Eccentrique* else) on Faith do strike."

Donne again advanced this argument in one of his sermons: "God is too large, too immense, and the man is too narrow, too little to be considered. . . . First for the incomprehensible-ness of God, the understanding of man, hath a limited, a determined latitude, it is an intelligence able to move in that sphere which it is fixed to, but could not move a greater." [1] Donne conceives God as beyond the knowledge acquired through reason and understanding: "I can comprehend *naturam naturatam,* created nature, but for that *natura naturans,* God himself, the understanding of man cannot comprehend." [1] This is in marked contrast to St. Thomas Aquinas' implicit confidence in the powers of intelligence and reason to comprehend God.

Donne in some of his most impassioned lines distrusted the knowledge acquired through the senses:

> "When wilt thou shake off this Pedantery,
> Of being taught by sense, and Fantasie?
> Thou look'st through spectacles; small things seem great
> Below; But up unto the watch towre get,
> And see all things despoyld of fallacies."
>
> *The Second Anniversary.*

In the discussion of Donne's conception of the relation of reason to faith it is important to notice that knowledge which was based on natural reason was to him of a limited nature and had no permanent character. He points out that we do not know the nature of even common things like grass or blood:

> "Why grass is greene or why our blood is red
> Are mysteries which none have reach'd unto."

The imperfect nature of knowledge is the constant theme of his poetry and prose alike:

> "What hope have we to know ourselves, when wee
> Know not the least things, which for our use be?"

"What Anatomist," he asks, "knows the body of a man

[1] *LXXX Sermons,* No. 7 (1629).

thorowly, or what casuist the soul? What Politician knowes the distemper of the state thorowly; or what master, the disorders of his own family? Princes glory *in Arcanis*, that they have secrets which no man shall know, and God knowes, they have hearts which they know not themselves; Thoughts and purposes indigested fall upon them and surprise them. It is so in naturall, in morall, in civill things; we are ignorant of more things than we know." [1]

Bacon wrote to Burghley (in 1592): "I confess that I have as vast contemplative ends as I have moderate civil ends; for I have taken all knowledge to be my Province." But Donne recognized that modern science and philosophy in the seventeenth century were still in their infancy and could not form a stable basis for the formulation of a theory of knowledge embracing science, ethics and metaphysics. Donne says: "Here in this world, knowledge is but as the earth, and ignorance as the Sea; there is more sea than earth, more ignorance than knowledge; and as if the sea do gaine in one place, it loses in another, so it is with knowledge too; if new things be found out as many as good, that were known before, are forgotten and lost." [1]

Donne recognized the value of the ancient learning; time divisions are artificial divisions, he had the sanity of a great poet to realize the importance of the Middle Ages in the eternal search of man for God. The craze to say something new so as to startle appeared to him shallow and meaningless:

> "For every man alone thinks he hath got
> To be a Phœnix, and that then can bee
> None of that kinde, of which he is, but hee." [2]

He said in one of his splendid sermons, "Almost all knowledge is rather like a child that is embalmed to make Mummy, than that is nursed to make a Man. . . . And if there be any addition to knowledge, it is rather a new knowledge, than a greater knowledge, rather a singularity in a desire of proposing something, that was not knowne at all before, than an empowering, and advancing, a multiplying of former inceptions; and by that means no knowledge comes to be perfect." [3]

[1] Sermon preached at St. Paul's upon Whitsunday, 1628.
[2] *The First Anniversary*, ll. 216–217.
[3] Sermon preached at the funeral of Sir William Cokayne, Knight, Alderman of London, December 12, 1626, *LXXX Sermons*, No. 80.

This distrust of knowledge and intellect does not exist in the system of St. Thomas; in fact the basis of his philosophy is a confidence in knowledge acquired through the senses and the operation of the intellect. St. Thomas defines truth as a perfection of understanding: "Truth is a perfection of the understanding and of its act" [1]; and he holds that intellect cannot err in acquiring knowledge: "The understanding is not liable to err in its knowledge of abstract being, as neither is sense in dealing with the proper object of each sense." [1]

Like intellect, understanding also, according to St. Thomas, is perfect inasmuch as it is never false: "An intellectual virtue is a perfection of the Understanding in Knowing. It never happens that the understanding utters anything false, but its utterance is always true when prompted by any intellectual virtue; for it is the part of virtue to render an act good, and to eternal truth is the good act of the understanding." [2]

Donne believed that this "perfection of the understanding in knowing" comes not through reason or intellect but faith and grace; he observes: "So is it for a Christian to enjoy the working of God's grace, in a faithful believing the Mysteries of Religion, though he enquire not into God's bed-chamber, nor seek into his unrevealed Decrees. It is . . . says Luther, a hatefull, a damnable Monosyllable, How, How God doth this or that, for, if a man come to the boldness of proposing such a question to himself, he will not give over till he finde some answer; and then, others will not be content with his answer, but every man will have a severall one." [3]

St. Thomas' and Donne's Conception of Grace.—Donne not only distrusted the power of intellect as an absolute entity not liable to err, but he also believed that faith came not through intellectual conviction but through the working of grace: "Salvation is the inward means of Salvation, the working of the spirit, that sets a seal to the eternal means: the *prope*, the nearness lies in this, that this grace, which is Salvation in this sense, grows out of that which is in you already, not only of any thing which is in you naturally, but God's graces that are in you, grows into more and more grace. Grace does not grow out of nature; for nature in the highest exaltation and rectifying thereof cannot produce grace.

[1] *Contra Gentiles*, p. 44.   [2] *Ibid.*, p. 45.   [3] *LXXX Sermons*, No. 30.

Corn does not grow out of the earth, it must be sowed; but corn grows only in the earth; nature and natural reason do not produce grace, but yet grace cannot take root in any other thing but in the nature and reason of man; whether we consider God's subsequent graces, which grow out of his first grace, formerly given to us, and well employed by us or his grace, which works upon our natural faculties and grows there." Grace thus does not grow out of nature, or reason, but out of the grace that is already within us, but it takes root in reason. God's knowledge is a gift, one cannot acquire it through one's intellectual effort, and so is salvation, which Donne defines as "the internal operation of the Holy Ghost in infusing grace." Religion in its higher and more spiritual form is thus above reason and rationalism.

To St. Thomas Aquinas also grace is the divine help which enables a man to surrender himself to God and thus prepare his intellect to receive the Word of God: "In like manner, before we arrive at our final end, which is the clear vision of the First Truth as it is in itself, the intellect of man must submit to God in readiness to take His Word: and that submission and readiness to believe is the work of divine grace." [1]

St. Thomas further defines the working and nature of this grace: "And therefore when we say that man needs the aid of grace for final perseverance, we do not mean that over and above that habitual grace first infused into him for the doing of good acts, there is infused into him another habitual grace enabling him to persevere; but we mean that when he has got all the gratuitous habits that he ever is to have, man still needs some aid of divine Providence governing from without." [2]

Donne thought that grace does not come so much from "without" as it grows out of "God's graces" that are in us; and like a true mystic he went further, and declared that grace and faith, though superior to reason and natural faculties of the soul, are inferior to the vision of God, which is the final aim of the human quest for God. Discussing the schoolmen's four ways of knowing God: faith, contemplation, apparition and vision, he says "their first way of assenting only, and their third way of apparition are weak, and uncertain wayes. The

---

[1] *Contra Gentiles*, pp. 323-324.   [2] *Ibid.*, p. 327.

other two, present faith and future vision, are safe wayes" [1];
but the object of man is not faith but the vision of God as He
is: "Faith is a blessed presence but compared with heavenly
vision, it is but an absence; though it create and constitute
in us a possibility, a probability, a kinde of certainty of Salvation, yet that faith which the best Christian hath, is not so far
beyond that sight of God which the naturall man hath as that
sight of God which I shall have in heaven, is above that faith
which we have in the highest exaltation." [2]

St. Thomas also held "that Happiness does not consist in the
knowledge of God by Faith," [3] and that "the final happiness
of man then will be in the knowledge of God, which the human
soul has after this life according to the manner in which pure
spirits know him." [4]

Higher Form of Reason.—Though Donne denied that certainty
to reason and intellect which St. Thomas had given to them
in his philosophy, we must remember in this connection that
St. Thomas himself thought that, in the higher stages of the
religious life, reason unguided by faith or unaided by grace
could not comprehend the mysteries of faith, and he holds that
the "points" which reason is unable to investigate [5] should be
believed as articles of faith, for he says: "There is also another
evident advantage in this, that, any knowledge, however
imperfect, of the noblest objects confers a very high perfection
on the soul.   And therefore, though reason cannot fully grasp
truths above reason, nevertheless it is much perfected by
holding such truths after some fashion at least, by faith." [5]

Thus St. Thomas, like Donne, also held that reason could
not go beyond a certain limit without the help of divine grace.
Rudolf Steiner discussing St. Thomas's conception of the
relation of faith and reason points out that he held that even
the truths which were comprehended as articles of faith,
though they could not be investigated by reason, were not
contradictory to reason, for St. Thomas believed that "man
penetrates up to a certain point into the spiritual nature of
things, but after that point comes faith.   And the two must
not contradict each other; they must be in harmony." [6]

[1] *LXXX Sermons*, No. 23.   [2] *Ibid.*
[3] *Contra Gentiles*, p. 213.   [4] *Ibid.*, p. 220.   [5] *Ibid.*, pp. 5–6.
[6] *The Philosophy of Thomas Aquinas*, by Rudolf Steiner (1932), p. 77.

It is also the position which Donne assumed in his explanation of the higher form of reason, which according to him is the result of the divine grace granted to the *regenerate* Christian and therefore not possessed by the *natural* man as such. This aspect of Donne's views in regard to the relation of faith to reason has so far been neglected by his critics.

The difference between Donne's and St. Thomas's views about the relation of reason and faith is that he had no such confidence in the "power" of reason as St. Thomas had and he gave it a subordinate place to faith; nature and reason can at best point to faith: "The light of nature, in the highest exaltation is not faith, but it bears witness to it"; and he recognized the contradiction which exists between reason and faith in the higher stages of religion; and to him the fact that certain doctrines of Christianity were above reason is a proof of its divine origin. Donne says, "If any state, if any convocation, if any wise man, had been to make a religion, a gospel; would he not have proposed a more probable, a more creditable gospel, to man's reason, than this?"

Donne, as we shall see, maintained that the reason of a *natural* man has a limited power to understand the mysteries of religion and that the reason of the *regenerate* Christian is a "new faculty" due to the divine grace which has been granted to him, and is therefore superior to the reason of a natural man, as such, and that reason in certain respects was subordinate to faith.[1] Donne divides reason into two forms. The lower form of reason he calls "natural reason," which is applied with profitable results to science and commerce and to the early stages of belief: "Some men by the benefit of this light of Reason have found out things profitable and useful to the whole world; As in particular printing. . . . It is this natural reason of man which also requires satisfaction in the elementary stages of faith."

Donne in his inimitable way shows how ridiculous it is to force a man to accept the dogmas of faith without satisfying his reasons: "He that should come to a *Heathen man*, a meere naturall man, uncatechised, uninstructed in the rudiments of the Christian Religion, and should at first, without any prepara-

---

[1] "Sermon preached at St. Paul's upon Christmasse Day, 1621," *LXXX Sermons*, No. 1.

tion, present him first with this necessitie; Thou shalt burn in fire, and brimstone eternally, except thou believe a *Trinitie of Persons, in a unitie of one God,* Except thou believe the Incarnation of the second Person of the Trinitie, the Sonne of God, Except thou believe that *a virgine had a Sonne,* and the same Sonne that God had, and that God was Man too and being immortall God, yet died, he should be so farre from working any spiritual cure upon this poore soule, as that he should rather bring the Christian mysteries into scorne, than him to a belief." [1]

The reason and conscience of man are bound to revolt against any process which denies full satisfaction to human reason. The victory of faith to Donne is not the triumph of blind faith and the unreasoning intellect. He declared: "Ignorance is not only the drousiness, the sillinesse, but the wickednesse of the soule: not onely dis-estimation in this world, and damnification here, but damnation in the next world, proceeds from ignorance. . . . Hell is darkness; and the way to it is the cloud of ignorance; hell itself is but condensed ignorance, multiplied Ignorance." [2]

Knowledge, he knew, was essential to the satisfaction of the mind as well as to the health of the soul. He said: "*Knowledge* cannot save us, but we cannot be saved without Knowledge; Faith is not on this side of knowledge but beyond it; we must necessarily come to *knowledge* first, though we must not stay at it, when we are come thither."

Donne held that knowledge, reason and intellect, though necessary in the initial stages, could not satisfy the hunger of the soul to behold God; the real bliss of the mystic's life lies beyond this stage of intellectual satisfaction. He knew that intellect and reason were poor guides in the search of the Infinite:

"Divers men may walke by the Sea-side, and the same beames of the Sunne giving light to them all, one gathereth by the benefit of that light pebles, or speckled shells, for curious vanitie, and another gathers precious Pearle, or medicinall Ambar, by the same light. So the common light of reason

---

[1] "Sermon preached at St. Paul's upon Christmasse Day, 1621," *LXXX Sermons,* No. 1.
[2] Sermon preached at the funeral of Sir William Cokayne, December 12, 1626.

illumines us all." But worldly men who use only the light of naturall reason would never reach their destination, for when "they have gone all these ways by the benefit of this light, they have got no further, then to have walked by a tempestuous sea, and to have gathered pebbles, and speckled cockle shells. Their light seems to be great out of the same reason, that a Torch in a misty night seemeth greater than in a clear, because it hath kindled and inflamed much thicke and grosse Ayre round about it." [1]

Donne believed that when through the process of self-purification the "naturall man" becomes the "regenerate Christian," reason also undergoes a change; new relations with the Infinite are established, then "reason" is no longer a faculty of arguments and understanding, but has been transformed into a faculty of vision.

"For a regenerate Christian," he points out, "being a new creature hath also a new facultie of Reason; and so believeth Mysteries of Religion out of another Reason, then as a meere naturall Man, he believed Naturall and Morall things. . . ." [2]

This conception of the transformation of reason into a higher faculty is the unique concept of Donne's relation of reason to faith.

But he believed that the function of "natural reason" was only to find out "sensible and material things," while faith alone could lead men to comprehend the Supreme Reality, God.

"Before the sunne was made, there was *a light* which did that office of distinguishing night and day; but when the sun was created, that did all the offices of the former light, and more. *Reason* is that first, and primogeniall light, and goes no farther in a naturall man; but in a man regenerate by faith, that light does all that reason did, *and more.*" [3] St. Thomas, as we have seen, never doubted the power of intellect to comprehend truth; he declared: "The intellect does not err over first Principles," [4] and he also believed that "mind alone can know the divine goodness. Therefore there needed to be intelligent creatures." [5]

---

[1] "Sermon preached at Saint Paul's upon Christmasse Day, 1621."
[2] *Ibid.*
[3] *Ibid.*
[4] *Contra Gentiles*, p. 44.
[5] *Ibid.*, p. 109.

To Donne reason has not only a limited scope but it is also subordinate to faith. "Men which seek God by reason, and naturall strength (though we do not deny common notions and generall impressions of a sovereign power) are like Mariners which voyaged before the invention of the compass, which were but coasters and unwillingly left the sight of the land, such are they which would arrive at God by this world, and contemplate him only in his creatures and seeming demonstration. . . . But as by the use of the compass, men safely dispatch *Ulysses'* dangerous ten years travell in so many dayes, and have found out a new world richer than the old; so doth Faith, as soon as our hearts are touched with it, direct and inform us in that great search of the discovery of Gods Essence, and the new *Hierusalem*, which Reason durst not attempt. . . . For all acquired knowledge is by degrees, and successive; but God is impartible, and only faith, which can receive it all at once, can comprehend him." [1]

Donne and Mysticism.—Donne had outgrown his belief in reason and knowledge to comprehend God, and like all great mystics he thought these "helps" to be deceptive which were "deduced from philosophy and naturall reason," and this defines his philosophical position, which is essentially that of a mystic. He declared in one of his celebrated sermons that those who believed in the light of reason and knowledge alone to find truth will *never* attain it:

"Their light shall set at noone; even in their height, some heavy crosse shall cast a damp upon their soule, and cut off all their succours, and devest them of all comforts, and thy light shall grow up, from a *faire hope*, to a modest assurance and *infallibility*, that, that light shall never go out, nor the *works of darknesse*, nor the *Prince of darkness* ever prevaile upon thee, but as thy light of *reason* is exalted by *faith* here, so thy light of *faith* shall be exalted into the light *of glory*, and fruition in the Kingdome of Heaven."

Donne has clearly said in one of his sermons that there are some decrees of God that cannot be searched by reason, and that His judgements should not be made the object of philosophical controversies. "Mysteries of Religion are not the less believ'd and embrac'd by Faith; because they are pre-

[1] *Essays in Divinity* (1615), pp. 37–39.

sented, and induc'd and apprehended by Reason. But this
must not enthrone, this must not exalt any mans Reason so
far, as that there should lie an Appeal, from Gods Judgements
to any mans reason: that if he see no reason why God should
proceed so, and so, he will not believe that to be Gods Judgement, or not believe that Judgement of God, to be Just: For,
of the secret purposes of God we have an example what to
say, given us by Christ himself. . . . *It is so, O Father, because
thy good pleasure was such*: All was in his own breast and bosome,
in his own good will and pleasure, before he Decreed it; And
as his Decree itself, so the wayes and Executions of his Decrees,
are often unsearchable, for the purpose and for the reason
thereof, though for the matter of fact, they may be manifest.
They that think themselves sharp-sighted and wise enough, to
search into those unreveal'd Decrees; they who being but
worms, will look into Heaven; and being the last of creatures,
who were made, will needs enquire, what was done by God,
before God did anything, for creating the World; *In ultiman
dementiam ruerunt*, says S. Chrysost. They are fallen into a
mischievous madness. . . . They will needs take up red hot
Irons, with their bare fingers, without tongs. That which is
in the centre, which should rest, and lie still, in this peace,
That it is so, because it is the will of God, that it should be so;
they think to toss and tumble that up, to the circumference, to
the Light and Evidence of their Reason, by their wrangling
Disputations." [1]

In the early stages of the triumph of scholasticism mystics
like St. Bernard were not influenced by the rational element in
scholasticism, but as the schools became more rigid and formal
in their application of the "new logic" of Aristotle to the
theology of the Church, mystics like Tauler and, later, Eckhart
revolted against the authority of scholasticism.

Hugo of St. Victor tried to effect a synthesis between
mysticism and scholasticism. He regarded ecstasy as an
additional power which should not impair the authority of
reason. Thus the dualism between "natural" pertaining
to reason, and "supernatural" pertaining to "contemplation"
and "ecstasy" became sharp in the mysticism of Hugo of St.
Victor, who is the only great scholastic mystic.

[1] *XXVI Sermons*, No. 6.

Scholasticism (of St. Thomas) and mysticism are not synonymous terms; some schoolmen systematized and reduced mysticism to scales of virtues and classified it into rigid stages.

Gerson, the Chancellor of the University of Paris, reduced mysticism to a science of the supernatural in which various stages of mystical life were clearly distinguished and classified, and the larger quest of mysticism, the union of the soul with God, was reduced to a code of ascetic life. It is a significant fact that scholasticism failed to produce a great line of mystics, except a few, like Hugo of St. Victor, Richard of St. Victor, Bonaventura (1221–1294), and Albert the Great. In the greatest German mystic of the fourteenth century, Eckhart, who mainly follows the Neo-Platonic tradition, the orthodox doctrines of the scholastic mysticism about the ladders of ascent and scales of virtue disappear. To Eckhart, the fundamental question is not these charts of virtues and stages of ascetic life, but the essential life of the soul and its relation to God. Though the system of St. Thomas did not prove favourable to the growth of mysticism, he seems to have clearly perceived the significance of *love* as a means of man's union with God. He concludes the analysis of the difference between *Love, charity* and *dilection* with this important observation on the powers of Love:

"But it is possible for man to tend to God by Love, being as it were passively drawn to Him, more than he can possibly be drawn thereto by his reason, which pertains to the nature of Dilection. And consequently Love is more God-like than Dilection." [1]

He knew that the "union" which is caused through *Love* is more lasting and intimate than that which is caused through *knowledge*:

"Again there is a union which is the *effect* of Love. This is real union, which the lover seeks with the object of his love. Moreover this union is in keeping with the demands of love . . . knowledge is perfected by the thing known being united, through its likeness, to the knower. But the effect of love is that the thing itself which is loved is in a way united to the lover, consequently the union caused by love is closer than that which is caused by knowledge." [2]

[1] *Summa Theologica*, 1a, 2a, c, qu. 26, arts. 3 and 4.
[2] *Ibid.*, 1a, 2a, c, qu. 28, arts. 1, 2 and 3.

St. Thomas recognizes the significance of the union through love, but he not only denies the possibility of the direct vision of God in this life,[1] he also asserts that God's presence in the human soul cannot be known with any certainty: "But the principle of grace and its object is God, who by His very excellence is unknown to us . . . and hence His presence in us and His absence cannot be known with certainty." [2]

Donne, on the other hand, rested his whole faith on the certainty of possessing the divine grace through Christ; he declared in one of his sermons: "I am that Christian man, who have seen this affliction in the cause thereof, so far off, as in my sin in Adam, and the remedy of this affliction, so far off, as in the death of Christ Jesus, I am the man, that cannot repine nor murmur, since I am the cause; I am the man that cannot despair, since Christ is the remedy." Donne believed firmly in the certainty of Christ's grace, but he recognized that before the soul could have this assurance of salvation through the grace of Christ, the reason of man must be satisfied, God infuses grace into the soul through its natural faculties. But Donne knows that grace can only have its growth in the natural faculties of the soul, which he calls the "reasonable soul." He says: "Let us reflect upon our beginning, upon the consideration of Gods first benefits, which he hath given to us all in Nature, *That light, by which he enlighteneth every man that commeth into the world*, That he hath given us a reasonable soule capable of grace here, (that, he hath denied no man, and no other creature hath that), That he hath given us an immortal soul capable of glory hereafter, (and that, that immortality he hath denied no man, and no other creature hath that) consider we alwaies the grace of God, to be the Sun itselfe, but the nature of man, and his naturall faculties to be the Sphear, in which that Sun, that Grace moves. Consider we the Grace of God to be the Soule itself, but the naturall faculties of man, to be as a body, which ministers Organs for that soule, that Grace to worke by." [3]

Donne the Mystic.—The regular stages of mystical life—conversion, purgation, illumination and union—have been

---

[1] See the first part of the *Summa Theologica*, where this problem is fully discussed.
[2] *Op. cit.*, 1a, 2a, c, qu. 112, art. 5.
[3] *LXXX Sermons*, No. 68, p. 685.

traced in Donne's life by Mrs. Simpson [1] and need not be repeated here. It must, however, be noticed that Donne attributes conversion wholly to the working grace: "Man in his Conversion is nothing, does nothing. His bodie is not verier dust in the grave, till a Resurrection, then his soule is dust in his body, till a resuscitation by grace. But then this grace does not worke upon this nothingness that is in man, upon this meere privation; but grace finds out mans naturall faculties, and exalts them to a capacity, and a suceptiblenesse of the working thereof, and so by the understanding infuses faith." [2]

Donne in his *Essays in Divinity* has given us a description of his own conversion which he attributes to the "visitation" of God: "though this soul of mine, by which I partake thee, begin not now, yet let this minute, O God, this happy minute of thy visitation, be the beginning of her conversion, and shaking away confusion, darknesse, barrennesse; and let her now produce creatures, thoughts, words and deeds agreeable to thee." [3]

Too much has been written about Donne's agonized sense of sin in general and of his own sins of youth in particular, to which he gave an intense expression in the *Holy Sonnets*, *Devotions* and *Sermons*, but his passionate belief in the mercy of God and the efficacy of prayer and repentance, and the Atonement of Sin through what he called "the inestimable price of his (Christ's) incorruptible blood," [4] is also evident in his *Sonnets* as well as in his *Sermons*.

> "Yet grace, if thou repent, thou canst not lacke;
> But who shall give thee that grace to beginne?
> Oh make thyself with holy mourning blacke,
> And red with blushing, as thou art with Sinne;
> Or wash thee in Christ's blood, which hath this might
> That being red, it dyes red soules to white." [5]

Donne in a remarkable passage in his *Sermons* says that though Christ has taken upon Himself the sins of all the world, every individual soul should bear the testimony of remission in his own conscience, and this he calls the "sealing" of the

---

[1] *A Study of the Prose Works of John Donne*, chap. v.
[2] *LXXX Sermons*, No. 61, p. 611.
[3] *Essays in Divinity*, p. 77.
[4] *LXXX Sermons*, Nos. 54 and 55, p. 548.
[5] *Holy Sonnets*, No. 4: Grierson, vol. i, p. 323.

pardon: "In the knowledge that Christ hath taken all the sins of all the world upon himselfe, that there is enough done for the salvation of all mankinde, I have a shadowing, a refreshing; But because I can have no testimony, that this generall redemption belongs to me, who am still a sinner, except there passe some act betweene God and me, some seale, some investiture, some acquittance of my debts, my sins . . . and covers my sin, from the eye of his father, *not onely obumbrando,* as hee hath spread himselfe as a cloud refreshing the whole world, in the value of the satisfaction, but *Attingendo* by coming to me, by spreading himself upon me, as the Prophet did upon the dead child, Mouth to mouth, Hand to hand." [1]

Donne, like the other mystics, seems to have received an assurance of the pardon of his sins in the stage of purgation, and so he relied on "some act between God and me." He also knows that the knowledge of the self comes only through suffering and privation which God inflicts on the individual soul. He declared: "So when the hand and sword of God hath pierced our soul, we are brought to a better knowledge of ourselves, than any degree of prosperity would have raised us to." [2]

Though Donne claimed for himself nothing but the guidance afforded to the Christian soul in the Holy Scriptures, and the ordinances, doctrines and ritual of the Church, we find a note of ecstatic joy in his contemplation of the love and mercy of God. Addressing God, he says: "O glorious beauty, infinitely reverend, infinitely fresh and young, we come late to thy love, if we consider the past daies of our lives, but early if thou beest pleased to reckon with us from this houre of the shining of thy grace upon us." [3]

These words remind us of St. Augustine's beautiful rhapsody about the love of God: "Too late loved I Thee, O Beauty so old, yet ever new! too late loved I Thee. And behold thou wert within and I abroad and there I searched for Thee. . . . Thou breathedst odours, and I drew in breath, and panted for Thee. I tasted, and hungered and thirsted. Thou touchedst me, and I was on fire for Thy peace," [4] Donne believed that

---

[1] *LXXX Sermons,* No. 56, p. 565.
[2] *Ibid.,* p. 563.   [3] *Ibid.,* p. 116.
[4] *Western Mysticism,* by Dom C. Butler, pp. 40, 41.

it is in the doctrine and Sacraments of the Church that God
has manifested Himself; but in order to recognize Him in His
Church, our spirit should bear witness to His Spirit in our
souls. He compares the Church to the Face of God and His
Spirit working in the Christian soul to His Eye: "God's
whole ordinance in His Church, is Gods face; For that is the
face of God, by which God is manifested to us; But then, that
eye in that face, by which he promises to guide us . . . is
that blessed spirit of his, by whose operation he makes that
grace, which does ever more accompany his ordinances,
effectual upon us; The whole congregation sees God face to
face, in the service, in the sermon, in the sacrament, but
there is an eye in that face . . . a piercing and operating spirit
that looks up that soul and foments and cherishes that soule,
who by a good use of Gods former grace, is become fitter for
his present." [1]

Illumination to Donne meant an ever-increasing sanctification of life resulting in a "holy cheerfulness" which he considers
to be the best evidence of the possession of Heavenly life on
earth. He seems to have frequently experienced this joy: "so
though he reserves that hemispheare of heaven, which is the
Glory thereof to the Resurrection, yet the other hemispheare,
the joy, God opens to our discovery, and delivers for our
habitation even whilst we dwell in this world. . . . And as
God doth inflict two deaths, and infuse two lives, so doth he
also passe two judgements upon man or rather repeats the
same judgement twice. For that which Christ shall say to thy
soule then at the last judgement, Enter into thy Masters joy,
He sayes to thy conscience now, *Enter into thy Masters joy.* The
everlastingness of the joy is the blessedness of the next life, but
the entering, the inchoation, is afforded here." [2]

The mystics believe that this joyful communion with God
is often interrupted by a state of intense spiritual isolation
in which God seems to desert the soul. Donne has several
times alluded to this state, which the mystics call the "Dark
Night of the Soul." "Love him not onely in spiritual trans-
figurations when he visits thy soule with glorious consolations,
but even in his inward eclipses, when he withholds his comforts,

---

[1] *LXXX Sermons*, No. 61, p. 617.
[2] *Ibid.*, No. 66, p. 672.

and withdraws his cheerfulness, even when he makes as though he loved not thee, Love him." [1]

Though Donne never seems to have attained the last stage of mystical life, the "unitive stage," which Evelyn Underhill has described as the state in which the mystic's "long sought correspondence with transcendental Reality, his union with God, has now been finally established: that his self, though intact, is wholly penetrated—as a sponge by the sea—by the ocean of Life and Love to which he has attained," [2] he seems to have believed in the soul's ultimate union with God as being the consummation of mystical life: "The other great effect of his guiding us with his eye, is, that it unites us to himselfe; when he fixes his eye upon us, and accepts the returne of ours to him, then he keeps us as the *Apple of his Eye—Quasi pupillam filiam oculi* (as S. Hierom reads it), as the Daughter, the issue, the offspring of his own eye. For then, *He that toucheth you, toucheth the Apple of his eye.* And these are the two great effects of his guiding us by his eye, that first, his eye turnes us to himselfe, and then turnes us into himselfe; first, his eye turnes ours to him, and then, that makes us all one with himselfe; . . . we cannot be safer than by being his; but thus, we are not onely His, but He." [3]

Christ and Scholasticism and Donne's Adoration of Christ.— Scholasticism failed to recognise the true significance of the life of Christ to the individual soul; Rudolf Steiner says: "And the question scholasticism could not answer was: How does Christ enter into human thought? How is human thought permeated with Christ? It is the question: How does one carry Christology into the thought? How is thought made Christ-like? At the moment when Thomas Aquinas died, in 1274, this question, historically speaking, confronted the world." [4]

It is a significant fact that the mystic contemplation of Donne is based on the mystical conception of Christology; in fact, like St. Paul and St. Augustine and the other great Christian mystics, Donne believed that all knowledge was to "know Christ" and all virtue was to be Christ-like. He once said:

[1] *Ibid.*, No. 40, p. 399.
[2] *Mysticism*, by E. Underhill, p. 499.
[3] *LXXX Sermons*, No. 61, p. 618.
[4] *The Philosophy of Thomas Aquinas*, by Rudolf Steiner, p. 76.

"one Philosopher thinks he is dived to the bottome when he says, he knows nothing but this, That he knows nothing. . . . S. *Paul* found that to be all knowledge, To know Christ." [1]

A passionate devotion to the Person of Christ is the keynote of Donne's mysticism. He observed, "that is enough which we have in St. John. Every spirit that confesses that Jesus is come in the flesh is of God; for since it was a coming of Jesus, Jesus was before; so he was God; and since he came in flesh, he is now made man; and that God and man are so met, is a sign to me that God and I shall never be parted." [2]

Donne defined his entering into the Church "a valediction to the world," and having divorced himself from worldly life he concentrated all his love on Christ:

> "Seale then this bill of my Divorce to All,
> On whom those fainter beams of love did fall;
> Marry those loves which in youth scattered bee
> On Fame, Wit, Hopes (false mistresses) to thee." [3]

He had prayed:

> ". . . let all mee elemented bee,
> Of power, to love, to know you unnumbred three" [4];

but he realized later, with all great mystics, that it was neither knowledge nor reason that could lead one to God, but faith and love. He declared in clear terms "we can humbly believe these mysteries of our religion, by faith, without the hand and help of reason." Love alone could save us:

> "Thy lawes abridgement, and thy last command
> Is all but love; Oh let this last will stand!" [5]

And this love was the love of Christ and his birth into the human soul, and he truly said "all these fulnesses I shall have, if I can find and feel in myself this birth of Christ."

Christ is the promise of regeneration in this life and hope and promise of salvation in the next as well; even the horrors of death give place to a spiritual joy when Donne thinks of the Redeeming character of his Saviour:

"If I can say (and my conscience doe not tell me that I

---

[1] *LXXX Sermons*, No. 4: Pearsall Smith, p. 94.
[2] *LXXX Sermons*, No. 2: Alford, vol. i, p. 33.
[3] *A Hymn to Christ (At the Author's Last Going into Germany)*.
[4] *The Litanie.*   [5] *Holy Sonnets*, No. 26.

belye mine own state) if I can say, that the blood of my Saviour runs in my veines, that the breath of his spirit quickens all my purposes, that all my deaths have their Resurrection, all my sins their remorse, all my rebellions their reconciliation, I will harken no more after this question as it is intended *de morte naturali*, of a naturall death, I know I must die that death, what care I? nor *de morte spirituali*, the death of sin, I know, I doe, and shall die so; why despair I? but I will finde out another death, *mortem raptus*, a death of rapture, and of extasie, and that death which St. Paul died more than once. The death which *S. Gregory* speaks of, *Divina Contemplatio quoddam sepulchrum animae*, the contemplation of God, and heaven, is a kinde of buriall, and sepulchre, and rest of the soule, and in this death of rapture, and extasie, in this death of the Contemplation of my interest in my Saviour, I shall finde myself and all my sins enterred, and entombed in his wounds, and like a Lily in Paradise, out of red earth, I shall see my soul rise out of his blade, in a candor, and in an innocence contracted there, acceptable in the sight of his Father." [1]

The significance of Christ's life and His Passion in the history of mysticism has been discussed by Miss Evelyn Underhill with a rare insight into the life of the Christian mystics:

"But from Jesus of Nazareth descends that whole spiritual race, that fresh creation, within which the Christian mystics stand as it were as the heads of great houses; the originators of those variations whereby the infinite richness and variety of the parent life has been expressed." [2]

It is thus clear that Donne belongs to that line of Christian mystics who, like St. Bernard and St. John of the Cross and St. Teresa, and others, have made the adoration of Christ and the contemplation of His Passion the aim of their mystical life, while St. Thomas belongs to the school of Dionysius, the Areopagite, who while recognizing the significance of Christ makes God Himself the central object of the mystic's life. [3]

St. Thomas and the Beatific Vision, and Donne's Views about it.— Though St. Thomas has passionately argued that the ultimate

---

[1] *LXXX Sermons*, No. 27.
[2] *The Mystic Way*, p. 147.
[3] This difference between the mysticism of Donne and of St. Thomas was suggested to me by Professor A. E. Taylor, to whom I am indebted for many a stimulating discussion on Donne's philosophy.

destiny of the human soul was to see God as He is, in the light of Glory in Heaven, and has devoted the third book of *Contra Gentiles* to this subject, he denied that we could see the Essence of God in this life. As all knowledge is derived through the senses, therefore the perception of Pure Spiritual Being, God, is beyond the capacity of the human mind: "If the connatural dependence of our understanding on Phantasms prevents us in this life from understanding other pure spirits, much less can we in this life see the divine essence, which transcends all angels. Of this fact the following may also be taken as an indication: The higher our mind is raised to the contemplating of spiritual things, the more it is abstracted from sensible things: but the final terminus to which contemplation can possibly arrive is the divine substance: therefore the mind that sees the divine substance must be totally divorced from bodily senses, either by death or by some rapture. Hence it is said in the person of God: *No man shall see me and live* (Exodus xxxiii, 20)." [1]

He holds that God can be known in this life by His effects alone: "Nor is it necessary for something greater than God to be conceivable if His non-existence is conceivable. For the possibility of conceiving Him not to exist does not arise from the imperfection or uncertainty of His being, since His Being is of itself most manifest, but from the infirmity of our understanding which cannot discern him as He is of Himself but by the effects which He produces, and so it is brought by reasoning to the knowledge of Him. As it is self-evident to us that the whole is greater than its part, so the existence of God is most self-evident to them that see the divine essence, inasmuch as His essence is his existence. But because we cannot see His essence, we are brought to the knowledge of his existence, not by what He is Himself but by the effects which He works." [2]

But what the mystic claims is that the attainment of the union of the soul with God, however fleeting, is possible, as Ruysbroeck declared "we behold that which we are, and we

---

[1] *Contra Gentiles*, translated by J. Rickaby, p. 216. He also says in the *Summa Theologica*, Part I, qu. 12, art. 2 (Dominican Fathers' Translation): "In order to see God there must be some similitude of God on the part of the visual faculty, whereby the intellect is made capable of seeing God. On the part of the object seen, which must necessarily be united to the seer, the essence of God cannot be seen by any created similitude."

[2] *Contra Gentiles*, translated by J. Rickaby, p. 10.

are that which we behold; because our thought, life and being are uplifted in simplicity, and made one with the truth which is God." [1] The last stage of mystical life is the unitive stage, when, as Dean Inge says, "man beholds God face to face and is joined to Him." [2] St. Thomas however denies that God could be seen (as He is) in this life or that the "object seen" could be "united to the seer." [3] St. Thomas has discussed in the *Summa Theologica* two typical examples, which the mystics have often quoted as pointing to the possibility of the Unitive Experience in this life: Jacob's seeing of God "face to face," and Moses' speaking to God "mouth to mouth." He assigns Jacob's vision to the "mode of Prophecy," "so when Jacob says, *I saw God face to face*, this does not mean the Divine Essence, but some figure representing God. This in itself is to be referred to some high mode of prophecy, so that God seems to speak, though in an imaginary vision; as will later be explained (II, 2, qu. clxxiv) in treating of the Prophetic grades. We may also say that Jacob spoke this to designate some exalted intellectual contemplation above the ordinary state." [3]

He holds that the vision of God granted to Moses and St. Paul, to whom St. Augustine has referred as men who saw God in His Essence, really belongs to "supernatural wonders"; St. Thomas points out that "as God works miracles in corporeal things, so also He does supernatural wonders above the common order, raising the minds of some living in flesh beyond the use of sense, even up to the vision of His own essence: as Augustine says of Moses the teacher of the Jews: and of Paul the teacher of the Gentiles." [3] St. Augustine speaking of St. Paul says that he "was rapt into this transcendent vision wherein we may believe that God vouchsafed to show him that life wherein, after this life, we are to live for ever," [4] and believes that Moses' desire "to see God in His own Nature as He will be seen by the saints in Heaven, as He is," [4] was fulfilled.

St. Thomas seems to have accepted the authority of St. Augustine in the case of St. Paul and Moses, but he regards these as exceptional cases belonging to the Prophetic grade

[1] Quoted by E. Underhill, *Mysticism*, p. 423.
[2] *Christian Mysticism*, Inge, p. 12.
[3] *Summa*, Part I, qu. 12, art. 2.
[4] Quoted by Dom C. Butler, *Western Mysticism*.

which does not apply to the ordinary mystics. He is quite definite in his view that God cannot be seen in this life.

In a passage which does not leave any doubt about St. Thomas's views, he maintains that the vision of God as He is cannot be granted to man in this life:

"*I answer that*, God can be seen in His Essence by man only if separated from this mortal life. The reason is, because, as was said above, the mode of knowledge follows the mode of existence of the knower. Our soul, as long as we live in this life, has its existence in corporeal matter; hence naturally it knows only what has a form in matter, or what can be known by such a form. It is evident that the Divine Essence cannot be known by the nature of material things. It was shown above that the knowledge of God by means of any created similitude is not the vision of His Essence. Hence it is impossible for the soul of man in this life to see the Essence of God. This can be seen in the fact that the more our soul is abstracted from corporeal things, the more it is capable of perceiving abstract intelligible things. Hence in dreams and alienations of the bodily senses Divine revelations and foresight of future events are perceived the more clearly. It is not possible, therefore, that the soul in this mortal life should be raised up to the supreme intelligible object, that is, to the Divine Essence." [1]

Wicksteed has also pointed out that St. Thomas denied the possibility of seeing God in His Essence in this life, which according to St. Thomas is a state proper to the state of glory which the soul can only attain in Heaven.

"Aquinas," Wicksteed points out, "it will be seen, wholly excludes the possibility of anticipating the vision of God while we are yet in the body; for the organic connection of the soul with the (not yet glorified) body makes it dependent ultimately upon the *species sensibiles* or Phantasmata, supplied by the senses, from which it can never shake itself free *in via*." [2]

Though St. Thomas did not believe that it was possible to have a vision of God in His Essence, he himself seems to have been granted such a vision of God in ecstasy, the nature

[1] *Summa*, Part I, qu. 12, art. 2.
[2] *The Reaction between Dogma and Philosophy*, by P. Wicksteed, p. 644. Also see Wicksteed's *Dante and Aquinas*.

of which he never related to another soul. He was staying at his sister's castle of San Severino, when he experienced a prolonged ecstasy, and when he returned to his normal self "He said with sighs: Son Rainaldo, I will tell thee a secret, forbidding thee to disclose it to any while I live. The end of my writing has come, for such things have been revealed to me that all that I have written and taught seems to me very little; and from this I hope in my God that, even as my teaching is ended so my life will soon close." [1]

Thus the supreme experience of the greatest exponent of scholasticism was in the end mystical.

Maritain has given several other recorded instances of the visions of the Virgin Mary and Christ which were granted to St. Thomas; once the sacristan' saw him raised above the ground. Maritain describing this incident says: "A similar incident occurred again at Naples. Friar Thomas was then writing the third part of the *Summa* dealing with the Passion and Resurrection of Christ, one day, before Matins, the Sacristan saw him raised nearly two cubits above the ground and stood a long time gazing at him. Suddenly he heard a voice proceed from the image on the crucifix to which the Doctor was turned, praying in tears: 'Thou has written well of me, Thomas, what reward shall I give thee for thy work ? '— None but Thyself, O Lord." [2]

Speaking of the mystical life of St. Thomas, Maritain says "we have information therefore regarding the mystical life of St. Thomas, in the testimonies of his brethren and exterior indications . . . there is however never a direct statement by himself. For he practised only too thoroughly the maxim of St. Anthony, the hermit, which he may have read in Cassian (every day he had read to him a few pages of Cassian), that 'there can be no perfect prayer, if the religious perceives himself to be praying.' And it was no part of his mission, like a St. John of the Cross or a St. Teresa, to expound the things of contemplation practically, from the point of view of introspection and experience." [2]

Having described the philosophical attitude adopted by

---

[1] *Dante and the Mystics,* by E. G. Gardner, p. 5. For a brief discussion of the Mystical Theology of St. Thomas see *The Mysticism of St. Thomas Aquinas,* by Fr. Vincent MacNabb.

[2] *St. Thomas Aquinas,* by J. Maritain, translated by J. F. Scanlan, p. 47.

St. Thomas on the problem of the Beatific Vision, we can now examine how far Donne agreed with his views.

Donne, following St. Thomas Aquinas, believed that we cannot behold God in His Essence, though a fleeting vision of God was possible in this life; he declared "that neither *Adam* in his extasie in Paradise, nor *Moses* in his conversation in the Mount, nor the other Apostles in the transfiguration of Christ, nor St. Paul in his rapture to the third heavens, saw the Essence of God, because it is admitted that these who have the sight of God, can never look off, nor lose that sight againe, only in Heaven shall God proceed to this patefaction, this mani-festation, this revelation of himself; and that by the light of glory." [1]   But he believed that St. Paul did enjoy a momentary vision of God while the eternity of His vision can only be enjoyed in Heaven. He says of St. Paul that God "gave him a Rapture, an Extasie, and in that, an appropinquation, an approximation to himselfe, and so some possession of Heaven in this life." [2]

There are several passages in his *Sermons* which show that Donne was familiar with the diverse views which were held by the different medieval philosophers, like St. Thomas and Duns Scotus, on "the Vision of God."   Donne says: "Blessed-nesse itself, is God himselfe; our blessednesse is our possession; our union with God. In what consists this? A great limbe of the schoole with their *Thomas*, place this blessednesse, this union with God, In *Visione*, in this, that in heaven *I shall see God*, see God essentially, *God face to face*, God as he is. We do not see one another so, in this world; In this world we see but outsides; in heaven I shall see God, and God essentially. But then another great branch of the schoole, with their *Scotus*, place this blessednesse, this union with God, *in Amore*, in this, that in heaven, I shall love God. Now love presumes know-ledge; for *Amari nisi nota non possunt*, we can love nothing, but which we do or think we do understand. There in heaven, I shall *know* God, so, as that I shall be admitted, not onely to an *Adoration* of God, to an *admiration* of God, to a *prosternation*, and reverence before God, but to an *affection*, to an office, of more familiarity towards God, of more equality with God, I shall *love* God. But even love itselfe, as noble a passion as it is, is

---

[1] *LXXX Sermons*, No. 23, p. 230.   [2] *Ibid.*, p. 476.

but a paine except we enjoy that we love; and therefore with
their *Aureolus*, place this blessednesse, this union of our souls
with God, in *Gaudio*, in our joy, that is, in our enjoying of God.
In this world we enjoy nothing; enjoying presumes perpetuity;
and here, all things are fluid, transitory: There I shall enjoy,
and possesse for ever, God himself.   But yet, everyone of these,
to *see* God, or to *Love* God, or to *enjoy* God, have *seemed* to some
too narrow to comprehend this blessednesse, beyond which,
nothing can be proposed; and therefore another limbe of the
Schools, with their *Bonaventure*, place this blessednesse *in all
these* together.   And truly, if any of those did exclude any of
these, so, as that I might *see* God, and not *Love* him, or love,
and not *enjoy* him, it could not well be called *blessednesse*; but
he that hath anyone of these, hath every one, all; And therefore the greatest part concurre, and safely *in visione*, that vision
is *beatification*, to see God as he is, that is blessednesse." [1]

But Donne does not argue like St. Thomas as a philosopher,
and he passes no opinion on the problem whether the bodily
senses can behold God or that the mind can ever be raised to
the level where it can behold the highest intelligible Being,
God.

He advances other than philosophical reasons for the in-
capacity of man to behold God in His Essence—it is the sinfulness of man, and the result of this sinfulness inherent in man
is that perfect purity (sanctification) cannot be attained in
this life, and significantly therefore it only has been affirmed
that the pure in heart alone shall see God.   He holds that man
can never altogether be free from sin and that the state of
sanctification and purification which can be attained in this
life can never be so perfect so as to enable us to comprehend
the Essence of God; and speaking of Philip Neri, and Ignatius
Loyola, he declared that "this pureness is not in their heart,
but in their fantasie," [2] and he further remarks that "they
meane, (and indeed, some of them say) that a man come to
that purity in this life, as that in this life, he shall be in possession of that very Beatificall vision, which is the state of glory in
heaven." [3]

[1] *L Sermons*, No. 48, p. 421.
[2] *XXVI Sermons*, p. 325.
[3] *LXXX Sermons*, No. 12, p. 116.

He rejects their claims to have attained such a purity in this life, but he knew that a momentary vision of God was possible in this life, as he himself says, "first His (God's) eye turnes ours to Him, and then, that makes us all one with Himself . . . we can not be safer than by being His; but thus we are not only His, but He." [1] Elsewhere he declared "the sight of God which we shall have in heaven, must have a *Diluculum*, a break of day here; If we will see His face there, we must see it in some beames here." [2]

He believed that the joys of Heaven did not begin after death but we have a foretaste of them in this life and they are only multiplied in the next: "Certainly as that man shall never see the Father of Lights after this, to whom the day never breaks in this life: As that man must never look to walk with the Lambe wheresoever he goes in heaven, that ranne away from the Lambe whensoever he came towards him, in this life; so he shall never possess the joys of heaven hereafter, that feels no joy here." [3]

To Donne "heaven and salvation is not a creation, but a multiplication; it begins not when wee dye, but it increases and dilates itself infinitely then," [3] and thus the true mark of the mystic is the possession of Heaven on earth.

"The pure in heart are blessed already, not onely comparatively that they are in a better way of Blessedness, then others are, but actually in a present possession of it: for this world and the next world are not, to the pure in heart, two houses, but two roomes, a Gallery, to pass thorough, and a lodging to rest in, in the same House, which are both under one roofe, Christ Jesus; the Militant and the Triumphant are not two churches, but this the Porch, and that the chancell of the same church, which are under one head, Christ Jesus; so the joy, and the sense of Salvation which the pure in heart have here, is not a joy severed from the joy of Heaven, but a joy that begins in us here, and continues and accompanies us thither, and there flows on, and dilates it selfe to an infinite expansion." [4]

This conception of ever-increasing blessedness and joy from this life to the next is a conception peculiar to all Christian mystics. St. Augustine says: "I entreat thee, O my God,

---

[1] *LXXX Sermons*, No. 61, p. 618.
[3] *L Sermons*, No. 26.

[2] *Ibid.*, No. 12, p. 122.
[4] *LXXX Sermons*, No. 12, p. 119.

that I may know Thee, that I may love Thee, that I may rejoice in Thee.   And even if I cannot do so fully in this life yet make me daily advance till my joy be full.   May I grow daily in knowledge of Thee while I am in this life, that here-after it may be full.   Make Thy love here increase in me, that there it may be full; that here my joy may in itself be great, that there it may be full in thee." [1]

Donne's imagination is ever kindled by the firm belief that he shall see God, it is a fact which he never doubted, and then his possession of God shall be timeless and so eternal.   He declared: "No man ever saw God and liv'd; and yet, I shall not live till I see God; and when I have seen him I shall never dye." [2]

It is almost the same desire which St. Augustine has expressed in one of his devotions: "Exceeding glorious will be the glory of seeing God as He is; of seeing Him and possessing Him and this to all eternity." [3]

In summing up, we may say St. Thomas's scholastic "reasoning" did not lead him to mystical faith; and it was mainly due to two reasons.   St. Thomas did not bring the religious experience of the human soul as one of the proofs of the existence of God; the Christian revelation is only proved on the basis of the miracles which Christ performed (*Contra Gentiles*, chap. vi.): and secondly he did not make *visio Dei* as an additional evidence of not only God's existence but also of His coming into the individual soul; and thus religious experience, which is the basis of all forms of mysti-cism, found no significant place in his majestic *Summa* of all knowledge.   But on that borderland of theology where moral and natural theology merge into mystical theology St. Thomas's philosophy is of great value.   His Holiness Pope Pius XI (in his Encyclical Letter "Studiorum Ducem") truly said: "Nor is his ascetical and Mystical Science any less noble.   He reduces the whole of moral discipline to the virtues and gifts; and he excellently defines the same method and discipline for various states of life, whether for those who follow the ordinary Christian life or for those who strive

---

[1] *Manual of Devotion of St. Augustine*, translated by the Rev. Marcus Dods, D.D., pp. 69–70.
[2] *LXXX Sermons*, No. 14, p. 117.
[3] *Devotions*, p. 33.

after consummate perfection, whether in a contemplative or active order." [1]

Donne was not the only great poet who in his search of God outlived the *rationalism* of St. Thomas; Dante, who had accepted the conception of the universe as revealed in the philosophy of St. Thomas Aquinas, also found the power of intellect inadequate in the realization of the supreme bliss, the vision of God.

Gardner has pointed out that in Dante, "Gradually discarding imagination and reason, the object of the mind's contemplation, becomes what is above reason and seems to be beside reason, or even against it." [2]   That the Mystical Vision in its essence cannot be described is the experience of all great mystics.   Dante says: "Hence onward my sight was greater than our speech, which fails at such a vision, and memory fails at so great excess" (*Paradiso*, xxxiii, 55–57).   Donne knew that in these stages of religious life, intellect, memory and speech, all those things which belong to sense and imagination fail ; and this bliss could be achieved only through Christ's mercy and His grace.   He prayed: "Lighten our Darkness, we beseech thee, O Lord, with all these lights; that in thy light we may see light; that in this essential light which is Christ, and in this supernatural light which is grace, we may see all these, and all other beams of light, which may bring us to thee, and him, and that blessed spirit which proceeds from both.   Amen!" [3]

Donne and Salvation—his Attitude towards Platonism.—Donne, it has been claimed by his critics like Miss Ramsay, "never knew that inner *unification* which is an essential element in the ethical teaching of Plotinus." [4]

That Donne attained "Illumination" and the peace that comes of the assurance of salvation becomes evident from a close study of his *Sermons*, but we must bear in mind the fact that Donne as a Christian mystic had outlived the experience of such non-Christian philosophers as Plato and Plotinus, as St. Augustine had done before him.   A critical estimate of the

[1] *The Mysticism of St. Thomas Aquinas*, by Fr. V. MacNabb, p. 1.
[2] *Dante and the Mystics* (London), by E. G. Gardner, pp. 157–177.   See also *Paradiso*, xxxiii, 142, and iv, 37–42.
[3] *XXVI Sermons*, No. 24, p. 325, and *LXXX Sermons*, No. 12, 122.
[4] "Donne's Relation to Philosophy" (*A Garland for John Donne*), p. 116.

influence of Neo-Platonism on Christian mysticism has been made in recent years by critics like Dean Inge, Dr. William Temple and George Santayana[1]; to my mind Dean Inge has exaggerated the influence of Plotinus on Christian thought, for Neo-Platonism differs from Christianity in many important respects. Plotinus conceived God, the Supreme One, as essentially impersonal, while the Christian conception of God is wholly personal. The Platonic Logos cannot be identified with Christ, for Christ is not only the Creative Principle emanating from God, he is also the God become Man: Plotinus has thus given no place to the Incarnation in his philosophy, which is the corner-stone of Christian mysticism.[2] W. K. Fleming has remarked, "The Incarnation with all that it implies was out of the range of his (Plotinus) thought." Plotinus did not believe in Redemption through suffering, and so the two cardinal dogmas of the Christian faith, the Incarnation and Crucifixion, have no place in the system of Plotinus, and these two central aspects have their basis in the exalted Christian Conception of Love, which Plotinus has also neglected in his philosophy.[3]

Though Donne admired and respected Plato, Socrates and Plotinus he knew that their philosophy was no substitute for Christian religion. He knew that without the inner working of Christ's grace and the help of the Sacraments there could be no belief or salvation. In a significant passage he has ridiculed those Platonists who "think that we can believe out of Plato, where we may find a God but without a Christ." [4] Donne held that without accepting the mysteries of the Incarnation and the Crucifixion we could not achieve salvation. But Miss Ramsay says: "Here I can but mention Spenser as a contrast to Donne, and indicate by this suggestion that path of escape from insecurity not found by the latter." [5] Spenser had never been troubled by any "immoderate desire" of human learning and languages, and he was not interested in such diverse systems of

---

[1] See Inge's *Philosophy of Plotinus* and *The Platonic Tradition in English Religious Thought*; Temple's *Plato and Christianity* and George Santayana's *Plato and Spiritual Life*.

[2] *Mysticism in Christianity*, by W. K. Fleming, p. 66.

[3] Dr. Bigg (*Neo-Platonism*, p. 248) has pointed out that "according to Plotinus God is goodness without love. Man may love God, but God cannot love man."

[4] *LXXX Sermons*, No. 62, p. 623.

[5] "Donne's Relation to Philosophy," p. 116.

philosophy which Donne's curiosity explored, nor had he Donne's agonized sense of sin and the equally vehement desire for redemption and the resolution of intellectual perplexities.

Spenser's personality is much more simple when compared to that of Donne; and moreover Spenser was not so deeply religious as Donne was, and Spenser's interest in Neo-Platonism was a philosophical and theoretical interest; he did not live on those planes of devotional life with which Neo-Platonism deals. St. Augustine best illustrates in his life the relation of Christian mysticism to Neo-Platonism.

Though St. Augustine was deeply influenced by Neo-Platonism, he found it inadequate for the higher stages of Christian life. Dom Butler has pointed out that "there is a tendency, I think, to exaggerate greatly the Neo-Platonism of the early treatises, particularly those composed between conversion and baptism, and to minimize the element of very real Christian and religious feeling that pervades them; still they are an ordered attempt to provide a philosophy of Christian belief in the ideas and terms of the most generally accepted and more spiritual philosophic system of the time, the Neo-Platonism, which Augustine loves as the means, humbly speaking, that had led him back to his Catholic faith." [1]

Donne, like St. Augustine, discovered another kind of beauty to which Spenser in his *Epithalamion* or *Hymns* did not give any importance, and that beauty was Christ: the constant theme of Donne's poetry and prose alike is:

"Love him as he is the *Lord*, that would have nothing perish that he hath made; And love him as he is *Christ*, that hath made himself man too, that thou mightest not perish; Love him as the *Lord* that could shew mercy; and love him as *Christ*, who is that way of mercy, which the Lord hath chosen. Returne againe, and againe, to that mysterious person, *Christ*." [2]

It is significant that Donne classed Plato and Socrates as "natural man" and distinguished them from the "regenerate Christian." Donne believed that philosophy and reason can

[1] *Western Mysticism*, by Dom Cuthbert Butler, pp. 57, 70. St. Augustine's early attitude towards Platonists is summed in the following sentence, when he said "The Platonists with the change of very few words and opinions would become Christians" (*De Vera Relig.*, 7); see Montgomery, *St. Augustine*. Also see "The Philosophy of St. Augustine," by M. C. D'Arcy S.J., in *A Monument to Saint Augustine*, chapter v.
[2] *LXXX Sermons*, No. 40, pp. 400–401.

sustain our moral life only to a certain limit: "as long as these helps of reason and learning are alive and awake and actuated in us they are able to sustain us from sinking under the afflictions of this world, for they have sustained many a Plato and Socrates and Seneca in such cases"; but when part of the "affliction" that God sends to us is the darkening of the powers of intellect and reason, these "helps" of philosophy are of no avail, and then the Christian is saved through Christ alone, for he exclaims: "I am the man that cannot despair, since Christ is the remedy."

Donne, like St. Augustine, had outlived the Neo-Platonic philosophers, and so it is idle to compare him to poets like Spenser. In speaking of Salvation to non-Christians before Christ, like Plato and Socrates, Donne could not say definitely that they will be saved: "To me, to whom God hath revealed his Son, in a Gospel, by a Church, there can be no way of salvation but by applying that Son of God, by that Gospel, in that Church. Nor is there any other foundation for any, nor other name by which any can be saved but the name of Jesus. But how this foundation is presented and how this name of Jesus is notified to them amongst whom there is no Gospel preached, no church established I am not curious in inquiring. I know God can be merciful as those tender Fathers present him to be; and I would be as charitable as they are. And therefore humbly imbracing that manifestation of his Son, which he hath afforded me, I leave God, to His unsearchable ways of working upon others, without farther inquisition." [1]

But he makes it clear that we cannot find God without the help of Christ, and Plato had no Christ to offer to his followers; he observes: "To know a better state, and to desire it, is not pride; for pride is onely in taking wrong wayes to it. So that, to think we can come to this by our own strength, without Gods inward working, or to thinke that we can believe out of *Plato*, where we may find a God but without a Christ, or come to be good men out of *Plutarch or Seneca*, without a Church and sacraments, to pursue the truth itselfe by any other way than he had laid open to us, this is pride, and the pride of the Angels."

Donne, as we have now seen, was interested in different

---

[1] *LXXX Sermons*, No. 26, pp. 261–262.

schools of philosophy; he knew the sceptical philosophers, like Sextus Empiricus, the Greek philosophers, like Plato and Socrates, and the whole body of scholastic philosophy before and after St. Thomas Aquinas, and his critics like Duns Scotus and Occam—he had read all these philosophers with special reference to his own ever-deepening religious life, but in his later years he took up a position which is essentially that of a mystic. Thus it was in the mystical form of faith and experience that he at last found *peace* and *certainty*. He had declared in one of his sermons that the man who has repented for his past sins sincerely will receive the testimony of his pardon on his death-bed and will be reconciled to God and possess Heaven before his bodily eyes be shut: "So if thou have repented before, and settled thyself in a religious course before, and have nothing to doe then, but to wrastle with the power of disease, and the agonies of death, God shall fight for thee in that weake estate; God shall imprint in thee a *cupio dissolvi*, S. Paul's, not onely contentednesse but desire to be dissolved; And God shall give thee a glorious Resurrection, yea an Ascension into Heaven before thy death, and thou shalt see thy selfe in possession of his eternall Kingdome, before thy bodily eyes be shut . . .; that even thy death-bed bee as Elias Chariot, to carry thee to heaven." [1]

Donne here seems to have prophesied the assurance and certainty of his own salvation which he was to receive in his last illness. Walton, who has given a first-hand account of the strange drama of the passing of Donne, has described how he was seized with the desire to be dissolved: "He lay fifteen days earnestly expecting his hourly change; and in his last day, as his body melted away, and vapoured into spirit, his soul having, I verily believe, some revelation of the Beatific Vision, he said 'I were miserable if I might not die.'"

Walton refers to a friend (I believe this to be Walton himself) to whom Donne declared that he was confident of his salvation: "His strength being much wasted . . . a friend that had often been a witness of his free and facetious discourse asked him, 'why are you sad?', to whom he replied with a countenance so full of cheerful gravity, as gave testimony of an inward tranquility of mind, and of a soul willing to take

[1] *LXXX Sermons*, No. 78, p. 802.

a farewell of this world, 'I am not sad. . . . And though of myself I have nothing to present to him but sin and misery, yet I know he looks not upon me now as I am of myself, but as I am in my Saviour, and hath given me even at this present time some testimonies by his Holy Spirit, that I am of the number of his Elect: I am therefore full of inexpressible joy and shall die in peace.' " [1]

[1] *Life of Dr. John Donne*, by Izaak Walton, edited by George Saintsbury (The World's Classics), p. 77.

It is, however, strange to find that Miss Evelyn Hardy (in *John Donne: A Spirit in Conflict*, 1942) has laid an exaggerated emphasis on Donne's "fear of death" and remarked that even in death "serenity was alien to Donne." The "insatiable whirlpools," "the furnaces" of his "spirit" "suffocated him up to the last" (p. 254). There is no evidence in Donne's writings to support sweeping generalizations of this nature!

PEN PORTRAIT OF JOHN DONNE

HE was of stature moderately tall; of a straight and equally-proportioned body, to which all his words and actions gave an unexpressible addition of comeliness.

The melancholy and pleasant humour were in him so contem-pered, that each gave advantage to the other, and made his company one of the delights of mankind.

His fancy was unimitably high, equalled only by his great wit; both being made useful by a commanding judgement.

His aspect was cheerful, and such as gave a silent testimony of a clear knowing soul, and of a conscience at peace with itself.

His melting eye shewed that he had a soft heart, full of noble compassion; of too brave a soul to offer injuries, and too much a Christian not to pardon them in others.

He did much contemplate—especially after he entered into his sacred calling—the Mercies of Almighty God, the Immortality of the Soul, and the Joys of Heaven: and would often say in a kind of sacred ecstacy—"Blessed be God that he is God, only and divinely like himself."

He was by nature highly passionate, but more apt to reluct at the excesses of it. A great lover of the offices of humanity, and of so merciful a spirit, that he never beheld the miseries of mankind without pity and relief.

He was earnest and unwearied in the search of knowledge, with which his vigorous soul is now satisfied, and employed in a continual praise of that God that first breathed it into his active body: that body, which once was a Temple of the Holy Ghost, and is now become a small quantity of Christian dust:

But I shall see it re-animated.   ISAAK WALTON.

February 15, 1639.

CHAPTER III

THE MYSTICAL ELEMENT IN THE POETRY OF GEORGE HERBERT

THE earlier Renaissance of Sidney, Surrey and Spenser was an age of consolidation in politics, religion and literature. The dangers of foreign invasion had made the whole nation rally round the Queen, who became the symbol of national solidarity; the leaders in the State as well as in the Church recognized the immediate need of uniformity, and so dissenters in the Church were treated as traitors to the Crown. Elizabeth's Act of Supremacy, "Restoring Ancient Jurisdiction," 1559, laid down that "all usurped and Foreign power and authority spiritual and temporal may for ever be clearly extinguished and never to be used or obeyed within this realm."

Shakespeare in his historical plays emphasized the virtues of orderly government; Spenser tried to interpret, through the richness of romance and allegory, the ideals of order and beauty; while Jewell and Hooker reasoned out a system of an organized Church government, and it is therefore not surprising that it was in drama, the most communal of artistic forms, that Elizabethan genius found its supreme expression. Hooker declared that royal authority was supreme in matters of religion[1]; the theory that the power of the Crown was supreme in the Church as well as in the State led to the consolidation of the national power; Einstein says:

"Churchmen were regarded as subjects of the Crown taking out commissions like other officers, and religion became merely one side of the State. The frequent shifts of men like Gardiner, Paget and Cecil cannot be laid down solely to indifference, fear or ambition, but were due to belief as well—sincere belief in the royal supremacy to decide questions of faith."[2]

But as the seventeenth century advanced, this conception

[1] Hooker's *Ecclesiastical Polity*, Book VII, chap. 2.
[2] *Tudor Ideals*, by L. Einstein, pp. 24, 25.

of uniformity in the Church and the State was assailed by the new individualism. Palmer has called it the "second period of the Renaissance"; it was "a period of introspection where each man was prone to insist on the importance of whatever was his own. . . . In science Bacon had already questioned established authority and sent men to nature to observe for themselves. In government, the King's prerogative was steadily questioned, and Parliament became so rebellious that they were often dismissed. A revolution in poetic taste was under way; Spenser's lulling rhythms and bloodless heroes were being displaced by the jolting and passionate realism of Donne. . . . The changes wrought in religion were of a deeper and more varied kind . . . personal religion, the sense of individual responsibility to God, was regarded as the one thing needful. . . . The call to individualism was the most sacred summons of the age." [1] The new individualism which Palmer ascribes to the second Renaissance was in fact no new movement in itself, but was the product of the earlier Renaissance. In the sixteenth century, circumstances had contrived to break all the strongholds of tradition and authority, thus liberating the individual; the destruction of feudalism, of monasticism, of scholasticism inevitably led to the growth of a new conception of human personality and the rôle assigned to it in human affairs. The culture of the Renaissance was based on the individual, while that of the Middle Ages was based on the ideals of communal and corporate life. The Renaissance had given to man a new conception of his moral worth and dignity; and the equality of opportunity which the new conditions offered to man led to the assertion of his wildest dreams.

The Reformation carried this individualism further into matters of faith; the abolition of the Papal authority is supposed to have liberated the conscience of man, and the translation of the Bible placed in his hands a new criterion of truth. Protestantism gave a new significance to the responsibility of the individual soul to God, and this was the logical outcome of the break-up of Catholicism; as Ernst Troeltsch has rightly observed: "A bond of union absolutely superior to individualism can only be supplied by a power as tremendous as that of

[1] *The Works of George Herbert*, by G. H. Palmer, vol. i, pp. 99, 100.

the belief in an immediate supernatural Divine revelation, such as Catholicism possessed and organized in the Church as the extension and continuation of the Divine incarnation." [1]

Elizabeth did not claim like the Pope the infallibility of judgement in all matters concerning faith; she declared in the Proclamation issued after her excommunication that she did not intend to enter into the conscience of her subjects and what she insisted upon was the observance of the outward forms of uniformity in the Church. Henry VIII had tried to be the Pope and King in one; but the Crown in England soon realized that it could not assume the dignity of the Pope and this was an important factor in the growth of individualism in religion.

Though Donne and Herbert taught the virtues of obedience to the established authority in Church as well as State, their emphasis is on personal holiness, on self-mortification, on the relations of the individual soul to God.[2]

Donne in one of his sermons justified the claims of the authority to legislate in matters "indifferent," where the Scriptures do not enjoin any definite form of ceremony or ritual: "That which Christ's Example left indifferent, the Authority of that church, in which God hath given thee thy station, may make necessary to thee; Though not absolutely necessary, and *Ratione medii*, that none can be saved that doe not kneele at the Sacrament, therefore because they do not kneel at the Sacrament, yet necessary *Ratione praecepti*, as it is enjoyned by lawful authority, and to resist lawful authority is a disobedience, that may endanger any man's salvation." [3]

Herbert went so far as to assert that though "spiritual men" cannot be judged by learned men they can be judged by a magistrate. He remarked: "Allowing no jurisdiction over the godly, this cannot stand, and it is ill doctrine in a commonwealth"; and he further declared: "Worldly learned cannot judge spirituall men's actions, but the magistrate

---

[1] *Protestantism and Progress*, by Ernst Troeltsch, p. 19.

[2] "Foole and wretch, wilt thou let thy soule be tyed
To mans lawes, by which she shall not be tryed
At the last day?"—Donne, "Third Satire."

[3] *LXXX Sermons*, p. 116, No. 12. Recently Dr. Tillyard has shown the preoccupation of Shakespeare with the extent and limits of the power of the Crown and its relation to the ideal of balance between the temporal and spiritual spheres of society. (*Shakespeare's History Plays*, by Dr. E. M. W. Tillyard. London, Chatto & Windus, 1944.)

may." [1] The personal problems of salvation, election and
good works are the things which engage the attention of
Donne and Herbert. The interest of Cranmer, Jewell and
Parker was in proving the antiquity of the Anglican Church,
in justifying the breach with Rome, in defending the ritual
and ceremony of their Mother Church; but Donne and
Herbert discern symbolic significance in the ritual, they preach
the gospel of a humanism based on charity and tolerance but
grounded on discipline and personal purity; they analyse
their own soul and meditate on its hopes and aspirations, they
reveal the contradictions of human nature; their interest in
the complex development of the human soul is almost dramatic.
Donne's ideal of purity extends far beyond its physical or
practical bounds. He, like Shakespeare, probes deeper into
our thoughts and intentions: "And though I may have done
thus much towards this purity, as that, for a good time, I have
discontinued my sin, yet if my heart be still set upon the
delight, and enjoying of that was got by former sins, though I
be not that dog that returnes to his vomit, yet I am still that
sow, that wallows in her mire; though I doe not thrust my
hands into new dirt, yet the old dirt is still baked upon my
hands, though mine own clothes doe not defile again; as *Job*
speaks (though I do not relapse to the practise of mine old
sin) yet I have none of *Icremies nitre*, and *sope*, none of *Jobs
snow-water*, to wash me cleane, except I come to Restitution.
As long as the heart is set upon things sinfully got thou sinnest
over those years sins, every day: thou art not come to the
Purity of this text, for it is *pure*, and *pure in heart*." [2]

Herbert with a more practical bent of mind is less concerned
with the metaphysical aspects of theology; he is mainly
concerned with personal holiness, the problems of sin, salvation and grace; to him "the country parson's library is a
holy life," [3] and "Law is Practice," [4] and his effort is to live
"the holy and unblamable life " [5]; but, like Donne, he is also
preoccupied with the relation of the individual soul to God:
"for their obligation to God and their own soul is above

[1] Herbert's "Notes on John Valdesso": Palmer, vol. i, p. 361.
[2] *LXXX Sermons*, p. 117.
[3] "The Country Parson," chap. xxxiii,: Palmer, vol. i, p. 307.
[4] *Ibid.*, chap. xxxii, p. 304.
[5] *Ibid.*, chap. xxxviii, p. 289.

any temporal tye. Do well and right and let the world sinke." [1]

It is this conception of the responsibility of the individual soul to God that produced the religious poetry of Donne and Herbert.

It was from Donne that Herbert learned the metaphysical manner, and when he wrote his two sonnets to his mother he seems to have already come under the bewitching influence of Donne.

Herbert himself tells us ("Second Jordan") that when he resolved to dedicate all his poetic powers to the Sacred Muse he chose the metaphysical style peculiar to Donne:

> "When first my lines of heav'nly joyes made mention,
>   Such was their lustre, they did so excell,
>   That I sought out quaint words, and trim invention."

Herbert's adoption of the metaphysical manner was not confined to his choice of "quaint words" but also extended to his thoughts:

> "My thoughts began to burnish, sprout and swell,
>   Curling with metaphors a plain intention,
>   Decking the sense, as if it were to sell."

When Herbert wrote to his mother, "For my own part, my meaning (dear Mother) is in these sonnets, to declare my resolution to be, that my poor Abilities in Poetry shall be all and ever consecrated to God's Glory; and I beg you receive this as one testimony." He had perhaps Donne's example in mind who, after writing some of the finest love lyrics of the century, had devoted himself to the writing of sacred verse. It is significant that Herbert asks of God:

> "Why are not sonnets made of thee? and layes
>   Upon thine Altar burnt?"

And Donne was the great poet who had not only composed divine sonnets, but also sent them to Herbert's mother. Donne wrote (1607) to Lady Herbert: "I commit the enclosed Holy Hymns and Sonnets (which for the matter, not the workmanship have yet escaped the fire) to your Judgement and to your protection 'too, if you think them worthy of it and I have appointed this inclosed sonnet to usher them to your happy hand."

[1] "The Country Parson," chap. xxix, p. 293.

Lady Herbert could not help showing these divine poems to Herbert, whom she was training for the Church. Donne had lamented the "Idolatrie" of "Profane Mistresses"[1] and had emphasized the virtues of bestowing all our affections upon God alone. He declared in one of his sermons later on: "What poems and what orations we make, how industrious and witty we are, to over praise men, and never give God his due praise."[2] It is in the same spirit that Herbert resolved that all his "poor Abilities in Poetry shall be all and ever consecrated to God's Glory."[3]

The influence of Donne is felt in Herbert's quality of poetic sensibility and his choice of conceits. The spontaneous quality of the Elizabethan song is absent from the poetry of Herbert; the song in Donne's hands had become a subtle, argumentative poem in which the poet feels and thinks at the same time.

T. S. Eliot has defined metaphysical poetry as "that in which what is ordinarily apprehensible only by thought is brought within the grasp of feeling or that in which what is ordinarily felt is transformed into thought without ceasing to be feeling." Herbert, like Donne, makes available for feeling the content of his thought. In the "Church Monuments," which is an early poem, we come across lines such as these:

> "While that my soul repairs to her devotion,
> Here I intombe my flesh, that it betimes
> May take acquaintance of this heap of dust;
> To which the blast of death's incessant motion,
> Fed with the exhalation of our crimes,
> Drives all at last."[4]

The quality of thought in Herbert's poems such as "Praise," "Mortification," "Parodie" and "Church Porch" is peculiarly Donnean.

Nothing is so important in studying the progress of a poet on the Mystic Way as the chronological order in which the poems were composed. Though Palmer says that the evidence drawn

[1] Grierson, vol. i, p. 299.
[2] *LXXX Sermons*, p. 88.
[3] *Walton' Lives*, edited by George Saintsbury, p. 268.
[4] All quotations have been cited from Palmer's edition of George Herbert's *Works*, but they have been compared with the definitive edition of Herbert's *Works* by the Rev. F. E. Hutchinson (Oxford, 1941), which appeared after this chapter had been written.

from the manuscript sources and the style of Herbert "is too slender to establish a thoroughgoing chronological sequence," he has grouped the poems in three main divisions to correspond with the three distinct periods of Herbert's life:

(1) The Cambridge period, from the beginning of his writings to 1627.
(2) The second period of crisis, 1627 to 1630, when he was instituted at Bemerton on April 26, 1630.
(3) 1630 to 1633, when he died, on March 3.

This classification is based on the assumption that the Williams MS., discovered by Dr. Grosart (in 1874, in the Williams Library, Gordon Square, London), contains the poems which Herbert wrote before 1630, when he settled down as a priest at Bemerton. No poem included in the Williams MS. contains reference to its author as a priest, though it contains seventy-three of the hundred and sixty-nine poems of the Bodleian MS.[1] The difference in the readings of these seventy-three poems common to both Williams and the Bodleian MSS. is due to the fact that Herbert was continuously revising his poems; the Williams MS. preserves the earlier draft of the revised poems which he sent to Nicholas Ferrar at the time of his death. A close study of the poems arranged thus in their probable chronological order enables us to comprehend the various stages in the religious life of Herbert. These can be divided into two main divisions:

(1) Awakening of the Self, and Purgation.
(2) Illumination.

The higher stages of the Mystic Way, the Dark Night of the Soul, and the Unitive Experience are not to be found in Herbert's poetry; in the end, however, we shall discuss the quality of his mystical experiences of God and discuss the reasons which Palmer has given to prove the "non-mystical" [2] quality of Herbert's religious poetry.

---

[1] The Williams MS. also contains six English poems and two series of Latin poems not found in the Bodleian MS. This chronological arrangement is merely indicative of the dates of revision, and not necessarily of the exact date of composition; and Palmer's subdivisions are of an arbitrary character and even misleading as to developments in Herbert's religious experience.

[2] Palmer, vol. i, p. 74.

The poems which Herbert wrote before 1627 (the year of the death of his mother; his other patrons—King James and the Marquis of Hamilton—had died two years earlier, in 1625), when he resigned the oratorship, reveal his conception of the Church, the Church ritual and festivals, the Holy Scriptures, prayers and the Sacraments.

The Anglican Church was peculiarly suited to effect a compromise between the Roman Catholic Church and the spirit of Protestantism. It recognised the Apostolic Succession, the need of priesthood and of ritual, while it encouraged the reading of the Bible in the English tongue, and upheld the Protestant conception of the individual responsibility of the soul to God, and the constant need of preaching. The Anglican Church in the hands of such ardent and sincere divines as Parker, Hooker, Andrewes and Laud became the repository of a new kind of Anglican polity which was based on the principles of tolerance and sweet reasonableness in matters of faith. Donne considered different Christian churches as "co-natural pieces of one circle" and not so "contrary as the North and South Poles. . . . Religion is Christianity, which being too spiritual to be seen by us doth therefore take an apparent body of good life and works, so salvation requires an honest Christian." [1] Moreover the Anglican divines did not consider, like the Puritans, the Pope to be Antichrist; they recognized him to be the true Bishop of Rome. Hooker said "that the church of Rome is a true church of Christ, and a sanctified church by profession of that truth which God hath revealed unto us by His Son, though not a pure and Perfect church." It is to this Church of Andrewes, Laud and Donne that Herbert belongs. To him the Anglican Church was not based on a convenient compromise; it essentially represented the Christian humanism, the spirit of moderation, tolerance and charity. Herbert defines the true character of the Church:

> "A fine aspect in fit aray,
> Neither too mean, nor yet too gay,
> Shows who is best."

He thought England to be a "land of light" in an age of religious persecution and intolerance; when he recommended

---

[1] *The Life and Letters of John Donne*, by Gosse, vol. i, p. 226.
[2] Palmer, vol. i, p. 367.

Ferrar to publish *The Divine Considerations of Valdesso*, a Spanish Catholic, he remarked that he considered Valdesso "to have been a true servant of God . . . who being obscured in his own country, he would have to flourish in this land of light and religion of the Gospell among His chosen." [1] This is the voice of Anglican humanism and religious polity.

Herbert's preoccupation with the ideals of the Church is shown again in "The Church Porch" and "The Church-Militant," the two long poems which belong to the period before 1630. In "The Church Porch" there is little religion or mysticism, Herbert displays his shrewd common sense in judging men; this poem was evidently written by a friend of Bacon, the orator and the courtier, and the lover of pregnant epigrams; good taste, fine breeding, refinement and culture were the qualities which Herbert thought indispensable for any serious vocation in life. He approves of courtesy and wit in discourse:

> "In thy discourse, if thou desire to please,
> All such is courteous, usefull, new, or wittie.
> Usefulnesse comes by labour, wit by ease;
> Courtesie grows in court; news in the citie.
> Get a good stock of these, then draw the card
> That suites him best, of whom thy speech is heard." [2]

He mixes worldly wisdom with the cultivation of such Christian virtues as Truth (stanza liii), Kindness (lv), Love (lix); his aim, in short, is to build the character of the Christian who lives an honest, pure, but ambitious life in the crowded world of men. This poem also shows Herbert's interest in the priest's work; he even prefers public prayer to private ones:

> "Though private prayer be a brave designe,
> Yet publick hath more promises, more love." [3]

And though the Puritans in Herbert's time exalted preaching, at the expense of prayer, Herbert declares that sermons are necessary but prayers are more important:

> "Resort to sermons, but to prayers most:
> Praying's the end of preaching." [4]

---

[1] Palmer, vol. i, p. 367. [2] "The Church Porch," Palmer, vol. ii, p. 49.
[3] *Ibid.*, p. 61. [4] *Ibid.*, p. 63.

Herbert sums up his conception of life when he declares:

"In brief, acquit thee bravely; play the man." [1]

In the warfare of life he counsels us to fight bravely and live dangerously like a soldier:

"Chase brave employments with a naked sword
Throughout the world. Fool not: for all may have,
If they dare try, a glorious life or grave." [2]

The Archbishop of Armagh rightly thinks that it is one of the "highest notes of style which Herbert has ever struck." [3]

In "The Church Militant" Herbert treats of the growth of the Church throughout the preceding ages: Palmer calls it "the first sketch of general church history in our language." Herbert does not trace the various stages in the development of the ecclesiastical organization of the Church, his main concern is to show the coming of righteousness and true religious life on earth:

"But above all, thy Church and Spouse doth prove
Not the decrees of power, but bands of love." [4]

He exalts the English Church above all the other Reformed churches, and, like the true High Churchman, defends the union of the Church and State. England achieved "the higher victorie" [5] by

"Giving the Church a crown to keep her state
And not go lesse than she had done of late." [5]

Herbert also shows here his strong bias against the Roman clergy. He tells us that sin resolved,

"To be a Church-man too and wear a Mitre," [6]

and that the Catholic ministers were

"Statesmen within, without doores cloisterers." [7]

Herbert's conception of the Church is that it is an embodiment of righteousness; and this conception, as his religious life deepened, assumed a mystical form. In the poems which are

[1] "The Church Porch," Palmer, vol. ii, p. 67.   [2] Ibid., p. 25.
[3] Poems by George Herbert, Introduction by Archbishop of Armagh (Red Letter Library, 1905), p. v.
[4] "The Church Militant," Palmer, vol. iii, p. 359.
[5] Ibid., p. 365.   [6] Ibid., p. 371.   [7] Ibid., p. 373.

not found in Williams MS., and therefore were written after 1630, such as "Sion" and "The Church Floore," he conceived the Christian Church, in contrast to Solomon's Temple, "where most things were of purest gold," [1] as built within the soul, the human aspirations and Christian virtues being its liturgy. St. Paul had said: "Know ye not that ye are the temple of God, and that the spirit of God dwelleth in you?" (1 Corinthians iii, 16). Herbert knew that the real temple was the human soul where the spirit of God made its home:

> "And now thy Architecture meets with sinne
> For all thy frame and fabrick is within." [1]

Herbert thought that the real dwelling-place of God was the human soul; in one of his letters to his mother he wrote: "God intends that [the soul] to be a Sacred temple for Himself to dwell in." [2]

Herbert's Church is "all within"; and even the "Church Floore" becomes symbolic of "Patience," [3] and "Humilite" [3]; while the choir is "Confidence," [3] and the "sweet cement" [3] and what binds the whole frame is "Love and Charity." [3] In the "Church Porch" he tries to refine the human nature and prepares the Christian to become worthy of tasting the delicacies of Divine Love; while the significance of "Perirrhanterium" (the Greek term for a sprinkling instrument) which, in Ferrar's edition, is inserted between "the Church Porch" and "The Church," is that "self-Purification" is necessary for entering the Church of God.

It is significant that Herbert, who was to express the serious spirit of Anglicanism, wrote his first poem (in Latin) to defend its church government and ritual against the attack of Andrew Melville (1543–1622), a leader of the Presbyterian party. [4]

Herbert's epigrams "concerning the use of ceremonies"

---

[1] "Sion," Palmer, vol. iii, p. 265. He had said in an earlier poem, "Man":
> "Since then, my God, thou hast
> So brave a Palace built, O dwell in it" (Palmer, vol. ii, p. 223).

[2] Palmer, vol. i, p. 405.

[3] *Ibid.*, vol. iii, p. 167. In an earlier poem, "The Altar," he had said that the real altar was "made of a heart and cemented with teares" (ii, 121).

[4] For further particulars of Herbert's controversy with Melville see *Walton's Lives* (edited by Saintsbury), pp. 271, 272, and A. G. Hyde's *Herbert and his Times*, pp. 55–58.

reveal the importance which he attached to ritual in the
church services; he argues that to adopt the Puritan austerity
would make us an easy prey to the Roman Church:

> "When Cæsar steer'd to Briton's shore
> With his great fleet in the days of yore,
> Seeing the natives of the place
> To have of clothing not a trace,
> He cried out as they caught his eye,
> O certain and easy victory."

Herbert thinks that if we give up the ceremonies, history
would repeat itself and we shall again be conquered by the
Roman Church:

> "Just so, the Puritans austere
> While they the Lord's spouse would strip bare
> Of all Ceremonies holy—
> Howe'er reverent and lowly,
>
> .   .   .   .
> Thus would they straightway her expose
> Destitute of seemly clothes
> To the Devil and enemies
> Conqu'ring easily as so she lies." [1]

In "The British Church," which belongs to the Bemerton
period, Herbert again disapproved of the Puritan rejection of
all ceremony. He held that though nothing was too mean
"to clothe the Sunne," the Anglican moderation in the use of
ceremonies was the only course open to the Reformed churches;
he did not approve of the Roman Catholic Church with her
"painted shrines" [2] or the Calvinistic Church which is "shie
of dressing" [2]; and addressing his own Church he says:

> "But, dearest Mother, what those misse,
> The mean, thy praise and glorie is,
> And long may be." [3]

Herbert recognizes the spiritual need of beauty and reverence
in worship and justifies the ritual and ceremony because they
lead to edification: "And all this he [the priest] doth not as
out of necessity or as putting a holiness in the things, but as
desiring to keep the middle way, between superstition and
slovenlinesse, and as following the Apostle's two great and
admirable Rules in things of this nature: The first whereof is,

[1] *The Complete Works of George Herbert*, edited by A. B. Grosart, vol. ii, p. 136.
[2] Palmer, vol. iii, p. 103.   [3] *Ibid.*

Let all things be done decently and in order; The second, Let all things be done to edification"[1] (1 Corinthians xiv).

Donne had also justified the ceremonies as "helps to excite and awaken devotion"; and pointing out the cause of their abuse in the Roman Catholic Church he had observed: "They were not practised as they should, *significative* but *effective*, not as things which should signifie to people higher mysteries, but as things as Powerfull, and effectual in themselves as the greatest Mysteries of all, the Sacraments themselves." [2] He further remarks: "All that I strive for is, but Moderation." [2]

This conception of ceremonies as "significative" but not "effective" was the Anglican viewpoint adopted by Herbert. The poems like "Prayer," "Scripture," "Baptisme," " Communion," "Love" (belonging to the pre-Bemerton period) form an important group, for they reveal to us Herbert's method of approach to God through prayer, meditation, and the Sacraments; these are his means of attaining personal holiness in the first two stages of the mystical life, the awakening of the self, and the purification of the self. Prayer for Herbert is the highest form of devotion. He calls prayer "the churches' banquet." It is,

> "The soul in paraphrase, heart in Pilgrimage,
> The Christian plummet sounding heaven and earth."

In "The Country Parson" he pointed out that "Private praying is a more voluntary act in them than when they are called to other's Prayers." [3] Herbert always considered prayer an important form of communication with God; it was to him an easy way of access to Him:

> "Of what an easie quick accesse,
> My Blessed Lord, art thou!"
> "Prayer" (ii).

The Anglican liturgy, like the Bible, had coloured the imagination of Herbert; and when, at his death-bed, Mr. Duncan wanted to know what prayer he should read, Herbert replied: "O Sir, the prayers of my mother, the Church of

1 "The Country Parson," chap. xiii, Palmer, vol. i, p. 248.
2 *LXXX Sermons*, p. 80.
3 In "The Church Porch" he had said that public prayer had "more promises, more love."

England, no other prayers are equal to them." Herbert is the poet of the Anglican Church, for his devotion found full satisfaction in the prayers, ritual and ordinances of the Church.

Like all the Protestant divines, Herbert laid great emphasis on the constant study of the Holy Scriptures, its correct and reverent interpretation.

To the Roman Catholic Church the essence of worship lies in the ministering of the consecrated and mystic rites by which God had ordained His ministers to symbolize to humanity the infinite mysteries of His Truth; thus the main duty of the priests was not preaching but ministering the Sacrament. Protestantism declared that truth was not so much in the mystical rites of the Sacrament as in the tradition of the Bible; hence the importance of preaching, of interpreting the Holy Scriptures. Herbert said:

> "Oh Book! Infinite sweetnesse! Let my heart
> Suck ev'ry letter, and a hony gain,
> Precious for any grief in any part;
> To cleare the breast, to mollifie all pain."
>
> "The Holy Scriptures."

In "The Country Parson" he also declared that "the chief and top of his knowledge consists in the book of books, the store house and magazene of life, and comfort, the Holy Scriptures. There he sucks and lives." [1]

Herbert in his "Notes on Valdesso" disapproved of his assigning the Holy Scriptures "only an elementary use." He points out that the Holy Scriptures have also "a use of perfection and are able to make the man of God Perfect" (1 Timothy iv.). [2]

Protestantism has often been defined as the revival of the Pauline and Augustinian religion of grace, but we must understand the differences which exist between the Catholic and Protestant conception of grace, for it is the Protestant conception of grace and sacrament which underlies such poems of Herbert as "The Holy Communion" and "The Holy Scriptures." Though Catholicism is a religion of grace, its conception of grace was that of sacramental grace, of supernatural and mystical power; its ministering by the

---

[1] "The Country Parson," chap. iv, Palmer, vol. i. 215.
[2] *Ibid.*, p. 369.

Church had a twofold effect on the recipient, the forgiveness of sin, and the mystical exaltation of humanity in partaking of the body and blood of Christ, that is, sharing in His Passion. The Protestant conception of grace is not that of the mystical substance, to be ministered through sacraments, but that of a divine temper of faith and spirit, which the believer can find in the Bible and in the love of Christ for humanity. Protestantism rejected the priesthood, for it maintained the doctrine of the universal priesthood of believers; the idea of the direct relation of the soul to Christ which is involved in the doctrine of the Justification by Faith modified the Catholic conception of the efficacy of the sacraments in this sense, that it was made dependent on the spiritual state of the recipient; anything like magical efficacy was denied to the sacraments.

In "The Holy Communion" Herbert traces the subtlety of God's approaches. God comes to his soul not externally:

> "Not in rich furniture, or fine aray,
>   Nor in a wedge of gold,"

but God enters the human soul bringing peace and rest with Him:

> "But by the way of nourishment and strength
>   Thou creep'st into my breast;
>   Making thy way my rest,
>   And thy small quantities my length";

God destroyes the "force and art of sin" and He purifies the soul as well as the flesh:

> "Leaping the wall that parts
>   Our souls and fleshy hearts";

The grace of Christ alone could enter the innermost recesses of the human soul:

> "Onely thy grace, which with these elements comes
>   Knoweth the ready way,
>   And hath the privie key,
>   Op'ning the soul's most subtile rooms."
>   "The Holy Communion."

This conception of the grace in the Sacrament of the Altar is characteristically Anglican and underlies several poems of Herbert which deal with this subject. The actual partaking of bodily "nourishment and strength" is the perfect symbol of God's grace stealing into the soul. It is the conception which Cranmer and Ridley had offered, and Hooker and Donne had defended. Cranmer had maintained that it is "the grace, the virtue, and benefit of Christ's Body" that are "really and effectually present" with him, and not that Body itself. Hooker had pointed out that the spiritual state of the receiver was an important factor: "the real presence of Christ's most blessed body and blood is not therefore to be sought for in the sacrament, but in the worthy receiver of the sacrament." [1] Donne with the spiritual energy which always characterized his sermons also declared: "Woe unto them who present themselves that day without such a preparation as becomes so fearful and mysterious an action upon any carnal or collaterall respects . . . before you come to that day, if you come not to a crucifying of yourselves to the world, and the world to you, *ut quid vobis?* . . . you shall prophane that day and the Author of it, as to make even that day of Christ's triumph, the triumph of Satan, and to make that body and blood of Christ Jesus, *Vehiculum Satanae*, his Chariot to enter into you." [2]

Concerning the real presence, Herbert's attitude is also characteristically Anglican. In the autobiographical poem called "Love Unknown" he says:

> "I found a callous matter
> Began to spread and to expatiate there":

and so he washed it with the holy blood of Christ:

> "I bath'd it often, ev'n with holy bloud,
> Which at a board, while many drank bare wine,
> A friend did steal into my cup for good,
> Ev'n taken inwardly, and most divine
> To supple hardnesses."

In Herbert's poetry the sacramental element of Christian worship is heightened by his love of elaborate ritual and symbolism. The Sacrament of the Holy Communion appealed to the imagination of Herbert for he insists on its frequency; "the parson celebrates it, if not duly once a month, yet at least five or six times a year; as, at Easter, Christmasse,

---

[1] *Laws of Ecclesiastical Polity*, Book V, lxviii, 5, 6; for further discourse see also Book V, lxvii, 3; and "A Christian Letter."

[2] *LXXX Sermons*, No. 14, p. 143.

Whitsuntide, afore and after Harvest, and the beginning of Lent." [1]

That Herbert had accepted the Anglican doctrine of the Eucharist is evident from his poem "The Holy Communion." He assumes the non-controversial position when he says,

> "First I am sure, whether bread stay
> or whether Bread doe fly away,
> concerneth Bread, not mee."

Hooker had also declared that the controversial aspect of the doctrine of Christ's presence in the Eucharist was immaterial to him: "What these elements are in themselves it skilleth not, it is enough that to me which take them they are the body and blood of Christ, his promise in witness hereof sufficeth, his word he knoweth which way to accomplish." [2]

Herbert rejects the Roman Catholic doctrine of transsubstantiation; the physical changes in the nature of the Bread are not important to him:

> "That flesh is there mine eyes deny."

The Anglican is eager not for the flesh of God but His Spirit:

> "This gift of all gifts is the best
> Thy flesh the least that I request.
>
> .   .   .   .   .   .
>
> Or give mee that so I have more
> My God, give mee all Thee."

Besides prayer, the Scriptures and the Sacraments, Herbert believed in another mode of divine communication; it was music.

Herbert's love of music is well known, it was developed during his Cambridge residence, and became his comfort and recreation at Bemerton. Walton says: "Though he was a lover of retiredness, yet his love of Musick was such that he went twice every week on certain appointed days to the cathedral church in Salisbury, and at his return would say: That his time spent in Prayer and Cathedral music elevated his soul and was his 'Heaven upon Earth'" [3]; and we also

---

[1] "The Country Parson," chap. xxii, Palmer, vol. i, p. 272.
[2] *Ecclesiastical Polity*, Book V, lxvii, 12
[3] See Herbert's *Epigrammata Apologetica*, xxvi: "De Musica Sacra,"

know the significant episode when he raised himself from his death-bed and sang the beautiful lines:

> "The Sundaies of mans life,
> Thredded together on times string,
> Make bracelets to adorn the wife
> Of the eternal glorious King."

Devotional music, Herbert tells us, in "Church Musick," was his comfort and refuge:

> "Sweetest of sweets, I thank you! When displeasure
> Did through my bodie wound my minde,
> You took me thence, and in your house of pleasure
> A daintie lodging me assign'd."

Herbert's knowledge of music made him conscious of the rich harmony of the English language. His poetic thought discovers its appropriate musical forms as in the poems called "The Church Monuments" and "The Pulley." Having discussed Herbert's method of approach to God through prayer, meditation and the Sacraments, we now come to his festival songs, which deal with the spiritual significance of the various stages of Christ's life.

Herbert's festival songs and the poems which deal with baptism and crucifixion are closely allied to his Church poems and were, like them, composed in his pre-Bemerton period. In poems like "Easter," "Whitsunday," "Christmas" and "Lent" Herbert symbolizes the various aspects of Christ's life; these songs of Christian festivals became the analogies of the soul's experience of Christ's living presence. Herbert's religious experience in these poems is simple, pious and undisturbed by any acute consciousness of sin; he sings in passionate but clear accents:

> "I got me flowers to straw thy way;
> I got me boughs off many a tree;
> But thou wast up by break of day,
> And brought'st thy sweets along with thee."
>
> "Easter."

In "Whitsunday" Herbert also relates the joyous experience of Earth when Christ was alive:

> "That th'earth did like a heav'n appeare";

and he prays to God to fulfil His promise "which he had made to his disciples at or before his ascension; namely that though he left them, yet he would send them the Holy Ghost to be their comforter." [1]

In "Trinitie Sunday" the threefold aspects of life as creation, redemption and sanctification (God as Father, Son, and the Holy Ghost) became to Herbert three cardinal virtues, faith, hope and charity:

> "Enrich my heart, mouth, hands in me,
> with faith, with hope, with charitie;
> That I may runne, rise, rest with thee."

The happy serene note of the close and intimate experience of God is maintained in "Christmas" and "Sunday." Herbert imagines a time when

> "His beams shall cheer my breast, and both so twine,
> Till ev'n his beams sing, and my musick shine."

But he sums up his attitude towards Christ when he says:

> "Who goeth in the way which Christ hath gone,
> Is more sure to meet with him than one
> That travelleth by-wayes."

Christian mystics throughout the ages have recognized Christ's path to be the only Mystic Way leading to God. Christ's coming to earth was not only an evidence of God's love for humanity, it also held out the promise that human nature could be raised to the heights of divine nature. Origen pointed out the true significance of Christ's life to the human soul when he said, "from Him there began the interweaving of divine and human nature, in order that the human, by communion with the divine, might rise to be divine." [2]

The whole effort of the life of the Christian mystic is to *know* Christ and be *transformed* in his Image, for Christ Himself raised life to its height and fullness as the perfect fusion of the "natural" and the "divine."

Herbert knows that those who have set their hearts on realizing the love of Christ in their lives must undergo the arduous process of self-purification:

> "Avoid, Profaneness! come not here!
> Nothing but holy, pure and cleare." [3]

---

[1] Walton's *Life*. [2] Quoted by Underhill, *The Mystic Way*.
[3] "Superliminare," Palmer, vol. ii, p. 119.

In "The Sacrifice" Herbert dwells at length on the spiritual and redeeming character of Christ's crucifixion, and in "Good Friday" he tries to apply the agony of the Passion of Christ to wipe off his sins:

> "That when sinne spies so many foes,
> Thy whips, thy nails, thy wounds, thy woes,
> All come to lodge there, sinne may say,
> *No room for me,* and flie away." [1]

The real consciousness of sin which is accompanied by the awakening of the self comes to Herbert when he approaches the crisis of his life (1627). In poems like "The Thanksgiving" and "The Reprisall" his self awakens to recognize its imperfection and unworthiness and at the same time there is an intense longing to be blessed with the love of God. He cries out:

> "O make me innocent, that I
> May give a disentangled state and free" [2];

and he resolves to discipline his self with God's help:

> "Though I can do nought
> Against thee, in thee will I overcome
> The man, who once against thee fought."

In "The Sinner" and the "Deniall" he recognizes the fact that God did not answer his prayers because of the imperfection of his own soul; he had cried:

> "*Come, come, my God, O come!*
> But no hearing." [3]

His soul was "untun'd and unstrung" and was not pure enough to receive His "favours."

We must note an important fact here; the consciousness of sin in his earlier poems is not strong; in poems like "The World," "Sinne" and "Faith" he seems to believe that Christ's death has atoned for our sins and thus the problem of the Fall and Sin has been solved for ever:

> "And where sinne placeth me in Adam's fall,
> Faith sets me higher in his glorie." [4]

---

[1] "Superliminare," Palmer, vol. ii, p. 151.
[2] *Ibid.*, p. 293: "The Reprisall."
[3] *Ibid.*, p. 297: "Deniall."   [4] *Ibid.*, p. 233: "Faith."

But in the later poems, when his self awakens to the need of purification, the consciousness of sin becomes very acute, as in poems such as "Nature" "Repentance" and "Grace":

> "Sinne is still hammering my heart
> Unto a hardness, void of love:
> Let suppling grace, to crosse his art;
> Drop from above." [1]

He recognizes the need of attaining simplicity, humility and surrender to the will of God:

> "Give me simplicitie, that I may live;
> So live and like, that I may know, thy wayes,
> Know them and practise them." [2]

His desire to surrender himself to the Divine Will is vehement:

> "Yet take thy way, for sure thy way is best,
> Stretch or contract me, thy poore debtor.
> This is but tuning of my breast,
> To make the musick better." [3]

Herbert's was a complex character; while one side of his nature drew him to the Church, and a life of the spirit, the other side (perhaps an inherited one) drew him to Court, a life of pleasure, learning and wit. Pride and ambition were the characteristics of his family and as his Cambridge years showed he was not free from them. Walton has told the story of his life as a courtier and orator when he had the "laudable ambition to be something more than he was." [3]

When Herbert's ambitions of becoming a Secretary of State were shattered to pieces by the death of all his patrons [4] he retired into the country; and in this period the awakening of the self which we have noticed in the earlier poems soon developed into the "Purgative Way." In his period of retirement, he seems to have felt a rebuke from God and his sense of sin became very acute. When he looks into his soul he finds nothing but vanity and sin there:

---

[1] "Superliminare," Palmer, vol. ii, p. 311: "Grace."
[2] *Ibid.*, p. 319: "A Wreath."
[3] His elder brother, Edward, was Ambassador to the French Court, while Henry was Master of Revels at the English Court.
[4] Herbert says: "Thou took'st away my life,
   And more; for my friends die."
                                    "The Collar," *ibid.*, vol. ii, p. 343.

"I find there quarries of pil'd vanities
But shreds of holiness, that dare not venture
To shew their face, since crosse to thy decrees,
There the circumference earth is, heav'n the centre." [1]

Herbert's resistance to the destiny which was drawing him closer to God was obstinate and intense and this conflict he has recorded in poems like "The Pearl," "Obedience" and "Affection," where he asks God:

"Now I am here, what wilt thou do with me?
None of my books will show."

When in "The Pearl" he records his decision to enter the priesthood he recounts all that he has renounced for the love of God;

"I know the wayes of Pleasure, the sweet strains,
The lullings and the relishes of it;
The propositions of hot blood and brains;
What mirth and music mean; what love and wit
Have done these twentie hundred years, and more."

He is proud to have abandoned "the wayes of honour" and "the quick returns of courtesie and wit" in order to have the love of God:

"I know all these, and have them in my hand;
Therefore not sealed but with open eyes
I flie to Thee. . . . "

Like the true lover he is glad that he has made a heavy sacrifice for his love; for he fully understands "at what rate and price I have thy love." [2]

Henceforth Herbert endeavours to surrender himself completely to the will of God to realize the virtue of humility and strive to win His love. He prays to God to conquer his heart:

"O tame my heart!
It is thy highest art
To captivate strongholds to thee." [3]

Herbert is not one of those poets who lose themselves in the luxury of language or find satisfaction in the external world; he knows the exquisite beauty of the world but he is intent on realizing the love of God in his own soul.

[1] *Ibid.*, vol. ii, p. 295: "The Sinner."
[2] "The Pearl."   [3] "Nature."

> "My stuffe is flesh, not brasse; my senses live,
> And grumble oft, that they have more in me
> Than he that curbs them, being but one to five:
> Yet I love thee." [1]

The external in fact throws him back into himself, and he begins to examine his inner self and realizes the need of repentance, confession and obedience:

> "Lord, I confesse my sinne is great;
> Great is my sinne, oh! gently treat
> With thy quick flow'r, thy momentarie bloom
> Whose life still pressing,
> Is one undressing,
> A steadie aiming at the Tombe." [2]

In poems like "Content," "Vanitie" and "Frailtie" he recognized the illusory character of worldly joys, which are now "a scourge," and he feels that repentance is a spiritual necessity and purge:

> "For they all produce repentance,
> And repentance is a purge." [3]

The consciousness of the need of repentance, confession and obedience was accompanied with the desire to realize the love of God in his own soul:

> "But as thy love shall sway,
> Resigning up the rudder to thy skill." [4]

He has resigned his soul to the working of Divine Love and his actions to His Will:

> "So disengag'd from sinne and sicknesse,
> Touch it with thy celestiall quicknesse,
> That it may hang and move
> After thy love." [5]

The mystic tries to be filled with the love of God and prepare his soul through purgation and discipline to be worthy of His grace. Evelyn Underhill says: "the Mystic Way has been a progress, a growth in love: a deliberate fostering of the inward tendency of the soul towards its source, an eradication of its disorderly tendencies to Temporal good." [6] Herbert

---

1 "The Pearl."   2 "Repentance," Palmer, vol. ii, p. 305.
3 "The Rose," *ibid.*, vol. ii, p. 389.
4 "Obedience," *ibid.*, vol. ii, p. 385.
5 "The Starre," *ibid.*, vol. ii, p. 365.
6 *Mysticism*, Evelyn Underhill, p. 512.

also realizes that the measure of the mystical life is *nearness* to God through the grace of Christ:

> "For as thou dost impart thy grace,
> The greater shall our glorie be.
> The measure of our joyes is in this place,
> The stuffe with thee." [1]

Besides repentance, Herbert also felt another phase of the purgative way: the need for *acts* of piety and devotion, such as the re-decoration of Leighton church. Evelyn Underhill has pointed out that the true mark of the mystic is that the new acquisition of spiritual energy should lead him to grapple with the practical problems of life. [2] Mystical experience is an enrichment, not an escape from life, it is an activity rather than a state; the mystic in fact becomes "a weapon and warrior" in one.

Herbert's main interest in the devotional life was practical; he defined the true character of purgation as "abhorring and renouncing of sin and turning unto God in truth of heart and newness of life" [3]; and this "newness of life" which is the mark of a regenerate Christian was not a theoretical condition, it must become evident in the holiness of life, as "the country parson's library is a holy life." [4]

In the last two poems of the period of crisis, "Praise" and "Love," we find a note of reconciliation and joy which is maintained in the poems which Palmer has classed under the suggestive heading "The Happy Priest."

Herbert seems to have received some favour of Divine Love, for he says:

> "Thou hast granted my request,
> Thou hast heard me." [5]

A strange tenderness and pathos creeps into his poem "Love," which seems to be an intimate record of his personal experience of the love of God. Like the true lover he says that he cannot behold the beauty of his Beloved:

---

[1] "Employment," Palmer, vol. ii, p. 103.
[2] Underhill, *op. cit.*, p. 495.
[3] "The Country Parson," Palmer, vol. i, p. 309.
[4] *Ibid.*, p. 307.
[5] "Praise," Palmer, vol. ii, p. 397.

> "I, the unkinde, ungratefull? Ah my deare,
> I can not look on thee.
> Love took my hand and smiling did reply,
> Who made the eyes but I?" [1]

He sat down and tasted the delicacies of love:

> "So I did sit and eat." [1]

In the poems which Herbert wrote just after his ordination, like "The Call," "Aaron," "The Odour" and "Clasping of Hands," we find a new lyric note of joy in his priestly office; the period of self-purification seems to have ended, doubts and fears no longer assail him; but the significance of these poems lies in the fact that Herbert establishes intimate relations with Christ. He addresses Him not with fear and awe, but in tender and affectionate accents:

> "Christ is my onely head,
> My alone onely heart and breast,
> My onely musick, striking me ev'n dead;
> That to the old man I may rest,
> And be in him new drest." [2]

He declares that Christ "lives in me" and that without Christ he shall have no rest:

> "Without whom I could have no rest:
> In him I am well drest." [2]

This joy has come to him through trust in God and he has realized the deeper truth that the surrender to the will of God is an enrichment of life itself:

> "Much troubled, till I heard a friend expresse,
> That all things were more ours by being his." [3]

And he knows that Christ's help "cannot fail or fall." [3]

The new deepening of Herbert's religious life seems to have come through his devotion to Christ. Walton tells us: "The same night that he had his Induction he said to Mr. Woodnot: I have this day taken Jesus to be my Master and Governor; and I am so proud of his service that I will always observe and obey and do his will, and alwaies call him Jesus my Master." [4] In "The Odour" the name Jesus Christ seems to perfume his mind and, as Walton remarks, to leave "an Oriental fragrancy

---

[1] "Love," Palmer, vol. ii, p. 401.   [2] "Aaron," *ibid.*, vol. iii, p. 13.
[3] "The Holdfast," *ibid.*, vol. iii, p. 17.   [4] Walton's *Life*.

in his very breath." The same note of passionate adoration is struck again in "A True Hymne":

> "My joy, my life, my crown!
> My heart was meaning all the day,
> Somewhat it fain would say:
> And still it runneth mutt'ring up and down
> With onely this, *My joy, my life, my crown*." [1]

His experience of God was the experience of the human soul feeling the abundance of Divine Love:

> "As when th' heart sayes (sighing to be approved)
> *O, could I love!* and stops: God writeth, *Loved*." [1]

Herbert seems to have received some favour and sign of His love:

> "My God, thou art all love.
> Not one poor minute 'scapes thy breast,
> But brings a favour from above;
> And in this love, more than in bed, I rest." [2]

He again rejoices in the consciousness of having received the gift, the nature of which he does not reveal:

> "Gift upon gift, much would have more,
> And comes." [3]

There is a strange familiarity in Herbert's discourse with God in the poems he wrote in this period. He evidently had received some sign or "gift" of God's favour (whether it was a vision of God in Illumination we cannot say), and he felt within himself peace and joy which he had not experienced before:

> "O what sweetness from the bowl
> Fills my soul,
> Such as is and makes divine!
> Is some star (fled from the sphere)
> Melted there
> As we sugar melt in wine?" [4]

It is a delight which cannot be described through language:

> "For thy neatness passeth sight,
> Thy delight
> Passeth tongue to taste or tell." [4]

---

[1] "A True Hymne," Palmer, vol. iii, p. 27.
[2] "Evensong," *ibid.*, vol. iii, p. 61.
[3] "Gratefullnesse," *ibid.*, vol. iii, p. 41.
[4] "The Banquet," *ibid.*, vol. iii, p. 53.

Was Herbert at this stage of his life granted a vision of reality? Did he achieve the bliss of "Illumination of the self"? These are the questions which can never be satisfactorily answered, but his language, his caressing intimate accents, show a peculiar likeness to the description given by the mystics of their "Illumination." The first characteristic of the "Illumination of the self," according to Underhill, is "A joyous apprehension of the Absolute, that which many ascetic writers call "the practice of the presence of God," and it was the Presence of God which seems to have filled Herbert's heart with "sacred cheer" and he felt Him as "sweetness" and "Love";

> "Here is love, which having breath
> Ev'n in death
> After death can never die." [1]

God had at last heard his call:

> "And yet when I did call,
> Thou heardst my call, and more." [2]

Herbert expresses his sense of *oneness* with God in the characteristic language of the mystic:

> "Without whom I could have no rest,
> In him I am well drest."

St. Augustine said: "When I shall cleave to thee with all my being, then shall I in nothing have pain and labour; and my life shall be a real life, being wholly full of thee." [3] His joyous apprehension of the presence of God found supreme expression in such lines as these:

> "Come, my Joy, my Love, my Heart:
> Such a Joy, as none can move:
> Such a Love, as none can part:
> Such a Heart, as joyes in love." [4]

Hugo of St. Victor had the same experience: "I am suddenly renewed; I am changed; I am plunged into an ineffable peace. My mind is full of gladness, all my past wretchedness and pain is forgot." [5]

Herbert even uses the favourite mystical symbolism of wine

---

[1] "The Invitation," Palmer, vol. iii, p. 49.
[2] "Praise," *ibid.*, vol. ii, p. 95.　　　　　[3] *Confessions*, Book X, chap. xxviii.
[4] "The Call," Palmer, vol. iii, p. 9.　　[5] *Mysticism*, E. Underhill, p. 294.

and cup; the celestial wine carries him high into the heavens and there he sees God. "No image, perhaps, could suggest so accurately," says Underhill, "as this divine picture of the conditions of Perfect Illumination; the drinking deeply, devoutly, and in haste of the Heavenly Wine of Life." [1]

Herbert says:

> "Having raised me to look up,
>   In a cup
> Sweetly he doth meet my taste." [2]

But Herbert drew back conscious of his own unworthiness to drink the heavenly wine:

> "But I still being low and short,
>   Farre from court,
> Wine becomes a wing at last." [2]

Having thus drunk the wine of life, he fearlessly mounts to the sky; and with a strange boldness he tells us of his experience:

> "For with it alone I flie
>   To the skie;
> Where I wipe mine eyes, and see
> What I seek, for what I sue;
>   Him I view,
> Who hath done so much for me." [2]

This mystical language of love and longing in which the poet could assert "Lord thou art mine and I am thine," [1] and realize that his personality apart from God will lose all its richness and significance, leaves no doubt about the quality of his religious experience, which was mystical in its essence:

> "If I without thee would be mine,
> I neither should be mine nor thine." [3]

But, like other Christian mystics, Herbert is eminently practical, he combined in a rare manner the practical aspects of the devotional life with the mystic's love of God.

In his insistence on personal holiness, and the love of Christ for the individual soul, Herbert's devotion is of the New rather than of the Old Testament. Herbert knows that to understand the Holy Scriptures your knowledge of them must be deep and learned. Ferrar tells us that Herbert's love of the

---

[1] *Mysticism*, E. Underhill, p. 285.
[2] "The Banquet," Palmer, vol. iii, p. 53.
[3] "Clasping of Hands," *ibid.*, vol. iii, p. 37.

Holy Scriptures was so great that he used to say that he would not exchange them for the riches of the whole world: "He hath been heard to make solemne Protestation, that he would not part with one leaf thereof for the whole world, if it were offered him in exchange." [1]

Herbert himself emphasized the importance of the Holy Scriptures in the life of the parson: "But the chief and top of his knowledge consists in the book of books, the storehouse and magazene of life and comfort, the Holy Scriptures. There he sucks and lives." [2]   But the real understanding of the Scriptures comes by *living* them: "But for the understanding of these means he useth are, first, a holy life; remembring what his Master saith, that if any do God's will, he shall know the Doctrine, John 7; and assuring himself that wicked men, however learned, do not know the Scriptures because they feel not and because they are not understood but with the same Spirit that writ them." [3]

That "Spirit" was to be cultivated from "within." He says that we should not "think that when we have read the Fathers or Schoolmen, a Minister is made and the thing done. The greatest and hardest preparation is within." [4]

This preparation in Herbert's life is revealed in the poems that belong to the purgative stage.

Herbert's critics, such as Courthope, Grosart, Beeching, Arthur Waugh, Ernst Rhys, have analysed the qualities of his religious poetry to determine his place among the English poets; but none of his critics has tried to study him from the mystical point of view.   J. B. Leishman says about Herbert's religion: "The outlines of his faith were simple perhaps—there is no trace of mysticism in his writings." [5]

He has been declared by Palmer to be "non-mystical" [6] because his religion has a strong vein of the institutional element in it.   He had found, as we have seen, great spiritual satisfaction in the rites and ceremonies of his Mother Church; but there have been few Christian mystics (and those were

---

[1] Ferrar, *The Printers to the Reader.*
[2] Palmer, i, p. 215.
[3] "The Country Parson," chap. iii, Palmer, vol. i, p. 215.
[4] *Ibid.*, p. 211.
[5] *The Metaphysical Poets*, by J. B. Leishman, 1934, p. 114.
[6] Palmer, vol. ii, p. 74.

never great) who have refused the aids of the Sacrament or the ritual and ceremonies of the Church. Herbert did not develop the mystical side of his religion at the expense of the other equally important elements. Palmer in his exhaustive study of Herbert's poems has not devoted a chapter to his mysticism, but his remarks dispersed throughout his notes and commentary show that he did not believe that Herbert was a mystic. His objections are (a) that Herbert's conception of God is not mystical, (b) that his religion was institutional rather than mystical, (c) that soon after settling at Bemerton "the conflicts of the crisis were renewed" [1] and thus he never achieved the peace of the mystic.

We shall discuss each of these three points separately to show that Palmer's views in some respects are incorrect and that he failed to realize the significance of the inner struggle of Herbert's later years, which was essentially spiritual and had no relation to the conflicts of the earlier crisis in his fortunes which were the result of worldly and material considerations and ambitions.

Herbert's conception of God is personal and mystical; Christ lives in him and through Christ he realizes his nearness to God. In his poem "The Flower" he calls God "Lord of Love," and it is the Lord of Love who wooes his soul, and for whose love he strives and suffers. Palmer thinks that Herbert thought of God as hostile and detached from human affairs: "Many will feel that this failure of inward unity was due to the separatist notions under which Herbert for the most part thought of God, conceiving Him not as immanent in human affairs but as detached and hostile." [2]

In the seventeenth century the Anglican divines like Donne and Andrewes, following St. Thomas Aquinas, held that God could not be seen in his essence by our bodily eyes, and moreover to the English mystics a close and intimate relationship with God (expressed through the symbolism of Divine Marriage) has never appealed as it has to the imagination of the Roman Catholic mystics. Donne said: "God is best seen by us, when we confess that he cannot be seen by us. . . . Here, in this life, neither the eyes, nor the minde of the most subtle,

---

[1] Palmer, vol. iii, pp. 171, 173.   [2] *Ibid.*, p. 174

and most sanctified man can see the Essence of God." [1]　In
Herbert's poetry there is no erotic familiarity with Christ as
we find in the Spanish mystics, especially St. Teresa, though he
conceived God as Love [2]; but love with the Anglican poets
is an intellectual rather than an emotional apprehension of
God.　Without God he feels a void in his life and his spirit
loses all its freshness and buoyancy:

> "Therefore my soul lay out of sight,
> 　　　Untun'd, unstrung;
> My feeble spirit, unable to look right,
> 　　Like a nipt blossome hung
> 　　　　Discontented." [3]

But it is through Christ that he apprehends God:

> "Christ is my onely head,
> My alone onely heart and breast." [4]

His presence brings "mirth," his absence dejection of spirit:

> "O what a damp and shade
> Doth me invade:
> No stormie night
> Can so afflict or so affright,
> As thy eclipsed light." [5]

　　It was Herbert's conception of God and His relation to the
individual soul that led him to mysticism.　Palmer has conceived mysticism as hostile to the established authority of the
Church or the Holy Scriptures; Herbert in his note on "The
Divine Consideration of Valdesso" maintained that to make
men of God "exempt from laws of God is dangerous and too
farre" [6]; and commenting on this Palmer says: "From it he
attacks mysticism in its central position, viz., its assertion that
the ground of authority lies in the individual's own feeling
and that no standards erected by past experience or by the
present needs of society can discredit that inner prompting." [6]
　　This is a charge which has always been brought against the
mystics, but we must remember that great mystics like St.
Paul, St. Augustine, St. Bernard and St. Francis have been
faithful sons of the Church.　St. Paul had declared the Church
to be the Body of Christ: "I, Paul . . . fill up that which is

[1] *LXXX Sermons*, p. 121.
[2] He says in "Evensong": "My God thou art Love," Palmer, vol. iii, p. 61.
[3] "Deniall," *ibid.*, vol. ii, p. 297.　　　　[4] "Aaron," *ibid.*, vol. iii, p. 1.
[5] "A Parodie," *ibid.*, vol. iii, p. 293.　　　[6] Palmer, i, p. 364.

behind [lacking] of the afflictions of Christ in my flesh, for
His Body's sake, which is the church" (Colossians i, 24).
G. Hodgson says: "Once more, to avoid misleading, it may
be well to say that the Mystic shares with the rest of us the
common life of the Church. It is an error to imagine that the
Catholic mystic, at any rate, is a law to himself, and has
peculiar methods of his own; it is no such thing" [1]; and she
has quoted at length from St. Catherine of Genoa, St. Francis,
St. Vincent Ferrer, and several other great mystics' writings,
to show that they were all dutiful sons and daughters of the
Church. St. Teresa said: "Experience is necessary throughout, so also is a spiritual director," and in the Church they
found a reliable "director" of their spiritual life. The
Anglican mystics like Donne, Herbert and Vaughan all
remained devout churchmen. Herbert thought that the
doctrines of the Church and the individual's devotional life
were intimately connected. He recognizes two "great helps"
—"a strict religious life" and "ingenuous search for truth";
and remarks, "which are two great lights able to dazle the
eyes of the misled, while they consider that God cannot be
wanting to them in Doctrine to whom he is so gracious in
Life." [2] He knew that any wavering from the doctrines of
the Church was dangerous:

> "Doctrine and life, colours and light, in one
> When they combine and mingle, bring
> A strong regard and aw." [3]

Doctrine and life should mingle like colour and light and thus
become one; and then alone the soul would feel the joy that
comes through a religious life lived intensely and strictly
according to the doctrines of the Church.

Palmer has emphasized the note of restlessness, of agony, of
disappointment in the poems which Herbert wrote at Bemerton
in order to prove that he never knew the inner peace and
calm which the mystic feels. We shall try to show that the
agony and restlessness of this period is not due to the fact
that "the conflicts of the crisis were renewed" due to his love
of a worldly career, but because after settling down at Bemerton

[1] *In the Way of the Saints*, G. Hodgson, pp. 108, 109.
[2] "The Country Parson," chap. xxiv, Palmer, vol. i, p. 280.
[3] "The Windows," Palmer, vol. iii, p. 15.

his religious life deepened and he felt that God had absented Himself from him; this is a phase of development experienced by every mystic.

Palmer says: "There came a reaction. The little parish which had seemed so attractive in its isolation and into which Herbert had thrown himself with such joyful eagerness proved painfully small. . . . The conflicts of the crisis were renewed. Human interests, personal desires, had never died in Herbert. They never did die." [1]

In "Submission," according to Palmer, "we hear of the painful contrast between the empty life at Bemerton and that to which he had aspired." His interpretation of line 23 of "The Pilgrimage" [1] is that Herbert's "parish life was stagnant and tasteless"; it would be nearer to truth to say that with the further deepening of his religious life Herbert knew that he had yet to travel a long way to realize in his soul a permanent and living Presence of God. "My hill was further" [2] is the common experience of the travellers on the mystic way; having attained a certain stage in their spiritual development they realize that the goal is still far off. A momentary supreme elevation in "Illumination" is generally followed by a recoil of the soul, and this falling away from the height brings sadness and disillusion to the human soul.

St. Augustine has described this phase with his usual insight into the psychology of mystical experience: "Thy invisible things, understood by those that are made, I saw, but I was not able to fix my gaze thereon; but my infirmity being struck back, I was thrown again on my normal experience (*solita*), carrying with me only a memory that loved and desired what I had, as it were, perceived the odour of, but was not yet able to feed upon" (*Confessions*, viii, 23).

Herbert says:

> "Soul's joy, when thou art gone,
> And I alone—
> Which cannot be,
> Because thou dost abide with me
> And I depend on thee." [3]

---

[1] Palmer, vol. iii, pp. 171, 173.
[2] A. G. Hyde, in *G. Herbert and His Times*, has compared this poem with Bunyan's *Pilgrim's Progress*.
[3] "A Parodie," Palmer, vol. iii, pp. 293–295.

When God's light is "eclipsed" from his soul, he fears that sin may return again. It is when mystics are most conscious of the living presence of Christ that they are most conscious of their own sin. Herbert says:

> "Ah Lord, do not withdraw,
> Lest want of aw,
> Make sinne appeare." [1]

But in this consciousness of sin there is no sense of complete alienation from God but a realization of the unworthiness of the soul. When Herbert asks Christ to return again to him, there is a strange tenderness in his address:

> "*My love, my sweetnesse, heare!*
> And heal my troubled breast which cryes,
> Which dyes." [2]

This phase of Herbert's mystical experience, when God seems to desert the soul, found expression in an acute distress of the soul, and though this was further heightened by his sense of approaching death, his Bemerton period cannot be described, as Palmer has done, as one of "disappointment, rebellion, dullness, self-reproach, penitence, mental perplexity, bodily pain, fear of God's alienation, and the bitterness of lifelong purpose coming to an end." [3] Much of the agony and pain in the poems written at Bemerton (*i.e.* those not found in the Williams MS.) are more spiritual than physical. Herbert seems to have experienced that affliction and dejection of spirit on which Donne loved to dwell in his sermons. "But when part of the affliction shall be, that God worketh upon the spirit itself, and damps that, . . . divest, strip the man of the man."

Herbert also knew that the affliction that God sends to the human soul is severe indeed:

---

[1] "A Parodie," Palmer, vol. iii, pp. 293-295.
[2] "Longing," *ibid.*, vol. iii, p. 287.
[3] Palmer, vol. iii, p. 245. The Rev. F. E. Hutchinson also thinks that there are still "echoes" of this conflict in the Bemerton poems and that Herbert questions the "utility" though not the "rightness" of his decision, as his health was failing so rapidly (Introduction, p. xxxvii, *The Works of George Herbert*, 1941). I do not agree with this view, for I hold that Herbert is here expressing that phase of his inner life which mystics call "The Dark Night of the Soul," and not the sense of frustration, depression and disappointment at his worldly failure as Palmer and, following him, the Rev. F. E. Hutchinson believe.

> "No scrue, no piercer can
> Into a piece of timber work and winde,
> As God's afflictions into man,
> When he a torture hath design'd." [1]

That this affliction was spiritual and religious Herbert has told us several times; he even imagines that his "grones" are making music for the Lord:

> "But grones are quick, and full of wings,
> And all their motions upward be;
> And ever as they mount, like larks they sing;
> The note is sad, yet musick for a King." [2]

In fact the struggle was a struggle of love and conquest between the soul and God, who woos the human soul:

> "The fight is hard on either part.
> Great God doth fight, he doth submit." [3]

This "fight" has ever been the theme of great mystical poetry: "I chased thee, for in this was my pleasure," says the voice of Love to Mechthild of Magdeburg; "I captured thee, for this was my desire; I bound thee, and I rejoice in thy bonds; I have wounded thee, that thou mayst be united to me. If I gave thee blows, it was that I might be possessed of thee." [4] The feeling of being hunted by the Divine Love is a common experience of medieval mystics. Eckhart declared: "He who will escape Him only runs to His bosom; for all corners are open to Him." [5]

Herbert in his poem "Affliction" has clearly declared that his grief is religious in the sense that it is another phase of divine love:

> "Thou art my grief alone,
> Thou Lord, conceal it not: and as thou art
> All my delight, so all my smart." [6]

That the restlessness which God has given to the human soul tosses it again to the bosom of the Lord was a favourite theme of Herbert's poetry. The "repining restlessness," [7] he thought,

[1] "Confession," Palmer, vol. iii, p. 259.
[2] "Sion," Palmer, vol. iii, p. 265.   [3] *Ibid.*
[4] *Mysticism*, by E. Underhill, Part I, chap. 6.
[5] This feeling found its supreme expression in Francis Thompson's *The Hound of Heaven.*
[6] "Affliction," Palmer, vol. ii, p. 339.
[7] "The Pulley," *ibid.*, vol. iii, p. 149.

could lead man to God; moreover this spiritual grief and smart
are in a way welcomed by the mystics, for they reveal to
them the reality of the Passion and thus they realise their
Fellowship with Christ in his suffering. Herbert realizes
that it is Christ who is grieving in Him:

> "Thy life on earth was grief, and thou art still
>   Constant unto it, making it to be
>   A point of honour now to grieve in me,
> And in thy members suffer ill." [1]

The absence of God was also the greatest of torments to him:
"Bowels of pitie, heare," he cries, and he prays: "Lord of my
soul, love of my minde, bow down thine eare!"

> "Lord Jesu, heare my heart,
>   Which hath been broken now so long,
>   That ev'ry part
>   Hath got a tongue." [2]

But this is the agony of a man who has experienced love;
and this state is a common occurrence in the life of the mystics.
"The periods of rapid oscillation between a joyous and painful
consciousness occur most often at the beginning of a new
period of the mystic way: between Purgation and Illumination,
and again between Illumination and the Dark Night," [2] is
how Underhill has defined the restlessness of the human soul
who has known the bliss of divine love; and thus even in
the agony of separation Herbert calls Christ "My love, my
sweetnesse, heare!" [3]
Herbert's wounds are the wounds of love:

> "Wounded I sing, tormented I indite," [4]

and he prays:

> "Pluck out thy dart,
>   And heal my troubled breast which cryes,
>   Which dyes." [3]

The consciousness of alienation from God after the experience
of this love causes great distress to the soul of the mystic. St.
John of the Cross describing his suffering says: "The greatest
affliction of the sorrowful soul in this state is the thought that

---

[1] "Affliction," Palmer, vol. ii, p. 339.   [2] *Mysticism*, E. Underhill, p. 467.
[3] "Longing," Palmer, vol. iii, p. 281.
[4] "Joseph's Coat," *ibid.*, vol. iii, p. 301.

God has abandoned it, of which it has no doubt; that He has cast it away into darkness as an abominable thing . . . the shadow of death and the pains and torments of hell are most acutely felt, that is, the sense of being without God, being chastised and abandoned in His wrath and heavy displeasure." [1]

The last few lines of this passage might well be taken as a description of the poetry of Herbert at Bemerton, the longing for Christ is so intense that every particle of Herbert's dust cries "come!"

> "Wilt thou deferre
>   To succour me,
>   Thy pile of dust, wherein each crumme,
>   Sayes, come?" [2]

Herbert knew that his end was fast approaching but he was ready to meet death calmly and cheerfully:

> "O show thy self to me,
>   Or take me up to thee." [1]

He had experienced the bliss of the love of God and he constantly refers to its happiness and joy:

> "I felt a sugred strange delight,
>   Passing all cordials made by any art,
>   Bedew, embalme, and over-runne my heart,
>   And take it in." [3]

d

And when Herbert imagines the joy which awaits him in Heaven, when he shall see God face to face, he is ready to welcome death:

> "If thy first glance so powerfull be,
>   A mirth but open'd and seal'd up again;
>   What wonders shall we feel when we shall see
>   Thy full-ey'd love!" [4]

And he uses the mystic's favourite symbol of light to denote the nature of the Presence of God:

> "And one aspect of thine spend in delight,
>   More than a thousand sunnes disburse in light;
>   In heav'n above." [4]

But it is pleasant to note that he seems to have again

---

[1] *Noche Oscura del Alma* (Lewis' translation), I, ii, chap. vi.
[2] "Longing," Palmer, vol. iii, p. 281.
[3] "Home," Palmer, vol. iii, p. 325.
[4] "The Glance," Palmer, vol. iii, p. 331.

experienced the love of God after this acute period of longing, agony and affliction:

> "How fresh, O Lord, how sweet and clean
> Are thy returns!" [1]

At the return of the "Lord of Love" he recovers "greennesse" of soul and "buds" again, and he wonders at the strangeness of this new experience:

> "O my onely light,
>   It cannot be
>   That I am he
> On whom thy tempests fell all night." [2]

He had felt the agony of the dark night of the soul; his "flesh and bones and joynts" [3] had prayed for the return of God, his thoughts had even become as it were sharp wounding weapons:

> "My thoughts are all a case of knives,
>   Wounding my heart
>   With scatter'd smart." [4]

But we should remember that this sense of grief and separation is inevitable in the life of the mystic, even such a great apostle as St. Paul experienced it: "Lest I should be exalted above measure by the abundance of revelation, there was given unto me a thorn in the flesh." [5] Christ seems to have returned to Herbert towards the end of his life. In a poem probably composed during the last Easter of his life he wrote:

> "Thy Saviour comes, and with him mirth:
>   Awake, Awake!" [6]

He knew that death was fast approaching—"the harbingers are come." [7] But death had lost its "ancient sting," it now meant Everlasting Life and Peace in Heaven:

> "Spare not, do thy worst.
>   I shall be one day better than before:
>   Thou so much worse, that thou shalt be no more." [8]

Having overcome his last conflict with his last enemy, by

[1] "The Flower," Palmer, vol. iii, p. 305.   [2] *Ibid.*
[3] "Home."   [4] "Affliction," iv.
[5] *The Mystic Way*, Underhill, p. 174.   [6] "The Dawning."
[7] "The Forerunners."   [8] "A Dialogue—Antheme."

the merits of his Master, Jesus, as Walton says, "he breathed
forth his Divine soul without any apparent disturbance," and
thus serenely and quietly passed away the "saint" of the
Anglican Church.[1]

Though Herbert perhaps never lived at the higher levels of
mystical life associated with the Unitive stage, the development
of his religious consciousness in the years of the crisis no doubt
belongs to the period of Purgation; while in the early years,
the Awakening of his self is closely akin to that of the mystics.
Whether he ever experienced Illumination cannot be definitely
known, but that his description of God's wooing his soul and
his own experience of God's Love is mystical in its essence
cannot be denied. The acute sense of alienation that the soul
feels in "the dark night" of its separation from God also finds
expression in his later poems. Herbert has neither the
sepulchral majesty of Donne's imagination, nor the ardour of
Crashaw, nor the mystical joy of Henry Vaughan, but in his
poetry the soul of the Church of Hooker and Laud found its
supreme expression, with its primitive piety and devotion to
tradition, its love of ritual and symbolism, and through him
the Church has spoken "more directly than the mystic, and
more temperately than the enthusiast." [2] In his poetry the
institutional and mystical elements were quietly and happily
blended together.

Though he has not the intensity and passion of a great
mystic, his poetry is rich in mystical content. He is the
poet who has known God and has felt the peace and joy of
His presence and also the pain and agony of His absence in a
manner peculiar to the mystics, and he has communicated
his experience to us with the complexity and richness
characteristic of a sensitive and sincere artist.

[1] Walton called him "Holy Mr. Herbert." His brother, Lord Herbert of
Cherbury, also says: "His life was most holy and exemplary; insomuch, that
about Salisbury, where he lived, beneficed for many years, he was little less than
sainted" (*Autobiography*, p. 11). Henry Vaughan also called Herbert "a most
glorious true saint, and a Seer" (1652).
[2] *The Poems of George Herbert* (Introduction by Arthur Waugh), p. iv.

CHAPTER IV

THE MYSTICAL ELEMENT IN THE RELIGIOUS POETRY OF RICHARD CRASHAW

RICHARD CRASHAW has been so widely hailed as a mystic that it is essential to analyse the elements of his religious poetry to determine the quality of his mystical experience.

Crashaw's religious poetry was largely written under the influence of the Counter-Reformation, which followed the Council of Trent and sent a wave of religious ardour and mystical faith through the Catholic countries. It ended the secular and pagan Renaissance in Italy, created the Order of the Jesuits, and gave rise to the mystical poetry of Vondel in Holland and Crashaw in England, and it was under its influence that the mystical soul of Spain flowered in the writings of St. Teresa, St. John of the Cross and Ignatius Loyola. The Counter-Reformation in England gave rise to the Laudian ideals of "beauty in holiness," of more reverence and decorum in church ceremonial and service, in the decoration of the churches, in the elaboration of the ritual; another aspect of the Counter-Reformation was the revival of asceticism within the Anglican Church. Donne had declared from his pulpit in St. Paul's: "And therefore, if when I study this holinesse of life, and fast, and pray, and submit my selfe to discreet, and medicinall mortifications, for the subduing of my body, any will say, this is Papisticall, it is a blessed Protestation, and no man is the lesse a Protestant, nor the worse a Protestant for making it, Men and brethren, I am a Papist, that is, I will fast and pray as much as any Papist, and enable myself for the service of my God, as seriously, as sedulously, as laboriously as any Papist." [1]

This ascetic ideal of life found its expression in the piety of George Herbert, and the saintliness of the life of the members of the religious colony at Little Gidding of Nicholas Ferrar, which was called the "Arminian Nunnery" by the Puritans.

[1] *LXXX Sermons*, No. 47: "Preached on the Conversion of S. Paul," 1629.

Crashaw is closely allied with these two great movements of his times which deeply influenced his poetic art and mystical faith. Though Crashaw's father was an ardent Puritan divine, and held the Pope to be Antichrist,[1] we should remember that he was deeply interested in the Roman Catholic devotional as well as the doctrinal and controversial literature of the Jesuits.

William Crashaw translated the verses of St. Bernard under the title of *The Complaint or Dialogue Betwixt the Soul and Bodie of a Damned Man* (1616), and wrote several Anti-Jesuit pamphlets, including the one dealing especially with the teachings of St. Ignatius Loyola named *Loyola's Disloyalty* (1610).[2]

In a very interesting letter William Crashaw requested "The Earl of Salisburye Lord High Treasurer of Englande" to send him the "popish books" which were recently confiscated —"And whereas I am informed some popishe bookes newely taken are in your lordships disposition, I beseche your lordship continue your wonted favoure and let me have of eche kind one, for my own use" (February 26, 1611).[3] This not only shows one of the many sources through which the Catholic devotional books found their way into the Puritan homes, it also makes it probable that Richard Crashaw, who early showed his interest in sacred themes, became acquainted with the Catholic devotional literature in his father's library long before he came to Cambridge, which was feeling the full tide of the Laudian reformation.

The aspect of Laud's reform of the Anglican Church which influenced Crashaw was the decoration of the churches and the institution of a reverent and elaborate ritual. Laud declared: "It is true the inward worship of the heart is the true service of God and no service acceptable without it; but the external worship of God in His Church is the great witness to the world that our heart stands right in that service of God. . . . These thoughts are they, and no other, which

[1] He declared even in his will: "I believe the Pope's seate and power to be the power of the greate Antichrist, and the doctrine of the Pope (as now it is) to be the doctrine of Antichrist."—Grosart, vol. ii.

[2] This was originally published in 1610 under the title *Jesuits' Gospell*, and was reissued in 1621 and in 1641 and 1643 under the above title, *Loyola's Disloyalty*.

[3] *State Papers—Domestic, James I*, lxi, No. 11, February 26 (1611).

have made me labour so much as I have done for decency and an orderly settlement of the external worship of God in the Church; for of that which is inward there can be no witness among men nor no example for men." [1]

The fruits of Laud's labour in this direction must have impressed Crashaw in the new chapel (1632) at Peterhouse, where Dr. Cosin, who was appointed master in 1634, had brought the services and ritual to the Laudian standard. Crashaw's taste in decoration and ritual seems to have been highly ornate and florid and the artistic and ceremonial aspect of Laud's Anglicanism appealed to his deep-seated poetic instincts.

Long before Crashaw migrated to Peterhouse the fame of N. Ferrar and his religious community at Little Gidding had reached Cambridge, and many ardent and devout men used to go over to Gidding to participate in their night vigils and Sunday devotions. "Several religious persons," says Dean Peckard, "both in the neighbourhood and from distant places attended these watchings: and amongst them the celebrated Mr. Richard Crashaw, Fellow of Peterhouse, who was very intimate in the family and frequently came from Cambridge for this purpose, and at his return often watched in Little St. Mary's Church near Peterhouse." [2]

It was perhaps the austere life of Nicholas Ferrar which aroused in Crashaw a similar desire to keep night vigils and devote himself to a life of prayer and mortification. His first editor (who L. C. Martin thinks was an inmate of Little Gidding) says that "he led his life in S. Marie's Church near St. Peter's College; there he lodged under Tertullian's roof of Angels; there he made his nest more gladly than David's Swallow near the House of God, where like a primitive Saint he offered more prayers in the night, than others usually offer in the day."

Regular watches were also kept throughout the night at Little Gidding, when the Psalms were recited every four hours by the watchers on their knees; these austerities of

---

[1] *The English Church from the Accession of Charles I to the Death of Queen Anne*, by W. H. Hutton, p. 53.

[2] *The Life and Times of Nicholas Ferrar*, by H. P. K. Skipton; *Cambridge in the 17th Century*, by J. E. B. Mayer; *Little Gidding and its Founder*, by Henry Collett; *John Inglesant*, by J. H. Shorthouse; *Ferrar Papers*, ed. B. Blackstone, Cambridge, 1938.

Nicholas Ferrar took a still severer turn after the death of his mother. After her death he never went to bed "but wraping himself in a loose frieze gown, slept on a bear's skin upon the boards. He also watched either in the oratory, or in the church three nights in the week." [1]

That Crashaw's relation with the Ferrars was intimate is further proved by the fact that Ferrar Collet was placed (May 1636) under Crashaw's charge at Peterhouse. A letter of Crashaw from Holland addressed probably to John Ferrar, the brother of Nicholas Ferrar, has been preserved which proves that Mary Collet,[2] the niece of Nicholas Ferrar, accompanied or joined Crashaw at Leyden.

Crashaw's conception of the night vigils is given in his "Description of a Religious House and Condition of Life":

> "A hasty Portion of prescribed sleep;
> Obedient Slumbers, that can wake & weep
> And sing, & sigh & work and sleep again;
> Still rowling a round sphere of still-returning pain."

It seems that Crashaw at Cambridge was a High Church man of the school of Laud and Andrewes.[3] As early as 1635 he had denied, in his verses prefixed to Shelford's *Five Pious Discourses*, the Puritan dogma that the Pope was Antichrist:

> "Why 'tis a point of Faith. What e'er it be
> I'm sure it is no point of charity."

He also denied the Protestant doctrine of Justification by Faith alone. He said (in *Fides Quae Sola Justificat*):

> "Faith is the body, Love the Soul.
> Take Love from it, you take the whole:
> Now, now indeed Thy Faith's alone,
> But being alone, lo, it is none."

But for the Civil Wars, Crashaw would still have remained an ardent High Church man, secure at Cambridge in "a little contentfull kingdom," [4] as he called his Patrimony in St. Peter.

---

[1] *Life and Times of Nicholas Ferrar*, by H. P. K. Skipton, p. 144.
[2] "Richard Crashaw and Mary Collet," *Church Quarterly Review*, vol. lxxiii.
[3] He also wrote a poem "Upon Bishop Andrewes his picture before his Sermons."
[4] L. C. Martin, Introduction.

His conversion, we should remember, did not depend like that of Donne on "controverted divinity"; it was not the Roman Catholic dogma, or philosophy, but the Catholic ritual and the reading of the Catholic mystics, especially of St. Teresa, which largely led him to seek repose in the bosom of the Roman Catholic Church. Crashaw's conversion was the confirmation of a spiritual state which had already existed, and this state was mainly emotional, an artistic abandonment to the ecstasy of divine love expressed through sensuous symbolism.

Grosart holds that Crashaw till 1634 was "as thoroughly Protestant, in all probability, as his father could have desired," [1] while R. A. Eric Shepherd states the viewpoint of the Roman Catholic critics when he says that Puritanism never had any influence on Crashaw: "Whether Puritanism can ever have had any influence on Crashaw, it is not possible to say. It is most probable that it never had." [2] The influence of Puritanism never seems to have been strong in his life and he soon adopted the tenets of the Laudian party, as is evident from his *Epigrammata Sacra*, a careful study of which shows that he had come early in life under the spell of the Catholic mystics, while such epigrams as "Mary Magdalene," "The Blessed Virgin seeks Jesus," "On the Wounds of our Crucified Lord" show the trend of his mind; these were the themes which were later on to occupy his mind as a devotional poet. He had already written his great hymn to St. Teresa while he was "yet among the Protestantes." [3] His conversion heightened his sense of ecstatic adoration of the Virgin Mary, Christ, and His Saints, and his piety and religious poetry became more characteristic of the Roman Catholic Church. He joined the Church which was already his spiritual home and cultivated, as H. C. Beeching has said, "that tone of familiarity which is so distressing in so many devotions used by Romanists and our own dissenters." [4] Nicholas Ferrar had given a prophetic

---

[1] Grosart, vol. ii, *Introduction to the Works of Crashaw*, p. xlii.
[2] *The Religious Poems of R. Crashaw*, Introduction, p. 3.
[3] Grosart quotes Crashaw's poems on the "Gunpowder Treason" as an evidence of Crashaw's puritanism, and compares them to "his father's wrath" (vol. ii, p. xli), but we must remember there was a large majority of the English Catholics who were against the conspiracies and plots of the Jesuits. See Donne's *Pseudo-Martyr*.
[4] H. C. Beeching, *Religio Laici*, 1902.

warning about the "coming troubles" a few days before his death to his brother John Ferrar: "I now tell you, that you may be forewarned and prepare for it, there will be sad times come, and very sad. But if you should live to see the divine service and worship of God by supreme authority brought to nought and suppressed, then look and fear the desolation is at hand, and cry mightily to God." [1] When this prophecy was fulfilled, and the Puritans ejected Crashaw from Cambridge in 1634, he *formally* became a Roman Catholic, and a few years later Cowley found him in great distress in Paris in 1646; thus by outward circumstances as well as by the inner urge of religious temperament his Rome-ward journey was completed.

A careful study of Crashaw's religious poetry shows that he was a poet with a mystical temperament, ornate and sensuous, rather than a mystic in the sense in which St. Augustine or Blessed St. Teresa were mystics. Algar Thorold holds that Dionysius the Areopagite's *Theologia Mystica* provides the solid basis on which the Roman Catholic mysticism rests. He explains; "The human soul, by an inverse movement to that of God towards the creature, rising step by step through the degrees of creation, remounts at last to God, enters the mysterious night of the Divinity, which no created light can pierce, and there unites herself intimately with her last end." [2] Pseudo-Dionysius in a passage which has become the classic of Roman Catholic mysticism says that the soul having become "purely free and absolute, out of self and of all things, thou shalt be led up to the ray of the divine darkness, stripped of all, and loosed from all." There is no evidence in Crashaw's poems that he was ever led up to the mysteries of "divine darkness" where the soul becomes united with God. Crashaw often appears to us as an ecstatic poet writing about the mystical experiences of a great saint (St. Teresa) rather than conveying the richness of his own mystical life. He does not express either the psychology or the sum-total of his mystical experience. Professor Grierson has justly remarked "neither spiritual conflict controlled and directed by Christian inhibitions and aspirations, nor mystical yearning for a closer communion with the divine, is the burden of his

---

[1] *The Life and Times of N. Ferrar*, Skipton, p. 145.
[2] *An Essay in Aid of the Better Appreciation of Catholic Mysticism*, Algar Thorold, p. 77.

religious song, but love, tenderness, and joy." [1] But the exaltation of joy and divine love do not seem to have been attained by any personal effort; there is no consciousness of sin in his poetry, no agony of purgation, no desolation of the "Dark Night of the Soul" such as we find in St. Bernard or St. John of the Cross.

Francis Thompson, who, like Crashaw, was also a Roman Catholic mystic, held that Crashaw's is "essentially a secular genius," and that he is attracted to religious themes "not by the religious lessons, but the poetical grandeur and beauty of the subject"—"he sings the Stable at Bethlehem, but he does not sing its lessons of humility, poverty, self-abnegation." [2]

Though Crashaw was attracted to these themes because they were religiously exalted, as the agony of Christ on the Cross, or the mysteries of the adoration of the Blessed Sacrament, or the heroic life of St. Teresa, and had great poetic possibilities in them, he never seems to have experienced the joys of an illuminated mystic. In spite of the advocacy of Mr. E. I. Watkin, to me Crashaw is a devotee rather than a mystic; even the tender intimacy of erotic mysticism is absent from his poetry.

St. Teresa describes her love for Christ in a way that has a ring of personal experience in it: "He also spoke other gracious words, which I need not repeat. His Majesty, further showing His great love for me, said to me very often: 'Thou art Mine, and I am thine.'" [3] We do not find any record of such intimate experience of the love of Christ in Crashaw's poetry.

The analysis of the divine poems according to their theme would help us in determining the quality of Crashaw's religious experience. A detailed grouping of the English poems according to their subject-matter will be found in the Appendix to this chapter, arranged in their chronological order (pp. 301–3). I have grouped the poems according to their themes in four sections as follows [4]:

---

[1] Introduction to *Metaphysical Lyrics and Poems of the Seventeenth Century* (1921), p. xlvi.

[2] See R. A. Eric Shepherd's Introduction, p. 9, and *Works of F. Thompson*, vol. iii (1913).

[3] *The Life of St. Teresa of Jesus written by Herself*, translated by David Lewis, p. 353.

[4] This is my own classification, which is based on the three original editions of 1646, 1648, 1652.

(1) Poems on Christ's life and His miracles.
(2) On the Catholic Church and its ceremonies.
(3) On the saints and martyrs of the Church.
(4) On several sacred themes such as the translation of the Psalms, and letters to the Countess of Denbigh, and "On Mr. George Herbert's *book intituled, the Temple of Sacred Poems sent to a Gentlewoman*," which contain Crashaw's reflections on the problem of conversion and on the efficacy of prayer.

The poems under the first section, on the life of Christ, published in 1646 are as follows:

(1) On the Water of our Lord's Baptisme.
(2) Upon the Sepulchre of our Lord.
(3) On the Still surviving markes of our Saviour's wounds.
(4) Come see the Place where the Lord lay.
(5) I am the Doore.
(6) Neither durst any man from that Day ask him any more Questions.
(7) Upon our Saviour's Tombe.
(8) Upon our Lord's last comfortable discourse with his Disciples.
(9) Upon the Thornes taken downe from our Lords head bloody.
(These nine are from *Divine Epigrams*, 1646.)
(10) Our Lord in his circumcision to his Father.
(11) On the wounds of our crucified Lord.
(12) On our crucified Lord Naked and Bloody.
(13) Easter day.
(14) On the bleeding wounds of our crucified Lord.
(15) A Hymne of the Nativity, sung by the shepherds.
(16) An Himne for the circumcision day of our Lord.
(17) New Year's Day.

The following poems dealing with the Life and Passion of Christ were added in 1648 and retained in the *Carmen Deo Nostro*, Paris (1652) [1]:

---

[1] No important poem dealing with Christ was added in 1652 and certain alterations were made in "For the Office of the H. Cross."

(1) To the Name Above Every Name.
(2) The Glorious Epiphanie of our Lord.
(3) The Office of the Holy Crosse.

Evensong; Compline (1652)—added to "The Office of the Holy Crosse)."

(4) Upon the H. Sepulchre.
(5) Charitas Nimia.   Poems from MSS.
(6) A Song.
(7) Out of Grotius his Tragedy of Christes sufferings.

There are only three poems (see the Appendix to this chapter) on church ceremonies, one being a translation of the famous hymn of St. Thomas in "adoration of The Blessed Sacrament." Except the two epigrams on the Virgin Mary, published in 1646, all the three great poems on the Virgin Mary—(1) "Sancta Maria"; (2) "Gloriosa Domina"; (3) "On the Glorious Assumption of our Blessed Lady "—were written after Crashaw's conversion and included in the 1648 edition. There are eleven poems dealing with the life of saints and martyrs of the Church like St. Magdalene, St. Teresa, St. Anthony and others. There are thirty-one poems dealing with other sacred subjects like the Prayer Book; "Description of the Religious House," and the poem addressed to the Countess of Denbigh, "Perswading her to Resolution in Religion." There are only six epigrams dealing with the miracles of Christ. This analysis of the divine poems shows the limited range of Crashaw's interest in the choice of his subjects which are mostly confined to Christ, the Virgin Mother, and the saints of the Church. There is not a single poem like Donne's "A Hymn to God the Father" or Herbert's poems like "The Affliction," "The Search" and "The Collar," poems which reveal the inner struggle for self-purification and the complexity of the aspirations of the soul in its attempt to apprehend God.

Crashaw's vision is more objective; he feels a kind of ecstatic ardour when he contemplates the life of the saints of Christ, or the mystery of Christ's birth and his relation to the Virgin Mary; he does not give us any insight into the inner struggle of his soul in what the Catholic mystics call the "progressive sanctification of life." His religious poetry is the song of thanksgiving and joy. In his famous hymn "To the Name above Every Name" he hails Christ with the passionate enthusiasm of a convert:

> "I sing the Name which None can say
> But touch't with An interiour Ray:
> The Name of our New Peace; our Good:
> Our Blisse: & supernaturall Blood:
> The name of All our Lives & Loves." [1]

He does not reveal any deep personal experience of the "interior-ray" of the love of Christ. The keynote of his hymn is

> "Awake & Sing
> And be All wing." [2]

He soars high on the wings of his imagination, but leaves us wondering about the nature and depth of his own religious experience.

Crashaw and the Dutch poet Vondel strike a new note in the religious poetry of the Counter-Reformation, the note of the ardour, exaltation and joy of the poet who has at last found peace and rest in the bosom of the Roman Catholic Church. In the study of Crashaw's devotional poetry we should bear in mind a simple biographical detail, that he was a *convert*. Edmund Gosse says that Crashaw "is the solitary representative of the poetry of Catholic Psychology which England possessed until our own days," [3] but it is the psychology of a convert to Roman Catholicism. The convert in his outburst of joy at the newly discovered truth forgets to dwell upon the lessons the Church teaches and instead sings of its saints and martyrs. Donne's religious poetry is also rich in its psychological content, but in Crashaw's poetry there is no subtle and argumentative evolution of feeling or its fusion with intellect; his poetry is controlled more by emotion than intellect. His ecstatic joy, like that of a convert, is uncontrollable. He feels the "Artfull Touch" of Christ which has led to his conversion and with him the whole creation sings:

> "All things that Are
> Or, what's the same,
> Are Musicall." [4]

---

[1] L. C. Martin, p. 239.　　[2] *Ibid.*, p. 240.
[3] *Seventeenth-century Studies*, by E. Gosse, pp. 154, 155.
[4] L. C. Martin, p. 241.

It is instructive to compare Crashaw with R. Southwell (1561-95). In this neglected Roman Catholic poet, the ecstatic phase, the desire for martyrdom which the Jesuits had kindled in many a religious soul, begins early in life. But what is significant in the life of Southwell is not the joy of the convert, for he was sent at an early age to Douay, and was educated there by the Jesuit Leonard and later at Paris by the Jesuit Thomas Derbyshire, and was duly ordained as a priest at the age of twenty-three (1584), but his passionate desire for martyrdom, which was at last satisfied, and he endured with great courage and fortitude tortures during his imprisonment at Topcliffe's house.[1]

On his way to England,[2] Southwell wrote a letter to the Father-General of the Jesuits (July 15, 1586) in which he declared: "nor do I so much dread tortures, as look forward to the crown."[3] Southwell often sings like Crashaw of the blessed state in Heaven:

"O State of Joys, where endless joye remains!
O haven of blisse, where none doth suffer wrack!
O happie house, which all delight containes!
O blessed state, which never feeleth lack!
O goodlie tree, which fruite dothe ever beare!
O quyette state, which danger neede not feare!"[4]

But the ecstatic note in Crashaw's poetry is not that of a martyr but that of a happy convert. His subjects are precisely those which would appeal to a convert, and moreover nearly all his poems are hymns. Crashaw's preoccupation with the "facts" of redemption, and the *means* by which it was accomplished, is more fully explained when we understand the psychology of a religious convert. Addressing Christ he says:

"How many Unknown Worlds there are
Of Comforts, which Thou hast in keeping!
How many Thousand Mercyes There
In pittys' soft lap ly asleeping!"[5]

Crashaw's main emphasis is on Christ, the Redeemer, rather than on Christ who is reborn in the soul of the mystic as St. Paul says: "I live yet not I, but Christ liveth in me."[6]

---

[1] *R. Southwell*, by M. Rodkin, p. 19.
[2] *The Book of R. Southwell*, P. C. M. Hood, p. 14.
[3] "Of the Joys of Heaven" from *A Foure-fould Meditation*.
[4] *The Religious Poems of R. Crashaw*, Introduction, p. 12, by A. Eric Shepherd.
[5] L. C. Martin, p. 244.   [6] Galatians ii, 20.

Crashaw does not establish any such intimate relation with Christ. If we analyse his three great hymns, in which he has celebrated the birth, life and Passion of Christ, we notice that he sings with ardour, and exaltation, and with infinite musical variations, the single theme of Christ, the Redeemer. In his "Hymn of the Nativity" he is eager to "Kiss thy feet, and crown thy head." [1] He seems to see, as if in ecstasy, the "Divine Babe" with his own eyes:

> "We saw thee in thy Balmy Nest,
>   Bright Dawne of our *Eternall Day*;
> Wee saw Thine Eyes break from the East,
> And chase the trembling shades away:
> Wee saw thee (and wee blest the sight)
> Wee saw thee by thine owne sweet light." [2]

It is in quite a different spirit that the Anglican Herbert wrote of the Nativity. Crashaw sings of the Birth of the Saviour, Herbert thinks of his own sin and the need of repentance. His prayer on "Christmas" is:

> "Furnish and deck my soul, that thou mayst have
>   A better lodging than a rack or grave." [3]

While Herbert *feels* the presence of Christ in the soul, Crashaw is satisfied with the *vision* of Christ only. His poems, says Gosse, "are not poems of experience, but of ecstasy, not of meditation, but of devotion" [4]; but the religious mood in these poems is not really that of "rapture" and "ecstasy" in the sense of being of a *rare mystical state* which St. Teresa herself experienced. St. Teresa describing the nature of the "rapture" says: "I have seen it myself and I know by experience, that the soul in rapture is mistress of everything. . . . O my God, how clear is the meaning of those words, and what good reason the Psalmist had, and all the world will ever have, to pray for the wings of the dove. It is plain that this is the flight of the spirit rising upwards above all created things, and chiefly above itself, but it is a sweet flight—a flight without noise." [5] In Crashaw's poetry there is no

---

[1] L. C. Martin, p. 108.   [2] *Ibid.*, p. 107.
[3] *The Works of G. Herbert*, edited by G. H. Palmer, vol. ii, p. 167.
[4] *Seventeenth-century Studies*, by E. Gosse, p. 153.
[5] *St. Teresa's Autobiography*, translated by David Lewis, p. 154. All the quotations are from this translation; unfortunately I could not obtain the standard edition of Professor Peers when I wrote this chapter.

consciousness of "a delicious flight" or "rapture" of the soul, which are the technical terms describing a rare mystical state. He has simply realized the sublimity and grandeur of the themes his imagination dwells upon—such as the life and Passion of Christ, and the martyrdom of the saints of His Church. It is the spirit of prayer, of thanksgiving, of singing hymns to the glory of the Lord and His spouse, the Holy Catholic Church which determines the character of Crashaw's mystical poetry; it is really the poetic apprehension of mystical experience rather than an account of his own journey on the Mystic Way. In his second great poem on Christ, "Charitas Nimia," he has approached the subject of redemption from a different point of view; he contemplates the sublimity of Christ's Sacrifice and the "faithlessnesse" of his own soul which His sacrifice has redeemed. He asks:

> "If I were lost in misery
> What was it to thy heaven & thee?
> What was it to thy pretious blood
> If my foul Heart call'd for a floud?" [1]

He recognizes that it was the sacrifice of Love; Christ gave away His life so that the sins of Man may be redeemed— "Love is too kind, I see." [2]

In his third important poem about Christ's life he chose a favourite theme of the Catholic poets, Christ as the "Bright Babe" (see Southwell's "Burning Babe").

In "The Glorious Epiphanie of our Lord" he meditates on the various aspects of Christ as the "Glorious Babe." He imagines the whole world lying in the loving grasp of the "Bright Babe" and being blessed by His kisses; it is an emblematic conceit:

> "O little all! in thy embrace
> The world lyes warm & likes his place.
> Nor does his full Globe fail to be
> Kist on Both his cheeks by Thee." [3]

Christ blesses the world with his "kiss" and the "mists" of false worship disappear from the earth. To him the "supernaturall Dawn of Thy pure day" [4] is the purification of all forms of worship; no longer shall man worship the Sun or "Ram, he-goat":

---

[1] L. C. Martin, p. 281.   [2] Ibid., p. 280.   [3] Ibid., p. 255.   [4] Ibid., p. 258.

> "The doting nations now no more
> Shall any day but Thine adore." [1]

The picture of Christ holding the world in His protecting arms is exquisite and sensitively drawn. Christ to Donne is also a Redeemer and the sublime agony of the Cross assumed a vital significance to Donne because of his own acute consciousness of sin, but Christ to Donne is a "feared" saviour; his sonnet on the "Nativitie" is solemn and aloof:

> " Seest thou, my soule, with thy faiths eyes, how he
> Which fills all place, yet none holds him, doth lye?
> Was not his pity towards thee wondrous high,
> That would have need to be pitied by thee? "
> "La-Corona."

He cannot address Christ with the familiarity of Crashaw, who called Him in his "Hymne of the Nativity" the "fair ey'd boy." It is not so much on the divinity of the "Bright Babe" that Crashaw dwells, the emotional concentration is more on the human side of the divine childhood, and Christ, the Babe, is not convincingly divine. It is this conception of Christ's Childhood which determines Crashaw's conception of the Heavenly Virgin Mother in which the Sanctity of Motherhood is more emphasized than the supreme Mystery of Christ's birth:

> "The Babe no sooner gan to seeke,
> Where to lay his lovely head,
> But straight his eyes advis'd his Cheeke,
> 'Twixt Mothers Brests to goe to bed.
> Sweet choise (said I) no way but so,
> Not to lye cold, yet sleepe in snow." [2]

The "tone of familiarity," which according to Beeching is "so distressing" to the Anglicans, may seem to be the keynote of Crashaw's poetry of religious ecstasy and exaltation. But Crashaw's imagery expressive of this "familiarity" is raised to a high level of devotional exaltation because it is suffused with his own feelings of reverence and affection for Christ:

> "Welcome to our wondring sight
> Eternity in a span!
> Summer in Winter! Day in Night!
> Heaven in Earth! and God in Man!
> Great little one, whose glorious Birth,
> Lifts Earth to Heaven, stoops heaven to earth." [3]

---

[1] L. C. Martin, p. 256.   *Ibid.*, p. 107.   [3] *Ibid.*

Even when Heaven stoops to earth, and eternity is shut in a span, Heaven remains Heaven, and it is only the feeling of wonder and reverence which elevates Crashaw's imagery to a religious significance.

Crashaw's worship of the Virgin Mary is closely associated with his conception of Christ, the "Bright Babe." It is significant to note that Crashaw, in his address to the reader in his *Epigrammata Sacra* (written before his conversion), declares that instead of writing poetry to celebrate Venus and Cupid, as the pagan epigrammatists had done, he would dedicate his poetry to the Virgin Mary and her Child:

> "Another Cypris holds me now,
> Another Love receives my vow:
> For Love is here and Mother kind,
> But she is a Virgin; He not blind." [1]

And, though still a Protestant, he invokes the Virgin Mary:

> "O child! O Lord! great Mother blest!
> O wonder of thy holy breast."

The Anglican Church does not make the worship of the Virgin Mary a fundamental article of her creed. Donne has treated the various controversies connected with the Virgin Mary in his sermon (Sermon No. 11 in *LXXX Sermons*) and declares: "*Pariet, & Pariet filium*, she shall bring forth a son; If a son, then of the substance of his Mother, that the Anabaptists deny; But had it not been so, Christ had not beene true Man, and then, man were yet unredeemed. He is her son, but not her ward; his Father cannot dye; Her son but yet he asked her no leave, to stay at Jerusalem. . . . His setling of Religion, his governing the church, his dispensing of his graces is not by warrant from her. They that call upon the Bishop of Rome; in that voyce, *Impera Regibus*; command Kings and Emperors, admit of that voyce, *Impera filio*, to her, that she should command her sonne: *Blessed are thou amongst women*, saies the Angell to her, Amongst women, above women; but not above any person of the Trinity that she should command her son."

Crashaw wrote his three great poems on the Virgin Mother

---

[1] He has several epigrams on the Virgin Mary, such as "Blessed be Paps" or "On the Blessed Virgin's Bashfulness."

after his conversion: (1) "Sancta Maria"; (2) "O Gloriosa Domina"; (3) "In the Glorious Assumption of our Blessed Lady."[1] The first poem celebrates her as "The Mother of Sorrows"; the second hails her as the "door of life," as the Mother of the Saviour:

> "Had not a Better Fruit forbidden it.
> Had not thy healthfull womb
> The worlds new eastern window bin
> And given us heav'n again, in giving Him."

And in the third he sings a solemn hymn at her hour of death. He expresses his own attitude towards the Virgin Mary when he says:

> "Hail, most high, most humble one!
> Above the world; below thy son." [2]

The doctrine embodied in the above lines was formulated during the period of the four great Councils (A.D. 324–451). E. B. Pusey says: "Yet it was self-evident, as soon as stated, that she of whom Christ deigned to take His human flesh was brought to a nearness to Himself above all created beings; that she stood single and alone in all creation or possible creations, in that in her womb He who in His Godhead is consubstantial with the Father deigned, as to His Human Body, to become Consubstantial with her" (*Eirenicon*, ii, 24).

In all the three poems Crashaw recognizes this fact, the sublimity of the Motherhood of the Divine Child. Her sorrow in "Sancta Maria" is the sorrow of a mother at the Great Affliction of her Son:

> "Each wound of His, from every Part,
> All, more at home in her own heart." [3]

We are not here concerned with the heresies and controversies about the Virgin Mary, which were closely associated

---

[1] Martin, p. 303. Courthope remarks that "The Virgin occupies a less prominent position in Crashaw's poetry than either St. Mary Magdalene or St. Teresa" (*History of English Poetry*, vol. iii, p. 222). This remark is hardly justified, for he wrote three of his famous poems on the Virgin Mary and she is present in his "Hymn of Nativity" and other poems as well.

[2] There is no evidence of the cult of the Virgin Mary in the first few centuries of the Christian era; the cult of the Virgin Mary assumed a great significance with the growth of monasticism and the idealization of virginity and chastity. Cardinal Newman admitted that no prayer to the Virgin Mary is found in the works of St. Augustine.

[3] Martin, p. 284.

with the controversies about the Incarnation, the mystery of the Word made Flesh (the Arian controversy was largely due to this fact) [1]; it is enough to remark here that Crashaw's worship of the Virgin Mary breathes the spirit of the Roman Breviary as reformed by the Council of Trent, where she is invoked as follows:

"Hail, O Queen, Mother of Mercy! Hail, our life, our sweetness, our hope! To thee we fly, the banished sons of Eve."

Crashaw, it is significant, also refers to the Fall through Eve and the restoration of the state of *grace* which existed before the Fall through the Virgin Mary:

"The first Eve, mother of our Fall,
E're she bore any one, slew all." [2]

It is the Virgin Mary who "renders all the stars she stole away." [2] Crashaw's Blessed Mary is more human than divine, and it is as the Mother of the Saviour rather than as the Saint of the Church that Crashaw invokes her:

"MARIA, men & angels sing
MARIA, mother of our King.
Live, rosy princesse, Live." [3]

He does not establish any personal relation to the Virgin Mary like that of the devotee to the Patron Saint, he sings of the Blessed Queen as if with the congregation rather than in the serene peace of private prayers. She is the "mistress of our song," and he does not seem to have entered into a mystic communion with her.

Another theme of Crashaw's religious poetry is the Contemplation of the Passion of Christ. Besides the long poem, "The Office of the Holy Crosse," Crashaw is never tired of mentioning the wounds, the blood, and the pierced hands and sides of Christ. Gosse says that Crashaw has "an hysterical delight in blood and details of martyrdom." [4] Mario Praz has traced this characteristic feature of Crashaw's religious poetry to the Jesuit's delight in and glorification of martyrdom:

---

[1] See Newman's *The Arians of the Fourth Century*, 1876.
[2] "O Gloriosa," Martin, pp. 302, 303.
[3] *Ibid.*, p. 306: "The Glorious Assumption."
[4] Gosse, *Seventeenth-century Studies*.

"Contrition and indulgence were the hinges of Jesuit morality; remorse for the life of flesh, the repentance of the eleventh hour, the gesture of the supreme refusal, the dramatic moment of conversion, the welcome given to the erring soul in the loving bosom of divinity—these were the most popular elements of the tormented and sophisticated faith and casuistry." [1]

Crashaw does not dwell upon the physical details of the crucifixion as minutely in his later poems ("The Office of the Holy Crosse" or "Charitas Nimia") as he had done in the earlier poems, such as "On the Wounds of our Crucified Lord" or "On the Bleeding Wounds of our Crucified Lord." In the later poems the Sublimity of Christ's Passion, the banishment of sin, and the attempt to realize the affliction of Christ in his own life are the themes of his contemplation of the Passion:

> "O teach those wounds to bleed
> In me; me, so to read
> This book of loves, thus writ
> In lines of death, my life may copy it
> With loyal cares." [2]

Throughout the Middle Ages the Passion of Christ was the theme most frequently treated in the mystery plays and devotional literature, but it was not till the time of St. Bernard and St. Francis of Assisi that the contemplation of the Passion reached its climax. [3]

Crashaw must have read St. Teresa's devotion to the Passion in her *Autobiography*. She remarks that it was the contemplation of the Passion of Christ which helped her to concentrate on prayer:

"It seemed to me that the being alone and afflicted, like a person in trouble, must needs permit me to come near unto Him. . . . I thought of the bloody sweat, and of the affliction He endured there; I wished, if it had been possible, to wipe away that painful sweat from His face; but I remember that I never dared to form such a resolution—my sins stood before me so grievously." [4] At another place she recommends

---

[1] *Secentismo e Marinismo in Inghilterra* (Firenze, 1925).
[2] Martin, p. 286, "Sancta Maria."
[3] The first recorded instance of the Stigmata was that of St. Francis of Assisi.
[4] *Life of St. Teresa*, David Lewis, pp. 59–60.

contemplation of the Passion as one of the best forms of meditation: "We set ourselves to meditate upon some mystery of the Passion: let us say, our Lord at the pillar. The understanding goeth about seeking for the sources out of which came the great dolors and the bitter anguish which His Majesty endured in that desolation." [1]

But Crashaw's meditation on the Passion is not mainly due to the fact that he became a Roman Catholic, but also to the general tendency of the devotional literature of his age; Guevara's *Mount of Calvary, or The Passion of Our Lord,* was one of the most popular books of devotion in the seventeenth century. Donne, Herbert and Vaughan all wrote great poems on the Passion of Christ. [2]

Vaughan recognizes that it is the covenant of "blood" which binds him to Christ:

> "That Thou forgott'st Thine own, for Thou didst seal
>   Mine with Thy blood, Thy blood which makes Thee mine,
>   Mine ever, ever and me ever Thine."
>
> "Love-sick."

There is no restraint and austerity and agonized sense of sin as in Donne's contemplation of the Passion. In Crashaw's art the theme of the Passion has acquired a baroque luxuriance of emotion.

Crashaw in the glow and heat of his religious feeling is eager to be intoxicated with the wounds of Christ, it is a kind of ecstasy in meditation, which St. Teresa held could be attained by contemplating certain aspects of the physical suffering of Christ on the Cross:

> "Till drunk of the dear wounds, I be
>   A lost Thing to the world, as it to me." [3]

Algar Thorold holds that the peculiar distinction of the Catholic mystic consists in his relation to the Church:

"The Catholic mystic, apart from his individual vocation to real apprehension of spirit, finds himself in relation to the Church, *i.e.* to humanity organized from the religious point of view, and it is, of course, in this relation, and what comes of it, that his peculiar note consists. . . . The task of the Catholic

---

[1] *Life of St. Teresa*, David Lewis, p. 91.
[2] W. A. Lewis Bettany in his Introduction to *Silex Scintillans* says that Vaughan has used the word "blood" ninety times.
[3] *Poems*, ed. Martin, p. 287.

mystic is so to adjust these social claims to this individual vocation that not either be defrauded, but that each subserve the other." [1]

He holds that it is the Church alone which can help the mystic in the "progressive fructification" of dogma in the human soul; he points out "the saint alone is the real proof of Christianity, he alone renders its dark sayings intelligible. The obligatory dogmata of the Church says Coventry Patmore are only the seeds of life." [1]

Though Crashaw's psychology is that of a Catholic devotional poet, his poetry is peculiarly free from any *doctrinal* implications. In his church hymns (which are elaborate versions of the Latin hymns), such as "The Hymn of the Church," "Lauda Sion Salvatorem," "The Office of the Holy Crosse," and "The Hymn of St. Thomas in Adoration of the Blessed Sacrement," he does not try to give a philosophical interpretation of the manifold life of the Church. They are in his own language "a descant upon plain song." [2]

His poem "Easter-Day" is free from all speculation as to the nature of the Resurrection [3]; he is content to sing of the glorious Resurrection of Christ and his conquest of death:

> "Rise, Heir of fresh Eternity,
> From thy virgin Tombe:
> Rise mighty man of wonders and thy world with thee.
> Thy tomb, the universall East,
> Natures new wombe,
> Thy Tombe, faire Immortalities perfumed Nest." [4]

His poem "The Hymn of the Church in Meditation of the Day of Judgement" does not emphasize that salvation shall be achieved through the protecting care and love of the Catholic Church. He relies on God's mercy and His love for Man, and hopes to find shelter at the Day of Judgement from God's wrath in Himself:

> "But thou giv'st leave (dread Lord) that we
> Take shelter from thyself, in thee;
> And with the wings of thine own dove
> Fly to thy scepter of soft love." [5]

---

[1] *An Essay in Aid of the Better Appreciation of Catholic Mysticism,* by Algar Thorold, p. 3.   [2] *Ibid.,* p. 45.

[3] As we find in Donne and Vaughan; see Vaughan's poem "Death, Resurrection and Immortality."

[4] L. C. Martin, p. 100.   [5] *Ibid.,* p. 300.

Faith and Love are the two pillars on which his religion
rests; but his faith is nothing but the "progressive fructification
of dogma" in his own soul; and it is love which helps the
"seeds of life" to blossom forth:

"Faith is my skill.   Faith can believe
As fast as love new lawes can give.
Faith is my force.   Faith strength affords
To keep pace with those powerfull words.
And words more sure, more sweet, then they
Love could not think, truth could not say." [1]

Crashaw's religious mind is intensely Catholic, but free
from any controversial and doctrinal bias.   Baron Von Hügel's
definition of the Catholic mind and its relation to the "Mind
of the Church" may well be applied to Crashaw.   He explains
thus: "For it is indeed certain that the special characteristic
of the Catholic mind is not, necessarily, universally and finally,
the conception and practice of sanctity under the precise form
of the devotional spirits and habits special to the particular
part or period of the Church in which that individual Catholic's
lot may be cast.   What *is* thus characteristic, is the continuous
and sensitive conviction that there is something far-reaching
and important beyond the Church's bare precepts, for every
soul that aims at sanctity, to find out and do. . . . For the
Church's life and spirit, which is but the extension of the spirit
of Christ Himself, is, like all that truly lives at all, not a sheer
singleness, but has a mysterious unity in and by means of
endless variety." [2]

Crashaw found a resting home in the Catholic Church
because it satisfied his conception of worship and faith, and he
harmonized his life with the life of the Church as expressed
in her devotions and ritual.

Another characteristic of Catholic mysticism is its conception of the created universe and the rôle assigned to Man in it.
According to the Catholic conception, the spheres of the
senses and spirit are not separated by any rigid line of demarca-
tion; they melt into each other, though the distinct duality
of matter and form has been recognized and accepted.   Dr.
Martineau says: "Hence the invariable presence of some
physical element in all that Catholicism looks upon as

[1] L. C. Martin, p. 292.
[2] *The Mystical Element in Religion*, by B. von Hügel, vol. i, pp. 122-123.

venerable.   Its rites are a manipular invocation of God . . . the
Catholic, looking on the natural universe, whether material
or human, not as an antagonist but as the receptacle of the
spiritual, seeks to conquer the World for the Church." [1]
This conception is implicit in the view of creation in which
the Roman Catholic Church believes.

The Catholic Church holds that "creation" is not "making,"
for making implies means, and God created all the things in
the universe as regards the whole of their substance Himself
out of nothing (as St. Thomas says: "*Productio alicujus rei
Secundum suam totam substantiam nullo praesupposito*" [2]).

Crashaw seems to have accepted this Catholic conception
of the created universe; in his poetry the sphere of the senses
melts into the sphere of spirit, and he frequently uses materialistic imagery to symbolize spiritual "states":

> "Heavens Golden-Winged Herald, late hee saw
> To a poore *Galilean* virgin sent:
> How low the Bright youth bow'd, and with what awe
> Immortall flowers to her faire hand present." [3]

Strangely, Courthope says that "this materialistic imagery
produces not horror but disgust." [4]   But before passing any
judgement on Crashaw's use of materialistic imagery we must
bear in mind that it was the result of his accepting the Catholic
conception of Creation; the Catholic mind uses a sensuous
vehicle to express spiritual states and tries to interpret the
invisible with the help of the visible, hence the frequent use
of erotic symbolism in the Roman Catholic mysticism (often
based on the Song of Songs).   Crashaw's devout imagination
is as much stirred by the unknown rites of the "mystical death"
of ecstasy as by imagining the physical suffering of Christ on
the Cross.   Crashaw freely invokes his senses to aid him in his
devotions.   He prays to God:

> "O fill our senses, And take from us
> All force of so prophane a Fallacy
> To think ought sweet but that which smells of Thee." [5]

---

[1] Dr. Martineau's review of Francis Newman's *Phases of Faith*; also see *Puritan
and Anglican Studies in Literature*, by Edward Dowden.   Courthope has confused
the physical element in Crashaw's mysticism with the "pagan Muse," see *History
of English Poetry*, vol. iii, pp. 229–230.
[2] *Summa Theologica*.   [3] L. C. Martin, p. 112: "Sospetto d'Herode."
[4] Courthope, *History of English Poetry*, vol. iii, p. 227.
[5] Martin, p. 244: "To the Name, etc."

God must fill the soul as well as the senses. Crashaw was
ever eager to bring

> "Flowers of never fading graces
> To make Immortal dressings," [1]

for "the Virgin's Son," but sensuous and amorous symbolism
formed an essential part of these "Immortal dressings" of his
divine songs.

The intensifying of religious life which followed the Council
of Trent deeply influenced Catholic devotion and gave new
strength and vitality to the monastic ideals in Italy, England
and France, but neither Italy nor France can be compared
with Spain in the eminence of her mystical achievement.

Spanish was a popular language in England in the last
decade of the sixteenth century when Vives, who was the tutor
of the Princess Mary, was at Oxford; and that the interest in
Spanish literature was widespread is further proved by the
presence of a large number of Spanish and Portuguese books
in the new library of Sir Thomas Bodley. The most popular
Spanish devotional writer in England was Fray Luis de Granada.
In 1582 his two famous books of devotion, *Meditaciones* and
Memorial de la Vida Cristiana, were translated by the English
Catholic Richard Hopkins, the first under the title *Prayer and
Meditation*; it ran into six editions in France before one was
published in London; in 1598 [2] Francis Meres translated the
essentially mystical work of Granada, *Granada's Devotions*;
earlier in the same year he had translated Granada's *The
Sinners Guyde*. As for one of the greatest Spanish mystics, St.
Teresa, no effort was made to translate her works into English
at this time. A French translation of her *Interior Castle*
appeared as early as 1601 and a Jesuit published an English
version of her *Autobiography* at Antwerp in 1611. It was,
however, the publication of the *Acta Authentica Canonizationis* at
Vienna, in 1628, which carried the story of her life of sanctity
and prayer far and wide in Europe.

Crashaw's interest in Spanish literature and mysticism seems

---

[1] L. C. Martin, p. 127.

[2] For other editions see *Spanish Influence on English Literature*, by Martin Hume,
p. 225. The Spanish books in Bodley's library were those which the Earl of Essex
had brought with him from his Spanish expedition in 1596.

to have been aroused during his early years at Cambridge. Dr. Lloyd, "sometime of Oriel College in Oxon," tells us that "Hebrew, Greek, Latine, Spanish, French, Italian were as familiar to him as English" [1]; moreover we must remember that Nicholas Ferrar, with whose family Crashaw was on intimate terms, had travelled in Spain, and when we also recall that Ferrar knew German, Dutch, Italian and Spanish it is almost certain that he must have brought with him a large number of Spanish books, for we are told that he brought home from his Continental travels "many scarce books in various languages, chiefly treating of a spiritual life of religious retirement." [2]   It was probably due to the influence of St. Teresa that Crashaw while at Cambridge, like "a primitive saint, . . . offered more prayers in the night, than others usually offer in the day." [3]

St Teresa's main contribution to the *psychology* of mysticism is her differentiation and classification of various forms of prayer into vocal and mental prayers; she laid great emphasis on a life of prayer and mortification in her *Autobiography*: "Only this will I say: prayer is the door to those great graces which our Lord bestowed upon me.   If this door be shut, I do not see how He can bestow them; for even if He entered into a soul to take His delight therein, and to make that soul also delight in Him, there is no way by which He can do so; for His will is, that such a soul should be lovely and pure, with a great desire to receive His graces." [4]

The influence of St. Teresa moulded to a great extent the devotions of Crashaw and helped in his conversion to the Roman Catholic Church.   Crashaw says that the "holy fires" in his soul were kindled "from reading thee":

> ". . . O Pardon if I dare to say
> Thine own dear bookes are guilty.   For from thence
> I learn't to know that love is eloquence." [5]

---

[1] *Memoirs of the Lives, Sufferings & Deaths of those Nobell, Reverend and Excellent Personages that suffered for the Protestant Religion.*   Also see Anthony à Wood's *Athenae Oxonienses* (1691), vol. ii, col. 688.

[2] See *Cambridge in the Seventeenth Century*, edited by J. E. B. Mayer, Part I, p. 201. For an account of Nicholas Ferrar's travels in Spain see *Nicholas Ferrar* by H. P. K. Skipton, pp. 54–57.

[3] Original Preface to the Reader, 1646.

[4] *The Life of St. Teresa*, translated by David Lewis, pp. 56–57.

[5] Martin, p. 322.

But St. Teresa held that the Love of God, which Crashaw calls "Wine of Immortall mixture," was a love that was born of ascetic life, the complete dedication of one's life to the service of God to the exclusion of all other interests:

"A love without self-interest small or great: all it desires and seeks is to see such a soul rich in celestial goods. This indeed is love, and not these unhappy affections here below: yet I mean not vicious ones: from these God deliver us." [1] Crashaw's ascetic and devotional life must have been influenced by the ideals which St. Teresa had held in such high esteem and expressed so forcefully in her writings. His friend "R. C." described the ascetic bent of Crashaw's mind:

> "Nor would he give, nor take offence; befall
> What might; he would possess himself: and live
> As deade (devoyde of interest) t'all might give
> Disease t'his well composed mynd; forestal'd
> With heavenly riches: which had wholy call'd
> His thoughts from earth, to live above in th'aire
> A very bird of paradice." [2]

He had completely "call'd his thoughts from earth" and in the moulding of his religious life St. Teresa's writings must have played a significant part. Crashaw was attracted by Spanish mysticism while "yet a Protestant" because one of the characteristics of Spanish mysticism, as Martin Hume has remarked, is "that it has little to do with theology or doctrine, and the works of Fray Luis de Granada can be read with as much edification by a Puritan as by a Roman Catholic if once the spirit can be exalted to the level necessary to understand them." [3]

Crashaw perhaps recognized this characteristic of Spanish mysticism as congenial to his own ecstatic mode of devotional life:

> "What soul so e'er, in any language, can
> speak heav'n like her's is my souls countryman." [4]

Crashaw's idealization of the "sweet deaths of love" and martyrdom is perhaps the result of his close study of St. Teresa's work. L. C. Martin in his great edition of Crashaw's works

---

[1] "Camino de Perfeccion," vii, *Mysticism*, Underhill.
[2] Martin, p. 233.
[3] *Spanish Influence on English Literature*, by Martin Hume, p. 216.
[4] Martin, p. 322: "An Apologie."

has only quoted two parallel passages from St. Teresa's *Autobiography*.[1] No editor of Crashaw has pointed out the high esteem in which St. Teresa held St. Mary Magdalene, for "The Weeper" was perhaps suggested to Crashaw by St. Teresa's great devotion to this saint; moreover Crashaw has referred to several incidents of St. Teresa's life in his great hymn "To the Name and Honor of the Admirable St. Teresa" which have escaped the notice of his critics.

> "Scarse has she learn't to lisp the name
> Of Martyr; yet she thinks it shame
> Life should so long play with that breath
> Which spent can buy so brave a death." [2]

The incidents in the hymn to St. Teresa are not the creation of his imagination but relate the actual happenings in her life.

In the above lines Crashaw has referred to an incident related by St. Teresa in her *Life* which shows her impatience for martyrdom while yet a child:

"When I read of martyrdom undergone by the Saints for the love of God, it struck me that the vision of God was very cheaply purchased; and I had a great desire to die a martyr's death—not out of any love of Him of which I was conscious, but that I might most quickly attain to the fruition of those great joys of which I read that they were reserved in heaven; and I used to discuss with my brother how we could become martyrs. We settled to go together to the country of the Moors begging our way for the love of God, that we might be there beheaded; and our Lord, I believe, had given us courage enough, even at so tender an age, if we could have found the means to proceed; but our greatest difficulty seemed to be our father and mother." [3]

Crashaw has given an elaborate account of this incident in lines 14–70 of his hymn.

> "Farewell house, & farewell home!
> She's for the Moors, & Martyrdom." [4]

In this hymn Crashaw maintains that her eager desire for

---

[1] See Martin, notes to pp. 131 and 134.
[2] Martin, p. 317: "A Hymn to . . ."
[3] *The Life of St. Teresa of Jesus*, translated by David Lewis, p. 4.
[4] Martin, p. 318.

martyrdom was not fulfilled because God had reserved the nobler death of ecstasy and Love for her:

> "Thou art Love's victime; & must dy
> A death more mysticall & high." [1]

Crashaw has again referred to this "mystical death" in "The Flaming Heart" [2]:

> "Let mystick DEATHS wait on't; & wise soules be
> The love-slain witnesses of this life of thee";

and describing the "pain" of these mystical joys Crashaw says:

> "O how oft shalt thou complain
> Of a sweet & subtle Pain
> Of intolerable joys!" [3]

St. Teresa says that when "the waters of grace have risen to the neck of the soul this state can only be described by calling it a death":

"It is rejoicing in this agony with unutterable joy; to me it seems to be nothing else but death, as it were to all things of this world, and a fruition of God. I know of no other words whereby to describe it, or to explain it; neither does the soul then know what to do—for it knows not, whether it should laugh or weep." [4]

In "The Flaming Heart" Crashaw has mentioned the "wounds of love":

> "Leave her that; & thou shalt leave her
> Not one loose shaft but love's whole quiver.
> For in Love's field was never found
> A nobler weapon then a wound." [5]

St. Teresa has described at length the effect of these *wounds* of love:

"Another prayer very common is a certain kind of wounding; for it really seems to the soul as if an arrow were thrust through the heart, or through itself. Thus it causes great suffering which makes the soul complain; but the suffering is so sweet,

---

[1] Martin, p. 319.

[2] *Ibid.*, p. 326. Crashaw borrowed the title "The Flaming Heart" from the title of her *Autobiography* published at Antwerp: *The Flaming Heart or the Life of the Glorious St. Teresa.* . . . Antwerpe MDXLII. The translator signs himself "M. T."

[3] *Ibid.*, p. 319.

[4] *Life of St. Teresa*, p. 114.

[5] L. C. Martin, p. 326.

that it wishes it never would end. . . . At other times, this wound of love seems to issue from the inmost depth of the soul; great are the effects of it; and when our Lord does not inflict it, there is no help for it, whatever we may do to obtain it, nor can it be avoided when it is His Pleasure to inflict it. The effects of those longings after God, so quick and so fine that they cannot be described." [1]

In Crashaw's poems we frequently come across his favourite phrase, "fire of Love" [2]; this expression also occurs in St. Teresa's *Autobiography*. She thinks that every true lover of God must have this fire; accusing the preachers of her day, she remarked "they are not burning with the great fire of love of God, as the Apostles were, casting worldly prudence aside; and so their fire throws out little heat." [3] The "wounds of love," "the fire of love" and "mystical death" are symbolic of various states of mystical experience.

Every critic of Crashaw has tried either to justify "The Weeper" or condemn it as an absurdity of metaphysical conceit. M. Praz has related this poem to the widespread European cult of St. Mary Magdalene; and to the Jesuits' conception of repentance and self-sacrifice. "One of the most typical expressions" of the phenomenon he points out "is the abundant cult of the Magdalene. For the plastic arts as well as in literature this motive renews itself inexhaustibly in the beautiful Sinner, pictured in the flower of her youth, who despoils herself of mundane pomps, and, ungirt and clothed in coarse garb, pours the silver stream of her tears on the feet of the Redeemer, wiping them with the golden river of her hair, the epoch must recognize itself as in a mirror." The technique of expression employed in "The Weeper," as in several other poems, is typically baroque.

Crashaw perhaps found in the *Autobiography of St. Teresa* an evidence of the efficacy of the prayers to St. Mary Magdalene, for she had declared:

"I had a very great devotion to the glorious Magdalene, and used to think of her conversion—especially when I went to communion. As I knew for certain that our Lord was then

---

[1] *Life of St. Teresa*, translated by David Lewis, pp. 427–428.
[2] See L. C. Martin, pp. 326, 327.
[3] *Life of St. Teresa*, p. 118.

within me, I used to place myself at His feet, thinking that my
tears would not be despised. I did not know what I was
saying; only He did great things for me, in that He was
pleased I should shed those tears, seeing that I soon forgot that
impression. I used to recommend myself to that glorious
Saint, that she might obtain my pardon." [1]

Crashaw also refers to the tears and sorrows of the
Magdalene, and, like St. Teresa, he also desires to sit at the
feet of Christ.

> "We go to meet
> A worthy object, our Lord's feet."
>   "The Weeper."

St. Teresa, it is evident, was to Crashaw the ideal type of the
contemplative mystic and she became one of the greatest
shaping influences in his life. It was her mystical experience
of "ecstasy" and "rapture" and sweet "deaths of love" that
aroused the piety and fired the imagination of Crashaw with
the desire to attain the mystic's direct vision of God. He
prays:

> "Lord, when the sense of thy sweet grace
> Sends up my soul to seek thy face,
> Thy Blessed eyes breed such desire,
> I dy in love's delicious Fire." [2]

It has been remarked by Crashaw's critics that his religious
muse is that of ecstasy,[3] but we must remember that ecstasy
has a definite place in Roman Catholic mysticism. A
desire for ecstasy, there is no doubt, lies at the root of our
nature.[4] And Francis Thompson declared that the main
characteristic of Crashaw's religious poetry is "ardorous
abandonment" and "rapturous ethereality,"[5] a quality of
religious lyric in which Crashaw's genius found its supreme
expression. The ".ecstasy" and "rapture" to which Crashaw
constantly alludes in his poems is not "a religious mood,"
as Courthope seems to believe, but is a "state" of mystical
experience, which St. Teresa has also defined: "It is a glorious

---

[1] *St. Teresa's Life*, translated by David Lewis, p. 59. Also see xxi, 9; xxii, 19.
Donne, Herbert and Vaughan also wrote poems on the Magdalene.
[2] L. C. Martin, p. 327: "A Song."
[3] See Courthope, *History of English Poetry*, vol. iii, pp. 222-227, and Gosse,
Seventeenth-century Studies, p. 153.
[4] See *The Dialogue of the Seraphic Virgin, St. Catherine of Siena*, introduction by
Algar Thorold.
[5] *The Works of Francis Thompson*, vol. iii (1914), pp. 175-177.

folly, a heavenly madness, wherein true wisdom is acquired; and to the soul a kind of fruition most full of delight." [1] Ardour, abandonment and the rapturous soaring qualities of Crashaw's lyrics are not literary devices, but expressions of the state of mystical life. [2]

In his description of the mystical experience there is no evidence of self-analysis and self-introspection, which we find in Donne and Herbert; all other religious moods are absorbed in the single mood of joy and thanksgiving.

A careful analysis of the themes of his poetry has shown that he does not give us any intimate account of his own struggles of self-purification and purgation as St. Teresa or St. Augustine or St. John of the Cross have done. St. John of the Cross makes love the motive of purgation. He points out that "in order to overcome our desires and to renounce all those things, our love and inclination for which are wont so to inflame the will that it delights therein, we require a more ardent fire and a nobler love—that of the Bridegroom." [3]

The keynote also of Crashaw's religious passion in its exalted heights is Divine Love; and as he has told us in his "Apologie" for the hymn on St. Teresa it was his "reading" of St. Teresa's works that revealed to him the true conception of this love. She is always relating the real significance of that mystical state when "the flames of that most vehement love of God which His Majesty will have perfect souls to possess." [4]

Crashaw has employed the imagery of the Song of Songs to express the ecstatic state of this divine love:

> "What Joy, what blisse,
> How many Heav'ns at once it is
> To have her God become her Lover." [5]

Canon Beeching says: "The world is justly suspicious of any mixture of compliment with devotion, especially when the devotion is of a type that uses freely the imagery of the Song of

---

[1] *Life of St. Teresa*, p. 114.
[2] For an elucidation of the emblem-motive in the imagery of Crashaw see *Studies in Seventeenth-century Imagery*, by Mario Praz, 1939, pp. 150, 151, 205. He has traced the actual emblems which adorned the manuscripts of *Carmen Deo Nostro*, presented to the Countess of Denbigh, to *Imago Primi Soeculi*, S.J., to Hugo's *Pia Desideria*, to *Amoris divini et humani anti-pathia* and to *Typus Mundi*.
[3] *Mysticism*, by E. Underhill, p. 203.
[4] *Life of St. Teresa*, p. 105.
[5] L. C. Martin, p. 331.

Solomon . . . the temper of the English race, and indeed of
the English language, is against religious rapture of the soul;
and not even the genius of Crashaw has been able to make it
seem other than exotic." [1]

But we must remember that in certain poems Crashaw has
also given a chaste and exalted expression to the power of
Divine Love:

> "Love, thou art Absolute sole Lord
> Of Life & Death." [2]

The supreme example of the use of the imagery of the Song
of Solomon is that of St. Bernard in his sermons, where it is
free from any implications of "sensuous love." St. Bernard
declared: "'*Let Him kiss me with the kisses of His mouth.*' Who
is it speaks these words? It is the Bride. Who is the Bride?
It is the Soul thirsting for God. . . . Of all the sentiments of
nature this of love is the most excellent, especially when it is
rendered back to Him who is the principle and fountain of it—
that is, God." [3]

Evelyn Underhill says: "It was natural and inevitable that
the imagery of human love and marriage should have seemed
to the mystic the best of all images of his own 'fulfilment of
life'; his soul's surrender, first to the call, finally to the embrace
of Perfect Love." [4]

Courthope's remark that no poet except Crashaw "has
depended so exclusively on the amorous imagery and allusion
which inspire the genius of the Pagan Muse" is not justified.[5]
It was not the Pagan Muse which taught Crashaw to express
in terms of ecstatic ardour the mysteries of Divine Love, but
the Christian mystics like St. Teresa, who describing the secrets
of the "Spiritual Marriage" said: "He has thus deigned to
unite Himself to His creature: He has bound Himself to her
as firmly as two human beings are joined in wedlock and will
never separate Himself from her." [6]

But Crashaw does not describe the "spiritual marriage" as

---

[1] Introduction to *Crashaw's Poems*, p. xxxiv.

[2] Martin, *Crashaw*, p. 317. Eric Shepherd says: "Every Catholic should repeat
it each morning. It is a line that stuns the cosmos at one blow," p. 24.

[3] For a discussion of the Mystical Language of St. Bernard see Dom C. Butler,
Western Mysticism, p. 160; also Underhill, *Mysticism*, p. 138.

[4] *Mysticism*, Underhill, p. 136.

[5] *History of English Poetry*, Courthope, vol. iii, p. 222.

[6] *The Interior Castle*, cap. ii.

his own personal experience, it is not the record of his own
illumination:

> "Delicious Deaths; soft exaltations
> Of souls; dear & divine annihilations;
> A thousand Unknown rites
> Of joys & rarefy'd delights." [1]

These lines are charged with infinite suggestion but they do
not reveal the reality of his own actual experience.   We cannot
accept the common definition of a mystic that he is a man who
has fallen in love with God, for the love of God is an essential
element of every religious experience.

If the mystic does not relate to us his own actual experience
we have no evidence to call him a mystic.   The life of an artist
interests us only when it is transformed into the work of art,
but it is not so with the mystic, who is a mystic only because
of the experience he has lived through, which we can only
dimly understand through his writings.   His work is of abiding
value if it is based on his own actual experience, a condition
which is not applicable to the works of imagination.   While
from the artist we demand "concrete expression," as Praz says,
"the mystic's aim, in the words of St. John of the Cross, is a
general obscure contemplation. . . . His supreme confession
is the Sanskrit 'Neti, Neti, Neti!'   'It is not that, it is not that,
it is not that.'" [2]

Though Crashaw is ever describing with admiration
"amorous languishments; luminous trances," [1] he seems to
have known that the supreme experience of the mystic, his
direct vision of God, can with difficulty be translated into the
language of the senses, it is a "dark night" of the soul with a
deep but dazzling light within; for he says:

> "And teach obscure Mankind a more close way
> By the frugall negative light
> Of a most wise & well-abused Night
> To read more legible thine originall Ray." [3]

But this only shows that Crashaw was deeply read in the
mystical literature of his age.   He neither relates it as his own

---

[2] Martin, "Prayer," p. 330.
[3] *Unromantic Spain*, by Mario Praz.
[4] *Ibid.*, p. 259; this attitude might have led Crashaw, if he had lived longer, to
that "discipline" of the self which is essential for the mystic to attain illumination.

personal experience nor does he try to analyse it as such;
as Professor Grierson says: "One cannot speak of Crashaw
as a mystic, for mysticism implies thought—and Crashaw does
not think, he accepts." [1]

He accepts the experience of such great mystics as St.
Teresa or St. Thomas Aquinas. Though Crashaw never
seems to have enjoyed "ecstasy" or illumination, he does
express in poetry his own experience of the love of God.
Crashaw knew by the strength of his own experience of
"conversion" that God woos the human soul. He says,
"Man is alone wo'ed," and asks the Countess of Denbigh to
"yield to his siege," [2] and he gives us an accurate and abstract
conception of "mystic love" which is beyond the possibility
of description:

> "Words which are not heard with Eares
> (Those tumultuous shops of noise).
> Effectual whispers, whose still voice
> The soul itself more feeles than heares." [3]

St. Teresa also says that Love to make itself known requires
no words. Describing the "Way of Understanding," she
points out that "it is our Lord's will in every way that the soul
should have some knowledge of what passes in heaven; and I
think that, as the blessed there without speech understand one
another—I never knew this for certain till our Lord of His
goodness made me see it." [4]

Crashaw never tells us what God in his goodness made him
see. He strikes a personal note in his translation of St. Thomas'
"Hymn in Adoration of the Blessed Sacrament":

> "Down, down, proud sense! discourses dy,
> Keep close my soul's inquiring eye!"

He perhaps has given us his own first-hand experience of
"Conversion" in "Councel":

> "Thence he might toss you
> And strike your troubled heart
> Home to himself; to hide it in his breast
> The bright ambrosiall nest,
> Of Love, of life, & everlasting rest." [5]

---

[1] *Cross-Currents in English Literature of the Seventeenth Century*, Oxford, 1929, p. 182.
[2] Martin, "Against Irresolution," p. 350.
[3] *Ibid.*, "Prayer," p. 330.
[4] *Life of St. Teresa*, p. 213.   [5] L. C. Martin, p. 333.

This is an account of the spiritual state of conversion and not of the mystical experience of illumination, which is nothing but a direct and intimate though momentary vision of God.

Crashaw, however, is a great devotional poet; he has given supreme expression to the moods of religious ecstasy in English lyric; there is human tenderness and the fire of the lover of God which informs his divine poems and distinguishes them from the conventional forms of the Anglican sacred poetry with its "solemn aloofness from celestial things." He knows how to express in exquisite imagery, and soft musical cadences, the ardour, the rapture and the exaltation of Divine Love, and it has a ring of deep, sincere and authentic understanding of the almost inaccessible heights of mystical life.

CHAPTER V

HENRY VAUGHAN, THE MYSTIC

It has been declared by critics that Donne was an anguished, tortured and troubled soul who never knew the inner unification so essential for the peace and felicity of the true mystic; that Herbert was an ascetic more concerned with the practical piety of religious life than with the ardour and exaltation of mystical faith; but Henry Vaughan has been recognized as a mystic *par excellence*. Canon Beeching has even asserted that Vaughan's rank as a poet is determined by the quality of his mysticism. "Herbert was an ascetic, Vaughan a mystic. And it is undoubtedly the mystical element in Vaughan's writing by which he takes rank as a poet."[1] Hodgson has said: "If ever an Anglo-Catholic mystic existed after the Reformation, Henry Vaughan was one."[2] Professor Grierson has also emphasized the mystical quality of this thought: "Vaughan is a less effective preacher, a far less neat and finished artist than Herbert. His temper is more that of a mystic."[3]

But we must remember that Vaughan was a specialist in experience which he could only suggest in his poetry through nature symbolism, by the sudden illumination of a conceit, by the help of analogies drawn from Christian mysticism, Neo-Platonism and Hermetic physics; it is because he succeeded in communicating to us the ardour, the felicity and the nature of this mystical experience that we chiefly value him as a poet. But there are critics, like Mr. W. A. Lewis Bettany, who do not consider Vaughan a mystic because there is no "ecstasy" and "rapture" in his poetry; he says: "Yet when all is said, he cannot be deemed a true mystic. His bent was towards speculation and vision, scarcely towards ecstasy and

---

[1] Introduction to *Poems of Henry Vaughan*, ed. E. K. Chambers (1896), p. xli.
[2] *English Mystics*, by G. E. Hodgson, p. 226.
[3] Introduction to *Metaphysical Lyrics*, p. xlv.

rapture." [1] This is an amazing statement, for even "ecstasy" and "rapture," which are mystical states, ultimately lead to "vision."

Richard Garnett characterized Vaughan's mysticism as Pantheism: "Perhaps this may be best expressed if we define Herbert as theistic, and Vaughan as Pantheistic." [2]

The difference of opinion among critics about the nature of Vaughan's mysticism is due to the various conceptions of mysticism held by these critics; Garnett calls Vaughan a pantheist, but still considers him an orthodox mystic: "Herbert is devout according to recognized method, Vaughan is a devout mystic. Herbert visits the spiritual world as a pious Pilgrim, but Vaughan is never out of it." [2]

Underhill has pointed out that the rich diversity in the religious experience of the mystics cannot be reduced to a rigid formula: "This central fact, it seems to me, is an overwhelming consciousness of God, and of his own soul: a consciousness which absorbs or eclipses all other centres of interest. . . . Hence we must put first among our essentials the clear conviction of a living God as the primary interest of consciousness and of a personal self capable of communion with Him. Having said this, however, we may allow that the widest latitude is possible in the mystic's conception of his Deity. At best this conception will be symbolic; his experience, if genuine, will far transcend the symbols he employs." [3]

This definition is elastic enough to include such diverse mystics as Plotinus, who experienced God as the "bare pure one"; St. Augustine, who called Him "Perfect Beauty," "old yet new," and Ruysbroeck, who discovered that He was the "abyss of fathomless beatitude where the Trinity of divine persons possess their nature in essential unity." Underhill says that "we cannot refuse the title of mystic to any of these; because in every case their aim is union between God and soul. This is the one essential of mysticism, and there are as many ways from one term to the other as there are variations in the spirit of man." [4]

---

[1] Introduction to *Silex Scintillans*, by W. A. Lewis Bettany (1905), p. xxviii.
[2] *Dictionary of National Biography*.
[3] *The Essentials of Mysticism*, E. Underhill, pp. 2, 3.
[4] *Ibid.*, p. 6.

Vaughan had a vivid and sublime consciousness of God and his own self, and his aim, like that of the true Christian mystic, was to attain the union with God through the redemptive grace of Christ and the usual Christian method of Purgation, Penance and Illumination.   Though Vaughan saw the Spirit of God working in Nature as in Man, he knew only one way "to climb" to God, and it was the Way of Christ:

> "But now since we to *Sion* came
> And through thy bloud thy glory see,
> With filial confidence we touch ev'n thee;
> And where the other mount all clad in flame,
>   And threatening clouds would not so much
>   As 'bide the touch
> We climb up this, and have too all the Way
>   Thy hand our stay.
> Nay, thou tak'st ours, and (which full Comfort brings)
> Thy Dove too bears us on her sacred wings." [1]

The first volume of Vaughan's poems, entitled *Poems with the Tenth Satyr of Juvenal Englished, by Henry Vaughan, gent*, appeared in 1646; these were the secular poems of a young man, some in the manner of Donne; the second volume of the secular verse, *Olor Iscanus*, appeared in 1651 (though the dedication to Lord Kildare Digby bears the date 1647).   This volume perhaps contains the poems which, as Thomas Vaughan tells us, the author intended to destroy.   The first edition of *Silex Scintillans* appeared in 1651, and the second, with the enlarged and rich second part, in 1655.   The two important prose works which contain his meditations also appeared during this period, *The Mount of Olives or Solitary Devotions*, 1652—this also contains "Man in Glory" and "Flores solitudinis"—with the *Life of Paulinus* in 1654; the last volume of his poems, *Thalia Rediviva*, was published by one of his friends, who signs himself as J. W., in 1678.   It is thus evident that the period when Vaughan composed his important poems and prose treatises lies roughly between 1650–55, there being only a few important sacred poems in *Thalia Rediviva* (1678).   There is no chronological order of the poems in the original editions, nor has any of his modern critics attempted to arrange them in the probable order in which they were composed, but, as we shall see, the

[1] *The Law and the Gospel*, vol. ii, p. 465—all the quotations are from L. C. Martin's edition of the *Works of H. Vaughan*, 2 vols., Oxford, 1914.

various stages of mystical life can easily be traced in his poems.[1]

In order to understand the significance of Vaughan's mystical experience, and define clearly the nature of his mysticism, we must bear in mind the two great influences in his early life, the influence of George Herbert, and the influence of the Civil Wars, for both of these influences deepened his religious life and helped him to withdraw into himself to communicate with Nature and the God of Nature. As he tells us, he concentrated all the spiritual energies of his soul on its "secret growth":

> "Then bless thy secret growth, nor catch
> At noise, but thrive unseen and dumb;
> Keep clean, bear fruit, earn life and watch
> Till the white Reapers come!"[2]

Though the influence of the religious verse of Donne largely descended through George Herbert, Vaughan did not escape the direct influence of Donne, which is evident in his secular poems and also in the use of conceits and the subtlety of thought in his devotional poetry. In Vaughan's first poems, published in 1646, addressed "to all Ingenious Lovers of Poesie," the influence of Donne is felt not only in the direct imitation of his conceits and mannerisms, but also in the management of conceits and the argumentative structure of his love poems. The lines "To Amoret gone from Him" betray the influence of Donne:

> "If creatures then that have no sense
> But the loose tye of influence,
> Though fate, and time each day remove
> Those things that element their love
> At such vast distance can agree
> Why, Amoret, why should not wee?"

In "An Elegy" we come across such lines in the manner of Donne as:

> "And prove
> In them the Metempsychosis of Love."

But most obvious and direct borrowing from Donne appears in Vaughan's poem "To Amoret, of the difference, twixt him,

---

[1] For a fuller bibliography of the works of Henry Vaughan see E. K. Chambers, Preface to the *Poems of Henry Vaughan*, vol. ii, pp. lvii–lxiii.
[2] "The Seed growing secretly," vol. ii, p. 511.

and other Lovers, and what true Love is." In "A Valediction: forbidding Mourning," Donne had used the famous metaphysical conceit of the lovers having attained such a perfect state of the union of souls that "absence" and "distance" had no effect on them:

> "Dull sublunary lovers love
> (Whose soul is sense) can not admit
> Absence, because it doth remove
> Those things which elemented it.
>
> But we by love, so much refin'd
> That ourselves know not what it is,
> Inter-assured of the mind,
> Care lesse, eyes, lips, and hands to misse."

Vaughan employed this conceit in his poem "To Amoret of the Difference 'twixt him, and other Lovers":

> "Just so base, sublunarie Lovers hearts
>   Fed on loose prophane desires,
>   May for an Eye,
>   Or face comply:
> But those removed, they will as soone depart,
>   And shew their Art,
>   And painted fires.
> Whilst I by pow'rfull Love, so much refin'd,
>   That my absent soule the same is,
>   Carelesse to misse,
>   A glaunce or kisse,
> Can with those Elements of lust and sence
>   Freely dispence
>   And court the mind." [1]

Vaughan's modification of the conceit shows that there is not the passion, subtlety and vigour of Donne; the argumentative evolution of thought is also absent, and its place has been taken by the didactic element; Donne calls the "sublunary lovers" "dull" but their love is not "loose prophane desires," and the mystery and wonder of love—"that ourselves we know not what it is"—is also absent from Vaughan's poem.

Vaughan informs us that though his love poetry "may warme the Bloud, the fire at highest is but Platonick, and the commotion, within these limits, excludes Danger"; but it is a Platonism not of Spenser but of Donne, and has been saturated with the quality of Donne's passion as revealed in

---

[1] Martin, i, p. 12.

the use of sensuous and complex images employed in poems like "The Lampe" and "The Charnel House":

> "Come see your dissolution, and weigh
> What a loath'd nothing you shall be one day,
> As th' Elements by Circulation passe
> From one to th'other, and that which first was
> Is again, so 'tis with you."

Though Vaughan turned to Herbert as a master of "Sacred Verse," the influence of Donne is felt in Vaughan's interest in the scientific discoveries and speculations of his age, in the theories about the pre-existence of the soul and its relation to God, in his belief in the resurrection of the body and the soul alike, and above all in the metaphysical cast of his thought and manner of handling the bold images and conceits about Eternity, Life, and mystical experience. Vaughan's preface to *Silex Scintillans* is really an attack upon all secular poetry of his day, "those ingenious persons, which on the late times are termed wits"; and when he repudiated his own secular poems, and desired that "if the world will be so charitable, as to grant my request, I do here most humbly and earnestly beg that none would read them," he naturally went for imitation and instruction to Herbert, who did not waste his genius in composing love poems full of "lewdness and impieties." Vaughan was not in favour of a strict censorship of published books, but what he desired was a dedication of the muse to Christ rather than to Apollo:

"The suppression of this pleasing and prevailing evil, lies not altogether in the power of the Magistrate: for it will flie abroad in Manuscripts, when it fails of entertainment at the press. The true remedy lies wholly in their bosoms, who are gifted persons, by a wise exchange of vain and vitious subjects, for Divine Themes and celestial praise."

And when he resolved to follow the counsel given in the above passage he saw the shining example of Herbert, who had dedicated all his poetic powers to God and His Church. In "The Author's Preface" he generously acknowledged that his conversion was due to the example and genius of Herbert: "The first that with any effectual success attempted a *diversion* of this foul and overflowing *stream*, was the blessed man, *Mr. George Herbert*, whose holy *life* and *verse* gained many pious

Converts (of whom I am the least) and gave the first check to a most flourishing and admired *wit* of his time." Vaughan declared that most of the imitators of Herbert were unworthy of the master, for "they had more *fashion* than *force*," and that their poetry was not the intimate record of their own religious experience, "for not flowing from a true, practick piety, it was impossible they should effect those things abroad, which they never had acquaintance with at home; being onely the productions of a common spirit, and the obvious ebullitions of that light humour, which takes the pen in hand out of no other consideration, then to be seen in print." [1] Vaughan makes a truly holy life a condition of writing great devotional poetry: "but he that desires to excel in this kinde of Hagiography, or holy writing, must strive (by all means) for perfection and true holyness, that a door may be opened to him in heaven, Rev. iv. 1, and then he will be able to write (with *Hierotheus* and Holy *Herbert*) A true Hymn." This passage is important in this respect, that it shows not only Vaughan's attitude towards contemporary religious poets but also the spirit in which he himself wrote his devotional poems, it being a record of his own experience of God—he had seen the things that were in "heaven" before he could write of them. He calls Herbert "holy" and it seems that his influence on Vaughan was not only literary but also spiritual. Vaughan referred again to the holy life of Herbert in a passage in his prose meditation "Man in Darkness": "We have had many blessed Patterns of a holy life in the *British Church*, though now trodden underfoot and branded with the title of *Anti-Christian*"; and referring to Herbert in the marginal notes he continues: "I shall propose but one to you, the most obedient Son that ever his *Mother* had, and yet a most glorious true *Saint* and a *Seer*. Heark how like a *busie bee* he *hymns* it to the *flowers*, while in a handful of *blossome* gathered by himself, he foresees his own *dissolution*." [2] The relation in which Vaughan stands to Herbert has become a problem in itself. Mr. Lyte, Archbishop Trench, Dr. Grosart, all have taken sides either with Herbert or Vaughan. Dr. Grosart asserted that "I limit Vaughan's debt to Herbert wholly to spiritual quickening, and the gift of

[1] Martin, vol. ii, p. 391.
[2] "Man in Darkness," L. C. Martin, vol. i, p. 186.

gracious feeling; more than that is profoundly exaggerated."
Vaughan's editors, like Beeching, E. K. Chambers and L. C.
Martin, have pointed out the parallels which exist between
Herbert's and Vaughan's poems, while a fuller and comprehensive list of parallels is given by W. A. Lewis Bettany in his
edition of *Silex Scintillans*. He calls Vaughan a "deliberate
plagiarist," and remarks that "the really significant features of
resemblance between Herbert and Vaughan are to be discovered in that parallelism of phrase and of conceit which
can be seen right through the *Temple* and *Silex Scintillans*, a
parallelism so continuous and so close as to leave the reader
no alternative save to regard the younger poet as the elder's
deliberate Plagiarist." [1] We must, however, remember that
in the seventeenth century literary plagiarism was not considered to be a "crime" as it is in our own day, for it did
not entail any financial loss to the poets, there being no
copyright; moreover, in spite of his indebtedness to Herbert
in the choice of themes and conceits, and even in the
titles of poems (he borrowed twenty-eight titles of Herbert's
poems), we value him primarily for things which are peculiar
to his own genius. He is less didactic than Herbert and is
more mystical; though a devout churchman in private life,
his poetry does not belong to any single communion, while
Herbert is the typical Anglican poet who discovered in the
ritual and ceremonies of his Mother Church the satisfaction
of the æsthetic side of his devotional temperament. Herbert's
ideal is the beauty in holiness, and beauty in order, enjoined
by the National Church and sanctioned by the State, but
Vaughan, as Professor Dowden said, "is the poet of what cannot be methodized—the incalculable beams and irradiation
of the soul, the incalculable wind that blows where it listeth;
his garden is watered by the sudden shower and the invisible
dew." [2] Herbert in "Church Porch" and Vaughan in "Rules
and Lessons" gave their respective precepts about moral life,
and these poems reveal the religious temperament of both
the poets. While to Herbert private prayer is a "brave
design," he prefers public prayers to it:

[1] Introduction to *Silex Scintillans*, by W. A. Lewis Bettany, p. xxxv.
[2] *Puritan and Anglican Studies in Literature*, by Edward Dowden, p. 121.

"Though Private prayer be a brave design
Yet Public hath more promises, more love;
And love's a weight to hearts, to eies a signe.
We all are but cold suitours; let us move
Where it is warmest; leave thy six and seven;
Pray with the most; for where most pray, is Heaven." [1]

Vaughan recognizes the necessity of the larger communion between Nature, Man and God; to him the hour of prayer is before dawn, when there are "set, awful hours 'twixt heaven and us." Vaughan's prayer is a mystical communion between Man and God; but a man who is conscious of the glory of the created universe:

"Walk with thy fellow creatures; note the *hush*
And *whispers* amongst them. There's not a *Spring*
Or *Leaf* but hath his *Morning hymn*. Each *Bush*
And *Oak* doth know *I AM*."

Vaughan's poetry is of the "seed growing secretly" and flowering into a vision of God. We have dealt with the nature and extent of the influence of George Herbert on Vaughan; we now come to the second important influence at this period of his life which deepened his religious consciousness.

The influence of the Civil Wars consists in the spiritual agony which the defeat of the ideals of the High Church Party inflicted upon him; and what is important is the fact that the influence of George Herbert and that of the Civil Wars coincided. He says in his Latin poem "Ad Posteros" that when the Civil Wars shattered his hope of a worldly career he came under the influence of Herbert:

"... then I went
To learned Herbert's kind encouragement,
Herbert, the Pride of our Latinity;
Six years with double gifts he guided me,
Method and love, mind and hand conspired,
Nor ever flagged his mind, nor his hand tired.
This was my shaping season; but the times
In which it fell were torn with public crimes;
I lived when England against England waged
War, and the Church and State like furies raged." [2]

By the days of Vaughan's youth the Anglican Church had acquired a permanent character after the disruption of the

---

[1] "The Church Porch," lxvii.
[2] "To After Ages," *On the Poems of Henry Vaughan*, by Edmund Blunden, p. 9.

Reformation; uniformity in doctrine and ritual had been achieved, and she had devoted and learned sons to expound and uphold her system, and idealize her ceremonies; under Laud the ideals of beauty in holiness, and stately and elaborate ritual had given a catholic character to the Church. The English Church in the sixteenth and seventeenth centuries produced her greatest divines, like Parker, Jewell, Hooker, Donne and Laud, Lancelot Andrewes and Jeremy Taylor; and a great and distinguished line of devotional poets, like George Herbert, Henry Vaughan and Thomas Traherne. In the Civil Wars the unity of national ideals which had been attained in the Church and State was destroyed. All that men like Vaughan, ardent Royalists and devout High Churchmen, considered sacred and significant was lost; the King and his Archbishop both had been executed; an epoch had ended. Barrett Wendell has pointed out that "when Puritanism sought to remould the laws and rights of England into those new forms which it believed, and sanctioned by the Divine right set in Scripture and interpreted by the Saints, it was met by an equally unbending determination that those laws and rights should rather be reduced to other new forms, proclaimed and sanctioned by the divine right inherent in the King. Two doctrines in the Church as well as the State arrayed themselves, and in the ensuing strife between the King and Parliament, and between the Puritans and Anglicans, the disruption of the national life was completed." [1]

Vaughan's sensitive and delicately attuned mind was deeply affected by this vast "disruption," but his affliction under the Puritan régime was mainly spiritual, he was not concerned with the political aspects of the great controversy.

In his "A Prayer in Time of Persecution and Heresie" he says: "Most Glorious and Immortall God, the Prince of Peace, Unity and Order, which makest men to be of one mind in a house, heale I beseech thee these present sad breaches and distractions! Consider, O Lord, the tears of thy Spouse which are daily upon her cheeks, whose adversaries are grown mighty, and her enemies prosper. The wayes of Zion do mourne, our beautiful gates are shut up and the Comforter that should relieve our Souls is gone far from us. Thy service and thy

---

[1] *The Temper of the Seventeenth Century in English Literature*, p. 250.

Sabbaths, thy own sacred Institutions and the pledges of thy love are denied unto us; Thy Ministers are trodden down and the basest of the people are set up in thy holy place." [1]

He seems to have witnessed at close quarters the misery and savage cruelty of the Civil Wars, and it left a deep and abiding impression on his mind. Critics disagree about whether Vaughan ever actually fought in the Civil Wars, but there are lines in his poem "To Mr. Ridsley" which suggest that, like his brother, Thomas Vaughan, he also enlisted in the Royalist army.

> "When this juggling fate
> Of soldiery first seiz'd me."

And further remembers,

> "That day, when we
> Left craggy Biston and the fatal Dee."

In his "Elegy on Mr. R. W.," who fell in the battle of Rowton Heath (September 24, 1645), he describes the death of his friend in a manner which suggests that he was also present at the battlefield:

> ". . . O that day
> When like the *Fathers* in the *Fire* and *Cloud*
> I mist thy face!" [2]

On the other hand, in one of his Latin poems he definitely says that he took no part in actual fighting:

> "But, Honour led me, and a pious heart:
> In this great ravenous heat I had no part;
> It was my faith, that guiltless blood will cry
> Aloud, and has a power which does not die."

Vaughan seems to have a Christian horror of shedding blood, to which he gave a passionate expression in his poem "Abel's blood"; and in one of his prayers in *The Mount of Olives* he again said: "I know, O my God, and I am daily taught by that disciple whom thou didst love, that no murderer hath eternal life abiding in him. Keep me therefore, O my God, from the guilt of blood, and suffer me not to stain my soul with the thoughts of recompense and vengeance, which is a branch of thy great prerogative, and belongs unto thee." [3]

[1] *The Mount of Olives*, in *Solitary Devotions*, Martin, i, p. 166.
[2] *Olor Iscanus*, Martin, i, p. 50.
[3] *Works of Henry Vaughan*, L. C. Martin, i, p. 167.

Miss Morgan's suggestion that Vaughan was present at Rowton Heath not as a combatant but in the capacity of a physician seems plausible,[1] whether he actually bore arms or not is not after all an important fact; that he revolted against the tyranny of war and the spiritual emptiness of the Puritan régime is a fact that cannot be denied, and it alone is of significance to the students of his mind and art. He saw his friends and relations falling on battlefields, his brother ejected from his living at Llansanffread, and he found churches defiled and the Anglican ritual prohibited and ridiculed, but there is a strange dignity and calm in his protest against the régime of the usurpers. He saw "Princes brought to their graves by a new way, and the highest order of humane honours trampled upon by the lowest,"[2] and he cried out like an ancient prophet: "*Arise O God, and let thine enemies be scattered, and let those that hate thee flee before thee. Behold, the robbers are come into thy Sanctuary, and the persecuters are within thy walls. . . . Our necks are under persecution, we labour and have no rest. Yea, thine own Inheritance is given to strangers, and thine own portion unto aliens.*" [3]

Vaughan in the midst of persecution and misery prayed to God to give him strength to forgive his enemies in the true Christian way: "Though they persecute me unto death, and pant after the very dust upon the heads of thy poore, though they have taken the bread out of the children's mouth, and have made me a desolation, yet Lord give me thy grace, and such a measure of charity as may fully forgive them. Suffer me not to open my mouth in Curses but give me the spirit of my Saviour, who reviled not again, but was dumb like a Lamb before his shearers." [4]

He had prayed God in "The Men of War" to give him "humility and peace":

> "Give me humility and peace
> Contented thoughts, innoxious ease,
> A sweet, revengeless, quiet mind,
> And to my greatest haters, kind." [5]

And these virtues he was to find in the solitary countryside

---

[1] E. Blunden thinks he took part in the fighting.
[2] "Man in Darkness," Martin, i, pp. 170, 171.
[3] Martin, i, p. 166.
[4] *The Mount of Olives*, Martin, i, p. 167.
[5] "The Men of War," Martin, ii, p. 517.

near the Usk, where he was to commune in an undisturbed
way with Nature and the God of Nature:

> "But rural shades are the sweet sense
>   Of piety and innocence
>   They are the meeks calm region, where
>   Angels descend and rule the sphere." [1]

Vaughan's awakening of self, or conversion, was the outcome
of a real and acute struggle which has left its mark on his
poetry. The actual date of his conversion, when he renounced
the pleasures of the world and resolved to dedicate his life
to God, is not known. It is probable that it took place
during the period between December 1647, the date of the
dedication of *Olor Iscanus*, and the publication of the first
part of *Silex Scintillans* in 1650, when Vaughan tried to suppress
all his early poems, which Thomas Vaughan later printed
in 1651, without his approval. *"Here is a Flame,"* declared
Thomas Vaughan, *"hath been sometimes* extinguished: *Thoughts
that have been* lost and forgot, but now they break out
again like the Platonic eminiscencie. *I have not the Author's*
Approbation *to the* Fact, *but I have* Law *on my* side, *though never*
a sword: *I hold it no man's* praerogative *to* fire *his* own
House." [2]

Besides the influence of Herbert and of the Civil Wars,
two other important influences at this period seem to have
quickened the already awakened sense of the new values of
spiritual life: (1) his conversion and the dedication of self to
Christ, and (2) the effect of a long and serious illness.

Vaughan seems to have early received some sign of favour
from Christ, and this was really the cause of his conversion. In
The Garland he has told us the story of his conversion. In his
"youthfull, sinfull age" he had drowned himself in worldly
pleasures:

> "I sought choice bowers, haunted the spring,
>   Cull'd flowers and made me posies:
>   Gave my fond humours their full wing,
>   And crown'd my head with Roses." [3]

But at the height of "this Careire" of pleasure a strange experience befell him which changed his whole attitude towards
life:

---

[1] "Retirement," Martin, ii, p. 642: *Choice Poems on Severale Occasions.*
[2] The Publisher to the Reader.   [3] *The Garland*, ii, 492, 493.

> "I met with a dead man,
> Who noting well my vain Abear,
> Thus unto me began:
> Desist fond fool, be not undone,
> What thou hast cut to-day
> Will fade at night, and with this Sun
> Quite vanish and decay." [1]

Various explanations have been given by critics as to what Vaughan meant by "dead man," [2] but it seems quite probable that he is referring here to Christ.

In his dedicatory "Epistle to Jesus Christ," prefixed to *Silex Scintillans*, he definitely ascribes his conversion to the love of Christ, to his "all-quickening" touch of compassion and mercy:

> "Some drops of thy all-quickening blood
> Fell on my heart; those made it bud
> And put forth thus, though Lord, before
> The ground was curst, and voide of store." [3]

And this experience of the love of Christ he assigns in his epistle to the period of his "sinful youth." [3] Thus his "conversion" took place early in life, and may account for his revulsion against love-poetry.

Vaughan has referred to his illness, which seems to have been a long and serious one, in his preface to *Silex Scintillans*: "*I was nigh unto death*, and am still at no great distance from it; which was the necessary reason for that solemn and accomplished *dress*, you will now finde this *impression* in. *But the God of the spirits of all flesh*, hath granted me a further use of mine, then I did look for in the *body*; and when I expected and had (by his assistance) prepared for a *message* of *death*, then did he *answer* me with *life*; I hope to his *glory*, and my great *advantage*." [4]

An acute illness of this kind was afterwards associated in Vaughan's mind with the purgation and the cleansing of self; such sickness to him was "wholesome," and with reference to the sickness of blessed Paulinus he wrote: "this sickness was a pure stratagem of love; God visited him with it for this very

---

[1] *The Garland*, ii, 492, 493.
[2] It has been suggested that he is either referring to the death of a friend which he has celebrated in several poems, beginning "Fair and young light" (ii, 513), or that beginning "Thou that know'st for whom I mourne" (ii, 416), or to his own spiritual death; see the poems "The Obsequies" and "Death."
[3] Martin, ii, pp. 394, 395.
[4] *Ibid.*, p. 392.

purpose, that He himself might be his Cordial." [1]   And in
several poems in *Silex Scintillans* we find Vaughan referring to
his illness again, which he regarded as a form of purgation.
He says in "Begging":

> "Dear Lord! restore thy ancient peace,
> Thy quick'ning friendship, man's bright wealth!
> And if Thou wilt not give me ease
> From sickness, give my spirit health!" [2]

But whatever might have been the cause of his conversion,
the fact remains that it was *final* and it influenced his whole
outlook on life, and made him seek God with the sincerity and
earnestness characteristic of all great mystics. With the
awakening of the self came to Vaughan an agonizing sense of
sin, and the realization of the worthlessness and waste of his
youth spent in the pursuit of worldly pleasures and ambitions.
He calls upon his heart to awake, which has lain dead for all
these years, to the need of purgation and repentance:

> "Come my heart! come my head
> In sighes and teares!
> 'Tis now, since you have laine thus dead
> Some twenty years;
>   Awake, awake,
>   Some pitty take
>   Upon yourselves—
> Who never wake to grone, nor weepe,
> Shall be sentenc'd for their sleepe." [3]

Underhill has pointed out that in conversion "the self
awakes to that which is within, rather than to that which is
without: to the Immanent not the Transcendent God, to the
personal not the cosmic relation." [4]   Vaughan sees deep into
himself and realizes the need of purification before he could
enter into a life which is "newness in Christ":

> "Prepare, prepare me then, O God!
>   And let me now begin
> To feele my loving father's *Rod*
>   Killing the man of Sinne!" [5]

He recognizes the need of spiritual affliction for the purification
of the self:

---

[1] *Life of Blessed Paulinus*, Martin, i, p. 356.   [2] "Begging," vol. ii, p. 501.
[3] "The Call," ii, p. 416.   [4] *Mysticism*, E. Underhill, p. 237.
[5] "The Day of Judgement," ii, p. 403.

> "Thus by the Crosse salvation runnes,
>   Affliction is a mother,
> Whose painfull throes yield many sons,
>   Each fairer than the other." [1]

Thus Vaughan recognizes the need of faith and considers the grace of Christ essential for purification and illumination of the self:

> "Three things I'de have, my soules chief health!
>   And one of these seme loath,
> A living FAITH, a HEART of flesh
>   The WORLD an Enemie
> This last will keepe the first two fresh,
>   And bring me, where I'de be." [2]

He recognizes that a steady heart, holiness and purity of life, and the mercy of Christ are necessary for those who travel on the Mystic Way:

> "Then make my soule white as his owne,
>   My faith as pure, and steddy,
> And deck me, Lord, with the same Crowne
>   Thou hast crowned him already!" [1]

Vaughan knows that the Mystic Way is a long and arduous way beset with difficulties, and only men of pure faith and iron determination can hope to reach the goal:

> "   . . . The night
> Is dark, and long;
> The Rode foul, and where one goes right,
>   Six may go wrong." [3]

He recognizes the need of following in the footsteps of the Saints of God who are the "shining lights" to guide us on our way to Him:

> "They are (indeed) our Pillar-fires
>   Seen as we go,
> They are that cities shining spires
>   We travell to." [3]

Vaughan tried to discipline his mind as well as the body in the purgative stage, but his asceticism is of the Protestant type, and in his poetry there is no ritualistic grandeur of the Catholic Church. Ernst Troeltsch has pointed out that the Protestant

---

[1] "The Call," Martin, ii, p. 417.
[2] "The Day of Judgement," ii, p. 402.
[3] "Content," ii, p. 423.

acceptance of the world did not preclude the ideal of asceticism. The real problem now became detachment from the world while living in it, and not a withdrawal from life into the quietude of the monastery:

"At bottom, the acceptance of the world does not cease to be an asceticism, that is, denial of the world, only it is a different kind of asceticism from the heroic asceticism of the Church, and it also differs from the legalistic detachment from the world practised by the 'sects.' It is an asceticism in the impulse of the individual conscience. 'Good Works' exist no longer; all that matters is the general spirit and attitude of the individual." [1]

Vaughan does not reject the body, but he prays that his whole personality, body and soul alike, may be transformed through the grace of Christ to taste the real bliss of mystic experience:

"Arise O daughter of Sion, O my soul redeemed with the blood of Christ! sit no more in the dust of thy sins, but arise, and rest in that peace which is purchas'd by the Saviour's merits. Christ Jesus! my most merciful and dear Redeemer! as it is thy meer goodness that lifts up this mortal and burthensome body, so let thy grace lift up my soul to the true knowledge and love of thee; grant also that my body may this day be helper and servant to my soul in all good works, that both body and soul may be partakers of those Endless Joyes, where thou livest, and reignest with the Father and the Holy Ghost, one true God world without End. Amen." [2]

He does not *despise* the world, but he is eager to soar beyond the illusion of natural phenomena, and in this process he rejects reason and rationalism. He found that in worldly wisdom "all is vanity":

> "Those secret searches, which afflict the wise,
> Paths that are hidden from the *Vulturs* eyes,
> I saw at distance, and where grows that fruit
> Which others only grope for and dispute." [3]

He knew that the knowledge of God comes not through intellect and learning, but through faith and mystical illumi-

---

[1] Ernst Troeltsch, *The Social Teaching of the Christian Churches*, vol. ii, p. 471.
[2] *The Mount of Olives*, Martin, i, p. 144.
[3] "The Hidden Treasure," ii, 520.

nation. We must remember that Vaughan found philosophy
and science inadequate to solve the mystery of the universe.
He was eager to know,

> "Who gave the Clouds so brave a bow,
> Who bent the spheres, and circled in
> Corruption with this glorious Ring,
> What is his name, and how I might
> Descry some part of his great light." [1]

He seems to have studied Nature minutely and meditated
long over her multitudinous and mysterious life:

> "I summond Nature: pierc'd through all her store,
> Broke up some seales, which none had touch'd before." [2]

Having discovered nothing to unveil the underlying Reality,
he searched his own heart:

> "To search myselfe, where I did finde
> Traces, and sounds of a strange kind." [2]

He heard the "Echoes beaten from th' eternall hills," but these
were "Weake beames," a glimpse of Reality and not the full-
faced vision of God, and he was "griev'd" that the "little
light I had was gone," and so he realized the truth of the old
paradox that he who shall lose his life shall find it, and the
extinction of self will result in the rebirth of a new and purer
life:

> "At last, said I,
> *Since in these veyls my Ecclips'd eye*
> *May not approach thee, (for at night*
> *Who can have commerce with the light?)*
> *I'le disapparell, and to buy*
> *But one half glaunce, most gladly dye.*" [2]

He realized the truth which every mystic discovers for himself,
that in order to have even a momentary glimpse, all that is
extraneous to the contemplation of God must be stripped of
self. Vaughan laid great emphasis on personal holiness, of
which he had early seen a shining example in George Herbert:

"And as for a regular, sober, holy life; we should in all
places, and at all times labour for it, for *without holiness no man
shall see the face of God*, much less be partaker of His merits, and
by this spiritual eating and drinking become a member of that
body, whose life and head He is." [3]

[1] "Vanity of Spirit," ii, p. 418.   [2] Martin, ii, p. 418.
[3] *The Mount of Olives*, vol. i, p. 159.

This desire for sacramental purity and holiness in the purgative stage is due to an acute consciousness of sin; Vaughan was assailed with the sense of sin and he realized his own unworthiness in the sight of God, which is a way to humility:

> "O what am I, that I should breed
> Figs on a thorne, flowres on a weed!
> I am the gourd of sin, and sorrow
> Growing o'r night, and gone tomorrow," [1]

Even in "Christ's Nativity," when he tries to sing the glory of the "King," he is conscious of his own impure self:

> "I would I had in my best part
> Fit Roomes for thee! or that my heart
>   Were so clean as
>   Thy manger was!
> But I am all filth, and obscene,
> Yet if thou wilt, thou canst make clean." [2]

This phase of purgation is experienced by all mystics. St. Augustine said: "I was swept up to thee by Thy Beauty and torn away from Thee by my own weight." [3] St. Bernard says that contemplation and devotion do not entitle every soul to the Sight of God; but "that Soul only which is shown, by great devotion, vehement desire, and tender affection to be His Bride, and to be worthy that The Word in all His beauty should visit her as a Bridegroom." [4] The cleansing of the self, however, leads to a complete surrender of the soul to the Will of God, the soul lies like passive clay in Divine Hands to be moulded according to His desire and purpose. Vaughan knew that one has to forget the glory of the life of the senses, so that in the dimness of his own self he may have a glimpse of God.

> "I'le seal my eyes up, and to thy commands
> Submit my wilde heart, and restrain my hands;
> I will do nothing, nothing know, nor see
> But what thou bidst, and shew'st and teachest me.
> Look what thou gav'st; all that I do restore
> But for one thing, though purchas'd once before." [5]

---

[1] "Repentance," ii, pp. 448–449.
[2] "Christ's Nativity," ii, 442.
[3] *Confessions*, Book VII, chap. xvii.
[4] Canticle xxxii, 3, quoted by Dom C. Butler, *Western Mysticism*, p. 145.
[5] "The Hidden Treasure," ii, p. 520.

This surrender is the result of humility and the consciousness of the need of grace.

Vaughan tries to build his faith not on the merits of his own work but on the grace of Christ—"So give me grace ever to rest." [1] He thus discourages over-inquisitiveness and curiosity in the mysteries of religion, for it does not help one to become a worthy receiver of grace:

> "Let me thy Ass be onely wise
> To carry, not search mysteries;
> Who carries thee, is by thee lead, ·
> Who argues, follows his own head." [1]

Thus Vaughan is no Nature mystic like Wordsworth, for he realized that he could only apprehend God through the grace of Christ, and that, after having recognized the glory and grandeur of the created universe, one has to seal one's eyes to it. Vaughan clearly recognizes the function of purgation as the purification of self, and surrender to the Will of God, and the transformation of the whole personality for the higher purposes of religious life; but, like all great English mystics, Vaughan has a firm grasp of the practical aspects of the mystical life; and though he is eager to experience a direct vision of God in illumination, he knows that it is only within the bounds of Gospel and Law that Divine love could be crystallized:

> "O Plant in me thy *Gospel*, and thy *Law*,
> Both *Faith* and *Awe*;
> So twist them in my heart, that ever there
> I may as well as *Love*, find too thy *fear*." [2]

Vaughan knows that real purgation is a "baptism in fire," it is the burning away of the dross so that the gold may be refined, it is the annihilation of self so that a new self may emerge. He knows that God sends "dew" as well as "frost" to the soul, and that love and discipline both were necessary for a mystic's life: God knows how to sow His seed in the human heart and the man who has known the ecstasy of a complete "surrender" can only say with Vaughan "blest be thy skill." He recognizes that the affliction which God sends is a training and disciplining of the soul:

---

[1] "The Ass," p. 518.
[2] "The Law and the Gospel," Martin, ii, p. 465.

> "And happy I to be so crost,
> And cur'd by Crosses at thy cost." [1]

Mortification has been defined by E. Underhill as "the positive aspect of purification" which helps the remaking of the self for the higher stages of religious life, in fact it is a preparation for illumination. Unsanctified emotions and undisciplined acts cannot help the soul in realizing the presence of God.

Thomas à Kempis described the true purpose of mortification when he said: "Who hinders thee more than the unmortified affections of thy own heart? . . . if we were perfectly dead unto ourselves and not entangled within our own breasts, then should we be able to taste Divine things, and to have some experience of heavenly contemplation." [2]

Vaughan, like all true mystics, knew that purgation was a disciplining of the self for the bliss of mystical experience. In a thoughtful passage in *The Mount of Olives* he says: "Inlighten my soul, sanctifie my body, govern my affections, and guide my thoughts, that in the fastest closures of my eyelids my spirit may see thee, and in the depth of sleep be conversant with thee." [3] In short, Vaughan realized that the true purpose of self-purification was that Christ may be reborn in the human soul. St. Paul's experience that "yet I live, yet no longer I, but Christ liveth in me," [4] is repeated in the life of every mystic; the "new birth" transforms the whole personality and makes him a "new creature," as St. Paul said: "If any man be in Christ, he is a new creature." It was for this mystic birth of Christ in his soul that Vaughan longed:

> "And let once more by mystick birth
> The Lord of Life be borne in Earth." [5]

Vaughan's body and soul alike pined for the love of Christ, he knew that without Him his life would be meaningless and insignificant; the constant refrain of his poetry and prose meditations is: "Make my soul to thirst for thee, and my flesh also to long after thee." [6]

Having completed the process of purgation, and having realized the true significance of mortification, Vaughan

---

[1] "Love and Discipline," ii, p. 464.   [2] See *Mysticism*, Underhill, p. 261.
[3] *The Mount of Olives*, L. C. Martin, i, p. 152.
[4] Galatians ii, 20 (R.V.).   [5] "Christ's Nativity," ii, p. 442.
[6] L. C. Martin, i, p. 153.

embarked on the third stage of the Mystic Way, "The Illumination of Self." He knew that the soul to be fully disciplined must be refined by fire:

> "O come! refine us with thy fire!
> Refine us! we are at a loss." [1]

After such purgation his spirit was ready to behold God. Vaughan has described his experience of illumination in several poems, such as "Unprofitableness" and "The Check," but the classical description of the joys of illumination after the severe strain of purgation is to be found in "Regeneration." This poem is a symbolical representation of Vaughan's journey on the Mystic Way. Mr. Herbert Read has chosen this poem as characteristic of Vaughan's style, and after quoting the first four stanzas he remarks, "four stanzas, but only two sentences, so admirably controlled in rhythm and construction that we are carried along with a smooth and delightful ease, and yet the meaning is retained." [2] The "delightful" ease of the rhythm does not explain the difficulty inherent in the symbolism of the poem. Symbolism has a definite significance in mysticism; it is true that symbolism is a sign for something which could not be expressed in any other way, but the meaning of the mystic always transcends the symbolism he employs to communicate his experience. He has to contract the majesty and the infinite splendour of his vision in finite words, and the symbols that he uses suggest rather than describe the richness of his mystical experience. St. Catherine of Siena described the difficulty of the communication felt by all mystics when she said: "To explain in our defective language what I saw, would seem to me like blaspheming the Lord or dishonouring Him by my speech; so great is the distance between what the intellect, when rapt and illumined and strengthened by God, apprehends, and what can be expressed by words, that they seem almost contradictory." [3]

A mystic's experience of the eternal is communicated through symbolism and allegory to his fellow-men. Vaughan himself referred to the difficulty of the symbolism he had used in his

---

[1] "Whitsunday," ii, p. 486.   [2] *Phases of English Poetry*, p. 27.
[3] *The Legend of St. Catherine of Siena*, ii, p. 190.

poems like "Regeneration" when in his preface to *Silex Scintillans* he said : "In the *perusal* of it, you will (peradventure) observe some *passages*, whose *history* or *reason* may seem something *remote*; but were they brought *nearer*, and plainly exposed to your view (though that (perhaps) might quiet your *curiosity*) yet would it not conduce much to your greater *advantage*." [1]

The reality of his mystical experience could not be "plainly exposed" to our view, it could only be communicated indirectly through the meaning inherent in his symbols. Illumination is to him a "virgin-soile" which only the friends of God can tread upon, it retains its freshness and wonder for every soul who experiences it :

> "A virgin-soile, which no
> Rude feet ere trod,
> Where (since he stept there) only go
> Prophets, and friends of God." [2]

He suddenly realized that the afflictions of purgation were over; "a new spring" greeted his senses, a new life blossomed forth in his soul :

> "The unthrift sunne shot vitall gold
> A thousand peeces,
> And heaven its azure did unfold
> Checqur'd with snowie fleeces.
> The aire was all in spice,
> And every bush
> A garland wore; Thus fed my Eyes
> But all the Eare lay hush." [3]

He found in the "Fountain" of baptism that some souls were "bright" and "round" and some were "ill shap'd and dull," and as if in a vision he saw the "bank of flowers," where it was midday, and he heard the "Wind" of the Lord rushing through the world. He tried to know its destination—"where it was or where not"—but the wind whispered in reply: "Where I please," for the wind of the Lord bloweth where it listeth,[4] and then suddenly Vaughan prayed for the "death" of ecstasy :

> "Lord then said I, *on me one breath,*
> *And let me dye before my death.*" [5]

It is in the death of ecstasy that "oneness with the Absolute"

[1] Martin, ii, Preface, p. 392.   [2] "Regeneration," ii, p. 397.
[3] Martin, ii, p. 398.   [4] St. John iii, 8.   [5] Martin, ii, p. 399.

is attained. St. Catherine of Siena, describing her condition in this state, says: "The body loses its feeling, so that seeing eyes see not, and hearing ears hear not, and the tongue does not speak . . . the head does not touch and the feet walk not, because the members are bound with Sentiments of Love." [1]   The joys of illumination enabled Vaughan to write some of the finest mystical poems in English literature; there is new energy and directness of expression; even "a single glance" from the Lord gives new life and freshness to the bleak leaves of his life:

> " . . . I flourish, and once more
> Breath all perfumes, and spice;
> I smell a dew like Myrrh, and all the day
> Wear in my bosome a full sun; such store
> Hath one beame from Thy Eys." [2]

He is eager to be so close to God that he may forget the world and only concentrate on mystic contemplation:

> " . . . so Close
> And knit me to thee, That though in this vale
> Of sin, and death I sojourn, yet one Eie
> May look to thee, to thee the finisher
> And Author of my faith." [3]

His experience of God is expressed either through the symbolism of light which is ever present in his conception of God, or he feels Him as sweetness and myrrh:

> " . . . I felt through all my pow'rs
> Such a rich air of sweets, as Evening showrs
> Fan'd by a gentle gale Convey and breath
> On some parch'd bank, crown'd with a flowrie wreath;
> Odors, and Myrrh, and balm in one rich floud
> O'r-ran my heart, and spirited my bloud,
> My thoughts did swim in Comforts, and mine eie
> Confest, *The World did only paint and lie.*" [4]

A joyous sense of the presence of God which is the characteristic of illumination was felt in all its richness by Vaughan. He acknowledges that it was Christ's "art of love" [5] that brought him "home" and showed to him the "Pearl" he had sought elsewhere:

---

[1] *Divine Dialogue*, cap. lxxix, quoted by Underhill, *Mysticism*.
[2] "Unprofitableness," ii, p. 441.   [3] "The Mutinie," ii, p. 468.
[4] *Mount of Olives*, ii, p. 476.   [5] "To the Holy Bible," ii, p. 541.

"Gladness, and peace, and hope, and love,
  The secret favors of the Dove,
  Her quickning kindness, smiles and kisses,
  Exalted pleasures, crowning blisses,
  Fruition, union, glory, life
  Thou didst lead to. . . ." [1]

The richness of Vaughan's experience of illumination was
conveyed to us through the favourite symbolism of light.
Professor Dowden has called him the "Mystic of Light," but
we must remember that the experience of Divine Radiance
flooding the inmost corners of being is common to most of the
mystics. The imagery of Fire and Light enters into their
description of the state of illumination. St. John of the Cross
experienced God as a Fire that burns but heals:

"O burn that burns to heal,
  O more than pleasant wound!
And O soft hand, O touch most delicate
  That dost new life reveal
  That dost in grace abound
And slaying, dost from death to life translate." [2]

St. Teresa described her illumination as an "infused
brightness . . . a light which knows no night; but rather, as
it is always light, nothing ever disturbs it." But the classical
description of illumination is given by Dante in *Paradiso*,
where in exalted vision he becomes united with the Light,
which is Truth itself: "For my sight, becoming pure, was
entering more and more through the ray of that high Light,
which in itself is truth. . . . I believe that, through the keenness that I endured of the Living ray, I should have been lost
if mine eyes had turned aside from it. And I remember that
I was the bolder, for this, to sustain so far that I united my
gaze with the infinite worth. O grace abundant, by which I
presumed to fix my gaze through the eternal Light so far that
I consumed my power of vision therein." [3]

Vaughan saw Eternity as pure and dazzling light, and this
vision revealed to him the true nature of the world:

"I saw Eternity the other night
  Like a great *Ring* of pure and endless light." [4]

---

[1] " To the Holy Bible," ii, p. 541.
[2] St. John of the Cross, *Flama de Amor Viva*, translated by Arthur Symons.
[3] *Paradiso*, xxxiii, translated by T. S. Eliot.
[4] "The World," ii, p. 466.

He sees the "doting lover" with his lute and "his flights," the "darksome statesman" working "underground," using "churches and altars" to further his selfish ends: the "fearful miser" counting his hoards of money; and he also realized that only a few had the capacity to soar "up into the Ring" of immortality, others were content not to use their "Wings," or the latent faculties of the soul which God had given them. After seeing the misery, the folly and the distorted vision of his fellow-men he cries out:

> "O fools (said I,) thus to prefer dark night
> Before true light,
> To live in grots, and caves, and hate the day
> Because it shews the way,
> The way which from this dead and dark abode
> Leads up to God,
> A way where you might tread the Sun, and be
> More bright than he."

While he was thus lamenting the madness of the vast majority of men, someone whispered the truth into his soul that immortality and the radiance of the Ring of eternity were meant only for the adoring and loving souls, "Christ's Bride." [1]

He refers to God as Light in several of his poems. The Angel of Life which came to him with "bright and busie wing" pointed to him a place of Eternal Light:

> "and point me to a place,
> Which all the year sees the Suns face." [2]

Before Christ comforted him, his soul was in agony because he was "no childe of day" [2]; and even before he was blessed with the vision of Eternity as a ring of "pure and endless light" he had already discerned, "through a long night," the "edges" of the dazzling brightness of God:

> "Thy edges, and thy bordering light!
> O for thy Centre and mid day!" [3]

He addresses Christ: "O light of light, the brightnesse of thy Father's glory"; and describing his intimacy with Christ in illumination, in *The Mount of Olives*, he says:

"As long as thou art present with me, I am in the light . . .

---

[1] Called in the Bible the "Children of the Bridegroom."
[2] "The Agreement," ii, p. 528.
[3] "Childe-hood," ii, p. 521.

when thou art present, all is brightnesse, all is sweetnesse, I am in my God's bosome, I discourse with him, watch with him, walk with him, live with him, and lie down with him. All these most dear and unmeasurable blessings I have with thee, and want them without thee. Abide then with me, O thou whom my soul loveth! Thou Sun of righteousness with healing under thy wings arise in my heart; refine, quicken, and cherish it; make thy light there to shine in darknesse, and a perfect day in the dead of night." [1]

To him the greatest bliss of the mystic is that the glorious sun "never setteth, but is alwaies at the height, full of brightness and consolation" [1]; and the greatest misery of the wicked is that a "heavie night sits in the noone-day upon those souls," and that "they look for light, and behold darkness; for brightnesse, and they walk in obscurity." [1]

St. Augustine in his *Confessions* has described, with his usual insight into the psychology of mystical experience, the nature of this Light often beheld by the mystics:

"I entered, and beheld with the mysterious eye of my soul the Light that never changes, above the eye of my soul, above my intelligence. It was not the common light which all flesh can see, nor was it greater yet of the same kind, as if the light of day were to grow brighter and brighter and flood all space. It was not this, but different: altogether different from all such things. Nor was it above my intelligence in the same way as oil is above water, or heaven above earth, but it was higher because it made me, and I was lower because made by it. He who knoweth the truth knoweth that Light, and who knoweth it knoweth eternity. Love knoweth it. O eternal Truth, and true Love, and lovable Eternity." [2]

Vaughan, like St. Augustine, knew that he who has seen this Light has seen Eternity, but it was a vision granted only to those who had known Love. St. Augustine says "Love knoweth it"; and Vaughan also points out:

> "*This Ring the Bride-groome did for none provide
> But for his bride.*"

By Eternity the mystic does not mean infinity of time, nor even

---

[1] *The Mount of Olives*, i, p. 151.
[2] St. Augustine's *Confessions*, Book VII, cap. x.

everlasting life [1]; he conceives Eternity as Boëthius did, as "the complete and perfect possession of unlimited life at a single moment"; it is the realization in one supreme moment of life of the eternal "Now," when the true character of illumination is revealed to the mystic. Dante defined the mystic's conception of Eternity when he said: "every *where* and every *when* is brought to a point." [2]

The "light-imagery" is used in the Prologue of the Fourth Gospel, and the mystics have often used it to symbolize their unique personal experience; it is something they have known and felt and have tried to communicate to us through the suggestive richness of the symbolism of Divine Radiance.

In his poem "The Dwelling-Place" Vaughan says, almost like St. Bernard, that he did not know how and when God visited his soul, but the certainty of His visit was beyond doubt, and its memory a cherished possession:

> "My dear, dear God! I do not know
> What lodgd thee then, nor where, nor how;
> But I am sure, thou dost now come
> Oft to a narrow, homely room,
> Where thou too hast but the least part,
> My God, I mean *my sinful heart*." [3]

St. Bernard (in Canticle lxxiv, which is ascribed to the closing years of his life) has described his mystical experience with singular charm and eloquence:

"But although He has frequently entered into my soul, I have never at any time been sensible of the precise moment of His coming. I have felt that He was present. . . . It was not by His motions that he was recognized by me, nor could I tell by any of my senses that He had penetrated to the depths of my being. It was, as I have already said, only by the movement of my heart that I was enabled to recognize His presence, and to know the might of His power by the sudden departure of vices and the strong restraint put upon all carnal affections."

Another characteristic of illumination, the fleeting glimpse of God, which must be differentiated from the unitive stage of mystical experience, is that it is transient and it leaves behind an intense longing for the soul's union with God.

---

[1] For a fuller discussion see Wicksteed, *The Religion of Time and the Religion of Eternity*, pp. 23–25.

[2] *Paradiso*, xxix, 12.   [3] "The Dwelling Place," ii, p. 516.

Vaughan's description of the transiency of illumination
agrees with similar descriptions given by such great mystics
as St. Augustine and St. Bernard. The soul after enjoying a
moment of supreme exaltation of union with God falls back
to its normal state; the pain of separation is acute, in which
longing for a permanent union is present. Vaughan has
described this experience in many poems, as "The Retreate,"
"Content," "The Evening Watch," "The Relapse" and
"Cock-crowing."

> "Come, come, what doe I here?
>   Since he is gone
> Each day is grown a dozen year,
>   And each houre, one;
>   Come, come!" [1]

In "The Relapse" he tells us that it was the love of Christ that
saved his soul; but he is grieved to return to his normal self:

> "Sullen, and sad Ecclipses, Cloudie sphere,
>   These are my due." [2]

When Christ is present all is "brightness," while His absence
brings darkness and eclipses. St. Augustine has described this
state with his usual clarity: "Thy Invisible things, understood
by those that are made, I saw, but I was not able to fix my
gaze thereon; but my infirmity being struck back, I was
thrown again on my normal experience, carrying with me
only a memory that loved and desired what I had, as it were,
perceived the odour of, but was not yet able to feed upon." [3]

In Vaughan this fleeting glimpse of reality found its supreme
expression in his longing for a fuller experience. He, in his
imagination, ever goes back to the hour when God did visit
him:

> "So o'r fled minutes I retreat
>   Unto that hour
> Which shew'd thee last, but did defeat
>   Thy light, and pow'r,
> I search, and rack my soul to see
>   Those beams again." [4]

This phase in the growth of mystical consciousness is the
common experience of all great mystics. St. Bernard remarks:

[1] "The Retreate," ii, p. 420.
[2] "The Relapse," ii, p. 433.
[3] *Confessions*, vii, 23.
[4] "The Evening-Watch," ii, p. 426.

"Then have I felt on a sudden so great a joy and confidence arising in me, that . . . it seemed to me that I was
one of those blessed ones. O that it had lasted longer. Again
and again do Thou visit, O Lord, with thy salvation." [1]

This "Eden" Vaughan saw in Nature, in the Primitive
Church, in the innocence of childhood:

> "The Vally, or the Mountain
> Afforded visits, and still *Paradise* lay
> In some green shade, or fountain." [2]

The blood of Christ and his contact with the world has brought,
in however small a measure, a state of grace which existed
before the Fall, and this grace he saw operative in the life of
the primitive Christians:

"It was a blessed and glorious age the Primitive *Christians*
lived in, *when the wilderness and the solitary places were glad for them,
and the desert rejoiced and blossom'd as the rose.* When the blood
of *Christ* was yet warme with the memory of his *miracles* and
love fresh and vigorous; what *zeale*, what powerful faith, what
perfect *charity*, hearty *humility*, and true *holinesse* was then to be
found upon the earth! If we compare the *shining* and *fervent
piety* of those saints with the *painted* and *illuding appearance* of
it in *these our times*, we shall have just cause to fear that our
candlestick (which hath been now of a long time under a Cloud)
is at this very instant upon removing." [3]

Vaughan's tendency to "retreat" back into Time is not confined to his memory of illumination; he remembers the dawn
of creation, the purity of childhood, the vigour of the Primitive
Church; thus the "time-dimension" was no impediment to
the flight of his imagination. Vaughan's idealization of childhood and the state of innocence before the Fall should be
studied in relation to his conception of Time and Eternity.

Vaughan associated the Fall not with the doctrine of predestination but with the "fall from grace." Like childhood,
the state before the Fall was a state of innocence and purity,
and both were associated in his mind with "time-lessness"
(in the sense that a child has no "consciousness" of Time).
The glimpse of "home" which a child has was in fact related

---

[1] Canticle xxiii, 15.   [2] "Corruption," ii, p. 440.
[3] *The Mount of Olives*, Martin, i, p. 181.

to man's longing afterwards to recover that state of purity and innocence which existed before the Fall. It is to the Fall that Vaughan attributes man's longing for "home," because man

> "Drew the Curse upon the world and Crackt
> The whole frame with his fall.
> This made him long for *home*, as loath to stay
> With murderers, and foes;
> He sigh'd for Eden, and would often say
> *Ah ! what bright days were those.*" [1]

His conception of childhood is quite different from that of Wordsworth, who did not relate the passing away of the glory, or the fading away of the glimpses of the "celestial home," to the Fall or the Christian conception of "grace." He could not find consolation, like Wordsworth, in the strength of the "philosophic mind"; for Vaughan did not think it possible to achieve any philosophic calm without the help of Divine grace. Wordsworth's conception of childhood is purely romantic, and based on the Neo-Platonic theory [2] of the pre-existence of the soul, while Vaughan's idealization of childhood, as a state of innocence and purity, has its roots in the Christian conception of grace. Vaughan, unlike Wordsworth, could not depend on the *philosophic* strength of mind attained through the individual effort alone, unaided and unillumined by the grace of God. Man loses the glimpses of Heaven not because he becomes engrossed in the material things of life, as Wordsworth believed, but because of the *sinfulness* of man (due to the Fall), the consciousness of which grows stronger with years. This is why Vaughan's conception of childhood is closely related to the Fall.

His idealization of childhood as a state of grace has two aspects: he cherished it as an unsullied state of innocence, and he believed that it was through the recovery of this state of grace that man could attain the purity of self again. He

---

[1] "Corruption," ii, p. 440.

[2] Professor L. C. Martin, in his essay "Henry Vaughan and the Theme of Infancy" (*Seventeenth-century Studies presented to Sir Herbert Grierson*), has skilfully traced Vaughan's conception of childhood to the Neo-Platonism of Hermes Trismegistus; but we must remember that the Neo-Platonic theory of the pre-existence of the soul had been refuted by St. Thomas Aquinas, and this theory should not be given the dignity of a Christian doctrine, as Professor Martin seems to have done.

thought that the child still retained some memory of his
celestial home:

> "Wash till thy flesh
> Comes like a child's, spotless and fresh."

He remembers childhood as a time when sin had not yet
invaded his soul and he was happy in "flowry vales, whose
flowers were stars." He could still have a glimpse of "divine
light" in this state of innocence:

> "O then how bright
> And quick a light
> Doth brush my heart, and scatter night;
> Chasing that shade
> Which my sins made,
> While I so *spring*, as if I could not *fade*." [1]

He laments that when we grow up the memory of the Heavenly
Home fades away, sin triumphs, and man cannot pierce
through the veil of appearance to behold Reality:

> "I see, thy Curtains are Close-drawn; thy bow
> Looks dim too in the Cloud," [2]

Man with the triumph of sin becomes "restless and irregular,"
and though he has the memory of his home, he does not know
how to reach there:

> "He knowes he hath a home, but scarce knows where,
> He sayes it is so far
> That he hath quite forgot how to go there." [3]

Vaughan, following the ideas of Plato in *Phaedrus*, says that in
order to reach home we must travel back:

> "O how I long to travell back
> And tread again that ancient track." [4]

He does not praise the child as the " seer " and " prophet," but
idealizes the innocence of his spirit and his nearness to God:

> "Happy those early days, when I
> Shin'd in my Angell-infancy." [4]

And it was by this angelic quality of the soul that he could still
have "a glimpse of his bright face." [4]

Vaughan's poem "The Retreate" is less laboured than

---

[1] "Looking-back," ii, p. 640.   [2] Martin, ii, p. 440.
[3] "Man," ii, p. 477.   [4] "The Retreate," ii, p. 419.

Wordsworth's "Intimations," and is really a narrative of what he conceived to be his own experience of childhood. The memory of the "bright face" of God dazzles his eyes as did the vision of the pure and endless light of Eternity:

> "I cannot reach it; and my striving eye
> Dazzles at it, as at eternity." [1]

And though he could not attain that state of pure innocence again, he treasures its memory. He asks:

> "Why should I not love childhood still? " [1]

And in lines of remarkable poetic charm he embodies the saying of Christ that to enter the Kingdom of God one must become a child again. It is by becoming childlike again that we shall behold the Face of God:

> "An age of mysteries! which he
> Must live twice, that would God's face see;
> Which *Angels* guard, and with it play,
> Angels! which foul men drive away." [1]

Thus the conception of childhood in Vaughan's poetry is related to his larger conception of the Fall, its effect upon human nature, and the state of innocence which man must acquire again to behold the face of God. It is thus evident that the idealization of childhood by mystics like Vaughan and Traherne is based on the realization of the fact that the instinctive purity, innocence, and simplicity of childhood are the qualities which a man should cultivate before he can hope to enter the Kingdom of God. But Vaughan does not seem to have studied the objections of St Thomas Aquinas to the Neo-Platonic doctrine of the pre-existence of the soul. The nineteenth-century criticism of Wordsworth's "Intimations," and the recent commentaries on Vaughan's "The Retreate," give an impression as if the Neo-Platonic doctrine of the pre-existence of the soul is a *Christian* doctrine, which is far from being the truth.

St. Thomas holds that it is the soul's union with the body that makes the perfect man, and that though the Matter may be said to exist before the Form, potentially, the human body "when it is actually human, as being perfected by a human

---

[1] "Childhood," ii, p. 521.

soul, is neither prior nor posterior to the soul, but together with it." [1] St. Thomas ingeniously argues that the soul did not exist before the body. His main argument is that if "the soul is in a higher state away from body, especially according to the Platonists, who say by union with the body the soul suffers forgetfulness of what it knew before and is hindered from contemplation of pure truth, at that rate it has no willingness to be united with a body except for some deceit practised upon it. Therefore, supposing it to have pre-existed before the body, it would not be united therewith of its own accord." [2]

But if as an alternative it is argued they were united by a "divine ordinance," [2] this does not strengthen the position of the Platonists, for St. Thomas says: "If then he created souls apart from bodies, we must say that this mode of being is better suited to their nature. But it is not proper for an ordinance of divine goodness to reduce things to a lower state, but rather to raise them to a higher. At that rate the union of soul with body could not be the result of a divine ordinance" [3]; therefore the soul could not exist before the body, and both are created at the same time.

Vaughan's pilgrimage from a life that was a "False life! a foil and no more," [4] to a life that was "a fix'd, discerning light," [4] has been a growth in ever-deepening consciousness of God and the true realization of the nature of His relation to the human soul. He knows that the real life is one that has been infused with the spirit of God and has received the impression of the Divine Kiss—"*A quickness, which my God hath kist.*" [4] It is nothing but the discovery of the newness of life in Christ.

The three stages of the mystical experience—the awakening of self, purgation, and illumination—can be easily traced in Vaughan's poetry.

Vaughan tried to apprehend God by discerning a glory in the cloud, by trying to recover the innocence of childhood, by realizing the mystical significance of the Holy Communion.

He, like Herbert and Bishop Andrewes, celebrated the ideal of beauty in holiness, and reverence, and decorum in receiving

---

[1] *Contra Gentiles*, p. 170 (J. Rickaby's translation).
[2] *Ibid.*, p. 162.   [3] *Ibid.*
[4] "Quickness," Martin, ii, p. 538.

the Sacrament. Vaughan was acutely conscious of the harmful effect of the controversy between the Puritans and the Anglicans. He prays to Christ:

> "Give to thy spouse her perfect, and pure dress,
> *Beauty* and *holiness*.
> And so repair these Rents, that men may see
> And say, *where God is, all agree*." [1]

His ideal virtues are "Obedience, Order, Light," [2] and like a true Anglican he insists on the worthiness of the receiver of the Sacrament. The attitude of mind in which one should approach the Communion table is one of utter humility and awe. When he is receiving the Sacrament, Vaughan thinks himself to be before the "glorious and searching Eye" [3] of God. Addressing Christ, he says: "Many a time hast thou knockt, and I have shut the doors against thee, thou hast often called, and I would not answer. Sleeping and waking, early and late, day and night have I refused instruction, and would not be healed. And now, O my God, after all this rebellion and uncleannesse, wilt thou come and lodge with me? O Lord, where shall I prepare, and make ready for thee? *What communion can there be betwixt light and darknesse,* purity and pollution, perfection and deformity." [3]

It is through the "mercy and plenteous redemption" [4] of Christ that he hopes to become worthy of taking the Bread of Life. He considers that the receiving of the Sacrament should prevent him from returning to his former "iniquities and pollutions" [5]; it should become "a signet upon mine hand, and a bracelet upon my arme," [5] so that it may strengthen him in his "pilgrimage towards heaven." [6] The Sacrament of the Altar not only purifies his soul but it also strengthens his body against sin and corruption:

> "Thou dost unto thy self betroth
> Our souls, and bodies both
> In everlasting light." [7]

---

[1] "The Constellation," Martin, ii, p. 470. [2] *Ibid.*
[3] *The Mount of Olives*, Martin, i, p. 160. [4] *Ibid.*, p. 161.
[5] *Ibid.*, p. 165. [6] *Ibid.*, p. 163.
[7] "The Holy Communion," ii, 458.

He contemptuously refers to the manner of receiving the Sacrament under the Puritan regime:

"Some sit to thee, and eat
Thy body as their Common meat." [1]

Walton, in his *Life of Hooker*, has described how the "Genevan Minister" who was appointed to the living of Borne in the fourth year of the Long Parliament administered "the Sacrament as in Geneva": "The day was appointed for a select company, and forms and stools set about the Altar or Communion-Table, for them to sit and eat, and drink; but when they went about this work, there was a want of some joint-stools which the Minister sent the Clerk to fetch, and then to fetch cushions (but not to kneel upon)." [2] The irreverence of the Puritans so shocked the parish clerk that he resigned his post, and died within a few days.

To Vaughan the real significance of the Holy Communion is that it is partaking of His Life; these gifts are the "fore-runner" of the joys that await the sanctified soul in the higher stages of mystical experience:

"Give to thy wretched one
Thy mysticall *Communion.*
That, absent, he may see,
Live, die, and rise with thee." [3]

Vaughan had known the real ecstasy of the mystical com-munion with God in illumination when the Bridegroom had admitted him into the dazzling "ring" of his Love. God is present in illumination but the vision soon fades away, leaving the soul restless and conscious of its own unworthiness. When the soul soars high, aiming at the "stars and spangled halls," it soon falls back through its unworthiness upon its own normal self:

"Doth my weak fire
Pine and retire
And (after all my height of flames,)
In sickly Expirations tames . . .
Poor, falling star !" [4]

---

[1] "Dressing," ii, p. 456.
[2] *Lives*, by Izaak Walton, edited by George Saintsbury, p. 217.
[3] "Dressing," ii, p. 455; see also poems "Easter Day," "Easter Hymn," and "The Feast."
[4] "Disorder and Frailty," ii, p. 445–446.

Vaughan now enters on the fourth stage of the Mystic Way, called the "Dark Night of the Soul," in which God seems to withdraw Himself completely from the soul. The main characteristic of the early phase of the "Dark Night of the Soul" is what Underhill has called "the periods of rapid oscillation between a joyous and a painful consciousness." [1]

In Vaughan the joyous apprehension of the Absolute assumed the form of passionate longing for union with God, and it was a longing which was crossed with the pain of separation. He recognizes that the veil which separates him from God must be first broken in him before he could stand face to face with Him:

> "This veyle thy full-ey'd love denies
> And onely gleams and fractions spies." [2]

He is impatient of this veil which separates him from God:

> "O take it off! make no delay,
> But brush me with thy light, that I
> May shine unto a perfect day.
> And warme me at thy glorious Eye!" [2]

The night of God's eclipse is to him a terrible agony; he cries out:

> "My dew, my dew! my early love,
> My soul's bright food, thy absence kills!" [3]

His prayer in "Anguish" is that God should either visit his soul with his "holy feet" or end his agonized life. In this great affliction he exclaims:

> "My God, could I weep blood,
> Gladly I would." [4]

And he even longs for death as a liberation of the soul from the prison-house of the body:

> "O my God, hear my cry;
> Or let me dye!" [4]

The soul longs for the freedom which will end this life of separation from God:

---

[1] *Mysticism*, p. 457.
[3] "The Seed growing Secretly," p. 510.
[2] "Cock-crowing," ii, p. 489.
[4] "Anguish," p. 526.

> "O then, just then! break or untye
> These bonds, this sad captivity,
> This leaden state, which men miscal
> Being and life, but is dead thrall." [1]

St. John of the Cross in his classical treatise on *The Dark Night of the Soul*, describing the true nature and purpose of this affliction of the soul, remarks:

"Souls begin to enter the dark night when God is drawing them out of the state of beginners . . . and is leading them into that of proficients, the state of contemplatives, that, having passed through it, they may arrive at the state of the perfect, which is that of the divine union with God." God leads men into this night, for here "the soul is established in virtue and made strong for the inestimable delights of his love." [2]

Vaughan, describing the nature of the experience of knowing "God by night," says:

> "Most blest believer he,
> Who in that land of darkness and blinde eyes
> Thy long expected healing wings could see,
> When thou didst rise,
> And what can never more be done,
> Did at midnight speak with the sun!" [3]

When the soul in the "dark night" beholds the "sun," that is God, it is the total being of man which takes part in this impassioned perception. The reality of this unique and strange experience can only be described through "negative symbols." Dante in the unitive stage is blinded with the Divine light flashing around him; this light can only be described as "dazzling darkness." Dante says: "As sudden lightning-flash that scatters the visual spirits, so that it deprives the eye of action towards the strongest objects; so shined round about me a living light, and left me swathed with such a veil of its effulgence, that naught appeared unto me." [4]

This dazzling darkness which the mystic finds in God is in reality his vision of the Supreme Reality. Vaughan knew this:

> "There is in God (some say)
> A deep, but dazzling darkness; As men here

---

[1] "The Ass," Martin, ii, p. 519.
[2] *The Dark Night of the Soul*, by St. John of the Cross, translated by David Lewis.
[3] Martin, ii, p. 522.   [4] *Paradiso*, xxx.

> Say it is late and dusky, because they
>   See not all clear;
> O for that night! where I in him
> Might live invisible and dim." [1]

St. John of the Cross explaining the true significance of this "dim contemplation" says that it is secret, *i.e.* unseen and undisturbed. He continues: "The second blessing is that because of the spiritual darkness of this night . . . the soul seeing nothing, and unable to see, is not detained by anything which is not God from drawing near unto Him, and, therefore, advances unhindered by forms and figures and natural apprehensions." [2]

St. John of the Cross has described his own experience of the union with God in a hushed voice quivering with tenderness and love:

> "All things I then forgot,
> My cheek on Him who for my coming came,
>   *All ceased, and I was not,*
> Leaving my cares and shame
> Among the lilies, and forgetting them." [2]

Vaughan does not seem to have enjoyed this state of union with God, which is granted to the sanctified soul after it has endured the privations of the "dark night" of the soul; he could not say with St. John of the Cross "*All ceased, and I was not.*" Vaughan does not claim to have experienced even the state of "dim contemplation" when God appears to the soul as "dazzling darkness." In the last stanza quoted above, Vaughan is describing the state of the soul in the "dark night," but he does not suggest that it is his own personal experience that he is describing; in fact he is careful to add "*some say*":

> "There is in God (some say)
> A deep, but dazzling darkness." [3]

He is here only referring to the experience of the other mystics and expresses his own longing to be also blessed with a similar experience; the description of his own state of bliss in *Thalia Rediviva* is really an account of illumination, for there is no evidence in Vaughan's poems of his ever having experienced

---

[1] "The Night," Martin, ii, p. 522.   [2] *The Dark Night of the Soul*, p. 182.
[3] "The Night," ii, p. 523.

the higher stages of mystical life, the "dark night" of the soul,
or the union with God. He says in "The Revival":

> "Hark! how his *winds* have chang'd their *note*,
> And with warm *whispers* call thee out.
> The *frosts* are past, the *storms* are gone:
> And backward *life* at last comes on.
> The lofty *groves* in express Joyes
> Reply unto the *Turtles* voice,
> And here in *dust* and *dirt*, O here
> The *Lilies* of his love appear!" [1]

This description does not refer to any intimate union with
God which generally follows the "dark night" of the soul.
These joys to him are only the foretaste of the glory that awaits
him, as the sanctified soul, in Heaven:

> "And what the men of this world miss,
> Some *drops* and *dews* of future bliss." [1]

Vaughan seems to have believed, with St. Augustine, St.
Thomas Aquinas and Donne, that we cannot see the Essence
of God as He is, what Vaughan calls "The Fulness of the
Deity," in this life. St. Thomas Aquinas remarks:
"The Divine Essence cannot be seen by a created intellect,
save through the light and glory, concerning which it is said
in the Psalm (xxxv, 10, or xxxvi, 9): In Thy light shall we see
light. This, however, can be participated in two ways: in
the one, by way of it becoming the immanent form (of the
intellect) and thus it makes the saints blessed in Paradise; and
in the other, by way of a certain passing passion as we have
said in the light of prophecy; and, in this latter way was in
Paul, when he was caught up. And therefore, by such a
vision he was not blessed absolutely, so that it overflowed to
his body, but only relatively; and therefore such a *being
caught* up pertains in some sort to prophecy." [2] St. Augustine,
discussing the nature of St. Paul's experience when he was
"caught up" into Heaven, says: "St. Paul was rapt into this
transcendent vision, wherein we may believe that God vouchsafed to show him that life wherein, after this life, we are to
live for ever." [3] The idea embodied in these discussions of St.
Augustine and St. Thomas is that while a transient glimpse of

---

[1] "The Revival," Martin, ii, p. 643.
[2] *Summa Theologica*, ii, 11, q. 175 a 2, 3.
[3] *Western Mysticism*, by Dom C. Butler, p. 81,

the *lumen gloriae* is granted to the mystic in illumination and
the unitive stage, the permanent vision is the privilege of the
blessed saints in Heaven.

Vaughan also believed that "eternal felicity" could only be
granted to the soul in Heaven, "therefore in my opinion
eternal Beatitude, or eternal felicity, is nothing else but a
sufficiency, or fulnesse of all good things, according to our own
desire, and without any indigency, which felicity all the friends
of God shall fully enjoy in the life which is to come." [1]

Eternal felicity, Vaughan considers, is possible only after
death, when Christ will "adopt us for his sons, making us his
Consorts in his own Kingdome. . . . But he himself is the
God deifying and we are but *deified*, or *gods* made by him." [2]

Vaughan believes that in this glorified resurrection the body
will be blessed like the soul, and the deified spirit of man shall
make him "co-heires with his only begotten Son who is in
everything co-equal with himself, *changing our vile bodies, that
they may be like unto his glorious body.*" [2]

St. Thomas Aquinas discussing the resurrection of the body
uses almost the same language: "Our resurrection shall be on
the model of the resurrection of Christ, *who will reform the body
of our humiliation*, so that it shall become conformable to *the body
of his glory* (Phil. iii, 21). But Christ after His resurrection had
a body that could be felt and handled, as He says: *Feel and see,
because a spirit hath not flesh and bones* as you see me to have (Luke
xxiv, 39): in like manner therefore also other risen men." [3]

Vaughan, like St. Thomas, believes that our resurrection
shall be the resurrection of the body and soul alike; he even
asserts that the souls of the elect "have not yet enjoyed the
fulness of felicity, until their bodies shall be restored unto
them incorruptible." [4] Vaughan says that the body, like a
"Spruce Bride,"

> "Shall one day rise, and cloath'd with shining light
>   All pure, and bright
>   Re-marry to the soule, for 'tis most plaine
>   Thou only fal'st to be refin'd again." [5]

It is after understanding Vaughan's conception of the

---

[1] *Man in Glory*, Martin, i, p. 209.   [2] *Ibid.*, p. 206.
[3] *Contra Gentiles*, lxxxiv.   [4] *Man in Glory*, Martin, i, p. 196.
[5] "Resurrection and Immortality," ii, p. 402.

Resurrection that we can realize the significance and beauty
of such lines as the following:

> "They are all gone into the world of light!
> And I alone sit lingering here." [1]

Vaughan's conception of life was governed by his view that it
was preceded by a luminous eternity and will be followed by an
eternity of light after the darkness of the grave. He knew that
"full-eyed" vision of God was not possible in our present life
and therefore he was ready to be dissolved and thus achieve
eternal life:

> "Since in these veyls my ecclips'd eye
> May not approach thee, (for at night
> Who can have commerce with the light?)
> I'll disapparell, and to buy
> But one half glaunce, most gladly dye." [2]

In this pilgrimage there is no fixity and permanence of
vision; His light "*thus wee saw there, and thus here,*" [3] and it is
only in rare moments of insight that we can transcend the
limitations of our self and "into glory peep." [4]

The glory of the star, that is, the soul, cannot be confined in
the tomb of the body, but by its very nature must shine forth
out of its confinement:

> "If a star were confin'd into a Tomb
> Her captive flames must needs burn there;
> But when the hand that lockt her up, gives room
> She'l shine through all the sphaere." [5]

To Vaughan death is "beauteous," for he is eager to know
the mysteries which lie beyond death and possess the freedom
that awaits the soul in heaven:

> "Resume thy spirit from this world of thrall
> Into true liberty." [5]

Death has no terrors for him, he is longing to be dissolved
so that he may ever "triumph in the security of everlasting
Beatitude" [6]:

> "Dissolve, dissolve! death cannot do
> What I would not submit unto." [7]

---

[1] "They are all gone," Martin, vol. ii, p. 483.
[2] "Vanity of Spirit," *ibid.*, p. 419.
[3] "The Pilgrimage," *ibid.*, p. 464.
[4] "They are all gone," *ibid.*, p. 484.
[5] *Ibid.*
[6] *Man in Glory*, vol. i, p. 210,
[7] "The Day-spring," ii, p. 644.

He believes that in Heaven both the body and the soul shall be "wing'd and free," [1] and that he will stand face to face with God:

> ". . . we shall there no more
>   Watch stars, or pore
> Through melancholy clouds, and say,
>   *Would it were day !*
> One everlasting *Saboth* there shall runne
> Without *Succession*, and without a *Sunne*." [2]

I have briefly described in the foregoing pages the characteristics of Vaughan's mysticism. He is a mystic in the only sense in which a poet can be a mystic—while possessing all the felicity and magic of the true poet, his devotional poetry is based on his own mystical experience. He had declared in his preface to *Silex Scintillans* that a poet should strive for "*perfection* and true *holyness, that a door may be opened to him in heaven* (Rev. iv, 1), and then he will be able to write (with Hierotheus and holy *Herbert*) a true *Hymn*." [3]

I have tried to show, by giving parallel quotations from such great mystics as St. Augustine, St. Bernard and St. John of the Cross, that Vaughan had passed through those phases of mystical life (which have been conveniently divided into the three stages of conversion or the awakening of the self, purgation or the purification of the self, and the illumination of the self) which these great mystics had also experienced. But of the higher stages of mystical life (*i.e.* the "dark night" of the soul and the unitive stage) we do not find any clear record either in Vaughan's poetry or prose. Though he has described the "dazzling darkness" of the "dark night" of the soul he does not claim to have experienced it himself; it was only an expression of his intense longing for such an experience.

He has not described this important stage of mystical life in terms of his own personal experience; moreover we do not find any evidence in his poems of his ever having reached the highest stage of the mystical life known as the unitive stage— which, as Miss Underhill says, is "the final triumph of the spirit, the flower of mysticism, the consummation towards which the contemplative life, with its long slow growth and costly training, has moved from the first" [4]—but we must

---

[1] "Resurrection and Immortality," *ibid.*, p. 402.   [2] *Ibid.*
[3] "The Preface," *ibid.*, p. 392.   [4] *Mysticism*, by E. Underhill, p. 413.

remember the important fact that Vaughan during the last thirty years of his life was silent, his latest poem which survives being his elegy on his brother's death in 1666,[1] included in *Thalia Rediviva* (1678); and thus we have no record of his further progress on the Mystic Way; perhaps, like St. John of the Cross, he had realized that the higher stages of mystical life relate "to matters so interior and spiritual as to baffle the powers of language," and so remained silent.[2]

[1] Vaughan died in 1695 (April 23).
[2] *The Living Flame of Love*, by St. John of the Cross, translated by David Lewis, p. 1.

CHAPTER VI

THE NATURE MYSTICISM OF HENRY VAUGHAN AND THOMAS VAUGHAN

DEAN INGE has defined religious mysticism in such broad terms as to include the search of God in nature as a form of mysticism.

"Religious mysticism," he says, "may be defined as the attempt to realize the presence of the living God in the soul and in nature, or more generally, as *the attempt to realize*, in thought and feeling, the immanence of the temporal in the eternal, and of the eternal in the temporal." [1]

This view of mysticism is based on the assumption that the universe is a manifestation of the creative activity of God, and everything, according to its measure, reflects the nature of its Creator. The mystic discerns an essential unity running through creation, which to him is the unity of the creative Intellect of God. In nature, mystics have discerned the spirit of God flowering in its manifold richness; to Philo nature is the language of God, but with "this difference, that while the human voice is made to be *heard*, the voice of God is made to be *seen*: what God says consists of acts, not of words." [2] Nature mysticism of a high order is present in St. Francis of Assisi; he sees the world around him through the "many-coloured glass," and is delighted to behold the workmanship and glory of God's creation; to him all the created things are the children of the same Divine spirit. In his "Hymn of the Sun" (*Il cantico de Sole*) St. Francis praises God "for all thy creation"; to him the sun is "Brother," the moon "Sister," and earth "Mother," which bringeth forth divers fruits and bright flowers and herbs.

This tender reverence for nature is one of the characteristics of nature mysticism. John Smith, the Cambridge Platonist, justifying it said: "God made the universe and all the creatures contained therein as so many glasses wherein He might reflect His own glory. He hath copied forth Himself in the creation;

[1] *Christian Mysticism*, by W. R. Inge, p. 5. [2] *Ibid.*, p. 254.

and in this outward world we may read the lovely characters of the Divine goodness, power and wisdom." This endeavour of man to discern God in nature gave rise to animism in primitive religion, to sublime pantheism in Hindu mysticism, and has brought Christian mystics like Shelley nearer to a form of pantheism, which Inge calls "pantheistic determinism," [1] an irrevocable power determining human actions.

Though Vaughan has been called by Richard Garnett a pantheist,[2] Nature did not provide him with the same devotional and religious stimulus as the Church's sacraments. Vaughan's religious life is bound up with the conception of Christ as the Redeemer, and the Church as the repository of His divine spirit, and though his religion, as expressed in poetry, is free from institutional formalism, it is essentially orthodox. To him the Eucharist is a "private seal," [3] and the symbol of mystical union with the spirit and body of Christ:

> "Give to thy wretched one
> Thy mystical *communion*,
>   That, absent, he may see
> Live, die, and rise with thee." [4]

Nature did not provide him with the same means of communion with Christ as the Holy Communion. Pantheism, as A. E. Garvie has defined it, "is the view that all is God, and that God is all, but since thought may move from God to all, or from all to God, it can assume two forms. If it begins with the religious or the philosophical faith in God as infinite and eternal reality, then the finite temporal world is swallowed up in God, and pantheism becomes acosmism (*q.v.*), *i.e.*, the world is an illusion in comparison with God as Reality. If it begins with the scientific conception of the poetic vision of the world as unity, then God is lost in the world, and pantheism becomes pancosmism." [5]

Vaughan's conception of nature, if viewed in the light of the above definition, is not pantheistic. To him the world is not an illusion, nor is his God lost in the world. He affirms the

---

[1] *Studies of English Mystics*, by W. R. Inge, p. 181.
[2] *Dictionary of National Biography.*   [3] "Dressing," Martin, ii, p. 456.
[4] *Ibid.*, p. 455.
[5] *Encyclopædia of Religion and Ethics*, edited by J. Hastings, vol. ix, p. 609.

reality of created nature and enjoys the glorious manifestation
of God's spirit in it, but he also realizes that supreme reality is
God, and thus enjoys the divine fellowship with Christ. His
God is *in* nature and yet *above* nature. Nature has its independent life, perhaps more permanent and well ordered than
the life of man, but it is equally dependent upon God. Neither
is all God nor is God completely manifested in nature. Life is
a quickness [1] touched with the Kiss of the Lord, and the pulse
of this quickness is felt in the human soul as well as in nature:

> "All were by thee,
> And still must be,
> Nothing that is, or lives,
> But hath his quicknings, and reprieves
> As thy hand opens, or shuts." [2]

It is God who sustains man as well as nature; nature has no
independent life of its own. Vaughan could not pray like
Wordsworth that he might become a "pagan suckled in an
outworn creed" in order to enjoy nature. But nature did
bring peace to his troubled spirit, as it did to Herbert's. He
rejects the life of "glory and gold" in preference to a life of
humility and devotion:

> "Let glory be their bait, whose mindes
> Are all too high for a low cell." [3]

In "The Seed growing Secretly" he wants to shine dimly
and "thrive" unknown in calmness and peace:

> "Then bless thy secret growth, nor catch
> At noise, but thrive unseen and dumb;
> Keep clean, bear fruit, earn life and watch
> Till the white winged Reapers come." [3]

In "Resignation" he tells us that he found that the joys of
the world were a hindrance to the growth of his devotional
life; he wants to tread the path of Christ, a path of humbleness
and poverty:

> "I hear, I see all the long day
> The noise and pomp of the *broadway*;
> I note their course and proud approaches;
> Their silks, perfumes and glittering coaches." [4]

---

[1] "Quickness," Martin, ii, p. 538.
[2] "The Holy Communion," Martin, ii, p. 457. T. Vaughan also says that
God is "the quickening of all," *Anthroposophia Theomagica*, p. 53.
[3] "The Seed growing Secretly," Martin, ii, p. 511.
[4] "The World," Martin, ii, p. 651.

The noise and pomp and glory are not for him; he had lived
the active life of the gallant of his day, and recoiled from its
vanity and hollowness at his conversion. In "A Rapsodie" he
has given us a glimpse of his life of gaiety before the influence
of Herbert so radically changed the trend of his life:

> "*Let's laugh now, and the prest grape drinke,*
> *Till the drowsie Day Starre winke;*
> *And in our merry, mad mirth run*
> *Faster, and further than the Sun;*
> *And let none his Cup forsake,*
> *Till that Starre again doth wake :*
> *So we men below shall move*
> *Equally with the gods above.*" [1]

The gallant cavalier became the recluse and the mystic, he
renounced the glitter of gilded coaches and the finery of silk
to choose a life of poverty and humble devotion:

> "But in the *narrow way* to thee
> I observe only poverty,
> And despis'd things: and all along
> The ragged, mean and humble throng
> Are still on foot, and as they go,
> They sigh and say: *Their Lord went so.*" [2]

He resolved to tread the narrow way of poverty and humbleness leading to Christ:

> "Thus, thus and in no other sort
> Will I set forth, though laugh'd at for't." [3]

He thus tried to retreat from the pomp and vanity of the world
to a life of contemplation in the solitude and peace of the
countryside. In "Retirement" he has told us the significance
of this step which was closely related to his conception of the
Mystic Way:

> "'Tis not th' applause, and feat
>   Of dust and clay
>   Leads to that way,
> But from those follies a resolv'd Retreat." [4]

Though Vaughan resolved to retreat, he never adopted the
Puritan attitude of condemning all forms of innocent pleasure
as detrimental to the life of the soul. Vaughan's sense of
mystical consciousness of the processes of life as manifested in

[1] Martin, i, p. 12.
[2] "The World," *ibid.*, ii, p. 651.
[3] *Ibid.*, ii, p. 651.
[4] "Retirement," *ibid.*, p. 463.

nature is keen, for he delighted in the eternal "change and flow" of created forms:

> "Beauty consists in colours; and that's best
> Which is not fixt, but flies and flows;
> The settled *Red* is dull, and *Whites* that rest
> Something of sickness would disclose." [1]

Even in his seclusion he valued the health and vigour of body; and translated the treatise of Henry Nollius on *Hermetical Physics* to show "the right way to Preserve and to restore Health." [2]

In nature he discovered a new world of beauty and æsthetic pleasure, and the peace and solitude necessary for communion with God through nature. In "Retirement" he has given us three reasons for preferring the country life to that of the city.

Nature in the countryside not only shows the "Earth's fair face" in all its virgin beauty, but it also reveals the fact that Earth is "God's *foot-stool*." When man sees the hills, trees, meadows, flowers, and "the boundless *skie*," his pleasure is not merely æsthetic, he also realizes the power and beauty of the creative energy of God:

> "And ev'ry minute bless the King
> And wise Creatour of each thing." [3]

The second reason which Vaughan advances is that the cities are "thrones of ill"; they are "cages with much uncleanness fill'd"; while in the countryside there is innocence and freedom:

> "But *rural shades* are the sweet fense
> Of piety and innocence." [3]

He retained that simplicity of vision which could enable him to see the angels ascending and descending from Heaven. To him nature is the calm region where

> "Angels descend, and rule the sphere;
> Where heav'n lyes *Leiguer*, and the *Dove*
> Duely as *Dew* comes from above." [3]

The countryside is thus to him an Eden on earth:

> "If Eden be on Earth at all,
> 'Tis that, which we the country call." [4]

---

[1] "Affliction," *ibid.*, p. 460.   [2] *Ibid.*, p. 547.   [3] *Ibid.*, p. 642.   [4] *Ibid.*, p. 643.

In nature he found that sense of peace and contentment which he thought necessary for the healthy growth of his devotional life. Vaughàn has himself declared that in the country even the days are lengthened and that the beauties of nature are easily accessible there:

"The day it self (in my opinion) seems of more *length* and *beauty* in the Country, and can be better enjoyed than any where else. There the *years* pass away calmly, and one *day* gently drives on the other, insomuch that a man may be sensible of a certaine *satietie* and *pleasure* from every *houre*, and may be said to feed upon *time* it self, which devours all other things." [1]

Vaughan recognized that he could only cultivate his love of nature in the solitude of the country:

> "Lord! what a busie, restles thing
> Hast thou made man !" [2]

And this restlessness inherent in the nature of man was accentuated by his love of ostentation and display of wealth; he points out that "one *day* spent in the recesse and privacie of the *Country*, seems more pleasant and lasting than a whole year at *Court*." [3]

> "Man is the shuttle, to whose winding quest
> And passage through these looms
> God order'd motion, but ordain'd no *rest*." [4]

Vaughan's conception of nature as the revelation of an aspect of the creative energy of God was influenced by Hermetic Physics, medical astrology and alchemy, and to a certain extent by the Platonic conception of Beauty in the sensible world ultimately leading to the supreme Beauty, God. The influence of his twin brother Thomas Vaughan, a student of occult sciences and mysticism, has been recently traced in Henry's conception of the physical world and its relation to God. A. C. Judson [5] has shown the affinity between the two brothers in their interest in natural sciences, alchemy and Platonism.

---

[1] "The Praise and Happiness of the Country Life," Martin, i, p. 129.
[2] "The Pursuite," Martin, ii, p. 414.　[3] *Ibid.*, i, p. 129.　[4] "Man," *ibid.*, ii, p. 477.
[5] "The Source of H. Vaughan's Ideas concerning God in Nature," *Studies in Philology*, xxiv.

Vaughan's translations and prose treatises not only show his interest in the various aspects of devotional life, as in *The Mount of Olives*, *Man in Darkness* and *Man in Glory*, but also in Hermetic Physics and in the occult sciences of his day. He translated Nierembergius' observations "on the need of Temperance and Patience," Plutarch's essays "on the Benefits we may get from our Enemies," and Eucherius' epistle "on despising the world when compared to the glories of heaven." Of the four translations which more or less must be considered Vaughan's own personal work, one is Guevara's treatise in praise of the country life, and the other three translations show Vaughan's interest in medicine; two are on the diseases of mind and body, one by Maximus Tirus, and the other by Plutarch, and the third is more important, it being the translation of Nollius' work on *Hermetical Physics*.[1]

This work gives us an insight into the complex relation of occult sciences to medicine and philosophy in the seventeenth century. Vaughan kept an open mind on these subjects, and he defines his attitude to such medical philosophers as Galen and Paracelsus in his preface to *Hermeticall Physicks*: "For my owne part, I honour the truth where ever I find it, whether in an old, or new Booke, in *Galen* or *Paracelsus*; and Antiquity (where I find it gray with errors) shall have as little reverence from me, as *Novelisme*. . . . I wish we were all unbiassed and impartiall learners, not the implicit, groundlesse Proselyts of Authors and opinions but the loyall friends and followers of truth." [2]

Henry Vaughan shared with Donne and Sir Thomas Browne their interest in the uncommon and remote regions of knowledge. In one of his letters to Aubrey he wrote: "I had but little affection to the skirts and lower parts of learning; where every hand is grasping and so little to be had —but neither nature nor fortune favoured my ambition." [3]

I am not concerned here with the larger relation of the occult sciences to mysticism, my limited aim is to point out the influence of occult philosophers like Paracelsus, Cornelius Agrippa and Pymander on Vaughan's conception of nature and its relation to God. The concept which underlies

---

[1] For a detailed list of prose translations see L. C. Martin, i and ii.
[2] Martin, ii, p. 548: "The Translator to the Ingenious Reader."
[3] Martin, ii, p. 673.

the occult sciences, as Underhill has pointed out, is common both to magic and mysticism. The starting-point of all magic, and of all magical religion—the best and purest of occult activities—is, as in mysticism, man's inextinguishable conviction that there are "other planes of being than those which the senses report to him, and its proceedings represent the intellectual and individualistic results of this conviction— his craving for the hidden knowledge." [1]

But the resemblance ends here; though religion, in its ceremonial aspects, has affinities with magic, religious mysticism adopts quite a different method and technique to apprehend reality from that followed by occult philosophers. Magic [2] and mysticism represent the two different but abiding passions of the self—"the desire to love and the desire to know." Mysticism, as Underhill has defined it, is "the science of ultimates," [3] and the true mark of the mystic is not to *know* but *to be*.

In the seventeenth century the two exponents of occult philosophy who had obtained wide popularity among the philosophers and scholars of the age were Cornelius Agrippa (1486–1535) and Paracelsus. Agrippa was a German soldier, physician and occult philosopher. For seven years (1511–18) he was in Italy, in the service of William VI of Monferrato and of Charles III of Savoy. His lectures on the *Pimander* of Hermes Trismegistus at Pavia in 1515 brought him in conflict with the Church. His work *De occulta Philosophia* (1510) brought him the antagonism of the Inquisition; it was printed at Antwerp in 1531. In his other work, *De incertitudine et vanitate scientiarum et artium atque excellentia Verbi Dei declamatio*, he advocated a return to Primitive Christianity. The complete edition of his works was published at Leyden in 1550. [4]

The reason why Henry Vaughan, like his brother Thomas Vaughan, became interested in Hermetic Physics was that he believed that the truth (fact) of science agreed with the truth of religion. Elias Ashmole, the alchemist, declared, in his pre-

---

[1] *Mysticism*, Underhill, p. 151.
[2] I have used the term "magic" in its ancient sense of occult philosophy, which is based on "an actual, positive, and realizable knowledge concerning the worlds which we denominate invisible."—A. E. Waite, *The Occult Sciences*, p. 1.
[3] *Mysticism*, Underhill, p. 72.
[4] See H. Morley, *Life of H. C. Agrippa* (London, 1856).

face to *Theatrum chemicum Britannicum* (1652), that the man who
can peer into the secrets of nature does not rejoice "that he
can make gold and silver," but because "he sees the Heavens
open, the Angells of God Ascending and Descending, and that
his own name is fairly written in the Book of Life." Henry
Vaughan himself defined medicine or "Physick" as "an Art,
laying down in certain Rules or Precepts, the right way of
preserving or restoring the health of Mankind." [1]

But this way of "restoring" the health of man was not limited
to medicine or physics, but also included occult philosophy
and Christian theology. In his treatise on *Hermetic Physicks*
Vaughan, describing the means "of the Preservation of
Health," remarks that "a pious and an holy life" are necessary
for maintaining health:

"For Piety (as the apostle teacheth) is Profitable for all
things, having the promise of this present life, and of that
which is to come. Now all piety consists in this, that we
love God with all our Souls, and our Neighbours as
ourselves." [2]

This connection between medicine, theology and astrology
was the favourite doctrine of Paracelsus (*c.* 1490–1541).[3]
Paracelsus, whom Henry Vaughan has mentioned with respect
in his Preface to *Hermetic Physicks*, was considered in the seventeenth century as a great authority on Hermetical Physics.
Paracelsus had little respect for the authority of Aristotle in
sciences, for he advocated a form of experimental science in
which occult sciences and theology were also included. He
discerned a direct relation between Nature (by which he meant
the infinite variety of God's creation) and Man and God. He
observes: "It is to learn the mysteries of Nature by which we
can discover what God is and what man is and what avails a
knowledge of heavenly eternity and earthly weakness. Hence
arises a knowledge of Theology, of Justice, of Truth, since the
mysteries of Nature are to be imitated which can be known
and obtained from God as the Eternal God." [4]

The system of Paracelsus is based on a visionary Neo-

[1] Martin, ii, p. 549.
[2] *Ibid.*, p. 552.
[3] See Waite, *The Hermetical and Alchemical Writings of Paracelsus* (1894), and also
A. M. Stoddart, *The Life of Paracelsus*, 1915.
[4] Waite, *op. cit.*, ii, p. 4.

Platonic philosophy in which the life of man is regarded as a part of the larger life of the universe.

Henry Vaughan's conception of nature seems to have been influenced by Paracelsus, for he also says: "He only is true Physician, created so by the light of Nature, to whom Nature herself hath taught and manifested her proper and genuine operations by experience." [1] Agrippa had tried to effect a synthesis between religious truth and natural sciences, and Thomas Vaughan was naturally attracted by his genius. Thomas wrote a poem appreciating Agrippa (1651), in which he described him as:

> "Nature's apostle and her choice high priest
> Her mystical and bright evangelist."

Anthony à Wood, describing Thomas Vaughan's debt to Agrippa, remarked: "Vaughan was a great admirer of the labours of Cornelius Agrippa, whose principles he followed in most of his works, and to whom, in matters of Philosophy, he acknowledged that next to God he owed all that he had." [2] Though Henry Vaughan does not mention Agrippa in his treatise on *Hermetic Physicks*, his interest in occult philosophy, like that of his brother, makes it probable that he had also studied the works of Agrippa, who was the greatest exponent of Hermetical physics and occult sciences in his age. Henry Vaughan, like Thomas Vaughan, mainly relies in his treatise on the authority of the Hermetists. Thomas had repudiated the authority of Galen and Aristotle alike. He declared: "I acknowledge the schoolmen ingenious: they conceive their principles irregular and prescribe rules for method, though they want matter. Their philosophy is like a church that is all discipline and no doctrine. . . . Besides their Aristotle is a poet in text. . . ." [3]

Henry Vaughan, while giving his reasons for preferring Hermetists to Galenists, says: "Now all the knowledge of the *Hermetists* proceeds from a laborious manual disquisition and search into Nature, but the *Galenists* insist wholly upon a bare received *Theorie* and prescribed Receits, giving all at adventure

---

[1] Grosart, ii, p. 333.
[2] Also see *The Works of T. Vaughan*, edited by A. E. Waite, p. 50.
[3] *Ibid.*, p. 7.

and will not be persuaded to inquire further than the mouth of their leader." [1]

The conception of the physical world as propounded by Hermetic philosophers like Cornelius Agrippa deserves a careful study for the proper understanding of Vaughan's conception of nature. In his *Occult Philosophy* Agrippa gave a reasoned exposition of the Hermetical conception of a *threefold division* of the world: (1) the realm of pure Intelligence; (2) the world of elements (earth, air, fire and water), and between them (3) a spiritual world which served as a link between the other two worlds. Agrippa, like Henry Vaughan, was, a physician, and they both maintained the ancient alliance between medicine and religion. Henry Vaughan says: "For true and perfect medicines, and the knowledge of them, can nowhere be had, but from God, whom we can serve by no other means in this life, but onely by piety and piety hath included in it fervent and incessant supplications unto God, hearty and frequent thanksgiving for his gracious and free benefits, with sincere and actuall love towards our Neighbours." [2]

Henry Vaughan, being thus interested in Hermetical physics, alchemy and medicine, must have come across this ordered exposition of the threefold division of the world according to Hermetical philosophy in the magical writings of his twin brother Thomas Vaughan. Thomas Vaughan declared (following Cornelius Agrippa) that "the great world consists of three parts—the elemental, the celestial and the spiritual— above all which God Himself is seated." [3] In this conception of nature, the physical and spiritual worlds were indissolubly linked together, and Henry Vaughan must have discovered in the philosophy of his brother, which is a curious mixture of Hermetical physics, Neo-Platonism, and Christian theology, many mystical ideas about the creation of the universe and its relation to God. Thomas Vaughan's first three works on magic were published in 1650, which is also the date of the publication of the first part of *Silex Scintillans*.

Thomas Vaughan's magical theories about heat and light

---

[1] Henry Vaughan, *Hermetical Physicks*, Martin, vol. ii, p. 550.
[2] Martin, ii, p. 579.
[3] *Anthroposophia Theomagica*, p. 40.

and magnetism help us to understand Henry Vaughan's constant references to them in his sacred poems. A. C. Judson has been able to trace almost a parallel idea to that embodied in "Cock-crowing" in Thomas Vaughan's *Anima Magica Abscondita*, 1650 [1]; but my purpose in this chapter is only to suggest certain similarities in Henry Vaughan's conception of nature and that of his brother, Thomas Vaughan, who was also a mystic and an ardent Anglican. A. E. Waite has pointed out the relation of magic to Neo-Platonism, the Jewish Kabbala, and Christian theology; magicians like Thomas Vaughan, he says, were "Christian mystics who never dreamed of looking further than Christianity for light, and what they pretend to have possessed was the key of miracles and not the key of religious symbolism." [2] Thomas Vaughan himself said that he was "neither papist nor sectary but a true, resolute protestant in the best sense of the Church of England." [3]

Henry Vaughan and Thomas Vaughan both conceived God as immanent in nature but still transcending nature. God sits in Heaven above "the morning-starre," and the glories of the created universe are mean shows when compared to the glory of Heaven:

> "Who on yon throne of Azure sits,
>   Keeping close-house
> Above the morning-starre,
>   Whose meaner showes,
> And outward utensils these glories are
>   That shine and share
> Part of his mansion." [4]

Nature is the manifestation of God, and though we can behold a glimpse of God in nature, He cannot be identified with it, for nature is an incomplete manifestation of His glory; it is only a "part of his mansion." Thomas Vaughan, like the Platonists, held that God created nature because He was in love with His own Beauty; moreover nature itself was too beautiful to be eternally hidden in the Mind of God. Speak-

[1] A. C. Judson, *Studies in Philosophy*, vol. xxiv.
[2] *The Magical Writings of T. Vaughan*, London, 1888, p. xxiii.
[3] *The Works of T. Vaughan*, edited by A. E. Waite, 1919, p. 58
[4] "Retirement," Martin, ii, p. 462.

ing of God's creatures he says: "He considered them first and made them afterwards. God in His eternal idea foresaw that where as yet there was no material copy. The goodness and beauty of the one moved Him to create the other, and truly the image of this prototype, being embosomed in the second, made Him so much in love with His creature that when sin had defaced it, He restored it by the suffering of that pattern by which at first it was made." [1]

Though Thomas Vaughan conceived God as manifesting His love for His creation in nature, the source of this creative energy, heat and light were manifestations of His power in nature, but He was above it: "So that hee overlooks all that he hath made, and the whole fabric stands in his heat and light, as a man stands here on earth in the sun-shine." [2] Thomas Vaughan's conception of nature is complex because it rests on his important and ingenious exposition of the Trinity—the "process of the Trinity from the centre to the circumference." [3] He conceives creation as an act of God revealing Himself in His creation, though essentially remaining apart from it: "God the Father is the Metaphysical super-celestial sun; the Second Person is Light; and the Third is Fiery Love or a Divine Heat proceeding from both. Now without the presence of this Heat there is no reception of the Light and by consequence no influx from the Father of Lights. For this Love is the medium which unites the Lover to that which is beloved, and probably 'tis the Platonic's chief Daimon, who doth unite us with the Perfect of Spirits." [3]

God before this act of creation was "wrapped up and contracted in Himself." Thomas Vaughan says: "Thus we read that 'darkness was upon the face of the deep' and 'the spirit of God moved upon the face of the waters.' Here you are to observe that, notwithstanding this process of the Third Person, yet was there no light, but darkness on the face of the deep, illumination properly being the office of the Second. Wherefore God also, when the matter was prepared by Love for Light, gives out His *Fiat Lux*, which was no creation—as most think—but an emanation of the word, in whom was life,

---

[1] *Anthroposophia Theomagica*, by T. Vaughan, edited by A. E. Waite.
[2] *Coelum Terrae*, pp. 142–143.
[3] *The Works of T. Vaughan*, edited by A. E. Waite, p. 14.

and that life is the light of men. This is the light whereof St. John speaks, that it 'shineth in darkness; and the darkness comprehended it not.' " [1]

This Divine Light, which was not only creation but an emanation of the Word, was infused into the matter and the Holy Ghost modelled the world according to the pattern which was in the Mind of God. He explains: "No sooner had the Divine Light pierced the bosom of the matter but the idea or pattern of the whole material world appeared in those primitive waters, like an image in a glass. By this pattern it was that the Holy Ghost framed and modelled the universal structure." [2] Now this structure was only an image of the original pattern which existed before the act of creation in the Mind of God. In a very interesting passage Thomas Vaughan says: "This is it which the Divine Spirit intimates to us in that Scripture where He saith that God created 'every plant of the field before it was in the earth, and every herb of the field before it grew.' But, notwithstanding this presence of the *idea* in Matter, the creation was not performed 'by the projection of something from the essence of the idea,' for it is God that comprehends His creature and not the creature God." [3] It is in the *manner* of creation, the Divine Light piercing the "bosom of matter," that the two worlds, the visible and the invisible, become linked; and Love is the link which united these two worlds. This conception of nature also explains the spirituality of matter which is a favourite idea of Henry Vaughan. He conceives nature as being conscious of life:

> "*Hedges have ears*, said the old *Sooth*,
> *And ev'ry bush is somethings booth*;
> This cautious fools mistake . . . ." [4]

Henry Vaughan thinks that not only do these two worlds co-exist but they also communicate with each other:

> "But I (alas!)
> Was shown one day in a strange glass
> That busie commerce kept between
> God and his Creatures, though unseen." [4]

Thomas Vaughan thought that God was immanent in nature

---

[1] *The Works of T. Vaughan*, edited by A. E. Waite, p.15.
[2] *Ibid.*, p. 16.   [3] *Ibid.*, p. 18.
[4] "The Stone," Martin, ii, p. 515.

as He was immanent within the individual soul; he conceives
the union of God with nature as a "Kiss"—"mysterious Kiss
of God and Nature" [1]—and thinks that "to speak then of God
without Nature is more than we can do, for we have not
known Him so; and to speak of Nature without God is
more than we may do, we should rob God of His glory and
attribute." [2]

In Thomas Vaughan we also meet the clear exposition of
the Hermetical conception of the two worlds, the visible and
the invisible, a conception which is ever present in Henry
Vaughan's nature poetry. Thomas Vaughan says in *Coelum
Terrae*: "Here we have two worlds, visible and invisible, and
two universal Natures, visible and invisible, out of which both
these worlds proceeded. The passive universal Nature was
made in the image of the active universal one, and the conformity of both worlds or Sanctuaries consists in the original
conformity of their principles." [3] He argues that spirituality
of matter is based on the fact that God created nature in His
own image as He created the soul in His own likeness. He
points out that when God "was disposed to create, He had no
other pattern or exemplar whereby to frame and mould His
creatures but Himself. But having infinite inward ideas or
conceptions in Himself, as he conceived so He created: that
is to say He created an outward form answerable to the inward
conception of figure of His mind." [4]

The Act of Creation was thus the result of God's own love for
Himself, for "God in love with His own beauty frames a glass,
to view it by reflection." [5] And man, Vaughan points out in
Lumen de Lumine, is "employed in a perpetual contemplation of
the absent beauty." [6] We can get a glimpse of this hidden
beauty of God in His creation; this conception of creation
gives us an insight into Henry Vaughan's conception of nature
as a revelation of the creative energy of God. He sees in
nature a shadow of eternity:

> "My gazing soul would dwell an houre
> And in those weaker glories spy
> Some shadows of eternity."

---

[1] *The Works of T. Vaughan*, edited by A. E. Waite, p. 93. (Henry Vaughan also
defined life as "A quickness, which my God hath Kist.")
[2] *Ibid.*, p. 395.   [3] *Ibid.*, p. 192.   [4] *Ibid.*, p. 193.
[5] *Ibid.*, p. 5.   [6] *Ibid.*, p. 298.

He believes that God's "absent" beauty is "present" in His creation and thus in nature is revealed the creative glory of God. He views nature as calling man to God:

> "O that man could do so! that he would hear
> The world read to him! all the vast expence
> In the creation shed, and slav'd to sence
> Makes up but lectures for his eie, and ear."

He holds that all things in God's creation "shew him heaven," [1]

> ". . . trees, herbs, flowers, all
> Strive upward still, and point him the way home." [1]

Henry Vaughan's conception of nature is not pantheistic, for he does not *identify* God with nature; nature only points the way to God, who is *above* nature. His soul is eager not to drown itself in the beauties of nature but to fly high above it to God:

> ". . . It was time
> To get thee wings on, and devoutly climbe
> Unto thy God." [2]

The soul in its flight towards God would soar

> "Above the stars, a track unknown and high." [2]

This view of nature may be termed the Christian conception of nature; speaking from the orthodox Christian point of view, mysticism is the attempt of the human soul to pierce through the veil of appearance to behold reality, and a synthetic and comprehensive vision of things is an essential quality of the mystic's mind; he perceives things as finally related to each other in an organic whole. The Christian who believes that God alone created the world cannot belittle the manifold and wondrous expression of His creative power and beauty.

The religious significance of nature symbolism goes back to the significant ritual in paganism. Nature poetry is not a typical modern phenomenon, it is only a secular version of the religious element in the pagan poetry of ritual and mystery play.

Dean Inge thinks that the Divine in nature has been discovered more fully by the Christian poets and theologians,

---

[1] "The Tempest," Martin, ii, p. 461. [2] "Isaac's Marriage," *ibid.*, p. 409.

and justifies this attitude towards nature as religious, but calls it "more contemplative than practical." He says: "Our Lord's precept, 'consider the lilies,' sanctions this religious use of Nature; and many of His parables, such as that of the Sower, show us how much we may learn from such analogies.   And be it observed that it is the normal and regular in Nature which in these parables is presented for our study; the yearly harvest not the three years' famine; the constant care and justice of God, not the 'special providence' or the 'special judgement.' We need not wait for catastrophes to trace the finger of God . . . but we may perhaps extract from the precept quoted above the canon that the highest beauty that we can discern resides in the real and natural, and only demands the seeing eye to find it." [1]

It is the "seeing eye" of the poet which discerns in the life of nature the handiwork of God, and this discovery of the poet leads him to "nature mysticism," which rests on the belief that everything in the world is symbolic of something higher and nobler.   This attitude towards nature is present in "the doctrine of signatures" which was current in the seventeenth century, and which held that "though Sin and Satan have plunged mankinde into an ocean of Infirmaties, the mercy of God, which is over all His workes, maketh grasse to grow upon the Mountaines and Herbes for the use of Men, and hath not only stamped upon them a distinct forme, but also given them particular signatures, whereby a man may read, even in legible characters, the use of them." [2]

To this doctrine there are repeated allusions in Vaughan's poems, not only herbs and flowers but also dust and stone "all have signature or life."   Herbalism thus provides another connecting link between medicine and mysticism in the seventeenth century.   Hermes Trismegistus held that the visible world mirrors the invisible world; Sir Thomas Browne expressed the attitude of the physicians of his day towards Hermetical philosophy when he said: "The severe Schools shall never laugh me out of the Philosophy of Hermes (*i.e.* Trismegistus) that this visible world is but a picture of the invisible, wherein, as in a portrait, things are not truly but in

[1] *Christian Mysticism*, W. R. Inge, p. 301.
[2] "Henry Vaughan, Silurist," *The Nineteenth Century*, vol. lxvii, p. 502.

equivocal shapes, and as they counterfeit some real substance in that invisible framework." [1]

The doctrine of the immanence of God in nature was fully developed by Eckhart, and it was embodied by Cornelius Agrippa and Paracelsus in their exposition of occult philosophy,[2] with which, as I have shown, Henry Vaughan, like his twin brother, Thomas Vaughan, was quite familiar.

Henry Vaughan was a student of natural philosophy, and in his poems he has claimed to have carried on some scientific experiments about the nature of things. This is an important phase in the development of his nature mysticism, for he in later years distrusted the scientific method of apprehending reality.[3] John Aubrey, writing to Anthony à Wood, says that he has written for Henry Vaughan the natural history of Surrey:

"I desire from kindness to tell him (Dr. Plott of Magdalen Hall) that I have writt out for him the Natural History of Metshire and of Surrey, and a sheet or two of other counties; and am now sending to my cosn. Henry Vaughan, silurist, in Brecknockshire, to send me the natural history of it, as also of the other circumjacent counties: no man fitter." [4]

In his poems Henry Vaughan displays an intimate knowledge of herbs and birds which is more scientific than poetic; the Hermetic physician is present in such observations as:

> "harmless violets, which give
> Their virtues here
> For salves, and syrups, while they live."

And he displays the interest of a naturalist in his observations on the life of birds in some of his poems, like "The Bird"; and there are many allusions to wild flowers in his poems, such as "Man." In "Vanity of Spirits" he says:

> "I summon'd nature: peirc'd through all her store,
> Broke up some seales, which none had touch'd before." [5]

But he realized the futility of the scientific method in knowing the ultimate reality; having searched nature, he came to search himself, where he found the echoes of "eternal hills." In

---

[1] *Religio Medici.*   [2] *Christian Mysticism*, Inge, p. 273.
[3] Martin, ii, p. 616.   [4] *The Nineteenth Century*, vol. lxvii, p. 501.
[5] Martin, ii, p. 418.

"The Search" he has definitely said that "The Skinne, and Shell of things," though fair can never lead us to God:

> "Search well another world; who studies this,
> Travels in Clouds, seeks Manna, where none is." [1]

And when he had searched the other world (by which he means the invisible world of Hermetical philosophy) he realized that the echoes of eternity were not in external nature but within his own self. Vaughan conceived God immanent in nature as *Spirit*, but transcendent as a *Source*. God fills the world unseen, and still remains above it:

> "Up to those bright, and gladsome hils
> Whence flowes my weal, and mirth,
> I look, and sigh for him, who fils
> (Unseen) both heaven, and earth." [2]

It is not nature but God Himself who is Henry Vaughan's "sole stay":

> "He is my Pillar, and my Cloud,
> Now, and for ever more." [2]

He realizes that God is present as an unseen spirit in nature, but one cannot have the mystic's "full-eyed" vision of God in nature, and so he longs to "climb" to God and leave these "masques and shadows" of His glory in created nature behind:

> "That in these masques and shadows I may see
> Thy sacred way,
> And by those hid ascents climb to that day
> Which breaks from thee
> Who art in all things, though invisibly." [3]

He knows that the ultimate reality is God; and that it is only when the mystic lives and has his being in God that he can apprehend reality:

> "There, hid in thee, shew me his life again
> At whose dumbe Urn
> Thus all the year I mourn." [3]

Nature has a reality of its own, and being the creation of God embodies His "active breath." Thomas Vaughan held the same faith: "for Nature is the voice of God, not a mere sound or command but a substantial, active breath, proceeding

[1] Martin, ii, p. 407.   [2] "Psalm-121," Martin, ii, p. 458.
[3] "I Walk'd the Other Day," Martin, ii, p. 479.

from the Creator and penetrating all things." God Himself is "a spermatic form," and this is the only sense in which a form may be defined as "the outward expression of an inward essence." [1] In this manner, nature, Thomas Vaughan points out, can reveal God to us. He, like Henry Vaughan, tries to climb to God through visible nature. He says that God can be known by "using and trying His creatures. For in them lies His secret path." [2] The object of knowledge is not nature but God Himself. He says: "Let them approach with confidence to the Almighty God who made the world, for none can give a better account of the work than the Architect." [2]

It is God alone who can reveal the true story of His creation. Henry Vaughan also declares that God can be known in His creatures, they lead man to God:

> "Sure, mighty love foreseeing the descent
> Of this poor creature, by a gracious art
> Hid in these low things snares to gain his heart,
> And layd surprizes in each Element." [3]

Though God is present unseen in nature, He is ultimately above it; the immanence and transcendence are the two inseparable aspects of the Deity. Henry Vaughan recognizes that God's Hand is visible in His creation:

> "The beams of thy bright Chambers thou dost lay
> In the deep waters, who no eye can find;
> The clouds thy chariots are, and thy path-way
> The wings of the swift wind." [4]

He is searching God in Heaven as on earth; he quotes the significant lines of Psalm lxxiii, verse 25: "Whom have I in heaven but thee? and there is none upon earth, that I desire besides thee." [5]

In the freshness of childhood the "gilded Cloud" and flowers were to him "Bright *Shootes* of everlastingness" [6]; and later he maintained that nature though speechless is not dumb:

> "And stones, though speechless, are not dumb." [7]

And he believed that herb and flower are "shadows of His

---

[1] *The Works of T. Vaughan*, Waite, p. 84.   [2] *Ibid.*, p. 85.
[3] Martin, ii, p. 461.   [4] *Ibid.*, p. 494.
[5] *Ibid.*, p. 505.   [6] *Ibid.*, p. 419.   [7] *Ibid.*, p. 531.

wisdome, and His Pow'r." [1] He says that nature receives the quickening of its life from God:

> "Darkness, and daylight, life and death
> Are but meer leaves turn'd by thy breath." [2]

Nature depends for its life on God, as does the soul of man:

> "Spirits without thee die
> And blackness sits
> On the divinest wits,
> As on the Sun Ecclipses lie." [2]

He sees the hand of God working in nature; but God is not in nature, He is "far" above it:

> "There's not a wind can stir
> Or beam pass by
> But strait I think (though far)
> Thy hand is nigh." [3]

God drew the circle of creation and His presence now fills it; days and nights to Henry Vaughan are the blinds through which he can have a glimpse of God:

> ". . . who drew this circle even
> He fills it; Dayes and hours are Blinds." [4]

He knows that everything that subsists has its "Commission from Divinitie," [5] and in "The Rainbow" he gives us a complete exposition of his conception of God as being immanent and transcendent at the same time. Addressing the rainbow he says:

> "When I behold thee, though my light be dim,
> Distant and low, I can in thine see him,
> Who looks upon thee from his glorious throne
> And mindes the covenant 'twixt *All* and *one*." [6]

Thus God looks from His throne on the glorious and colourful pageant of nature which He has created; He is *all* in nature and *one* above it. Thomas Vaughan has also quoted a passage from Pseudo-Dionysius with approval where he expounds a similar idea: "Nay also (sayeth the Areopagite) they declare him to be present in our minds, and in our souls, and in our bodies, and to be in Heaven equally with earth, and in himself at the same time; the same also they declare to be in the

---

[1] Martin, ii, p. 438. [2] *Ibid.*, p. 457. [3] *Ibid.*, p. 420.
[4] *Ibid.*, p. 425. [5] *Ibid.*, p. 482. [6] *Ibid.*, p. 510.

world, around the world, above the world, above the Heaven, the Superior Essence, Sun, Star, fire, water, Spirit, dew, cloud, the very stone, and rock, to be in all things which are, and himself to be nothing which they are." [1]

God is in all things and still He is not identified with them, He is "nothing which they are."

Though Henry Vaughan recognized the presence of God in nature, and declared that His spirit "feeds" "all things with life," [2] he has a clear conception of God's transcendence. God is "above the morning-starre," [3] he wants to "climb unto thy God," [4] and Heaven to him is "a countrie far beyond the stars," [5] and he speaks of the "transcendent bliss" [6] of knowing God.

Thomas Vaughan also conceived God as sitting on His throne and filling the world with His creative energy, which he identified with Light. He imagines "the great world . . . above all which God Himself is seated in that infinite, inaccessible Light which streames from His own nature." [7]

Henry Vaughan conceived God as Light and Heat filling the whole "frame" of the world:

"O thou immortal light and heat!
Whose hand so shines through all this frame,
That by the beauty of the seat
We plainly see who made the same." [8]

He conceived nature as having life of its own; and, being conscious of its life, nature also prayed to God:

". . . There is not a *spring*
Or *Leaf* but hath his *Morning-hymn*; Each Bush
And *Oak* doth know *I AM*." [9]

Nature, which did not share in the Fall to the same extent as man did, has a better memory of its "home." Man strays from the path leading to his home:

"Nay hath not so much wit as some stones have
Which in the darkest night point to their homes." [10]

---

[1] *Anthroposophia Theomagica*, p. 35.   [2] Martin, ii, p. 515.   [3] *Ibid.*, p. 462.
[4] *Ibid.*, p. 408.   [5] *Ibid.*, p. 430.   [6] *Ibid.*, p. 539.
[7] *Anthroposophia Theomagica*.
[8] Martin, ii, p. 488; for other poems where H. Vaughan speaks of God as Heat and Light see "I Walk'd the Other Way" and "Love-Sick"; see also T. Vaughan, *Coelum Terrae*, 1650, p. 218.
[9] Martin, ii, p. 436.   [10] *Ibid.*, p. 477.

In "The Constellation" he asserts in the Franciscan manner that the herbs which man treads upon "know much, much more."[1] He believes that all nature shared in the "Law and ceremonies"[2] and "had equal right"[2] to be benefited with the appearance of "the Sun of righteousness," Christ. Nature, like man, was expecting to be redeemed by the death of Christ:

"Trees, flowers, & herbs; birds, beasts, & stones
That since man fell, expect with groans
To see the lamb, which all at once
Lift up your heads and leave your moans." [3]

He says that the death of Christ was man's life and nature's "full liberty." [3]

Henry Vaughan has thus clearly recognized the same "divine spark" in nature which he finds in the human soul:

"And so the flowre
Might have some other bowre." [4]

Thomas Vaughan likewise said: "There is not an herb here below but he hath a star in heaven above." [5]

Henry Vaughan again declared:

"Dear *Soul*! thou knew'st, flowers here on earth
At their Lords foot-stool have their birth." [6]

He holds that the herbs even know the Providence of God and "praise thy bounteousness" [7]; the hills and valleys also sing the praises of their Creator, for they were taught their lesson "when first made" [8]:

"So hills and valleys into singing break,
And though poor stones have neither speech nor tongue,
While active winds and streams both run and speak,
Yet stones are deep in admiration." [8]

To Henry Vaughan the presence of the "Divine spark" in nature was the proof that the spirit of God was still operative in nature:

"It seems their candle, howe'er done
Was tinn'd, and lighted at the sun." [9]

The Divine image in his own heart gives him hope that God would dwell in him:

---

[1] Martin, ii, p. 409.   [2] *Ibid.*, p. 451.   [5] *Ibid.*, p. 501.
[4] *Ibid.*, p. 478.   [5] *The Works of T. Vaughan*, p. 299.   [6] Martin, ii, p. 508.
[7] *Ibid.*, p. 506.   [8] *Ibid.*, p. 497.   [9] *Ibid.*, p. 488.

> "Seeing thy seed abide in me,
> Dwell thou in it, and I in thee." [1]

Thomas Vaughan advanced a similar theory of creation in *Anima Magica Abscondita*. Speaking of the soul he says: "She is guided in her operations by a spiritual, metaphysical *grain*, or *seed*, or *glance* of light, simple and without any mixture, descending from the first *Father of Lights*. For though His *full-eyed love* shines on nothing but man, yet everything in the world is in some measure directed for his preservation by a spice touch of the First Intellect." [2]

So Henry Vaughan declared:

> "This veyle thy full-ey'd love denies,
> And only gleams and fractions spies." [3]

Henry Vaughan's enjoyment of the beauties of nature was to a certain extent determined by the mystic's vision of the universe as the "Shadow" or reflection of God. To him the green trees, mountains and living streams were the "boundless Empyrean themes" and commentaries on His Creative Power. Vaughan's landscape is typically Welsh; he does not paint scenes of vast spaces or sublime mountains; nor does he try to create imaginary landscapes like those of Shelley. The Celtic spirit in him flowered with all its delicate sensitiveness to the sensible world and its power of vision. He met "surprise in each element" [4] and discerned God and Heaven in the pageant of earth and sky:

> "All things I see,
> And in the heart of Earth, and night
> Find Heaven, and thee." [5]

As a nature poet his favourite themes are dawn and night. Mornings are "mysteries" [6] to him, and it is in the hour of dawn that he waits with the eagerness and wonder of a great lover for the "*Bridegroome's coming*" [7]:

> "Unlock thy bowres,
> And with their blush of light descry
> Thy locks crown'd with eternity." [7]

---

[1] Martin, ii, p. 488.
[3] Martin, ii, p. 489.
[5] *Ibid.*, "The Evening Watch," p. 426.
[6] *Ibid.*, p. 436.

[2] *Anima Magica Abscondita*, p. 81.
[4] *Ibid.*, p. 461.
[7] *Ibid.*, p. 451.

It is in the morning that the whole world "awakes, and sings," and the mystic in him seems to hear "the great *chime and symphony* of nature." [1]   He even conceived prayer as "the world in tune," in which the spirit of man and the spirit of nature both take a solemn and joyous part.

Vaughan held that, in order to discern the spirit of God working and realizing itself in nature, man must first purify his inner self:

> "What sublime truths, and wholesome themes,
> Lodge in thy mystical, deep streams!
> Such as dull man can never finde
> Unless that spirit lead his minde,
> Which first upon thy face did move,
> And hatch'd all with his quickning love." [2]

The spirit that moved on the face of nature must also move in the soul of man before he can understand the mystery of creation.   This is the central theme of Vaughan's philosophy of nature mysticism.   Vaughan conceived that herbs and trees, birds and man, each had a "divine spark":

> "For each enclosed spirit is a star
> Inlightning his own little sphere." [3]

The light has been "borrowed from far," but it is the same light which is in the soul of man and the heart of nature.   The bond of union between the visible and the invisible world is God's love attained through holiness, which Henry Vaughan calls "the Magnet":

> "Sure, *holyness* the Magnet is,
> And *Love the Lure*." [4]

Thomas Vaughan also speaks of "the infallible Magnet, the Mystery of union," by which he conceives that "all things may be attracted, whether Physicall or metaphysicall, be the distance never so great," [5] and he defines this magnet as Love, "For this ' Love ' is the medium which unites the Lover to that which is beloved." [6]

Henry Vaughan recognized that the means to apprehend God were holiness and love; and though in the glories of nature the purified vision of the mystic may behold the spirit

---

[1] Martin, ii, p. 424.   [2] *Ibid.*, p. 538.   [3] *Ibid.*, p. 497.
[4] *Ibid.*, p. 539.   [5] *Anthroposophia Theomagica*, p. 20.   [6] *Ibid.*, p. 12.

of God working, this spirit could not be identified with God
Himself:

> "If the sun rise on rocks, is't right,
> To call it their inherent light?" [1]

The way leading to God was the narrow and the arduous way
which the mystics have ever travelled throughout the ages:
repentance, purgation, illumination are the stages which ultimately lead to the union of the soul with God. Repentance
to him is

> "The little gate
> And narrow way, by which to thee,
> The passage is." [2]

Though Vaughan possessed the mystic's capacity of seeing
the angels ascending and descending in nature, he, like the
orthodox Christian mystic, knew that the path leading to God
was "a narrow, private way," [3] the way of humility, poverty
and repentance.

The mystic may discern a glimpse of God in the glories of
His creation, but the "full-eyed" vision of God could only be
attained through purification and the mystical birth of Christ
in the human soul. Through these veils of appearance,
Vaughan's "Ecclips'd Eye" [4] could not behold the "Ultimate
Reality, God," and so he declared that he was eager to be
dissolved and be "nothing" in order to stand face to face with
God:

> "*I'le disapparell, and to buy*
> *But one half glance, most gladly dye.*" [4]

Thomas Vaughan also held that it was only through the dissolution of the body that we could see God; speaking of the
Divine origin of the soul he says, "thus her descent speaks her
original. . . . But the frailty of the matter excluding eternity,
the composure was subject to dissolution." [5] In *Lumen de
Lumine* he observes that it is after the dissolution of the body
that "we shall know the Hidden Intelligence and see that Inexpressible Face which gives the outward figure to the body." [6]
It is, he says, through the love of God that man would enter
into the bond of "Eternal Unity" with God and the soul shall

[1] Martin, ii, p. 395.   [2] *Ibid.*, p. 448; also see pp. 498 and 521.
[3] *Ibid.*, p. 498.   [4] *Ibid.*, p. 419.
[5] *Anthroposophia Theomagica*, p. 5.   [6] *Lumen de Lumine*, p. 299.

find "the true Sabbath, the Rest of God into which the Creature shall enter." [1]

It is thus evident that Henry Vaughan was influenced by the "doctrine of Signatures," the Hermetical conception of the world, and the relation of the invisible to the visible world as expounded by his twin brother Thomas Vaughan in his magical writings.   The constant references in Henry Vaughan's poetry to heat, light and magnetism, and the subtle processes of life in nature, can only be understood by a study of the occult philosophy of his brother, where they have a definite significance and value.   It was perhaps from occult philosophers like Cornelius Agrippa and Hermes Trismegistus that Henry Vaughan drew his conception of God as being immanent in nature, and still transcending it, which is the keynote of his mystical as well as his nature poetry.

[1] *Lumen de Lumine,* p. 302.

CHAPTER VII

THOMAS TRAHERNE, THE MYSTICAL PHILOSOPHER

THOMAS TRAHERNE alone of all the mystical poets of the seventeenth century has tried to give us a systematic exposition of his philosophy. The reality of his own mystical experience became the subject-matter of his philosophical speculations, which gives breadth, richness and intensity to his poems and prose alike. The abstract philosophy tinged with the Neo-Platonism of his times was thus transformed into an intensely personal faith. Traherne's claim to be regarded as a Divine philosopher, a claim which he himself advanced in his preface to *Christian Ethicks*, and in *Centuries of Meditations*, has been largely ignored by his critics:

"I will open my mouth in Parables, I will utter things that have been kept secret from the foundation of the world. Things strange, yet common; incredible, yet known; most high, yet plain; infinitely profitable yet not esteemed. . . . The thing hath been from the creation of the world, but hath not been so explained as that the interior Beauty should be so understood. It is my design, therefore, in such a plain manner to unfold it that my friendship may appear in making you the possessor of the whole world." [1]

That his quest was philosophical in the higher sense of the word, as the quest of Plotinus was, in which personal experience is woven into the fabric of an organic system of philosophy, is evident from a close perusal of his "fourth century" (*Centuries of Meditations*). The important fact in the study of the religious mysticism of Thomas Traherne is that he apprehended the truth of Christianity philosophically. He holds that the perfect man is a Divine philosopher: "But he that is Perfect is a Divine Philosopher, and the most glorious creature in the whole world. Is not a Philosopher a lover of Wisdom?" [2]

---

[1] Preface to *Christian Ethicks*.   [2] *Centuries of Meditations*, Dobell, 1908, p. 241.

And he further argues that as a Christian is a perfect man he must necessarily be a philosopher: "That is the signification of the very word, and sure it is the essence of a Christian, or very near to it, to be a lover of wisdom. . . . Every man, therefore, according to his degree, so far forth as he is a Christian, is a Philosopher." [1] The mystic always gives us his real experience and actual knowledge: and hence mystical doctrines in their turn are never merely speculative, even if they involve speculation. In its essence mysticism is experimental.

Professor Rufus Jones has pointed out that mysticism is "religion in its most acute, intense and living stage." [2]

Traherne has synthesized his mystical experience with his philosophy, they illustrate each other; a philosophy divorced from personal experience has no meaning for him: "Philosophers are not only those that contemplate happiness, but practise virtue. He is a philosopher that subdues his vices, lives by reason, orders his desires, rules his passion, and submits not to his senses, nor is guided by the customs of the world." [3] In short, he is a man who has proposed to himself "a superior end than is commonly discerned." [3] Such a man was a true and perfect Christian, and Traherne himself tried to live up to this ideal.

We shall study him primarily as a mystical philosopher. Underhill says that mysticism "is an art of establishing man's conscious relation with the Absolute," and that it is an "organic process which involved the perfect consummation of the love of God." [4] Traherne fulfils these conditions in a high degree; in his unique personality the active and the contemplative sides of mysticism were exquisitely harmonized, and he gave a supreme expression to the glory of "the perfect consummation of the love of God," which he declared was the end of all true felicity: "For besides contemplative, there is an active happiness, which consisteth in blessed operations. And some things fit a man for contemplation, so there are others fitting him for action: which as they are infinitely necessary to practical happiness, so are they likewise infinitely conducive to contemplation itself." [5] His philosophy is

[1] *Centuries of Meditations*, p. 241.
[2] *Studies in Mystical Religion*, p. 15.   [3] *Centuries of Meditations*, p. 244.
[4] *Mysticism*, E. Underhill, p. 96.   [5] *Centuries of Meditations*, p. 238.

instinctive and alive with his own personal experience; his personality is the reflection of his mystical philosophy. Behind the artistic and spontaneous simplicity of Traherne's poetry and prose we discover a mind highly trained, and original enough to steer its way safely through the complicated and involved theological controversies of his times. He was (as *Roman Forgeries* and *Christian Ethicks* show) a great scholar, an authority on ecclesiastical history, but his learning, as we find in *Centuries of Meditations*, was well assimilated. Though, like all mystics, he *rediscovered* for himself the "grandeur and glory of Religion," his debt to Plato is obvious. He had an extensive knowledge of the writings of Plotinus and the Neo-Platonic philosophers from Hermes Trismegistus to Mirandola.

His Christianity is essentially Platonic—the Christianity of the Gospel of St. John and the Pauline epistles, of St. Paul, the mystic who was "caught up" into the third heaven. But he is not a Neo-Platonic mystic like Plotinus; his conception of God as the "God of Love" is essentially Christian, and it differs from that of Plotinus, who conceived God as the "Pure One." This difference is often overlooked by Traherne's critics. "According to Plotinus," says Dr. Bigg, "God is goodness without love. Man may love God, but God cannot love man." [1] The central idea of Christianity, the Incarnation, has no place in the speculative system of Plotinus, while to Traherne it is the supreme act of love. Traherne's debt to Plato and Plotinus does not lie in the ideas and concepts which he borrowed from their philosophy, but in the support this philosophy gave to his own mystical experience: that reason and religion do not contradict each other, and that the religious life is the only reasonable life. As a Platonist and as an advocate of reason in the realm of "divine philosophy," Traherne takes his place in the group of the Cambridge Platonists. In his sweet reasonableness, in his conception of reason and faith, in adopting Neo-Platonic philosophy, he comes nearer to the group of the Cambridge divines than to the followers of Donne. We must remember that Sir Orlando Bridgeman, the patron of Traherne, was a Cambridge man, and his chaplain before Traherne was Hezekiah, one of the group, and the friend of Henry More. Thomas Burton and

[1] For a detailed discussion of this point of view see Bigg: *Neo-Platonism*.

Traherne were both present when their patron drew up his will and it is quite probable that they had met several times before this. Traherne thus had established direct personal contacts with the members of this group.

Traherne came rather late in the history of seventeenth-century mysticism. Donne lived from 1573–1631, Herbert, 1593–1633, Vaughan, 1621–95. The Cambridge Platonists were writing their philosophical and theological treatises about the middle of the seventeenth century; Traherne was born about 1636 and died in 1674. If we divide the mystics of the seventeenth century into two main groups—the devotional poets of the school of Donne and the mystical philosophers of the Cambridge group—Traherne has closer affinities with the latter than with the former group, though in the main he reflects the general spirit of the movement rather than any particular side of the Cambridge Platonists.

The themes of his mystical poetry and prose are the themes of "Divine Philosophy," as he himself says of St. Paul: "But there is also a Divine Philosophy of which no books in the world are more full than his own. That we are naturally the Sons of God (I speak of primitive and upright nature), that the Son of God is the first beginning of every creature, that we are to be changed from glory to glory, into the same Image, that we are spiritual Kings, that Christ is the express Image of His Father's Person, that by Him all things are made whether they are visible or invisible, is the highest Philosophy in the world; And so is it also to treat, as he does, of the nature of virtues and Divine Laws." [1] This may be taken as Traherne's comprehensive description of the themes of Divine philosophy which are also the themes of his poetry and prose alike.

Before attempting to analyse the themes of his mystical philosophy I would try to explain his conception of childhood, its relation (a) to his own personal experience as a child, and (b) the influence of this experience on his mysticism; for his mysticism, though highly philosophical, had its seeds in the intuitions of childhood.

Traherne, like Vaughan, recognized and felt the innocence and sanctity of childhood, which he ascribed to a child's nearness to God:

[1] *Centuries of Meditations*, pp. 239, 240.

> "He in our childhood with us walks
> And with our Thoughts mysteriously he talks." [1]

Both these poets believed that they were in communion with God in the innocence of their childhood and they looked back to it as a time of "Angell Infancy."

Vaughan asked:

> "Since all that age doth teach is ill
> Why should I not love childhood still?"

And in a similar vein Traherne declared:

> "And as I backward look again,
> See all his Thoughts and mine most clear and plain.
> He did Approach, He me did woo;
> I wonder that my God this thing would do." [1]

But here the resemblance ends. Vaughan's experience leads him to other planes of reality:

> "I cannot reach it; and my striving eye
> Dazzles at it, as at eternity." [2]

Traherne could not write of childhood as a period of life which man could not live again: he believes in the recovery of the vanished light. To him Christ's injunction that "*He must be born again and become a little child that will enter into the Kingdom of Heaven*" [5] is of real and immediate significance. He says that the blest state of childhood is to be achieved through our conscious effort: "It is not only in a careless reliance upon Divine Providence, that we are to become little children, or in the feebleness and shortness of our anger and simplicity of our passions, but in the peace and purity of all our soul, which purity also is a deeper thing than is commonly apprehended. . . . And therefore it is requisite that we should be as very strangers to the thoughts, customs, and opinions of men in this world, as if we were but little children, those things would appear to us only which do so to children when they are first born . . . and only those things appear, which did to Adam in Paradise, in the same light and in the same colours: God in his Works, Glory in the light, Love in our parents, men, ourselves and the face of Heaven: Every

---

[1] "The Approach," Dobell, p. 31.
[2] Martin, p. 520.

man naturally seeing those things, to the enjoyment of which he is naturally born." [1]

Man was to regain the child-like faculty of seeing spiritual things naturally and directly, to the enjoyment of which he is "naturally born," and in this process he was to recover again the freshness and wonder of a child's first impressions of the world. Traherne himself seems to have achieved it:

> "For till His works *my* wealth became,
> No Love, or Peace did he enflame:
> But now I have a DEITY." [2]

Traherne's idealization of childhood is based on the innocence and glory of his own childhood, the memory of which lingered in his soul throughout his life and largely determined the nature of his doctrine of felicity. In his "native health and innocence of childhood" he saw all the world in celestial light:

> "I felt a vigour in my sense
> That was all spirit. I within did flow
> With seas of life, like wine;
> I nothing in the world did know
>   But 'twas divine." [3]

He has given us a connected and vivid account of his own childhood in the "third century" of *Meditations*, where he tells us of his early "obstinate questionings" about the nature of the world and God. His main conception of childhood, however, is based on three important conceptions: (1) in his "Estate of Innocence" there is no trace of original sin; (2) the glory, wonder and freshness of vision in childhood ever remained a vivid experience with him; (3) he believed that the pure and virgin apprehensions of reality in childhood were intuitions of reality. He had no consciousness of sin in his childhood. "I knew not," he wrote, "that there were any sins, or complaints, or laws. I dreamed not of poverties, contentions or vices. All tears and quarrels were hidden from mine eyes." [4] He says:

---

[1] *Centuries of Meditations*, p. 161.

[2] "Poverty," *The Poetical Works of Thomas Traherne*, edited by G. I. Wade, p. 128. "Works" here refers not to the Bible but God working in the glory of the created universe.

[3] "Wonder," Dobell, p. 5.

[4] *Centuries of Meditations*, iii, 2.

> "Nor did I dream of such a thing
> As sin, in which mankind lay dead." [1]

He believes the child to be free from the taint of original sin: "And that our misery proceedeth ten thousand times more from the outward bondage of opinion and custom, than from any inward corruption or depravation of Nature: And that it is not our parents' loins so much as our parents' lives, that enthral and blind us." [2]

He lived in his childhood as if it was the state of grace before the Fall:

> "Only what Adam in his first estate,
> Did I behold;
> . . . my blessed fate
> Was more acquainted with the old
> And innocent delights which he did see
> In his original simplicity." [3]

While his soul in childhood was "a fort, Impregnable to any sin," [4] he was also blessed with the pure and virgin apprehensions about the nature of the world, its glory and richness reflected the beauty of its Creator:

> "And every stone, and every star a Tongue,
> And every Gale of Wind a curious song.
> The Heavens were an oracle, and spake
> Divinity: The Earth did undertake
> The office of a Priest." [4]

His life in childhood was free from all "Contagion" [5] and he saw things "Ev'n like unto the Deity." [5] This way of apprehending reality was based on the "Sacred Instinct" [6] which inspired his soul in childhood. Everything was transformed for him, even "the corn was orient and immortal wheat" which stood from "everlasting to everlasting." [7] And "All Time was Eternity and a perpetual Sabbath." [7] Though Traherne has given us the "sublime and celestial greatness" of childhood, he has not explained its mystery. The reason, perhaps, is that he did not believe in the pre-existence of the soul. This is why he did not express any definite opinion on its origin, as we find in Vaughan or Wordsworth:

---

[1] "Eden," Dobell, p. 8.   [2] *Centuries of Meditations*, iii, 8, p. 164.
[3] Dobell, p. 9.   [4] "Dumbness," *ibid.*, p. 35.   [5] Wade, p. 104.
[6] *Ibid.*, p. 113.   [7] *Centuries of Meditations*, p. 157.

> "The soul that rises with us, our life's star
> Hath had elsewhere its setting
> And cometh from afar." [1]

He has given us the wonder and mystery of childhood but he does not try to solve its mystery. He had accepted the Biblical story of Creation literally and he believed that God created the first man in his Image out of nothing:

> "From dust I rise,
> And out of nothing now awake!" [2]

This nothingness was an eternity:

> "I that so long
> Was nothing from Eternity." [2]

The miracle of birth remains a supreme mystery to him:

> "How like an Angel came I down!
> How bright are all things here!" [3]

He is at a loss to account for his early innocence:

> "Whether it be that Nature is so pure,
> And custom only vicious; or that sure
> God did by Miracle the guilt remove,
> And made my soul to feel His love
> So early." [4]

Traherne's speculations about God and His relation to the world were nevertheless influenced by His experience as a child, when he enjoyed the beauty and magnificence of the world and regarded it as his own:

> "A stranger here
> Strange things doth meet, strange glories see;
> Strange treasures lodg'd in this fair world appear,
> Strange all and new to me;
> But that they mine should be, who Nothing was,
> That strangest is of all, yet brought to pass." [5]

Traherne soon lost this capacity of enjoying and possessing the world, and he ascribes it to the corrupt customs and manners of civilization: "The first Light which shined in my Infancy in its primitive and innocent clarity was totally eclipsed: in so much that I was fain to learn all again. If you ask me how it was eclipsed? Truly by the customs and manners of men,

---

[1] Wordsworth's "Ode on Immortality."
[2] Dobell, p. 2, 1.
[3] *Ibid.*, p. 4.
[4] *Ibid.*, p. 13.
[5] *Ibid.*, p. 3.

which like contrary winds blew it out . . . and at last all the celestial, great, and stable treasures to which I was born, as wholly forgotten, as if they had never been." [1]

The story of his progress in felicity is then briefly told in the "third century": having been "swallowed up therefore in the miserable gulf of idle talk and worthless vanities" of the world, he did not find any longer the "bliss which Nature whispered and suggested to me," until he entered the University and there found a totally new world of fascinating ideas awaiting exploration: "Having been at the University and received there the taste and tincture of another education, I saw that there were things in this world of which I never dreamed; glorious secrets, and glorious persons past imagination. There I saw that Logic, Ethics, Physics, Metaphysics, Geometry, Astronomy, Poesy, Medicine, Grammar, Music, Rhetoric, all kinds of Arts, Trades, and Mechanisms that adorned the world pertained to felicity . . . there were received all those seeds of knowledge that were afterwards improved; and our souls were awakened to a descerning of their faculties, and exercise of their powers." [2]

Though his eager curiosity for knowledge was satisfied at the University, he did not learn there how to achieve felicity. He says: "There was never a tutor that did professly teach Felicity" [3]; and the means to achieve felicity were revealed to him at last in the Bible. Traherne's debt to the Bible is not confined to its imagery and diction, he himself confesses that the reading of the Bible was a central fact in his life, it confirmed his belief in the goodness of God and the beauty and wonder of the world he had known in childhood:

"And by that book I found that there was an eternal God, who loved me infinitely, that I was His son, that I was to overcome death and to live for ever, that He created the world for me, that I was to reign in His throne and to inherit all things. Who would have believed this had not that Book told me? It told me also that I was to live in communion with Him, in the image of His life and glory, that I was to enjoy all His treasures and pleasures, in a more perfect manner than I could devise, and that all the truly amiable and glorious persons in

---

[1] *Centuries of Meditations*, pp. 162, 163.
[2] *Ibid.*, pp. 186, 187.   [3] *Ibid.*, p. 187.

the world to be my friends and companions." [1] Here in a nut-
shell is the essence of the mystical philosophy of Traherne
which he learnt from the Bible. But his real conversion
to a new way of life perhaps occurred when he returned
to the country after finishing his University career and,
"being seated among silent trees, and meads and hills, had
all my time in my own hands," and resolved "to live upon
ten pounds a year" and devote himself to the study of felicity
and realize the truth of religion in his own life. He observes:
"For it is impossible for language, miracles, or apparitions to
teach us the infallibility of God's word, or to shew us the
certainty of true religion, without a clear sight of truth itself,
that is into the truth of things." [2]

His means of achieving felicity, and thus knowing "the truth
of things," was a return to the simplicity of childhood with its
naïve trust in God, its capacity of enjoying and thus possessing
the world: "So that with much ado I was corrupted, and
made to learn the dirty devices of this world which now I
unlearn, and become, as it were, a little child again that I may
enter into the Kingdom of God." [3] Elsewhere he declared:
"I knew by intuition those things which since my Apostasy I
collected again by the highest reason." [4]

His main ideas embodied in his mystical philosophy can be
conveniently studied under the following three headings:

(1) Traherne's Conception of God and His relation to the
    World.
(2) Traherne's Conception of the Soul and its way of
    apprehending Reality.
(3) The nature of the Union of the Soul with God and the
    manner in which it is achieved.

Under the last heading I will also be able to discuss the
quality of Traherne's own mystical experience apart from his
philosophical speculation about the nature of the soul's union
with God, and thus answer the question which is inevitable in
the case of every mystic—Did he enjoy a direct vision of God
in the illuminative or unitive stages of the Mystic Way?

Traherne's conception of God in many respects is that

[1] *Centuries of Meditations*, pp. 181, 182.   [2] *Ibid.*, p. 194.
[3] *Ibid.*, p. 158.   [4] *Ibid.*, p. 157.

of the New Testament; he holds that God is Love and the human soul and the created universe are both emanations of Divine Love. To him God is Love—"God is Love, and my Soul is Lovely!"[1]—and he remarks that "He is not an object of Terror but Delight."

Traherne points out the futility of knowing God through a *negative* way, by discovering what He is not. Many medieval mystics, following Dionysius the Areopagite, who held that "there is no contact with the Deity, nor has it any communion with the thing participating in it,"[2] had declared that no symbol was sublime enough to express the Infinite God and that the mind should be deliberately stripped of every earthly likeness or analogy of His being (these mystics were at the opposite pole of thought to the "pantheistic mystics" who tried to discover the *One* in Many). St. Augustine declared "we must not even call God ineffable, since this is to make an assertion about Him. He is above every name that can be named."[3]

The self thus emptied would attain to an abstraction which the mystics called the Desert of Godhead, or "the Divine Darkness" of the soul. Traherne holds that in order to apprehend the true nature of felicity we must not try to discover God through negatives: "Nevertheless great offence hath been done by the philosophers and scandal given, through their blindness, many of them, in making Felicity to consist in negatives. They tell us it doth not consist in riches, it doth not consist in honors, it doth not consist in pleasures. Wherein then saith a miserable man doth it consist?"[4]

He holds that the world is a means of beautifying the soul, which would be empty and deformed without the manifold ideas with which nature furnishes it: "Your soul, being naturally very dark, and deformed and empty when extended through infinite but empty space, the world serves you in beautifying and filling it with amiable ideas; for the perfecting of its stature in the eyes of God."[5]

Traherne saw God in all that was good and beautiful, and he remarked, as Plato had done before him, that "to know

[1] *Centuries of Meditations*, p. 49.
[2] See *Eternal Life*, by Von Hügel, p. 97.   [3] *De Trin.*, vii, 4, 7.
[4] *Centuries of Meditations*, pp. 153, 154.   [5] *Ibid.*, p. 139.

Him therefore as He is is to frame the most beautiful idea in all worlds." [1] He declared "to know God is to know Goodness. It is to see the beauty of infinite Love: To see it attended with Almighty Power and Eternal Wisdom; and using both those in the magnifying of its object." [2]

To know God as Goodness, Beauty and Love is "to see the King of Heaven and Earth take infinite delight in Giving." [4] Traherne thinks that this is the only way of *knowing* God: "Whatever knowledge else you have of God, it is but Superstition." [2]

The infinite goodness and beauty of God is made accessible to man; this is the significance of God's attributes:

"He delighteth in our happiness more than we: and is of all other the most Lovely object. An infinite Lord, who having all Riches, Honors, and pleasures in His own hand, is infinitely willing to give them unto me. Which is the fairest idea that can be devised." [3]

This goodness and beauty of God are not abstract attributes, they are transformed into what Traherne calls an *Act*, which is the becoming *actual* of what was potential in God:

> "His Essence is all Act; He did that He
> All Act might always be." [4]

It is the attribute of His nature to be possessed and enjoyed by all:

> "His nature burns like fire;
> His goodness infinitely does desire
> To be by all possesst." [4]

God was self-sufficient and could have subsisted without any *Creation*, but He not only revealed His attributes in the creation of man and nature but also communicated his goodness to the soul of man:

> "He is an Act that doth communicate." [4]

The beauty of God is also in conformity with *Law* and can be discerned by *Reason*: "It is an idea connatural to the Notion of God, to conceive Him Wise and Good, and if we can see some Reason in his ways, we are apt to suspect there is no

---

[1] *Centuries of Meditations*, p. 12. [2] *Ibid.*, pp. 11, 12.
[3] *Ibid.*, p. 12. [4] "The Anticipation," Dobell, p. 85.

Deity, or if there be, that he is Malevolent and Tyrannical, which is worse than none. For all Wisdom and Goodness are contained in Love." [1]

Though love, beauty and joy "adorn the God-head's dwelling-place," [2] it is a beauty which is well-ordered:

"Order the beauty even of beauty is,
It is the rule of bliss,
The very life and form and cause of Pleasure." [2]

Love, Beauty, Joy and Order are to Traherne the different aspects of the Deity.

In *Christian Ethicks* [3] Traherne has shown how far the Deity is limited by this law of "Order in Beauty." He holds that the Power of God could not exist without Wisdom, and in God there is no separation between these attributes; this is why nothing is possible to God which is not infinitely excellent, for in Him Power, Wisdom and Will are identical. The Wisdom of God is revealed in ordering and regulating His creation. To moderate God's Power "is to limit or extend it as Reason requires. Reason requires that it should be so limited as most tends to the perfection of the universe." [4] God is thus "the Law-giver of Heaven and Earth," [5] and in ordering, regulating His Power, He has revealed His infinite Wisdom and Love.

"His Wisdom did His Power here repress," [6]

and thus created a perfect pattern of Wisdom; thus God's Power is limited only so far as He is incapable of doing anything imperfectly. The greatest attribute of God is thus His unity.

"God is not a Being compounded of body and soul, or substance and accident, or power and act, but is all act, pure act, a simple Being whose essence is to be, whose Being is to be perfect so that He is most perfect towards all and in all. He is most perfect for all and by all. He is nothing imperfect, because His being is to be perfect. It is impossible for Him to be God and imperfect." [7] As God is perfect therefore He is Pure Act, or as Traherne says "all act": "All His power

---

[1] *Christian Ethicks*, p. 49. [2] "The Vision," Dobell, p. 20.
[3] Chapter xiii, "Of Temperance in God."
[4] *Christian Ethicks*, chapter xiii, p. 341.
[5] *Centuries of Meditations*, p. 52. [6] Dobell, p. 120.
[7] *Centuries of Meditations*, p. 208.

being turned into Act, it is all exerted; infinitely and wholly.
. . . Were there any power in God unemployed He would be
compounded of Power and Act. Seeing therefore God is
all Act, He is a God in this, that Himself is Power exerted.
An infinite Act because infinite Power infinitely exerted. An
Eternal Act because infinite power eternally exerted." [1]

Traherne declares that Knowledge and Wisdom are the
attributes of God as "Eternal Act," for "He is one infinite Act
of KNOWLEDGE and WISDOM, which is infinitely beautified
with many consequences of Love." [2] What is the *nature* of
God who is limited by Wisdom, enriched by Knowledge and
possesses infinite Power? Traherne has defined it as *Love*.
He calls God "Pure Love"; it is in love that the unity of His
Being is expressed: "God is not a mixt compound Being, so
that Love is one thing, and Himself another; but the most
pure and simple of all Beings, all Act, and pure Love in the
abstract." [3] To Traherne, God's Love is "The Fountain" of
"Heaven and Earth" [4]; and it is also

"Abridgement of Delights!
And Queen of sights." [5]

In "Anticipation" he has given a metaphysical conception
of the nature of God as an Act of bliss:

"From all to all Eternity He is
That Act: an Act of Bliss:
Wherein all Bliss to all,
That will receive the same, or on Him call,
Is freely given: from whence
'Tis easy even to sense
To apprehend that all Receivers are
In Him, all gifts, all joys, all eyes, even all
At once, that ever will or shall appear." [6]

God's Power was thus infinitely exerted towards a definite
end, that being Infinite Love. It is in the nature of love
to manifest itself: "for it seems all love is so mysterious
that there is something in it which needs expression and can
never be understood by any manifestation (of itself in itself)
but only by mighty doings and sufferings." [7] God's Love
could not be complete until "it has poured out itself in all

[1] *Centuries of Meditations*, p. 208.   [2] *Ibid.*, p. 139.   [3] *Ibid.*, p. 109.
[4] Dobell, "Another," p. 93.   [5] "Love," *ibid.*, p. 94.
[6] Dobell, "The Anticipation," p. 93.   [7] *Centuries of Meditations*, p. 284.

its communications."[1]   This idea is the keystone of Traherne's conception of the relation of God to the world:

> "In all His works, in all His ways,
> We must His glory see and praise;
> And since our pleasure is the end,
> We must His Goodness, and His Love attend." [2]

The creation of the world and its relation to God, according to Traherne, could be understood only by recognizing the end of creation, which is to please the object of God's Love, man. God, as he says, in "The Circulation,"

> ". . . the primitive eternal spring
> The endless ocean of each glorious thing." [3]

And the human soul is "spacious" enough to contain this Infinite Love of God:

> "The Soul a vessel is,
> A spacious bosom, to contain
> All the fair treasures of His bliss,
> Which run like Rivers, from into the main,
> And all it doth receive returns again." [4]

Thus he pictures the created universe as a vast "circulation" of God's Love and so all things ultimately return to Him. Traherne significantly remarks: "Socrates, perhaps, being an heathen, knew not that all things proceeded from God to man, and by man returned to God; but we that know it must need all things as God doth, that we may receive them with joy and live in His image." [5]

God created Heaven and earth so that man may recognize Him in the *symbolism* of Creation: "We needed Heaven and Earth, our senses, such souls, such bodies with infinite riches in the Image of God to be enjoyed." [5]

We must understand the two implications of creation: it was necessary for the perfection of God's Love, and it was equally necessary for the union of God and Man. In the work of His creation God desired to please man as well as Himself: "Infinite Goodness loves to abound, and to overflow infinitely with infinite treasures. Love loves to do somewhat for its object more than to create it. It is always more stately being surrounded with power, and more delighted being inaccessible

---

[1] *Centuries of Meditations*, p. 284.
[2] "The Recovery," Dobell, p. 88.   [3] "The Circulation," Dobell, p. 73.
[4] "The Demonstration," *ibid.*, p. 79.   [5] *Centuries of Meditations*, p. 28.

in a multitude of treasures, and more honourable in the midst of admirers; and more glorious when it reigneth over many attendants. Love therefore hath prepared all these for itself and its object." [1]

The world was created so that it may serve as a means of communication between God and Man, the Lover and the Beloved; thus the supreme attribute of God as Love is that He can be known, and does *communicate* Himself. "It is absolutely impossible," he declares, "that any power dwelling with Love should continue idle. Since God therefore was infinitely and eternally communicative, all things were contained in Him from all eternity." [2]

The things when created therefore bore an impress of His Divinity, Wisdom, Power and Love. To Traherne, thus, God is the "object" of felicity, the "manner" of our enjoyment of God is through the enjoyment and possession of the world, and the human soul is the means by which the man is to enjoy God—he says: "All which you have here, God, the World, yourself." [3]

In the "second century" he has explained God's "manner of revealing Himself" [4] in the world. He defends God's being invisible, for "whatsoever is visible is a body; whatsoever is a body excludeth other things out of the place where itself is. If God therefore being infinite were visible He would make it impossible for anything to have a being." [4] Moreover he could not assume any *body* for it would have been incapable of expressing His attributes. He points out that "the world is that Body, which the Deity hath assumed to manifest His Beauty and by which He maketh Himself as visible, as it is possible He should." [5]

He argues that it is only in the "manifold and delightful mixture of figures and colours" of this world that God's Beauty and Wisdom could be revealed:

"Ancient Philosophers have thought God to be the Soul of the World. Since therefore this visible world is the body of God, not His natural body, but which He hath assumed; let us see how glorious His Wisdom is in manifesting Himself thereby. It hath not only represented His infinity and

---

[1] *Centuries of Meditations*, p. 50.   [2] *Ibid.*, p. 209.   [3] *Ibid.*, p. 155.
[4] *Ibid.*, pp. 90, 91.   [5] *Ibid.*, p. 92.

eternity which we thought impossible to be represented by a body, but His beauty also, His wisdom, goodness, power, life, and glory, His righteousness, love, and blessedness: all which, as out of a plentiful treasury, may be taken and collected out of this world." [1]

It is difficult to assign any definite source for these Neo-Platonic ideas of God and His relation to the world; perhaps one of the "ancient philosophers" he has in mind is Plotinus, who in the "sixth Ennead" has expressed strikingly similar thoughts, as these: "God is not external to anyone, but is present in all things, though they are ignorant that he is so," and "God is not in a certain place, but wherever anything is able to come into contact with him there he is present."

This idea, however, underlies Traherne's conception of the world and its relation to God. The goodness and grandeur of God's creation was to Him a sufficient proof of His existence:

> "The Author yet not known
> But that there must be one was plainly shewn;
> Which Fountain of Delights must needs be Love
> As all the Goodness of the Things did prove." [2]

To Traherne the world is "the Paradise of God" [3]; it is the "glorious mirror" [4] wherein "you shall see the face of God," [4] and so "the brightness and magnificence of this world . . . is Divine and wonderful." [5]

The world is thus the symbolic expression of the manifold attributes of God, His Power, Wisdom, Glory and Love, and it provides man with the means of establishing communion with God, for "His omnipresence was wholly in every centre: and He could do no more than that would bear: communicate Himself wholly in every centre." [6]

The way of communion with God was the enjoyment and "possession" of the world, this is the central idea of Traherne's Doctrine of Felicity:

"He wanted the communication of His divine essence, and persons to enjoy it. He wanted worlds, He wanted spectators, He wanted joys, He wanted treasures," [7] for as he points out "want is the fountain of all his fulness," [7] and that "want in God is Treasure to us," [7] and thus "wants are the bands and

---

[1] *Centuries of Meditations*, p. 93. [2] *Nature*, H. I. Bell, p. 73.
[3] *Centuries of Meditations*, p. 21. [4] *Ibid.*, p. 90.
[5] *Ibid.*, p. 25. [6] *Ibid.*, p. 137. [7] *Ibid.*, p. 29.

cements between God and us." [1] Traherne maintains that unless man enjoys the world, and esteems it as his own, the end of creation is not attained, and God is infinitely grieved:

> "If we despise His glorious works,
> Such sin and mischief in it lurks
> That they are all made vain;
> And this is even endless pain
> To Him that sees it. Whose diviner grief
> Is hereupon (Ah me!) without relief." [2]

He imagines God as the Bridegroom who has built this palace of created universe for His Bride, Man; and therefore nothing would displease Him more than the rejection of the world:

> "As bridegrooms know full well that build
> A Palace for their Bride. It will not yield
> Any delight to him at all
> If she for whom he made the hall
> Refuse to dwell in it
> Or plainly scorn the benefit." [3]

To God, man's enjoyment of the world is more important than all the glorious universe He has created:

> "Her Act that's woo'd yields more delight and pleasure
> If she receives, than all the pile of treasure." [3]

Traherne's theory of *enjoyment* of the world deserves a fuller treatment, which however cannot be attempted in this brief survey.[4] It can be summed up in one of his most striking utterances on this subject. He says: "You shall be like Him, when you enjoy the world as He doth," [5] for by taking an infinite delight in His creation we shall be fulfilling the *end* for which He created the world:

> "Our blessedness to see
> Is even to the Deity
> A Beatific Vision! He attains
> His Ends while we enjoy. In us He reigns." [6]

Mere enjoyment is not sufficient, we must be conscious of possessing the world and then enjoying it as our own: "your enjoyment of the world is never right, till you so esteem it, that everything in it, is more your treasure than

---

[1] *Centuries of Meditations*, p. 34.
[2] Dobell, "The Recovery," pp. 88.   [3] *Ibid.*, pp. 88, 89.
[4] For further references see the following pages of *Centuries of Meditations*, 16, 18, 20, 29–32, 39, 54, 55, 90, 115.
[5] *Centuries of Meditations*, p. 90.   [6] Dobell, p. 87.

a King's exchequer full of Gold and Silver."[1] When we have developed the faculty of "possessing" and enjoying the world fully, then and then alone the magnificence of the world will truly be revealed to us :·

> "Here I was seated to behold new things,
> In the fair fabrick of the King of Kings.
> All, all was mine." [2]

But the world must be seen under a definite law; we must see things in their true perspective so that we may see them as God intended us to see them. He says "the World is unknown . . . till the Beauty and the serviceableness of its parts is considered." [3] In order to *know* the world we must conceive it as the manifestation of the divine law: "Everything in its place is admirable, deep and glorious, out of its place like a wandering bird, is desolate and good for nothing." [4] The first step to attain felicity was thus to recognize the truth that "All things were well in their proper places, I alone was out of frame and had need to be mended." [5] This process of possessing and enjoying the world is nothing but the establishment of a new spiritual relation with the world. The "outward things," he says, "lay so well, methought, they could not be mended : but I must be mended to enjoy them." [5]

Order, clarity, precision, beauty, unity and law are the qualities which the world shares in common with the attributes of God. The *wisdom* of God is revealed even in the minute parts of a grain of sand: "You never enjoy the world aright, till you see how a sand exhibiteth the wisdom and power of God." [6] When we have realized this truth we shall understand how everything "conduceth in its place, by the best means to the best of ends." [7]

Traherne's view of the manner of enjoying the world does not only consist in recognizing the fact that "all things were infinitely beautiful in their places," [8] but he also holds that this manner is essentially spiritual. You cannot enjoy the world and behold the beauty of God's creation without the aid of your *senses*, but this is an elementary stage of enjoy-

---

[1] *Centuries of Meditations*, p. 18.   [2] "Nature," Dobell, p. 52.
[3] *Centuries of Meditations*, p. 12.
[4] *Ibid.*, "Third Century," No. 55; also see ii, 13; iii, 62; iii, 60; i, 10.
[5] *Ibid.*, p. 206.   [6] *Ibid.*, p. 19.   [7] *Ibid.*, p. 126.   [8] *Ibid.*, p. 264.

ment: "By the very right of your senses you enjoy the World. Is not the beauty of the Hemisphere present to your eye? Doth not the glory of the sun pay tribute to your sight? Is not the vision of the World an amiable thing?" [1]

It is after you have realized the significance of the glory of the world and its beauty has entered into your soul that the real enjoyment begins—"you never enjoy the world aright, till the Sea itself floweth in your veins, till you are clothed with the heavens, and crowned with the stars." [2] Thus the true enjoyment of the world leads us to achieve oneness with nature.

Having assimilated the glory and beauty of the world till "your spirit filleth the whole world," [2] you realize the great truth that reality is not objective but subjective: "the services of things and their excellencies are spiritual: being objects not of the eye, but of the mind; and you are more spiritual by how much more you esteem them." [3] He shows in his beautiful poem "Nature" how the soul spiritualizes the material objects until life itself becomes

> "A Day of Glory where I all things see
> As t'were enriched with Beams of Light for me." [4]

This is the mystic's way of apprehending reality; he acknowledges the existence of Matter, but Matter without Spirit is of no significance to him. In his poem "Praeparative" he says:

> "'Tis not the object but the light
> That maketh Heav'ns 'tis a clearer sight.
> Felicity
> Appears to none but them that partly see."

Reality can thus be apprehended by what he calls the "Ministry of Inward Light." [5]

Ideas signifying the spiritual concepts are the only reality, and these alone can transcend the narrow boundaries of space and matter. In "Dreams" he observes:

> "Thought! Surely *Thoughts* are true;
> They please as much as *Things* can do:

[1] *Centuries of Meditations*, p. 15:
> "My senses were informers to my Heart,
> The conduits of His Glory, Power and Art" ("Nature").

[2] *Ibid.*, p. 20.　　　[3] *Ibid.*, p. 19.
[4] Dobell, p. 51.　　　[5] Dobell, "The Circulation," p. 72.

> Nay Things are dead,
> And in themselves are severed
> From souls; nor can they fill the Head
> Without our thoughts.   Thoughts are the Real Things
> From whence all joy, from whence all sorrow springs." [1]

He sometimes seems even to doubt the *reality* of matter apart from spirit:

> "... I could not tell
> Whether the Things did there
>   Themselves appear,
> Which in my spirit truly seem'd to dwell:
> Or whether my conforming Mind
> Were not ev'n all that therein shin'd." [2]

He affirms the superiority of "thoughts" to "things":

> "Compar'd to them,
> I *Things* as *Shades* esteem." [3]

Nature to him is subjective and not objective, and this explains the unreality of his "nature poetry"; he describes his *sense* of enjoyment of the glory of nature but there are no descriptions of visible nature, hills, flowers and streams, as in Wordsworth:

> "*Things* are indifferent, nor giv
> Joy of themselves, nor griev." [4]

Even true Things when unknown have no reality for us, but Mind can transcend Matter and apprehend them through *Ideas*:

> "*Things true* effect not, while they are known:
> But Thoughts most sensibly, tho quite alone." [4]

Mind being the only Reality, the enjoyment of the world consists in *ordering* our thoughts, so that they may present to the mind a true picture of the Thing:

> "... what care ought I
> (Since Thoughts apply
> Things to my Mind) those Thoughts aright
> To frame, and watch them day and night;
> Suppressing such as will my Conscience stain,
> That *Heav'nly Thoughts* me *Heav'nly Things* may gain." [4]

This conception of the relation of matter to mind elucidates

[1] "Dreams," *Poetical Works of T. Traherne,* edited by G. I. Wade, pp. 193, 194.
[2] "My Spirit," Wade, p. 162.
[3] "The Review," Wade, p. 207.
[4] "The Inference," Wade, pp. 194, 195.

many difficult passages in *Centuries of Meditations* where he affirms that the idea of the world is better than the world itself: "What would Heaven and Earth be worth were there no spectator, no enjoyer? As much therefore as the end is better than the means, the thought of the world whereby it is enjoyed is better than the world. So is the idea of it in the Soul of Man, better than the World in the esteem of God: being the end of the World, without which Heaven and Earth would be in vain." [1]

The end of the world is that man may enjoy it, and as it is enjoyed through ideas, the image of the world within our mind is more precious to God than the material world which He Himself has created. This is the startling result of Traherne's mystical speculation about the nature of Reality: "The world within you is an offering returned which is infinitely more acceptable to God Almighty, since it came from Him, that it might return unto him. Wherein the mystery is great. For God hath made you able to create worlds in your own mind which are more precious unto Him than those which He created; and to give and offer up the world unto Him, which is very delightful in flowing from Him, but much more in returning to Him." [2]

The world before its *actual* creation had existed in the Mind of God, and its image can again exist in the mind of man, and in this way man comes nearer to God's idea of the world: "Besides all which in its own nature also a Thought of the World or the World in a Thought, is more excellant than the World, because it is spiritual and nearer unto God. The material world is dead and feeleth nothing, but this spiritual world, though it be invisible, hath all dimensions, and is a divine and living Being, the voluntary Act of an obedient soul." [3] Man in this way comes nearer to the creative Consciousness of God.

The spiritual world within our mind is "nearer unto God," because all things exist in His mind; and in this manner of apprehending Reality we come nearer to His Mind, the Source of all Creation:

---

[1] *Centuries of Meditations*, pp. 143, 144.
[2] *Ibid.*, p. 144.   [3] *Ibid.*, pp. 144, 145.

"All Things appear
All things are
Alive in Thee! Super-Substantial, Rare
Above themselves, and nigh of kin
To those pure Things we find
In his Great Mind
Who made the World!" [1]

This concept of Reality also explains the nature of Traherne's imagination, which enabled him to feel so intensely the life of the past ages and the glory of new kingdoms beyond the seas; it almost becomes a "vision": "When the Bible was read, my spirit was present in other ages. I saw the light and splendour of them, the land of Canaan, the Israelites entering into it, the ancient glory of the Amorites, their peace and riches. . . . I saw all and felt all in such a lively manner, as if there had been no other way to those places, but in spirit only." [2] For one who has established such intimate relations with the divine consciousness, there is no past or future, for "time-divisions" are mainly confined to human minds.

Whether the object has any real existence apart from the observer appeared to him beside the point: "The sun would shine in vain to you could you not think upon it" [3]; and he further declares: "Dead things are in a room containing them in a vain manner; unless they are objectively in the Soul of a seer. The pleasure of an enjoyer is the very end why things placed are in any place. The place and the thing placed in it being both in the understanding of a spectator of them." [4]

In order to understand the mystical significance of these ideas we must bear in mind the fact that Traherne was occupied with the problem of how to attain *union* with God and he thought that this could be achieved by the exercise of three faculties in three *distinct* stages.

To sum up what I have explained in detail, he believed that—(1) the world must first be *known* through observation, (2) and the way in which it embodies the attributes of God must then be understood, and (3) man must develop the faculty of enjoying and possessing the world. The first implies the use of the senses in observing and realizing the beauty of the world, the second of the intellect in appre-

[1] "My Spirit"; this idea is again repeated in "Silence" and "Consummation."
[2] *Centuries of Meditations*, p. 176.
[3] *Ibid.*, p. 144.   [4] *Ibid.*, p. 78.

hending its significance, and the third of the soul in loving and prizing it as the glorious manifestation of the attributes of God.

I have described in detail the first two stages of what Traherne calls "the Way of Felicity." The perception of the material beauty of the world by the aid of the senses is man's first step towards God. He declared that "by the very right of your senses you enjoy the World." [1] The next stage concerns the intellect, when you turn from the observation of *things* to the contemplation of their *ideas*:

> "When I so in *Thoughts* did finish
> What I had in Things begun." [2]

This spiritual apprehension of Reality was better than the perception of the beauty of the material world through the senses, for he believed that "the idea of Heaven and Earth in the soul of Man is more precious with God than the things themselves and more excellent in nature." [3] Traherne seems to have anticipated the Berkleyan conception that the reality and permanence of the material world is due to its reality and permanence as an *idea* in the Mind of God: "If He would but suspend His power, no doubt but Heaven and Earth would straight be abolished, which He upholds in Himself as easily and as continually as we do the idea of them in our own mind." [4] God "upholds" the world in His Mind because it is "the Manifestation of Eternal Love" [4]: and this Divine process of sustaining the world, Traherne argues, must be repeated in the mind of man if he is to love God: "We likewise ought to show our infinite love by upholding Heaven and Earth, Time and Eternity, God and all things in our Souls, without wavering or intermission: by the perpetual influx of our life." [4]

This is the highest achievement of the mystic in the second stage, when in his soul he comprehends the world and re-creates it in his mind, for "were you able to create other worlds, God had rather you should think on this. For thereby you are united in Him." [5] The third stage, when the soul

[1] *Centuries of Meditations*, p. 15.   [2] Wade, p. 206.
[3] *Centuries of Meditations*, p. 143.
[4] *Ibid.*, p. 142.
[5] *Ibid.*, p. 144.

loves and prizes what the senses have observed and the intellect comprehended, involves the discussion of the nature of the soul, its relation to God, the effects of the Fall on man and his redemption through Christ, and Traherne's conception of the nature of the soul's union with God.

Traherne's whole conception of the soul and its relation to God is based on the belief common to all mystics that man was made in the image of God, and he is the noblest thing which God has created: "It is no blasphemy to say that God cannot make a God": and further adds that "Since there cannot be two Gods the utmost endeavour of Almighty Power is the Image of God."[1]

The Divine powers inherent in man's soul depend on its being an image of God: "God from all Eternity was infinitely blessed and desired to make one infinitely blessed. He was infinite Love, and being lovely in being so, would prepare Himself a most lovely object. Having studied from all Eternity, He saw none more lovely than the Image of His Love, His own Similitude, O Dignity unmeasurable."[2]

The soul in order to contain the infinite Love of God must be infinite in itself: "Infinite love cannot be expressed in finite room: but must have infinite places wherein to utter and shew itself,"[3] for God is as eager for our Love as we are for His:

"He seeks for ours as we do for His,
Nay, O my Soul, ours is far more His bliss
Than His is ours; at least it so doth seem
Both in His own and our esteem."[4]

The infinite capacity to love, to know, and to possess are to Traherne the *three* supreme attributes of the soul:

"Few will believe the soul to be infinite: yet infinity is the first thing which is naturally known. Bounds and limits are discovered only in a secondary manner. . . . That things are finite therefore we learn by our senses. But infinity we know and feel by our souls, and feel it so naturally as if it were the very essence and being of the Soul."[5]

This infinite capacity of the soul is due to God's presence in it: "the Truth of it is, it is individually in the Soul: for God

---

[1] *Centuries of Meditations*, p. 206.   [2] *Ibid.*, p. 49.   [3] *Ibid.*, p. 136.
[4] "Another," Dobell, p. 91.   [5] *Centuries of Meditations*, pp. 136, 137.

is there, and more near to us than we are to ourselves. So that we cannot feel our souls, but we must feel Him, in that first of properties, infinite space." [1]

Traherne has given us this conception of an ideal and pure soul in his poem "My Spirit," and he holds that the highest attribute of the soul in childhood is its infinite capacity for knowledge and love:

> "I felt no dross nor matter in my Soul,
> No brims nor borders, such as in a bowl
> We see. My Essence was capacity,
> That felt all things." [2]

Mind to Traherne is the instrument of knowledge; soul, the instrument of love, and they are both intimately connected. Love he holds is not independent of knowledge for love presupposes knowledge, and so he defines the soul as "mind exerted, reaching the Infinity." [3] In God, soul and mind are identical, He knows and loves together as a *simple* Act. "O Glorious Soul," he exclaims, "whose comprehensive understanding at once contains all Kingdoms and Ages! O Glorious Mind! whose love extendeth to all creatures!" [4] Soul in its uncorrupted state in childhood possessed this faculty of knowing and prizing things as they are.

> "But being simple like the Deity
> In its own centre is a Sphere
> Not shut up here, but everywhere." [5]

This infinite capacity of the soul is natural to it and is only lost through sin. He asks: "What shall we render unto God for this infinite space in our understanding? Since in giving us this He hath laid the foundation of infinite blessedness, manifested infinite love, and made us in capacity infinite creatures."

Man must show this infinite capacity of his soul in loving God who is Infinite Love.

"By Love alone is God enjoyed, by Love alone delighted in, by Love alone approached or admired. His Nature requires Love, thy nature requires Love. The law of Nature commands

---

[1] *Centuries of Meditations*, pp. 136, 137.
[2] "My Spirit," Dobell, p. 41.
[3] *Ibid.*
[4] *Centuries of Meditations*, p. 44.
[5] "My Spirit," Dobell, p. 41.
[6] *Centuries of Meditations*, p. 132.

thee to Love Him—the Law of His nature, and the Law of thine." [1]

It is the nature of God to be beloved and possessed by man, for the blessedness of man consists in His Love.

> "His goodness infinitely does desire
> To be all possesst;
> His Love makes others blest." [2]

Though the world is "a perfect Token of His perfect Bliss," [3] the supreme mystery of Divine Love is expressed in the person of Jesus Christ: "*God by loving begot His son. For God is Love, and by loving He begot His Love. He is of Himself and by loving He is what He is, INFINITE LOVE.*" [4]

God "begot" His son so that man may be restored to the original purity and happiness which he had enjoyed before the Fall. The *knowledge* of the state of blessedness before the Fall, Traherne holds, is essential to understand the full implication of redemption through Christ: "*Remember from whence thou art fallen and repent. Which intimates our duty of remembering our happiness in the estate of innocence. For without this we can never prize our Redeemer's love: He that knows not to what he is redeemed cannot prize the work of redemption.*" [5] He has given an exquisite description of man's glorious estate before the Fall in his poem "Adam's Fall," and in several poems [6] where he deals with the native innocence of the soul in childhood which resembles the blessed state before the Fall:

> "Encompass'd with the Fruits of Lov,
> He crowned was with Heven abov,
> Supported with the Foot-stool of God's Throne,
> A Globe more rich than gold or precious stone,
> The fertil Ground of Pleasure and Delight,
> Encircled in a sphere of Light." [7]

God's sending of Christ to redeem the sins of man and thus restoring him to his original purity was a supreme act of love: "His Love therefore being infinite, may do infinite things for

---

[1] *Centuries of Meditations*, p. 53.   [2] "The Anticipation," Dobell, p. 85.
[3] *Ibid.*, p. 83. He affirms the superiority of soul to created nature in poems like "Admiration" and "Insatiableness."
[4] *Centuries of Meditations*, p. 109.
[5] *Ibid.*, p. 83.
[6] These poems are, "An Infant Ey," "News," "Nature" and "My Spirit."
[7] "Adam's Fall," Wade, p. 116.

an object infinitely valued. Being infinite in Wisdom, it is able also to devise a way inscrutable to us, whereby to sever the sin from the sinner and to satisfy its righteousness in punishing the transgression, yet satisfy itself in saving the transgressor. And to purge away the dross and incorporated filth and leprosy of sin: restoring the Soul to its primitive beauty, health and glory. But then it doth this at an infinite expense, wherein also it is more delighted, and especially magnified, for it giveth Another equally dear unto itself to suffer in its stead. And thus we come again by the Works of God to our Lord Jesus Christ." [1]

Traherne holds that redemption could have been achieved through the death of Christ alone. He argues [2] that even angels were unworthy to perform man's redemption and suffer for his sins, for it was an act of supreme love reserved by God for His son who "would humble Himself to the Death of the Cross for our sakes." [2] He points out that "one great cause why no Angel was admitted to this office, was because it was an honour infinitely too great and sublime for them, God accounting none but His own Son worthy of that dignity." [3]

Having been restored to the original purity before the Fall, or even "to greater beauty and splendour than before," [4] it is a greater transgression of the Divine law of love for man to sin now:

"God cannot therefore but be infinitely provoked, when we break His laws. Not only because Love is jealous and cruel as the grave, but because also our duty being so amiable, which it imposeth on us with infinite obligations, they are all despised. His Love, itself, our most beautiful duty and all its obligations. So that His wrath must be very heavy and His indignation infinite." [5]

Sin to him is thus

". . . a Deviation from the way of God." [6]

Sin makes the soul a deformed and an ugly object, and God as Supreme Beauty cannot be *united* to an ugly object; this to Traherne is the greatest *misery* of sin: "Yet Love can forbear, and Love can forgive, though it can never be reconciled to an

[1] *Centuries of Meditations*, p. 103.   [2] *Ibid.*, pp. 104, 105, 106.
[3] *Ibid.*, pp. 104, 105.   [4] *Ibid.*, p. 103.
[5] *Ibid.*, p. 102.   [6] "Adam's Fall," Wade, p. 115.

unlovely object. . . . What shall become of you therefore since God cannot be reconciled to an ugly object? Verily you are in danger of perishing eternally. He cannot indeed be reconciled to an ugly object as it is ugly." [1] If God could be reconciled to an ugly object He would no longer be Supreme Beauty, and therefore it is against the nature of God to be reconciled to an ugly object.

Man was redeemed through Love, and sin is a transgression of the law of love; and as the union of God and man can only take place through love, sin is the greatest hindrance in the attainment of this union.

It is however evident that Traherne has no acute consciousness of sin, and though he recognizes the need of self-discipline in devotional life, it does not constitute what the mystics call the purgative stage. [2]

"No one," says the author of *Theologia Germanica*, "can be enlightened unless he is first cleansed or purified and stripped." [3]

The two aspects of the purification of the self which Underhill calls "the Negative Purification or self-stripping" and "the Positive Purification" or "Mortification," "a deliberate recourse to painful experience and difficult tasks," [4] are not to be found in the life of Traherne. He has not felt what St. Bernard calls "the sharp blade of sincere Repentance." [5] He has not known, like St. Augustine, "the tears of confession, the troubled spirit, the contrite heart." Traherne says: "I do not speak much of Vice which is a far more easie Theme, because I am entirely taken up with the abundance of Worth and Beauty in Virtue." [6]

He seems to have relied too much on the "sacred instincts" of childhood; and his views about the innocence of childhood being corrupted by the "vicious customs" of men resembles more those of the naturalists like Rousseau than those of the typical mystics like St. Bernard or St. Catherine of Siena, in

---

[1] *Centuries of Meditations*, p. 102.
[2] *Western Mysticism*, by Dom C. Butler, p. 143.
[3] *Theologia Germanica*, chapter xiv.
[4] *Mysticism*, by Underhill, pp. 204, 205.
[5] Also see *Western Mysticism*, by Butler, p. 143.
[6] *Christian Ethicks*, "Address to the Reader." Evelyn Underhill has truly observed: "Traherne is no use to me somehow: too meditative and not sufficiently contemplative. I want some one with a higher temperature, at whose fires I may re-enkindle my chilliness."—*The Letters of Evelyn Underhill*, edited by Charles Williams (Longmans, 1943), p. 122.

whom the consciousness of sin was so acute that they realized the need of utter humility; the Voice of God told St. Catherine: "by humbling thyself in the valley of humility thou wilt know Me and thyself, from which knowledge thou wilt draw all that is necessary." [1]

Traherne sees *Order*, *Beauty* and *Love* everywhere in God's creation but he does not try to solve the problem of evil and sin in this world. He recognizes that sin is ugly and therefore a hindrance to man's union with God, Who is the most Sublime Beauty we can conceive of; but he does not show the need of self-purification or mortification to subdue sin.

Plotinus does not recognize the reality of evil in God's creation. "Evil," he says, "is not alone. By virtue of the nature of Good, the power of Good, it is not Evil only. It appears necessarily, bound around with bonds of Beauty, like some captive bound in fetters of Gold." [2] Dean Inge remarks that Plotinus "cannot regard it [evil] as having a substance of its own." [2]

It was perhaps due to the influence of Plotinus that Traherne minimized the presence of evil in the world and called it merely a "deviation from the way of God." [3] It is significant that, like Plotinus, Traherne, as we have seen, has identified God with goodness and declared "To know God is to know Goodness." [4]

Plotinus, Dean Inge has pointed out, assumed "The moral aspiration for the Good. . . . Throughout the Enneads, it is regarded as too fundamental to need argument. Of the Beautiful he says that he who has not yet seen God desires Him as the Good; he who has seen Him adores Him as the Beautiful (I. vi, 7). . . . But he does not really subordinate Beauty to Truth and Goodness. Ultimately they are one and the same." [5]

Traherne also thinks that to apprehend God is to know Goodness, Beauty and Love. [6] Traherne's conception of God and evil and sin was undoubtedly influenced by the philosophy of Plotinus.

[1] *Mysticism*, by E. Underhill, p. 200.
[2] *The Philosophy of Plotinus*, by W. R. Inge, vol. i, p. 22.
[3] See his poem "Adam's Fall."
[4] *Centuries of Meditations*, pp. 11, 12.
[5] See Dean Inge's "Essay on Neo-Platonism, "*Encyclopædia of Religion and Ethics*, vol. ix.
[6] *Centuries of Meditations*, pp. 11, 12.

We do not find the three stages of mystical life—purgation, illumination and union—in any marked degree or in regular order in Traherne's life. The first does not exist, the last two are not separated by any development of mystical consciousness; moreover his conception of illumination differs from those of mystics like St. Augustine or St. John of the Cross.

Traherne does not show any psychological interest in his own religious experience such as we find in St. Augustine, nor does he analyse his mystical experience from a critical point of view as does St. John of the Cross in his great treatise *The Dark Night of the Soul.*

In order to understand the full significance of *Love* in the mystical philosophy of Traherne we must understand his conception of the Trinity, which like the Cambridge Platonists he had borrowed from Plotinus. The Father was the creative source of all things, Whom Traherne calls the Fountain; the Holy Spirit was the Divine spark in the human soul; the Son was the means of enabling the two to be united. To Traherne, God is Lover, Christ is His Love, becoming "in act what it was in power," and thus His Love comes to us through Christ. To realize the true significance of God's Love and Christ's Cross, and to love both the Father and the Son to the utmost of our capacity is to attain felicity.

"Love is the Spirit of God. In Himself it is the Father or else the Son, for the Father is in the Son, and the Son is in the Father: In us it is the Holy Ghost." [1] Thus the Trinity is the expression of the different aspects of the Love of God, as Traherne explains: "In all Love there is some Producer, some Means, and some End; all these being internal in the thing itself. Love loving is the Producer, and that is the Father: Love produced is the Means, and that is the Son; For Love is the means by which a lover loveth. The End of these Means is Love: for it is love by loving: and that is the Holy Ghost." [2] Thus Traherne expounded this characteristic conception of the infinite Love of God through the Trinity, for in "His being Love you see the unity of the Blessed Trinity, and a glorious Trinity in the Blessed unity." [3]

---

[1] *Centuries of Meditations*, p. 112.
[2] *Ibid.*, p. 113; for fuller quotation see pp. 106–111.
[3] *Ibid.*, p. 112.

Caroline Spurgeon has called Traherne a philosophical mystic [1]; but he is more properly a Love mystic, the mystic who found in the conception of God as "Infinite Love" an explanation of the relation of God to the world, the human soul, and Christ. He is certainly a philosopher, but his philosophy of felicity is based on his own personal experience of God as Love—speaking of his own experience of felicity, he remarks: "and by what steps and degrees I proceeded to that enjoyment of all Eternity which I now possess I will likewise shew you." [2]

It is obvious that in the formulation of his mystical philosophy he was influenced by the Platonic school at Cambridge, by the philosophy of such Neo-Platonists as Plotinus and Hermes Trismegistus, and above all by the Bible, in which he discovered (especially in the epistles of St. Paul and the Gospel of St. John [3]) the supreme conception of God as Love and Christ as the highest embodiment of that love. Traherne's mysticism, though expressed in terms of abstract philosophy, is crystallized within the bounds of orthodox Anglicanism, as the publisher of *Christian Ethicks* pointed out: "For he firmly retains all that was established in the Ancient Councils, nay and sees cause to do so, even in the highest and most transcendent mysteries; only he enriches all by farther opening the grandeur and glory of Religion with the interior depths and Beauties of Faith."

To Traherne, the incarnation of Christ was not only a token of God's Love, it was also a positive demonstration of the possibility of the union of God and man. His meditations on the Passion of Christ in the "first century" of *Meditations* show that he had a passionate love of Christ. The vision of the Cross was to Donne a symbol of Christ's sacrifice and humiliation which reminded him of his own sins of youth; to Traherne, in whom the consciousness of personal sin was not so strong, the Cross is a triumphant symbol of man's conquest over death, and his redemption from sin; he says: "our Saviour's Cross is the throne of delights. That centre of Eternity, that tree of Life in the midst of the Paradise of God." [4]

[1] *Mysticism in English Literature.*   [2] *Centuries of Meditations*, p. 162.
[3] Speaking of the illuminated mystic he says: "the revelations of St. John transport him."
[4] *Centuries of Meditations*, p. 39.

The Cross to him is the means of man's union with God:
"The Cross of Christ is Jacob's ladder by which we ascend
into the highest heavens. . . . That Cross is a tree set on fire
with invisible flame, that illuminateth all the world. The
flame is Love; the Love in His bosom who died on it." [1]
The Incarnation of the Son was to Traherne, as to Donne also,
a glorification of the Body. When God assumed the Flesh, he
sanctified the Body and the senses for ever. He remarks
"this Body is not the cloud, but the Pillar assumed to manifest
His love unto us. In these shades doth this sun break forth
most oriently." [2] All the bodily senses thus become the
means of apprehending the goodness and beauty of God:

> "There's not an Ey that's fram'd by Thee
> But ought thy Life and Love to see." [3]

This idea is again repeated in his poem "The Person," and
in his contemplations on the blessings of the body in "A Serious
and Patheticall Contemplation of the Mercies of God." [4]

It was Traherne's belief that "God never shewed Himself
more a God than when He appeared man," [5] for it was the
fulfilment of His Love, and the means of demonstrating the
possibility of the union between God and man, which is the
end of all his creation.

The Incarnation and Crucifixion were the two supreme
aspects of God's Love for man; and, as we have shown,
Traherne believed that the union between God and man could
only be achieved through Love.

He says that the soul was created to be the infinite measure
of God's Love, and "the Soul is shrivelled up and buried
in a grave that does not Love. But that which does love
wisely and truly is the joy and end of all the world, the
King of Heaven, and the Friend of God, the Shining Light
and Temple of Eternity: The Brother of Christ Jesus, and one
Spirit with the Holy Ghost." [6]

To be in *act* what man is in potentiality is Traherne's definition of the union of the soul with God. He declares: "Love
also being the end of souls, which are never perfect till they

---

[1] *Centuries of Meditations*, p. 43.   [2] *Ibid.*, p. 68.
[3] "The Estate," Dobell, p. 64; also see pp. 68, 69.
[4] See "Thanksgiving for the Body," Dobell, pp. 163, 164.
[5] *Centuries of Meditations*, p. 68.   [6] *Ibid.*, p. 116.

are in act what they are in power. . . . Till we become therefore all Act as God is, we can never rest, nor ever be satisfied." [1]

He believes that within certain limits it is possible for man
to become "all Act as God is," but his method of achieving it
is not that of the typical mystics like St. Augustine, St. Bernard,
or St. Teresa, the way of purgation, repentance and illumination; it is for Traherne more a form of *philosophical contemplation.* Speaking of his own speculations about the nature of
God and Eternity he observes: "Little did I think that, while
I was thinking these things, I was conversing with God." [2]
Though he believed that God was "eternally communicative," [3]
for Traherne the channels of communication were not those
of the orthodox Christian mystics.

Critics like G. E. Willett [4] and Rufus M. Jones [5] think that
Traherne believed in the possibility of perfect union with God,
but a closer study of *Centuries of Meditations* shows that Traherne
believed in the communion with God not in a direct vision of Him
in illumination, but in what he called our "Understanding."
This was to be achieved in three stages, in which the senses
in observing the world, reason in apprehending it, and
the soul in loving and valuing it were to play their respective
parts. The end of felicity was to "approach more near, or to
see more clearly with the eye of our Understanding, the
beauties and glories of the whole world: and to have communion with the Deity in the riches of God and Nature." [6]
The story of his own experience as told by him in the "third
century" falls into these three stages. To him the communion
with God is not, as with the other Christian mystics, a cul-
mination of the long process of purgation, a supreme gift of
grace from God to the mystic, it is to him an act of understanding which man can achieve through the powers of the
Senses, Intellect, and the Soul; but his description of the
state of communion with God resembles that of the typical
mystics: "To enjoy communion with God is to abide with
Him in the fruition of His Divine and Eternal Glory, in all His
attributes, in all His thoughts, in all His creatures, in His
Eternity, Infinity, Almighty Power, Sovereignty." [7]

[1] *Centuries of Meditations*, p. 115.   [2] *Ibid.*   [3] *Ibid.*, p. 209.
[4] *An Essay on Traherne*, by G. E. Willett, 1919.
[5] *The Spiritual Reformers of the 16th and 17th Centuries.*
[6] *Centuries of Meditations*, p. 211.   [7] *Ibid.*, p. 237.

This communion is to be enjoyed not in a direct vision of God but in the contemplation of God, His attributes and works: "We are to enjoy communion with Him in the creation of the world, in the government of Angels, in the redemption of mankind, in the dispensation of His Providence, in the incarnation of His Son, in His passion, resurrection, and ascension, in His shedding abroad the Holy Ghost, in His government of the Church, in His judgement of the world, in the punishment of His enemies, in the rewarding of His friends, in Eternal Glory." [1]

This mode of apprehending Reality, God, is peculiar to the mystical genius of Traherne. By communion with God he does not mean the illumination of the mystic, a direct and immediate vision of God; it is to him an "act of Understanding" which is the supreme expression of our spiritual powers. Traherne definitely says: "These things shall never be seen with your bodily eyes, but in a more perfect manner, you shall be present with them in your Understanding. You shall be in them to the very centre and they in you. As light is in a piece of crystal, so shall you be with every part and excellency of them." [2]

As we have shown in the foregoing pages, he believed that the image of an object in the mind was better than the object itself [3] and that the apprehension of an object re-creates it in the mind, and the understanding of a thing places it within the soul: "An object seen, is in the faculty seeing it, and by that in the soul of the seer." [4]   This applies not only to material objects; whatever can be conceived by man, no matter how abstract, can exist in the mind. The soul was to him eternal in a purely philosophical way; it could, like eternity, contain all Time. He says: "Thus all ages are present in my soul." [4] And he also declared that "the Eternity and Infinity of God are in me for evermore—I being the living Temple and comprehensive of them." [4]   It is, then, through "Understanding" that the soul becomes God-like; he has defined this "act of Understanding" as "the presence of the soul, which being no body but a living Act, is a pure spirit and mysteriously fathomless in its true dimensions." [5]

---

[1] *Centuries of Meditations*, p. 237.   [2] *Ibid.*, p. 132.
[3] *Ibid.*, p. 250.   [4] *Ibid.*, p. 78.   [5] *Ibid.*, p. 132.

He has described the manner in which the soul becomes united with its object in contemplation of the "act of Understanding": "For as light varieth upon all objects whither it cometh, and returneth with the form and figure of them: so is the soul transformed into the Being of its object . . . and by understanding becometh all Things."[1] The soul thus possesses what it understands, and through this act of understanding becomes united to the "Being of its object."

This mode of apprehending reality explains his conception of the union of the soul with God, which is not a direct union in illumination but through "Understanding," as Traherne has defined it. He says: "The true examplar of God's infinity is that of your understanding, which is a lively pattern and idea of it. It excludeth nothing, and containeth all things, being a power that permitteth all objects to be, and is able to enjoy them."[2] This is the original conception underlying the mystical philosophy of Thomas Traherne and which has escaped the notice of all his critics. He definitely says that it is not possible to see the Face of God in a direct vision, we can only recognize Him in His glory: "For so glorious is the face of God and true religion that it is impossible to see it but in transcendent splendour. Nor can we know that God is till we see Him infinite in Goodness. Nothing therefore will make us certain of His Being but His glory."[3] Discussing the illumination of David, Traherne declared: "He saw God face to face in this earthly Tabernacle"[4]; but further on he qualified this statement by the remark that "He saw these things only in the light of faith, and yet rejoiced as if he had seen them by the Light of Heaven."[5]

He also believed that all the powers of the soul could not be turned into an act of Understanding here as they shall be in Heaven: "We by the powers of the soul upon Earth, know what kind of Being, Person, and Glory it will be in the Heavens. Its blind and latent power shall be turned into Act, its inclinations shall be completed, and its capacities filled, for by this means is it made perfect."[6] Neither the soul can be perfected here, nor shall we see the Face of God on Earth; but we can see His Being in His glory.

---

[1] *Centuries of Meditations*, p. 78.   [2] *Ibid.*, p. 98.   [3] *Ibid.*, p. 236.
[4] *Ibid.*, p. 233.   [5] *Ibid.*, p. 234.   [6] *Ibid.*, p. 291; also see p. 130.

Thus the end of felicity is to "to be conformed to the Image of His glory: till we become the resemblance of His great exemplar. Which we then are, when our power is converted into Act, and covered with it, we being an Act of KNOWLEDGE and WISDOM as He is: when our souls are present with all objects, and beautified with the ideas and figures of them all." [1] Thus in order to become an "act of Knowledge and Wisdom," "all things must be contained in our souls," [1] so that we may become "the same mind with Him who is an infinite eternal mind." As Plato and the Apostle term Him:

> "If God, as verses say, a spirit be
> We must in spirit like the Deity
> Become: we must the Image of His mind
> And union with it, in our spirit find." [1]

Thus through this "act of Understanding" we become the *image* of the Mind of God, and are united to Him. This Union, we must remember, ultimately rests on God's love for us and our love for Him and His Son: "For Love communicateth itself: And therefore love in the fountain is the very love communicated to its object. Love in the fountain is love in the stream, and love in the stream equally glorious with love in the fountain. Though it streameth to its object it abideth in the lover, and is the love of the lover." [2]

Thus the paradox of mysticism is achieved: the soul is in "all things" and still capable of withdrawing "into the centre of his own unity," [3] where "he shall be one spirit with God, and dwell above all in the solitary darkness of His Eternal Father." [3]

The originality of Traherne's mystical philosophy is obvious from this brief survey: he has given to his mystical experience a rare logical lucidity and philosophical unity, and he has conveyed his mystical experience to us through intellectual concepts [4]; he has thus achieved the goal of the philosopher as well as that of the mystic, for as Dean Inge (paraphrasing Von Hartmann) has said: "The relation of the individual to the absolute, an essential theme of Philosophy, can only be mystically apprehended." [5]

[1] *Centuries of Meditations*, p. 140.   [2] *Ibid.,*, p. 111.   [3] *Ibid.*, p. 298.
[4] He said: "All men see the same objects, but do not equally understand them. Intelligence is the tongue that discerns and tastes them" (*Centuries of Meditations*, p. 211). T. S. Eliot has also said that in the Seventeenth Century intellect was at the tip of the senses.   [5] *Christian Mysticism*, by Dean Inge, p. 337.

APPENDIX TO CHAPTER IV

THE religious poems of R. Crashaw arranged according to their various themes:

Christ

1646 Edition

On Lords Baptisme.
Sepulchre of our Lord.
Christs wounds.
Come see the place where the Lord lay.
I am the doore.
And he answered nothing.
Neither durst any man from that day aske him any more questions.
Upon our Saviours Tombe wherein never man was laid.
Upon our Lords last comfortable discourse with his disciples.
But now they have seen and hated.
Upon the Thornes taken down from our Lords head, bloody.
She began to wash his feet with tears.
Our Lord in circumcision to his Father.
On the wounds of our crucified Lord.
On our crucified Lord naked and bloody.
On the bleeding wounds of our crucified Lord.
A Himne on the Nativity sung by Shepherds.
A Himne for the circumcision of our Lord.

1648 *Edition*

New Years Day.
To the Name above every name.
In glorious Epiphanie of our Lord.
The office of the Holy crosse.
The song of Divine Love.
Evensong.
Complaine.
Charitas Nimia.

1652 *Edition*

The office of the Holy crosse (enlarged).

The Virgin Mary

1646 Edition

On the blessed Virgin's bashfulnesse.
Blessed be the Paps which thou hast sucked.

1648 Edition

Sancta Maria.
The Virgin Mother.
On the Assumption.

The Saints and Martyrs of the Church

1646 Edition

The Weeper.
The Tear.
The sick implore St. Peters shadow.
To the Infant Martyrs.
Upon Lazarus his Teares.
Upon the Infant Martyrs.
On St. Peter casting away his nets at our Saviours call.
In memory of the Virtuous and Learned Lady, Madre de Teresa.
An Apologie for the precedent Himne.

1648 Edition

The Flaming Heart.

Church Ceremonies and Festivals

1646 Edition

Easter Day.

1648 Edition

A Hymn of the Church.
A Hymn on the Blessed Sacrament.
The Hymn of Sainte Thomas in Adoration of the Blessed Sacrament.

On Miracles

On the Miracle of Multiplyed Loaves.
The dumb healed.
On the Miracle of the Loaves.
The blind cured by the word of our Saviour.
To our Lord upon the Water made wine.
Upon the dum divell cast out.

Other Poems

1646 Edition

On a Prayer booke sent to Mrs. M. R.
On Master George Herberts booke . . . sent to a Gentlewoman.
On a Treatise of charity.
Upon Bishop Andrewes.
On Hope.

1648 Edition

Description of a Religious House.
To the Queen's Majesty.

1652 Edition

To the Countess of Denbigh.

BIBLIOGRAPHY

THIS Bibliography is not intended to be exhaustive. Only the important books consulted or referred to are given, and only modern editions of the works of the poets are mentioned here.

CHAPTER I. GENERAL, HISTORY AND CRITICISM (INCLUDING THE HISTORY OF THE CHURCH)

PHILIPS, EDWARD: *Theatrum Poetrarum.* 1675.
CATTERMOLE, R.: *Literature of the Church of England.* 2 vols. 1844.
GOSSE, EDMUND: *Seventeenth-century Studies.* 1883.
    Jacobean Poets. 1894.
GILLOW, JOSEPH: *Biographical Dictionary of the English Catholics.* 5 vols. 1888–1902.
JUSSERAND, J. J.: *Literary History of the English People.* 1894–1904. Trans. 3 vols. 1895–1900.
GEE, H., and HARDY, W. J.: *Documents Illustrative of English Church History.* 1896.
COURTHOPE, W. J.: *History of English Poetry,* vols. ii and iii. 1897–1904; 1903.
DOWDEN, E.: *Puritan and Anglican.* 1900.
SECCOMBE, T., and ALLEN, J. W.: *The Age of Shakespeare.* 2 vols. 1903.
HUTTON, W. H.: *The English Church from the Accession of Charles I to the Death of Anne.* 1903.
Cambridge Modern History, vols. iii and iv, 1904 and 1906.
HUME, MARTIN: *Spanish Influence on English Literature.* 1905.
GRIERSON, H. J. C.: *First Half of the Seventeenth Century.* 1906.
    Cross Currents in English Literature of the XVIIth Century. 1929.
    With J. C. SMITH: *A Critical History of English Poetry.* 1944.
Encyclopædia of Religion and Ethics. 13 vols. 1908–27.
Cambridge History of English Literature, vols. iii, ix, 1909–12.

WALES

MORRICE, J. C.: *Wales in the Seventeenth Century.* 1918.

SCOTLAND

SMITH, G. G.: *Scottish Literature.* 1919.
MACKENZIE, A. M.: *Historical Survey of Scottish Literature to 1714.* 1933.

HUNGERFORD, P. JOHN: *The English Catholics in the Reign of Queen Elizabeth.* 1920.

WHITNEY, J. P.: *Bibliography of Church History.* 1923.

WELLS, HENRY W.: *Poetic Imagery, illustrated from Elizabethan Literature.* Columbia University, 1924.

HUGHES, W. J.: *Wales and the Welsh in English Literature from Shakespeare to Scott.* 1924.

LEGOUIS and CZAMIAN: *History of English Literature.* Paris, 1924. Trans. 1926–27.

OGG, D.: *Europe in the Seventeenth Century.* 1925.

CLARK, G. N.: *The Seventeenth Century.* 1929.

HOLMES, ELIZABETH: *Aspects of Elizabethan Imagery.* 1929.

EMPSON, W.: *Seven Types of Ambiguity.* 1930.

TREVELYAN, G. M.: *England Under the Stuarts.* Fifteenth Edition. 1930.

WILLIAMS, CHARLES: *The English Poetic Mind.* 1932.

PEARSON, L. E.: *Elizabethan Love Conventions.* University of California, 1933.

ELTON, OLIVER: *The English Muse.* 1933.

WILLEY, BASIL: *The Seventeenth-century Background.* 1934.

SIMPSON, P.: *Proof-reading in the Sixteenth, Seventeenth and Eighteenth Centuries.* 1935.

MATHEW, D.: *Catholicism in England* (1535–1935). 1936.
        The Jacobean Age. 1938.

CROSS, F. L.: *Anglicanism.* 1935.

CRAIG, HARDIN: *The Enchanted Glass.* New York, 1936.

HARRISON, A. W.: *Arminianism.* 1937.

HARRISON, G. B.: *Elizabethan Journals.*
        A Jacobean Journal. London, 1941.

HALLER, W.: *The Rise of Puritanism.* Columbia, 1938.

MAGEE, BRIAN: *The English Recusants.* 1938.

MILLER, PERRY and JOHNSON, T. H.: *The Puritans.* New York, 1938.

JOHN, L. C.: *The Elizabethan Sonnet Sequence—Studies in Conventional Conceits.* Columbia, 1938.

BROOKS, C., and WARREN, R. P.: *Understanding Poetry.* New York, 1938.

KNAPPEN, M. M.: *Tudor Puritanism.* University of Chicago, 1939.

JONAS, L.: *The Divine Science.* Columbia, 1940.

EVANS, IFOR B.: *Tradition and Romanticism.* 1940.

ADDLESHAW, G. W. U.: *High Church Tradition.* 1941.

SAMPSON, GEORGE: *Concise Cambridge History of English Literature.* 1941.

TILLYARD, E. M. W.: *The Elizabethan World Picture.* Chatto & Windus, 1943.

BETTESON, H.: *Documents of the Christian Church.* World Classics, 1943.

BURN-MURDOCH, H.: *Church, Continuity and Unity.* Cambridge University Press, 1945.
WILSON, F. P.: *Elizabethan and Jacobean.* Oxford University Press, 1945.

GENERAL CRITICISM—METAPHYSICAL POETRY
(INCLUDING MYSTICISM IN RELATION TO POETRY)

JOHNSON, SAMUEL, DR.: *Cowley (Lives of the Poets, 1779).*
BARCLAY, ROBERT: *The Inner Life of the Religious Societies of the Commonwealth.* 1876.
SAINTSBURY, G.: *History of Criticism and Literary Taste in Europe.* 3 vols. 1900–4.
　History of English Criticism. 1911.
　Prefaces and Essays. 1933.
SMITH, G. G.: *Elizabethan Critical Essays.* 2 vols. 1904.
SPINGRAM, J. E.: *Critical Essays of the Sevententh Century.* 3 vols. 1908–9.
GRIERSON, H. J. C.: Introductions to his edition of *John Donne's Poems,* 1912 and 1929.
　Introduction to *Metaphysical Lyrics and Poems,* 1921.
SPURGEON, CAROLINE F. E.: *Mysticism in English Literature.* Cambridge University Press, 1913.
THOMPSON, GUY A.: *Elizabethan Criticism of Poetry.* Menasha, 1914.
JONES, RUFUS M.: *Spiritual Reformers in the 16th and 17th Centuries.* 1914.
　Mysticism and Democracy in the English Commonwealth. Harvard, 1932.
HODGSON, G. E.: *A Study in Illumination.* 1914.
COWL, R. P.: *Theory of Poetry in England.* 1914.
QUILLER-COUCH, ARTHUR: *Studies in Literature.* First Series. (Contains chapters on Donne, Herbert and Vaughan, Traherne and Crashaw.) Cambridge University Press, 1918.
OSMOND, P. H.: *Mystical Poets of the English Church.* 1919.
CLOUGH, BENJAMIN C.: "Notes on the Metaphysical Poets (Donne, Carew, Dryden, Butler)," *Mod. Lang. Notes,* 1920.
THOMPSON, E. N. S.: "Mysticism in Seventeenth-century Literature," *Studies in Philology,* 1921.
　Literary Bypaths of the Renaissance. Yale, 1924.
HODGSON, G. E.: *English Mystics.* London, Mowbray, 1922.
NETHERCOTE, A. H.: "The Term Metaphysical Poets before Johnson," *Mod. Lang. Notes,* 1922.
BENNET, C. A.: *Philosphical Study of Mysticism.* 1923.
READ, HERBERT: "The Nature of Metaphysical Poetry," *Criterion,* 1923.
LUCAS, F. L.: *Authors Dead and Living* (includes Donne, Vaughan, Marvell). London, Chatto & Windus, 1926.

NETHERCOTE, A .H.: "The Reputation of the Metaphysical Poets during the Seventeenth Century," *Journal of English and German Philosophy*, 1924.

    The Attitude toward Metaphysical Poetry in Neo-classical England. Chicago Abstracts of Theses, 1925.

    "The Reputation of the Metaphysical Poets during the Age of Pope," *Philological Quarterly*, 1925.

    "The Reputation of the Metaphysical Poets during the Age of Johnson and the Romantic Revival," *Studies in Philology*, 1925.

    "The Reputation of Native *versus* Foreign Metaphysical Poets in England," *Mod. Lang. Review*, 1930.

LEA, K. M.: "Conceits," *Mod. Lang. Review*, 1925.

ELIOT, T. S.: *Lectures on Metaphysical Poetry* (The Clark Lectures, Trinity College, Cambridge). Unpublished MS. at Eliot House, Harvard University, 1926.

    Selected Essays. London, 1932.

    The Idea of a Christian Society. 1939.

READ, HERBERT: *Reason and Romanticism.* 1926.

    Phases of English Poetry. 1928.

KNOWLES, DOM DAVID: *The English Mystics.* 1927.

KEMP, VIOLET A.: "Mystical Utterances in Certain English Poets," *Hibbert Journal*, 1928.

NEWBOLT, HENRY (Editor): *Devotional Poets of the Seventeenth Century.* London, 1929.

BLUNDEN, EDMUND: *Nature in English Literature.* London, 1929.

PEERS, E. ALISON: *Studies of Spanish Mystics.* 1930.

WILLIAMSON, GEORGE: *The Donne Tradition.* Oxford, 1930.

WHITE, HELEN C.: *English Devotional Literature (Prose)* (1600–1640). University of Wisconsin, 1931.

    The Metaphysical Poets, a Study in Religious Experience. New York, Macmillan, 1936.

HOWARTH, R. G. (Editor): *Minor Poets of the Seventeenth Century.* London, Dent, 1931.

BALD, R. C.: *Donne's Influence in English Literature.* Morpeth, 1932.

EWER, M. A.: *Survey of Mystical Symbolism.* 1933.

QUENNELL, PETER (Editor): *Aspects of Seventeenth-century Verse.* London, Cape, 1933.

GERBERT, C.: *Anthology of Elizabethan Dedications and Prefaces.* University Pennsylvania, 1933.

SHARP, R. L.: "The Pejorative Use of Metaphysical," *Modern Language Notes*, 1934.

    "Some Light on Metaphysical Obscurity and Roughness," *Studies in Philology*, 1934.

    "Observations on Metaphysical Imagery," *Sewanee Review*, 1935.

GRIERSON, H. J. C., and BULLOUGH, G.: *The Oxford Book of Seventeenth-century Verse.* Oxford, Clarendon, 1934.

GRIERSON, H. J. C., and SMITH, J. C.: *A Critical History of English Poetry.* 1944.

LEAVIS, F. R.: "English Poetry in the Seventeenth Century," *Scrutiny,* 1935; also see his *Revaluations,* 1936.

MARSHALL, L. BIRKETT: *Rare Poems of the Seventeenth Century.* Cambridge University Press, 1937.

Seventeenth-century Studies presented to Sir Herbert Grierson. Edited by John Purves. 1938.

PRAZ, M.: *Studies in Seventeenth-century Imagery.* 1939.

BROOKS, C.: *Modern Poetry and the Tradition.* University of North Carolina, 1939.

GILBERT, A. H.: *Literary Criticism: Plato to Dryden.* New York, 1940.

COLLINS, JOSEPH B.: *Christian Mysticism in the Elizabethan Age.* Johns Hopkins, 1940.

SHARP, R. L.: *From Donne to Dryden. The Revolt Against Metaphysical Poetry.* University of North Carolina, 1940.

BUSH, DOUGLAS: "Two Roads to Truth: Science and Religion in the Early Seventeenth Century," *Journal of English Literary History,* U.S.A., 1941.

    The Renaissance and English Humanism. University of Toronto Press and Oxford University Press, 1941.

    English Literature in the Earlier Seventeenth Century (1600–1660). Oxford, Clarendon, 1945. The Oxford History of English Literature Series, edited by F. P. Wilson and Bonamy Dobrée.

TUVE, ROSAMUND: "A Critical Survey of Scholarship in the Field of English Literature of the Renaissance," *Studies in Philology,* 1943.

GUINEY, L. I.: *Recusant Poets.* Sheed & Ward, 1943.

MERSCH, FR. E.: *Le Corps mystique du Christ.*

HALLETT, P. E.: *History of the Passion.* Translated by Mary Basset. London, Burns & Oates, 1941.

LANGUAGE

MOORE, J. L.: *"Tudor-Stuart" Views on the Growth, Status and Detinsy of the English Language.* Halle, 1910.

Dictionary of Printers and Booksellers, 1557–1640. Mackerrow, 1910.

SKEAT, W. W., and MAYHEW, A. L.: *A Glossary of Tudor and Stuart Words.* 1914.

MATHEWS, M. M.: *Survey of English Dictionaries.* 1933.

JESPERSON, O.: *Growth and Structure of the English Language.* Seventh Edition, 1933.

STARNES, D. T.: *Dictionaries of the Seventeenth Century* (**P.M.L.A.**, ii, 1937); also see *University of Texas Studies in English.* 1937.

Astronomy

STIMSON, DOROTHY: *The Gradual Acceptance of the Copernican Theory of the Universe.* New York, 1917.

SHAPLEY, H., and HOWRATH, H. E.: *A Source Book in Astronomy.* 1929.

COLLIER, K. B.: *Cosmogonies of Our Fathers.* Columbia, 1934.

NICOLSON, MARJORIE: "The Telescope and Imagination," *Modern Philology*, 1934–35.
"The New Astronomy and English Literary Imagination," *Studies in Philology*, 1935.
The Microscope and English Imagination. Smith College, 1935.
"Cosmic Voyages," *English Literary History*, 1940.

JOHNSON, FRANCIS R.: *Astronomical Thought in Renaissance England.* Johns Hopkins, 1937.

ALLEN, DON CAMERON: *Star Crossed Renaissance.* Duke University, 1941.

Bibliographies (General)

LOWNDES, W. T.: *Bibliographers' Manual of English Literature.* Revised Edition by H. G. Bohn. 6 vols. 1869.

HAZLITT, W. C.: *Hand-book to the Popular Poetical and Dramatic Literature of Great Britain.* 1867.
Collections and Notes. 6 vols. 1876–1903.

Bibliographies in *Cambridge History of English Literature*, vols. iii ix, 1902–12.

ARBER, E.: *British Museum General Catalogue of Printed Books* (new edition in progress), 1931.
Transcript of the Registers of the Company of Stationers, London; between A.D. *1554–1640.* 5 vols.
Transcript of the Same, 1640–1708, by G. E. B. Eyreand in 3 vols. (By H. R. Plomer. 1913 14.)

Register of Bibliographies of the English Language and Literature, by C. S. Northup. Yale, 1925.

Annals of English Literature, 1475–1925, by J. C. Ghosh and E. G. Withycombe. 1935.

PINTO, V. DE SOLA: *The English Renaissance* (1510–1688). 1938.

HARVEY, SIR PAUL: *Oxford Companion to English Literature.* Second Edition, 1937–38.
Concise Oxford Dictionary of English Literature. 1939.

Cambridge Bibliography of English Literature, by F. W. Bateson. 4 vols. 1941.

CROSS, T. P.: *Bibliographical Guide to English Studies.* Eighth Edition. University of Chicago, 1943.

General Works on Mysticism

BREMOND, ABBE H.: *La Provence Mystique.* Paris, 1908.
  Histoire Littéraire du Sentiment Religieux en France. 8 vols.
  Paris, 1916–28.
BERGSON, HENRI: *Prayer and Poetry.* London, 1928.
  *Time and Free Will: an Essay on the Immediate Data of
  Consciousness.* Translated by F. L.Pogson, 1910.
  Matter and Memory. Translated by N. Paul and W. Scott
  Palmer, London, 1910.
  Creative Evolution. Translated by A .Mitchell, London, 1911.
  The Two Sources of Morality and Religion. 1923.
BIGG, DR. C.: *The Christian Platonists of Alexandria.* Bampton
  Lectures, Oxford, 1885.
  Neoplatonism. London, 1895.
BUTLER, DOM CUTHBERT: *Western Mysticism.* (In *Encyclopædia* of
  Ethics.)
CONETON, G. G.: *Medieval Panorama.* Cambridge University Press,
  1938.
DELACROIX, H.: *Essai sur le Mysticisme Spéculatif en Allemagne au
  XIV. Siècle.* Paris, 1900.
  Études d'Histoire et de Psychologie du Mysticisme. Paris, 1908.
GREGORY, ELEANOR C.: *An Introduction to Christian Mysticism.*
  London, 1901.
  *A Little of Heavenly Wisdom. Selections from some English Prose
  Mystics.* With Introduction. A Library of Devotion.
  London, 1904.
GILSON, ÉTIENNE: *La Philosophie au Moyen Age.* Payot, 1930.
  Reasons and Revelation in the Middle Ages. London, 1939.
HERMAN, E.: *The Meaning and Value of Mysticism.* London, 1915.
INGE, W. R.: *Christian Mysticism.* Bampton Lectures, 1899.
  Studies of English Mystics. London, 1906.
  Personal Idealism and Mysticism. London, 1907.
  The Philosophy of Plotinus. 2 vols. London, 1918.
JAMES, WILLIAM: *The Principles of Psychology.* 2 vols. London, 1890.
  The Will to Believe. New York, 1897.
  The Varieties of Religious Experience. Gifford Lectures, London,
  1902.
  A Pluralistic Universe. Hibbert Lectures, London, 1909.
JEFFERIES, RICHARD: *The Story of My Heart.* Second Edition.
  London, 1891.
JONES, RUFUS M.: *Studies in Mystical Religion.* London, 1909.
  Spiritual Reformers in the 16th and 17th Centuries. London, 1914.
KINGSLAND, WILLIAM: *An Anthology of Mysticism and Mystical
  Philospohy.*
KNOWLES, DOM D.: *The English Mystics.* London, 1928.

MARITAIN, J.: *Art and Scholasticism.* London, 1930. (First published in 1923.)
    Prayer and Intelligence. London, 1928.
    An Introduction to Philosophy. London, 1930.
    Religion and Culture. 1931.
    Freedom in the Modern World. 1936.
    The Degrees of Knowledge. London, 1938.
    True Humanism. 1938.
MASSIGNON, L.: *Essai sur les Origines du lexique technique de mystique Musulmane.* Paris, 1922.
    La Passion de Al-Halladj. 2 tomes. Paris, 1922.
NICHOLSON, R. A.: *The Mystics of Islam.* London, 1914.
PATMORE, COVENTRY: *The Rod, the Root, and the Flower.* Second Edition. London, 1907.
PEERS, ALLISON: *Spanish Mysticism.* London, 1924.
    Studies in Spanish Mystics. 1927.
PLATO: *Opera.* Ed. J. Burnet. 5 vols. Oxford, 1899–1907.
    The Dialogues, with Introduction by B. Jowett. 1892.
    The Republic. Translated by B. Jowett, 1888.
PLOTINUS: *The Enneads.* Translated by Stephen Mackenna, London.
POWICKE, F. J.: *The Cambridge Platonists.* London, 1926.
SHARPE, A.: *Mysticism, its true Nature and Value.* London, 1910.
SPURGEON, CAROLINE: *Mysticism in English Literature.* London, 1913.
SMITH, MARGARET: *Studies in Early Mysticism in the Near and Middle East.* London, 1931.
TAYLOR, A. E.: *Plato; the Man and his Work.* London, 1926.
THOROLD, ALGAR: *An Essay in Aid of the better Appreciation of Catholic Mysticism.* London, 1900.
TOLLEMACHE, M.: *Spanish Mystics.* London, 1886.
TROELTSH, ERNST: *Protestantism and Progress.* 1929.
TULLOCH, J.: *Rational Theology and Christian Philosophy in England in the Seventeenth Century.* 2 vols. Edinburgh, 1872.
UNDERHILL, E.: *Mysticism.* 1911.
    The Mystic Way. London, 1913.
    Practical Mysticism. 1914.
    The Essentials of Mysticism. London, 1920.
    The Life of the Spirit and the Life of To-day. London, 1922.
    The Mystics of the Church. London, 1925.
    Man and the Supernatural. London, 1926.
VAUGHAN, R. A.: *Hours with the Mystics.* Third Edition. 2 vols. London, 1880.
VON HÜGEL, BARON F.: *The Mystical Element in Religion, as studied in St. Catherine of Genoa and her Friends.* 2 vols. London, 1908.
    Eternal Life. Edinburgh, 1912.
    Essays and Addresses on the Philosophy of Religion. Second Series. London, 1921, 1926.
    Selected Letters. 1927.

WAITE, A. E.: *Studies in Mysticism.* London, 1906.
WATKIN, E. I.: *Philosophy of Mysticism.* 1919.
   A Philosophy of Form. London, 1935.
   Catholic Art and Culture. 1942.
WEBB, C. C. J.: *History of Philosophy.* Home University Library, 1915.
WHITTAKER, T.: *The Neoplatonists: a Study in the History of Hellenism.* Cambridge, 1901.
WULF, M. DE: *History of Medieval Philosophy.* London, 1909.
   Scholasticism, Old and New. Dublin, 1907.
   Philosophy and Civilization in the Middle Ages. Princeton, 1922.

SAINTS MENTIONED IN THE BOOK

AUGUSTINE OF HIPPO, SAINT:

Works. Edited by Marcus Dods. 15 vols. Edinburgh, 1876. *The Confessions* (first nine books). Translated by C. Bigg. London, 1898. *The Confessions.* Translated by Dr. E. B. Pussey. London, 1907. Bertrand, L.: *St. Augustine.* 1913. *A Monument to St. Augustine,* by various authors. 1932.

BERNARD OF CLAIRVAUX, SAINT:

Trans. *Life and Works of St. Bernard.* Edited by Dom J. Mabillon, O.S.B. Translated and edited by S. L. Eales, M.A. 4 vols. London, 1889–96. *Cantica Canticorum: Sermons on the Song of Songs.* Translated by S. J. Eales, M.A. London, 1895. *Sermons on the Canticles.* 2 vols. Dublin, 1920. *St. Bernard on the Love of God.* Translated by Edmund Gardner. London, 1916. Williams, Watkin: *The Mystical Theology of St. Bernard.* London, 1940. *Studies in St. Bernard.* London, 1927. *The Mysticism of St. Bernard.* London, 1931. *St. Bernard of Clairvaux.* Manchester, 1935.

BONAVENTURA, SAINT:

Trans. *Théologie Seraphique,* extraite et traduite par C. et A. Alix. 2 vols. Paris, 1853. Gilson, E.: *La Philosophie de S. Bonaventura.* Paris, 1924.

CATHERINE OF GENOA, SAINT:

Trans. *The Treatise on Purgatory.* With a Preface by Cardinal Manning. London, 1858.

CATHERINE OF SIENA, SAINT:

Trans. *The Divine Dialogue of St. Catherine of Siena.* Translated by Algar Thorold. Second Edition. London, 1926. Gardner, Edmund: *St. Catherine of Siena.* London, 1907.

DIONYSIUS THE AREOPAGITE:

Trans. *The Works of Dionysius the Areopagite.* Translated by the Rev. J. Parker. 2 vols. Oxford, 1897. Muller, H. F.: *Dionysius, Proclies, Plotinus.* Munster, 1918.

IGNATIUS LOYOLA, SAINT:

The Spiritual Exercises. Spanish and English, with Commentary. by J. Rickaby, S.J. London, 1915. Peers, E. Allison, "St. Ignatius," in *Studies of the Spanish Mystics*, vol. i. London, 1927.

JOHN OF THE CROSS, SAINT:

Trans. *The Ascent of Mount Carmel.* Translated by David Lewis. New Edition. London, 1906. *The Dark Night of the Soul.* Translated by D. Lewis. London, 1916. *The Flame of Living Love.* Translated by D. Lewis. London, 1912. *A Spiritual Canticle of the Soul.* Translated by D. Lewis. London, 1911. Peers, E. Allison, "St. John of the Cross," in *Studies of the Spanish Mystics*, vol. i, with bibliography. Hoornaret, R.: *The Burning Soul of St. John of the Cross.* London, 1931. *Complete Works.* Translated by E. Allison Peers. 3 vols. London, 1934–35. (From the critical text of Padre Silverio. Supersedes all other versions. Detailed bibliography.) Frost, Bede: *St. John of the Cross.* Introduction to his Philosophy. London, 1937.

THOMAS AQUINAS, SAINT:

The Summa Theologica of St. Thomas Aquinas, translated by Fathers of the English Dominican Province. 12 vols. London, 1912–17. *Contra Gentiles.* Annotated translation by Father J. Rickaby, S.J. London, 1905. O'Neill, H. C.: *New Things and Old in St. Thomas Aquinas.* Conway, John P.: *A Biographical Study of St. Thomas Aquinas.* MacNabb, Fr. V. J.: *St. Thomas Aquinas* and *The Mysticism of St. Thomas Aquinas.* Maritain, J.: *St. Thomas Aquinas, Angel of the Schools.* 1931. *Art and Scholasticism.* London, 1930. Patterson, R. L.: *The Conception of God in the Philosophy of Aquinas.* 1933. Steiner, Rudolf: *The Philosophy of Thomas Aquinas.* 1932. Taylor, A. E.: *St. Thomas Aquinas as Philosopher.* Wicksteed, P. H.: *Dante and Aquinas.* Chesterton, G. K.: *St. Thomas Aquinas.* Hardy, L.: *Le Doctrine de la Redemption chez St. Thomas.* Gilson, E.: *The Philosophy of St. Thomas Aquinas.* Translated by E. Bullough.

SUSO, BLESSED HENRY:

Life of B. Henry Suso, by Himself. Translated by T. F Knox. London, 1913. *Little of Eternal Wisdom.* London, 1910.

TERESA, SAINT:

Trans. *The Life of St. Teresa of Jesus, written by Herself.* Translated by D. Lewis. Fifth Edition. London, 1916. *The Book of the*

Foundations of St. Teresa of Jesus, written by Herself. Translated by D. Lewis. London, 1913. *The History of the Foundations.* Translated by Sister Agnes Mason. 1909. *The Interior Castle.* Translated from the autograph of St. Teresa by the Benedictines of Stanbrook Abbey. London, 1912. *The Way of Perfection.* Translated from the autograph of St. Teresa by the Benedictines of Stanbrook Abbey, with Notes by Zimmerman. London, 1911. *Letters*, in 4 vols. translated by the Benedictines of Stanbrook Abbey. London, 1919–24. CRITICISM Coleridge, H. J. *Life and Letters of St. Teresa.* 3 vols. London, 1872. Colvill, H. H.: *Saint Treesa of Spain.* London, 1909. Peers, E. Allison: "St. Teresa" in *Studies of the Spanish Mystics.* London, 1927. With full bibliography. Whyte, A.: *Santa Teresa: an appreciation.* Edinburgh, 1897.

THOMAS À KEMPIS:

Trans. *Of the Imitation of Christ.* Revised translation by Dr. C. Bigg. Library of Devotion. London, 1901. Wheatly, L. A.: *The Story of the Imitatio.* London, 1891.

CHAPTER II. JOHN DONNE (1572–1631)[1]

POEMS

1. *Poems*, by J. D., with elegies on the author's death. London. Printed by M. F. for John Marriot, and are to be sold at his shop in St. Dunstan's Churchyard in Fleet Street. 1633, 1635, 1649, 1650, 1669.
2. *Poems on Several Occasions.* Written by the Reverend John Donne, D.D., Late Dean of St. Paul's. London. Printed for J. Tonson, and sold by W. Taylor at the shop in Paternoster Row, 1719.

---

[1] For a detailed description of the MS. collections of Donne's poems see *A Bibliography of Dr. John Donne* by Geoffrey Keynes (1932), pp. 114–116. This is the most exhaustive bibliography of all Donne's works; recently two more bibliographies have been published. This short bibliography of Donne is based on these three bibliographies supplemented with the books and articles which have appeared after 1942.
  (a) *Studies in Metaphysical Poetry* by Theodore Spencer and Mark Van Doren. *Two Essays and a Bibliography.* Columbia University Press, New York, 1939.
  (b) *John Donne since 1900.* A Bibliography of Periodical Articles by William White. Boston, F. W. Faxon, 1942.
  None of Donne's poems have survived as written by his own hand except a Latin epigram on Hooker written on the fly-leaf of William Covell's *Defence of the five books of Ecclesiastical Policie: Written by Richard Hooker.* London, 1603.

3. *The Poetical Works of Dr. John Donne.* In three volumes. With the life of the author. Edinburgh, at the Apollo Press, by the Martins. Anno 1779. [Bell's edition of the Poets of Great Britain, vols. 23–25.]

4. The Fuller Worthies Library. *The Complete Poems of John Donne, D.D., Dean of St. Paul's.* Edited with preface, essays on life and writings, and notes, by the Rev. Alexander Grosart. In two volumes. 1872.

5. *Poems.* Edited by E. K. Chambers. With an Introduction by George Saintsbury. In two volumes. London, Lawrence & Bullen, 1896. The Muses Library.

6. *Love Poems of John Donne*, selected and edited by Charles Eliot Norton. Boston, 1905.

7. *The Poems of John Donne.* Edited from the old editions and numerous manuscripts with introductions and commentary by Herbert J. C. Grierson. In two volumes. Oxford (at the Clarendon Press, 1912).

8. *John Donne Dean of St. Paul's Complete Poetry and Selected Prose.* Edited by John Hayward. The Nonesuch Press, Bloomsbury, 1929.

9. *The Poems of John Donne.* Edited by H. J. C. Grierson, Professor of Rhetoric and English Literature in the University of Edinburgh. London, Oxford University Press, 1929. There is a new introduction and it contains a few corrections and improvements, and the *apparatus criticus* is abbreviated. 1929.

10. *The Courtier's Library, or Catalogus Librorum Aulicorum incomparabilium et non Vendibilium*, by John Donne. Edited by Evelyn Mary Simpson, with a translation, 1930. The Nonesuch Press.

11. *The Poems of John Donne.* Edited with an introduction by Hugh I'Anson Fausset. Everyman's Library, No. 867. The text is modernized throughout. London, J. M. Dent & Sons. In New York by E. P. Dutton & Co.

12. *The Holy Sonnets of John Donne.* Introduction by Hugh I'A. Fausset, engravings by E. Gill. London, Dent, 1938.

13. *The Poems of John Donne.* Edited by Roger E. Bennett. Chicago, University Classics, 1942. Packard & Company. Professor Bennett has modernized the spelling; this edition is based on the Grierson text, but Professor Bennett had the advantage of examining at first-hand the four out of the thirty-seven MSS. on which Professor Grierson had based his text, as these four MSS. are at Harvard; and also the three other MSS. (one in the Morgan Library and two at Harvard College) which have been discovered since 1912, the date of Grierson's great edition. The four of these MSS. which were at Harvard could not be examined at first-hand by Professor Grierson when he prepared his 1912 edition.

PROSE

1. *Pseudo-Martyr.* London. Printed by W. Stansby for Walter Burre, 1610.
2. *Conclave Ignati.* 1621, 1626, 1634, 1635. (Two Latin editions were printed in 1611.) Since the seventeenth century the English version has been printed in full only in the Nonesuch Edition of the *Complete Poetry and Selected Prose*, edited by John Hayward, 1929. *Ignatius His Conclave.* Reproduced in facsimile from the edition of 1611, with Introduction by Charles M. Coffin. New York, Columbia University Press, and Oxford University Press, 1941.
3. Sermons:
    (i) *Sermon Judges* xx, 15 [v. 20]. London. Printed by William Stansby for Thomas Jones, 1622.
    (ii) *Sermon Acts* 1, 8. Printed by A. Mat for Thomas Jones, 1622.
    (iii) *Encaenia. The Feast of Dedication.* London. Printed by Aug. Mat for Thomas Jones, 1623.
    (iv) *Three Sermons. Three Sermons upon Speciall Occasions.* London. Printed for Thomas Jones, 1623.
    (v) *Sermons on Acts* 1, 8. Preached to the Honourable Company of the Virginian Plantation, 13th November 1622. London. Printed for Thomas Jones, 1624.
    (vi) *First Sermon Preached to King Charles.* London. Printed by A. M. for Thomas Jones, 1625.
    (vii) *Four Sermons. Four Sermons upon Speciall Occasions,* by John Donne, Dean of St. Paul's, London. Printed for Thomas Jones, 1626.
    (viii) *Sermon Preached at White Hall,* 1625. London. Printed for Thomas Jones, 1626.
    (ix) *Five Sermons upon Special Occasions.* London. Printed for Thomas Jones, 1626.
    (x) *Sermon of Commemoration. A Sermon of Commemoration of the Lady Davers, late wife of Sir John Davers.* London. Printed by I. H. for Philemon Stephens and Christopher Meredith, 1627.
    (xi) *Death's Duell.* London. Printed by Thomas Harper for Richard Redmer and Benjamin Fisher. 1632, 1633. (Two more editions of the *Sermons* came out in 1633.)
4. *Six Sermons.* Printed by the Printers to the University of Cambridge, 1634.
5. *Sermon on Eccles.* xii, 1. Printed in *Sapientia Clamitans.* London. Printed by I. Haviland, 1638.
6. *LXXX Sermons.* London. Printed for Richard Royston and Richard Marriot, 1640.

7. *Fifty Sermons.* London. Printed by Ja. Flesher for M. F. J. Marriot and R. Royston, 1649.
8. *XXVI Sermons.* London. Printed by T. N. for James Magnes, 1660 (twice in 1661).
9. *The Sacred Classics: or, Cabinet Library of Divinity.* Edited by the Rev. H. Stebbing, M.A., and the Rev. R. Cattermole. London, 1835.
10. *The Works of John Donne.* Rd. by Henry Alford, M.A. In six volumes. London, John W. Parker, 1939. [This is the only complete edition of all the sermons of John Donne since the seventeenth century. The text with its modernized spelling is of little value.]
11. *Donne's Sermons.* Selected passages, with an essay by Logan Pearsall Smith. Oxford, 1919.
12. *Sermon Psalm* xxxviii, v. 9. Now first printed. London. Privately printed, 1921. [Fifty copies were printed for Mr. Wilfred Merton from the Dowden MS.]
13. *Donne's Sermons XV and LXVI.* Cambridge. At the University Press, 1921. [From *LXXX Sermons.* Introductory note by "Q."]
14. *X Sermons preached by that late Learned and Reverend Divine John Donne.* Chosen from the whole body of Donne's *Sermons* by Geoffrey Keynes, 1923. The Nonesuch Press. [725 copies were printed on Dutch mould-made paper. Mr. Keynes has written a bibliographical note.]
15. *John Donne. Complete Poetry and Selected Prose.* Ed. John Hayward. (Nonesuch Press, 1929, pp. 555–760.)
16. *Sermon on Ec.* xii, 1. Ed. by Mrs. E. M. Simpson. London, The Nonesuch Press, 1932. [This sermon first appeared in *XXVI Sermons by John Donne,* 1660, under the title "A Sermon of Valediction at my Going into Germany." The text is based on the Lothian Manuscript, collated with the Ashmole MS. (Bodleian), and also on the version that appeared in *Sapientia Clamitans.* London, 1638.]
17. *The Easter Sermons of John Donne,* with introduction, commentary, textual notes, and a bibliography. Edited by Herbert H. Umbach. New York, Cornell University, 1934.

DEVOTIONS

18. *Devotions upon Emergent Occasions.* By John Donne, Dean of St. Paul's. London. Printed by A. M. for Thomas Jones, 1624, 1627, 1634 (printed by A. M. to be sold by Charles Greeve), 1638 (printed by A. M. to be sold by Richard Royston). This volume of meditations, expostulations and prayers was composed during Donne's illness in 1623 and published in 1624. It proved to be popular, and passed through three editions

(five issues) in his lifetime, and two editions appeared within seven years after his death.

19. *Devotions.* (In the *Works* of John Donne. Ed. Henry Alford, M.A. London, 1939. Vol. iii, pp. 493–614.)

20. *Devotions by John Donne with two Sermons*: 1. On the decease of Lady Danvers, mother of George Herbert; 2. Death's Duel —his own funeral sermon—to which is prefixed his life by Izaak Walton. London, William Pickering, 1840.

21. *Donne's Devotions.* Oxford, D. A. Talboys, 1841 (with many hideous woodcut pieces, tail-pieces and initials more representative of Victorian sentimentality than the sensibility of Donne).

22. *Devotions upon Emergent Occasions by John Donne.* Edited by John Sparrow, with a Bibliographical Note by Geoffrey Keynes. Cambridge, 1923. The text is based on the first three editions of 1624, 1625 and 1626; this is the standard edition now.

23. *Devotions upon Emergent Occasions, with Death's Duel.* By John Donne. With an Introduction by William H. Draper, M.A. Marshall, Hamilton, Kent & Co. Ltd., London, E.C. 4, 1925. Abbey Classics. [This edition is ornamented by Martin Travers Simpkin; Walton's life of Donne has been also reproduced; at the end the author has given an English version of the *Stationes*, erroneously attributed to Donne by Dr. Grosart, who had found an English translation of these lines on the fly-leaves of a copy of the third edition of 1627.

ESSAYS IN DIVINITY

24. These essays were composed by Donne in 1614 or 1615, before he entered into Holy Orders, but were printed for the first time by John Donne the younger, with his *Juvenilia*, in 1652, under the title *Paradoxes, Problems, Essays, Characters.*

25. *Essays in Divinity by the late Dr. Donne, Dean of St. Paul's. Now made publick by his son J. D., Dr. of the Civil Law.* London. Printed by T. M. for Richard Marriot, 1651.

26. *Essays in Divinity by John Donne.* Edited by Augustus Jessopp, M.A. London, John Tupling, 1855.

LETTERS

The majority of Donne's letters were published by his son, John Donne the younger, in 1651; he had included in this edition only 129 letters. John Donne the younger further edited twenty-five hitherto unpublished letters of his father for Sir Tobie Matthew's *Collection* (1660). Ten more letters were printed from MSS. at Loseley House, Surrey, by A. J. Kempe, in the *Loseley Manuscripts*, 1835;

eight of these Gosse included in his *Life and Letters of John Donne*; Gosse also discovered nineteen unpublished letters, which were included in his *Life* of Donne. Mr. Logan Pearsall Smith discovered another thirty-two letters, to Sir Henry Wotton and others, in a commonplace-book in the library of the late Mr. G. H. Finch at Burley-on-the-Hill. These letters were printed by Mrs. Simpson in her study of the *Prose Works*, 1924. Mr. Hayward added three more letters in his Nonesuch Edition of the *Complete Poems and Selected Prose*, 1929. One new letter was printed for the first time in the *London Mercury*, December 1925; and another was privately printed at Harvard in 1930.

The text of the 1651 and 1660 editions cannot be verified now, as the original manuscripts (except that of one letter) are not extant. Mr. I. A. Shapiro has been busy for many years in preparing the standard text of all the available letters of Donne, and he tells me his edition will include short biographies of Donne's correspondents also.

1. *Letters to Severall Persons of Honour*: written by John Donne, sometime Deane of St. Paul's, London. Published by John Donne, Dr. of the Civill Law, London. Printed by J. Flesher, for Richard Marriot, and are to be sold at his shop in St. Dunstan's Church-yard under the Dyall, 1651; 1654.

2. *A Collection of Letters, made by Sir Tobie Matthews, Kt., with a Character of the Most Excellent Lady, Lucy, Countess of Carleile*. By the Same Author. To which are added many Letters of his own, to severall persons of honour, who were contemporary with him (includes twenty-five new letters).

3. *The Loseley Manuscripts*. Manuscripts, and other rare documents, preserved in the Muniment Room of James More Mobynew, Esq., at Loseley House, in Surrey. . . . Now first edited, with notes, by Alfred John Kempe, Esq., F.S.A., London. John Murray, 1835 (includes ten unpublished letters).

4. *Letters to Several Persons of Honour*. Edited by C. S. Merrill, Junior. New York, 1910. (This limited edition of 600 copies is really a literal reprint of the 1651 edition, but the editor has added notes.)

5. *A Study of the Prose Works of John Donne*, by Enalyn M. Simpson. Oxford, 1924 (thirty-two letters were printed for the first time from transcripts of the MSS. at Burley-on-the-Hill).

6. *The London Mercury*, vol. xiii, London, 1925 (one letter from the Loseley MSS. was for the first time printed here).

7. *John Donne: Complete Poetry and Selected Prose*. Edited by John Hayward, 1929 (three letters were published here for the first time).

8. *John Donne's Letter to Sir Nicholas Carey* [Carew] (1625). (This was printed in 1929 with a note by T. Spencer.)

(For a detailed bibliography of letters see Keynes.)

Juvenilia

The sportive, humorous, often trifling, *Juvenilia* of Donne were probably composed before 1600. Mr. Keynes has called them "scurrilous," but they did not appear such to his contemporaries, for they were widely circulated in MS. form. They were, however, not published during Donne's lifetime. I think not because of their scurrilous nature (this did not shock the Elizabethans, for they were accustomed to worse things in their dramatists and poets, including Shakespeare and Marlowe), but because their author, having divorced the world, had concentrated all his attention on "Heavenly" things, and it would not have been proper for the famous Dean of St. Paul's to have published these "evaporations of wit" of his early and adventurous youth. Donne truly summed up his attitude to his earlier work in a letter to Sir Henry Wotton (1600?): "Only in obedience I send you some of my paradoxes . . . they were made rather to deceave tyme than her daughter truth . . . and they have only this advantage to scape from being caled ill things that they are nothings."

The first edition of *Juvenilia* was published by Henry Seyle in 1633, and was quite unauthorised. When John Donne printed *Paradoxes and Problems*, in 1652, he did not mention the earlier edition; he, however, increased the number of paradoxes from eleven to twelve; and added seven more problems, bringing their number to seventeen. In the same volume he included two characters; "An Essay on Valour"; "A Sheaf of Miscellany Epigrams"; a reprint of "Ignatius his Conclave," and also the "Essays in Divinity."

The two characters were: (1) "The Character of a Scot at First Sight," and (2) "The True Character of a Dunce"; one of these had already been included in the eleventh edition of Sir Thomas Overbury's *The Wife* (see "John Donne and Sir Thomas Overbury's Characters," *Mod. Lang. Review*, 1923).

Another problem, entitled "Why was Sir Walter Raleigh thought the fittest man to write the History of these Times?"—which has been preserved at Oxford (Tanner MS.)—was for the first time printed by Gosse (vol. ii, 52). Professor Sir Herbert Grierson has the transcript of another paradox which was printed by Mrs. Simpson in her article "Two MSS. of the *Paradoxes and Problems*" (*Review of English Studies*, 1927). This paradox is called "Why doth John Sarisburiensis writing de Nugis Curialibus handle the Providence and Omnipotence of God?"—and is included in O'Flaherty's MS. at Harvard. Mrs. Simpson has written another article, "More Manuscripts of Donne's *Paradoxes and Problems*" (*Review of English Studies*, 1934).

(1) *Juvenilia or certain Paradoxes and Problems*, written by J. Donne.

London. Printed by E. P. for Henry Seyle, 1633. (Another edition with slight variants came out in 1633. It had no *Imprimaturs* of Sir Henry Herbert, which shows that the publication was unlicensed.)

(2) *Paradoxes, Problems, Essayes, Characters, written by Dr. Donne, Dean of St. Paul's, to which is added a Book of Epigrams, written in Latin by the same Author*; translated into English by J. Maine, D.D. As also *Ignatius his Conclave, a Satyr*. Translated out of the originall copy written in Latin by the same Author, found lately amongst his own papers. London. Printed by T. N. for Humphrey Moseley at the Princes' Armes in St. Paul's Church-yard, 1652. (Another issue with slight variants came out in the same year.)

(3) *Paradoxes and Problems by John Donne, with Two Characters and an Essay of Valour*, now for the first time printed from the editions of 1633 and 1652 with one additional problem. London, The Nonesuch Press, 1923. (The additional problem is from the Tanner MS. Mr. Geoffrey Keynes has contributed a bibliographical preface.)

(4) A selection of "Paradoxes and Problems" was also published by Mr. John Hayward in his *Complete Poetry and Selected Prose of John Donne*, 1929. The text is based on the edition of 1652.

(5) BENNETT, R. E.: (Bibliographical note to) *Juvenilia or Certain Paradoxes and Problems*. From the first edition. New York, Facsimile Text Society, 1936.

BIOGRAPHY AND CRITICISM

(In chronological order, but all the essays of one author have been listed at one place.)

THE list is not exhaustive, only important books and articles have been mentioned.

BAKER, SIR RICHARD: *A Chronicle of the Kings of England*. London, 1643.

BELL, WILLIAM: *Comedies, Tragi-Comedies with other Poems*, by William Cartwright. London, 1651. (The reference to Donne occurs in the Commendatory Poem by William Bell: "With Donne's Rich Gold and Johnson's Silver Mine.")

WALTON, IZAAK: The *Life of Donne* first appeared as an introduction to *LXXX Sermons*, 1640. The first separate issue was published in 1658. In 1670 Walton included the *Life of Donne* in his famous volume of *Lives*.[1] In the edition of 1658, Walton had made many additions and alterations; but there were little changes in the edition of 1670 except that the letters printed at the end of the 1658 edition were omitted and "An hymn to

[1] For details of other editions see "Bibliography of Izaak Walton's Lives," *Oxford Bibliographical Society Proceedings and Papers*, vol. ii, 1930.

God, my God, in my sickness, March 23, 1630," and Walton's "Elegy on Dr. Donne," April 7, 1632, were added. There was another edition in 1675, which for the first time contained a long account of Donne's vision of his wife seen while he was in Paris in 1612, and "Valediction forbidding mourning." was also included. An important edition of the *Lives* was edited with scholarly annotations by Thomas Zouch in 1796. The only separate edition of the *Life of John Donne* was issued in 1852 by Thomas Edlyne Tomlins (*The Life of John Donne, D.D., Dean of St. Paul's Church, London.* By Izaak Walton, with some original notes by An Antiquary. London. Published by Henry Kent.) (The Contemplative Man's Library for the Thinking Few.) Tomlins had included nine letters from the Loseley MSS.[1]

FULLER, THOMAS: *The Church History of Britain.* London, 1655.

WINSTANLEY, WILLIAM: *England's Worthies.* London, 1660.

BARKSDALE, CLEMENT: *Memorials of Worthy Persons. Two Decades.* London, 1611.

PHILLIPS, EDWARD: *Theatrum Poetrum, or a Compleat Collection of the Poets.* London, 1675.

TEMPLE, SIR WILLIAM: *Miscellanea: In Two Parts.* London, 1680–90.

OLDHAM, JOHN: *Works.* London, 1684.

WINSTANLEY, WILLIAM: *The Lives of the Most Famous English Poets.* London, 1687.

DRYDEN, JOHN: *The Satires of Decimus Junius Juvenalis. Translated into English Verse.* London, 1693.

JOHNSON, SAMUEL: *The Lives of the Most Eminent English Poets.* London, 1779.

COLERIDGE, S. T.: *The Literary Remains.* London, W. Pickering, 1836–38.

LIGHTFOOT, DR. J. B.: *The Classic Preachers of the English Church.* London, 1877.

GOSSE, SIR EDMUND: *Gossip in Library.* London, Heinemann.
    "The Poetry of John Donne," *The New Review,* vol. ix, 1893.
    The Life and Letters of John Donne. London, Heinemann, 1899.
    "The Sepulchrall Dean," *Sunday Times.* London, 12th October 1919. Review of Pearsall Smith's *Donne's Sermons.*
    "Metaphysical Poetry," *More Books on the Table.* London, Heinemann, 1923.

DOWDEN, EDWARD: *New Studies in Literature.* Boston and New York, 1895.

JESSOPP, DR. AUGUSTUS: *John Donne, Sometime Dean of St. Paul's.* London, 1897

STEPHEN, SIR LESLIE: "John Donne," *The National Review,* vol. xxxiv, 1899.

---

[1] *The Lives of Dr. John Donne . . .* etc. Written by Izaak Walton. Printed by Tho. Newcomb for Richard Marriott, 1670.

CHADWICK, J. W.: "John Donne, Poet and Preacher," *The New World*, vol. ix, 1900.

BEECHING, CANON H. C.: "Religio Laici," Walton's *Life of Donne*. 1902.

HARRISON, JOHN SMITH: *Platonism in English Poetry of the 16th and 17th Centuries*. Columbia University Press, New York, 1903.

JONSON, BEN: *Conversations of Ben Jonson with William Drummond of Hawthornden*. Ed. Philip Sidney. London, 1906.

GRIERSON, SIR H. J. C.: "John Donne," *Camb. Hist. of Eng. Lit.*, vol. iv. Cambridge, 1909.

Review of Praz's "Scentismo e Marinismo in Inghilterra," *Rev. Eng. Studies*, London, 1926.

"Donne and Lucretius" (letter), *Times Literary Supplement*, 5th December 1929.

"The Oxford Donne" (letter), *Times Literary Supplement*, 20th February 1930.

Review of Legouis' "Donne the Craftsman," *Rev. Eng. Studies*, London, 1930.

"Donne and the Roman Poets" (letter), *Times Literary Supplement*, 26th February 1931.

"The Metaphysical Poets," in *The Background of English Literature*. Chatto & Windus.

Reprint of Introductory Essay to *Metaphysical Lyrics—Donne to Butler*. Oxford, 1921.

HUTCHINSON, REV. F. E.: "The English Pulpit from Fisher to Donne," *Camb. Hist. of Eng. Lit.*, vol. iv. Cambridge, 1909.

"Donne the Preacher," *Theology*, vol. xxii, London, 1931.

CHAMBERS, E. K.: "John Donne, Diplomatist and Soldier," *Mod. Lang. Review*, Cambridge, 1910.

Review of *Poems*, ed. Grierson, *Mod. Lang. Review*, Cambridge, 1914.

"An Elegy by John Donne" (from Holgate MS.), *Review of Eng. Studies*, 1931.

PICAVET, F.: "Medieval Doctrines in the Works of Donne and Locke," *Mind*, xxvi, 1917.

SAINTSBURY, GEORGE: *A History of English Prose Rhythm*. London, Macmillan, 1912.

"The Metaphysical Poets," *Times Literary Supplement*, London, 27th October, 10th November 1921.

SIMPSON, MRS. E. M. (*née* SPEARING): "John Donne's Sermons, and their relation to his Poetry," *Mod. Lang. Review*, Cambridge, 1912.

"A Chronological Arrangement of Donne's Sermons," *Mod. Lang. Review*, 1913.

"John Donne and Sir Thomas Overbury's Characters," *Mod. Lang. Review*, 1923.

A Study of the Prose Works of John Donne. Oxford, 1924.

"Two Manuscripts of Donne's *Paradoxes and Problems*," *Rev. Eng. Studies*, London, 1927.

"Essays in Divinity" (cancelled Dedication to Sir Harry Vane, Jr.), *Times Literary Supplement*, London, 21st January 1926.

"More Manuscripts of Donne's *Paradoxes and Problems*," *Rev. Eng. Studies*, 1934.

"A Note on Donne's Punctuation," *Rev. Eng. Studies*, London, 1928.

"Jonson and Donne," *Rev. Eng. Studies*, July, 1939.

"The Text of Donne's *Divine Poems*," *Essays and Studies*. 1941.

BROOKE, RUPERT: "John Donne, the Elizabethan," *The Nation*, London, 1913.

"John Donne," *Poetry and Drama*, vol. i, 1913.

SYMONS, ARTHUR: *Figures of Several Centuries*. London, Constable, 1916.

RAMSAY, MARY PATON: *Les Doctrines Médiévales chez Donne*. London, Milford, 1917.

Also see *A Garland for John Donne*, edited by Theodore Spencer. Oxford University Press, 1931.

BREVOLD, L. I.: "Review of Miss Ramsay's *Doctrines Médiévales*," *Jour. Eng. and Germ. Philology*, Illinois, U.S.A., 1922.

"The Naturalism of Donne in relation to some Renaissance Traditions," *Jour. Eng. and Germ. Philology*, 1923.

"Religious Thought of Donne in relation to Medieval and Later Traditions," in *Studies in Shakespeare, Milton and Donne*. Univ. of Michigan Publications, vol. i. Macmillan, 1925.

"Sir Thomas Egerton and Donne," *Times Literary Supplement*, London, 13th March 1924.

READ, HERBERT: "The Nature of Metaphysical Poetry," *The Criterion*, London, April 1923.

FAUSSET, HUGH I'ANSON: *John Donne; A Study in Discord*. London, Cape, 1924.

NETHERCOT, A. H.: "The Reputation of Jhone Donne as a Metrist," *Sewanee Review*, 1922.

"The Reputation of the Metaphysical Poets during the Seventeenth Century," *Jour. Eng. and Germ. Philology*, 1924.

"The Reputation of the Metaphysical Poets during the Age of Johnson and the Romantic Revival," *Studies in Philology*, 1925.

"The Reputation of the Metaphysical Poets during the Age of Pope," *Philological Quarterly*, 1925.

"The Reputation of Native *versus* Foreign 'Metaphysical Poets' in England," *Mod. Lang. Review*, 1930.

HUTTON, W. H.: "John Donne, Poet and Preacher," *Theology*, vol. ix. London, 1924.

SPARROW, JOHN: "On the Date of Donne's 'Hymne to God my
God in my Sickness,'" *Mod. Lang. Review*, Cambridge, 1924.

"Donne's Table-talk," *London Mercury*, 1928.

Review of "Poetry and Prose," ed. Hayward, *London Mercury*,
1929.

"John Donne and Contemporary Preachers," *Essays and
Studies by Members of the English Association*. Oxford, 1930.

"Donne's Religious Development," *Theology*, London, 1931.

"A Book from Donne's Library," *London Mercury*, 1931.

PRAZ, MARIO: *Scentismo e Marinismo in Inghilterra*. (John Donne—
Richard Crashaw.) Florence, 1925.

Studi sul Concettismo. Milan, 1934.

Studies in Seventeenth-century Imagery. vol. i. Warburg
Institute Studies, 1939.

SENCOURT, ROBERT: *Outflying Philosophy*. (John Donne, Sir Thomas
Browne, and Henry Vaughan.) London, Simpkin Marshall,
1925.

WILSON, F. P.: "The Early Life of John Donne," *Review of English
Studies*, London, 1927.

LEGOUIS, PIERRE: *Donne, the Craftsman*. (Paris, Didier.) Oxford
University Press, 1928.

"John Donne," *Times Literary Supplement*, 31st July 1937.

DARK, SIDNEY: "John Donne" in *Five Deans*. London, Cape, 1928.

TERRILL, T. E.: "Spanish Influence on John Donne." (Unpublished Harvard dissertation.) 1928.

"A Note on John Donne's Early Reading," *Mod. Lang.
Notes*, 1928.

BUTT, J. E.: "John Donne and Lincoln's Inn," *Times Literary
Supplement*, 10th April 1930.

"Walton's Copy of Donne's Letters," *Review of English Studies*,
1932.

ELIOT, T. S.: "Talks on Donne's Poetry, broadcast by T. S. Eliot,"
The Listener, London, 19th and 26th March 1930.

"The Metaphysical Poets," *Times Literary Supplement*, London,
20th October 1921.

"Lectures on Metaphysical Poetry," *The Clark Lectures*,
Trinity College, Cambridge. (Unpublished MS. at Eliot
House, Harvard University.) 1926.

"John Donne," *Nation*, London, 1923.

John Donne : A Garland for John Donne, editor T. Spencer, 1931.

SHAPIRO, I. A.: "John Donne and Lincoln's Inn," *Times Literary
Supplement*, 10th April 1930.

"The Text of Donne's Letters to Severall Persons," *Review
of English Studies*, London, vol. vii, 1931.

"John Donne and Parliament," *Times Literary Supplement*,
10th March 1932.

"Donne and Sir Thomas Roe," *Times Literary Supplement*, 7th February 1935.

"John Donne," *Times Literary Supplement*, London, 14th August 1937.

"John Donne the Astronomer and Date of the Eighth Problem," *Times Literary Supplement*, 3rd July 1937.

"Donne and Astronomy," *Mod. Lang. Review*, 1938.

WILLIAMSON, GEORGE: "The Donne Tradition," *A Study in English Poetry from Donne to the Death of Cowley*. Cambridge, Mass. Harvard Univ. (Oxford University Press, 1930.)

"The Donne Canon," *Times Literary Supplement*, London, 18th August 1932.

"The Libertine Donne," *Philological Quarterly*, 1924.

"Textual Difficulties in the Interpretation of Donne's Poetry," *Mod. Philology*, 1st August 1940.

ANON.: "John Donne, Preacher and Bencher of Lincoln's Inn," *The Times*, 31st March 1931.

BENNETT, R. E.: "John Manningham and Donne's Paradoxes," *Mod. Lang. Notes*, London, 1931.

"Addition to Donne's 'Catalogus Librorum,'" *Mod. Lang. Notes*, 1934.

"Donne and Sir Thomas Roe," *Times Literary Supplement*, 31st January 1935.

"Tracts from John Donne's Library," *Review of English Studies*, 1937.

"Walton's Use of Donne's Letters," *Philological Quarterly*, 1937.

"John Donne and Everard Gilpin," *Review of English Studies*, 1939.

"Donne's Letters from the Continent in 1611–12," *Philological Quarterly*, January 1940.

Donne's Letters to Severall Persons of Honour. Pub. Mod. Lang. Association of America, March 1941.

ASHLEY-MONTAGU, M. F.: "Donne, the Astronomer," *Times Literary Supplement*, p. 576, 1937.

WOOD, H. HARVEY: "A Seventeenth-century Manuscript of Poems by Donne and others," *Essays and Studies*, by Members of Eng. Ass., 1931.

"Donne's 'Mr. Tilman': A Postscript (letter)," *Times Literary Supplement*, 9th July 1931.

SPENCER, THEODORE: *A Garland for John Donne*. 1631–1931. Essays by T. S. Eliot, Evelyn M. Simpson, Mario Praz, John Hayward, Mary P. Ramsay, John Sparrow, George Williamson and Theodore Spencer. Oxford University Press, 1931.

Studies in Metaphysical Poetry, by T. S. and Mark Van Doren. New York, Columbia University Press and Oxford University Press, 1938.

LEAVIS, F. R.: "The Influence of John Donne on Modern Poetry,"
Bookman, London, 1931.

    English Poetry in the Seventeenth Century. Scrutiny, 1935.

BALD, R. C.: *Donne's Influence in English Literature.* 1932. Morpeth,
St. John's College Press.

WOOLF, VIRGINIA: "Donne after Three Centuries," *The Second
Common Reader*, London, 1932.

HUGHES, M. Y.: *Kidnapping Donne.* University of California.
Published in English. 1934.

    "The Lineage of the 'Extasie'," *Mod. Lang. Review*, 1932.

BENNETT, JOAN: *Four Metaphysical Poets: Donne, Herbert, Vaughan,
Crashaw.* Camb. Univ. Press, 1934.

    "The Love Poetry of John Donne. A Reply to Mr. Lewis,"
    Seventeenth-century Studies presented to Sir Herbert Grierson.
    Oxford, Clarendon, 1938.

LEISHMAN, J. B.: *The Metaphysical Poets: Donne, Herbert, Vaughan,
Traherne.* Oxford, Clarendon, 1934.

MOORE, J. F.: "Scholasticism, Donne, and the Metaphysical
Conceit," *Revue Anglo-Américaine*, 1936.

SAMPSON, ASHLEY: "The Resurrection of Donne," *London Mercury*,
1936.

WHITE, HELEN C.: *The Metaphysical Poets: a Study in Religious
Experience.* New York, Macmillan, 1936.

COFFIN, CHARLES M.: *John Donne and the New Philosophy.* New
York, Columbia Univ. Press, 1937.

UMBACH, HERBERT H.: *The Rhetoric of Donne's Sermons.* Modern
Language Association Publications, 1937.

    Also see *English Literary History*, vol. xii, 1945.

CROFTS, J. E. V.: *John Donne. Essays and Studies* (English
Association), Oxford, Clarendon, vol. xxii, 1937.

LEWIS, C. S.: "Donne and Love Poetry in the Seventeenth Century," *Seventeenth-century Studies presented to Sir Herbert Grierson.*
Oxford, Clarendon, 1938.

LEWIS, E. GLYN: "The Question of Toleration in the Works of
John Donne," *Mod. Lang. Review*, 1938.

HUSAIN, ITRAT: "John Donne on Conversion," *Theology*, London,
1936.

    The Dogmatic and Mystical Theology of John Donne. S.P.C.K.,
    London, 1938.

    "The Influence of Donne on the Post-War Poets," *The
    Visva-Bharati Journal*, Santi-Niketan, India, 1939.

    The Mystical Element in Metaphysical Poets. Oliver & Boyd,
    Edinburgh, 1946.

KEYNES, GEOFFREY: "Death's Duell," *Times Literary Supplement*,
24th September 1938.

SHARP, R. L.: *Donne to Dryden. The Revolt against Metaphysical Poetry.* Chapel Hill, University of North Carolina Press, and Oxford University Press, 1940.

BOWERS, FRENDSON I.: "An Interpretation of Donne's Tenth Elegy," *Mod. Lang. Review*, April, 1939.

MILTON, ALLAN RUGOFF: *Donne's Imagery.* Corporate Press, New York, 1940.

"Drummond's Debt to Donne," *Philological Quarterly*, 1937.

CARLETON, PHILLIPS D.: "John Donne's Bracelet of Bright Hair about the Bone," *Mod. Lang. Review*, May 1941.

BENHAM, ALLEN R.: "The Myth of John Donne the Rake," in the volume *In Honor of Hardin Craig.* 1941.

TILLYARD, E. M. W.: "A Note on Donne's 'Extasie'," *Review of English Studies*, January, 1943.

CAMERON, ALLEN DON: "Donne's Suicides," *Modern Language Notes*, February, 1941.

The Star-crossed Renaissance. The Quarrel about Astrology and its Influence in England. Durham, North Carolina. Duke University Press, 1941.
"Review of *The Poems of John Donne*, ed. by Roger E. Bennett" (Chicago, Packard & Company, 1942), in the *Journal of English and Germanic Philology*, 1942.
"John Donne's Knowledge of Renaissance Medicine," *Journal of English and Germanic Philology*, 1943.
"Dean Donne Sets his Text," *Journal of English Literary History*, U.S.A., September, 1943.

MATHEWS, ERNEST G.: "John Donne's 'Little Rag'," *Mod. Lang. Notes*, December, 1941.

HARDY, EVELYN: *John Donne, A Spirit in Conflict.* Constable, 1942.

STEIN, ARNOLD: "Donne and the Couplet," *P.M.L.A.*, September, 1942.

SIMPSON, PERCY: "The Rhyming of Stressed with Unstressed Syllables in Elizabethan Verse" (mentions Donne as a metrical innovator), *Mod. Lang. Review*, 1943.

MOLONEY, M. F.: *John Donne: His Flight from Mediævalism.* University of Illinois, 1944.

SCOTT, W. S.: *The Fantasticks, John Donne.* John West House, London, 1945.

POTTER, GEORGE R.: "Hitherto undescribed Manuscript Versions of Three Sermons by Donne," *Journal of English and Germanic Philology*, 1945.

RAINE, KATHLEEN: "John Donne and the Baroque Doubt," *Horizon*, London, 1945.

KNIGHT, L. C.: *On the Social Background of Metaphysical Poetry.* Scrutiny, Cambridge, 1945.

BIBLIOGRAPHY

Cambridge History of English Literature. 1909–12.

KEYNES, GEOFFREY: *The Bibliography of John Donne.* 179 pp. Quaritch, London, 1914. 2nd edition. 311 pp. Cambridge University Press, 1932.

Bibliographical Note to *Devotions upon Emergent Occasions.* Edited by John Sparrow. Cambridge University Press, 1923.

Bibliographical Notes to *Ten Sermons,* 1923, and *Paradoxes and Problems,* 1923.

MACCARTHY, DESMOND: "A Reader's Bibliography of John Donne," *Life and Letters,* 1928.

HEBEL, J. W., and F. A. PATTERSON, and assisted by C. M. COFFIN: *English Seventeenth-century Literature. A Brief Working Bibliography.* 1929.

HEBEL, J. W.: Bibliographical Note to *Biathanatos.* New York, Facsimile Text Society. Oxford, Blackwell, 1930

UMBACH, HERBERT H.: A Bibliographical Note to *The Easter Sermons of John Donne.* An edition with Introduction, Commentary, Textual Notes and a Bibliography. New York, Cornell University, 1934.

COFFIN, CHARLES M.: "Bibliography of John Donne," *Times Literary Supplement,* 2nd August 1934.

BENNETT, R. E.: Bibliographical Note to *Juvenilia; or Certain Paradoxes and Problems.* New York, Facsimile Text Society, 1936.

PINTO, V. DE SOLA: *The English Renaissance* (1510–1688). London, 1938.

SPENCER, T., and VAN DOREN, M.: *Studies in Metaphysical Poetry.* (Two Essays and a Bibliography.) 1939.

WHITE, WILLIAM: *John Donne since 1900—A Bibliography of Periodical Articles.* Boston, 1942.

CONCORDANCE

COMBS, H. C., and SULLENS, Z. R.: *Concordance of Donne.* Chicago, 1940.

CHAPTER III.   GEORGE HERBERT (1593–1633)

Only the English works are included in this bibliography

The Temple, Sacred Poems and Private Ejaculations. Cambridge, 1633; also 1633, 1634, 1635, 1638, 1641, 1656 (London); 1660, 1667, 1674 (including Walton's *Life,* 1679, 1703, 1709).

A Treatise of Temperance, by Ludowick Cornaro, translated by G. Herbert (contained in *Hygiasticon*), 1634.

Letter and Notes prefixed to Ferrar's translation of *The Hundred and Ten Considerations of John Valdesso*, 1638. Edited by Chapman, 1905.

"Outlandish Proverbs, selected by Mr. G. H." (in Witt's *Recreation*), 1640; included in Herbert's *Remains*, 1652.

Select Parts of Herbert's Sacred Poems, 1773 (prepared by John Wesley).

"A Priest to the Temple" (in Herbert's *Remains*), 1652. Edited by H. C. Beeching, 1898.

The Works of G. Herbert, with Preface by W. Pickering, and Notes by S. T. Coleridge. 2 vols. 1835.

Works. Edited by R. A. Willmott, 1854.

The Complete Works. Edited by A. B. Grosart. 3 vols.

RHYS, ERNEST: *The Poems of George Herbert* (1885), Introduction.

PALMER, GEORGE H. (Editor): *The English Poems of George Herbert*. New York, Houghton Mifflin, 1916.
> *The English Works of George Herbert*. Newly arranged and annotated and considered in relation to his life. 3 vols. London, Hodder, 1920. (Reprint of 1905 edition.)

BEECHING, H. C. (Editor): *The Country Parson*. Oxford, Blackwell, 1915. (Reprint of 1898 edition.)

BISHOP OF NORTH CAROLINA (Editor): *The Priest to the Temple; or, The Country Parson, His Character and Rule of Life*. Wisconsin, Marehouse, 1916.

HERBERT, GEORGE: *Poems, English and Latin*. Editor, G. C. Moore Smith. Oxford, 1923.
> *Poems*. Selected by Sir H. Walford Davies. Newton, Gregynog Press, 1923.
> *Poems*. Augustan Books of English Poetry. London, Benn, 1927.
> *The Temple and a Priest to the Temple*. Introduction by Edward Thomas. London, Everyman's Library, 1927.
> *Works in Prose and Verse*. Chandos Classics. London, Warne, 1927.

MEYNELL, FRANCIS: Nonesuch Edition of *The Temple*, with a Bibliographical Note by G. Keynes. 1927.

The Works of George Herbert. Edited by the Rev. F. E. Hutchinson. Oxford, Clarendon, 1941.

CRITICISM

WALTON, IZAAK: *The Life of Mr. George Herbert*. 1670.

AUBREY, JOHN: *Brief Lives*. Edited by Andrew Clark. 2 vols. 1898.

ADDISON, JOSEPH: "On False Wit," *Spectator*, 7th May 1711.

Herbert, Edward (Baron Herbert of Cherbury). Autobiography. 1764. Edited by Sir Sidney Lee, 1886 and 1907.

Cowper, William, The Correspondence of. 1802.

COLERIDGE, S. T.: *Biographia Literatia,* sections xix and xx. 1817.

DANIELL, J. J.: *Life of George Herbert.* 1848.

BENSON, E. W.: *The Praise of George Herbert.* 1851.

MAYER, J. E. B.: *Nicholas Ferrar's Two Lives.* Edited by. 1855.

DANIELL, J. J.: *Life of George Herbert.* 1893.

GIBSON, E. C. S.: *The Temple.* 1899.

DOWDEN, E.: *Puritan and Anglican Studies.* 1900.

BEECHING, H. C.: *Religio Laici.* 1902.

ARCHBISHOP OF ARMAGH: *Poems of George Herbert,* Introduction.

HUTCHINSON, REV. F. E.: *Camb. Hist. Eng. Lit.,* vol. vii, cap. ii.

HYDE, A. G.: *George Herbert and his Times.* 1905.

PALMER and MORE, P. E.: *Shelbourne Essays.* Fourth Series. New York, 1906.

BUCHANAN, E. S.: *G. Herbert, Melodist.*

BULLOCK, C. *An Hour with George Herbert.*

CURRIER, ALBERT H.: "George Herbert." *Biographical and Literary Studies.* Boston, The Pilgrim Press, 1915.

WAUGH, ARTHUR: *The Poems of George Herbert,* Introduction.

CLUTTON-BROCK, ARTHUR: "George Herbert," *More Essays on Books.* London, Methuen, 1921.

MERRIL, L. R.: "The Church Porch," *Mod. Lang. Notes,* 1921.

GRIERSON, H. J. C.: *Metaphysical Lyrics and Poems of the Seventeenth Century: Donne to Butler. With an Essay.* Oxford, Clarendon, 1921.

> *The Background of English Literature.* London, Chatto & Windus, 1925.

> *Cross Currents in English Literature of the Seventeenth Century* (The Messenger Lectures, Cornell). London, Chatto & Windus, 1929.

> *The Oxford Book of Seventeenth-century Verse.* Chosen by, and G. Bullough. Oxford, Clarendon, 1934.

HODGSON, G. E.: *English Mystics.* London, Mowbray, 1922.

LUCAS, F. L.: *George Herbert. Life and Letters.* 1928.

> *Studies, French and English.* 1934.

NAYLOR, E. W.: "Three Seventeenth-century Poet-Parsons and Music (Traherne, George Herbert, Robert Herrick)," *Proceedings of the Musical Association,* London, 1928.

ROBBIE, H. J. L.: "George Herbert," *Church Quarterly Review,* 1928.

EINSTEIN, L.: *Tudor Ideals.*

TROELTSH, ERNST: *Protestantism and Progress.*

WILLIAMSON, GEORGE: *The Donne Tradition. A Study in English Poetry from Donne to the Death of Cowley.* Oxford University Press, 1930.

BEACHCROFT, T. O.: "Nicholas Ferrar, his Influence on and Friendship with George Herbert," *Criterion,* 1932.

ELIOT, T. S.: "George Herbert," *Spectator,* 1932.

BLUNDEN, EDMUND: "George Herbert's Latin Poems," *Essays and Studies of the English Association*, 1933.

SLADE, HILDA M.: "The Tercentenary of George Herbert," *Poetry Review*, 1933.

HUTCHINSON, F. E.: "George Herbert. A Tercentenary," *Nineteenth Century*, 1933.
"John Wesley and George Herbert," *London Quarterly Review*, 1936.

ORANGE, U. M. D.: "Herbert's Poetry," *Poetry Review*, 1933.

HERBERT, GEORGE (1593–1633): *Times Literary Supplement*, 22nd December 1905; 1st April 1920; 2nd March 1933; 12th July 1941; and *Cambridge Review*, 1933.

HALL, BERNARD G.: "The Text of George Herbert," *Times Literary Supplement*, 26th October 1933.

SPARROW, JOHN: "The Text of George Herbert," *Times Literary Supplement*, 14th December 1933.

THOMAS GILBERT: "George Herbert," *Contemporary Review*, pp. 143, 706–716, 1933.

BARRET, K. I.: "Studies in the Life and Writings of George Herbert." Unpublished dissertation. University of London, 1934.

BENNET, J.: *The Four Metaphysical Poets (Donne, Herbert, Vaughan and Crashaw)*. Camb. Univ. Press, 1934.

LEISHMAN, J. B.: *The Metaphysical Poets (Donne, Herbert, Vaughan, Traherne)*. Oxford, Clarendon, 1934.

WARREN, AUSTIN: "George Herbert," *American Review*, 1936.

HARPER, G. M.: "George Herbert's Poems," *Quarterly Review*, 1936.

WHITE, HELEN C.: *The Metaphysical Poets: a Study in Religious Experience*. New York, Macmillan, 1936.

LUKE, S.: "An Old Handbook on the Pastoral Office: A Priest to the Temple," *London Quarterly Review*, 1937.

BLACKSTONE, B.: *The Ferrar Papers*. Edited by. 1938.

FREEMAN, MARY ROSE: "George Herbert and the Emblem Books," *Review of English Studies*, April, 1941.

LUCAS, MARY: "Imagery in George Herbert's Poetry." Unpublished dissertation. University of Liverpool.

GRIERSON, H. J. C.: "Review of *The Works of George Herbert* edited with a Commentary by Rev. F. E. Hutchinson, Oxford, Clarendon Press," in *Mod. Lang. Review*, April, 1942.

WILSON, F. P.: "A Note on George Herbert 'The Quidditie,'" *Review of English Studies*, 1943.

KNIGHT, L. C.: *George Herbert*. Scrutiny, Cambridge, 1944.

CONCORDANCE

MANN, CAMERON: *A Concordance to the English Poems of George Herbert*. New York, Houghton Mifflin, 1927.

BIBLIOGRAPHY

PALMER, G. H.: *Herbert Bibliography.* Cambridge, Mass., 1911.
SPENCER, T., and VAN DOREN, M.: *Studies in Metaphysical Poetry*
    (*Two Essays and a Bibliography.*) New York, Columbia
    University Press, 1939.
KEYNES, GEOFFREY: "Bibliographical Note to Nonesuch Edition of
    The Temple," 1927.

NICHOLAS FERRAR (1592–1637)

WORKS

The Hundred and Ten Considerations of Signior John Valdesso. 1838.

CRITICISM

SHORTHOUSE, J. H.: *John Inglesant.* 1880–81.
MACDONOUGH, T. M.: *Brief Memoirs of Nicholas Ferrar.* Chiefly
    collected from a Narrative by Dr. Turner. 1837.
MAYOR, J. E. B.: *Nicholas Ferrar* (Two Lives by his brother and by
    Doctor Jebb). 1855.
CARTER, T. T.: *Nicholas Ferrar; his Household and his Friends.* 1892.
SHARLAND, E. C.: *The Story Books of Little Gidding.* 1899.
ACLAND, J. E.: *Little Gidding and its Inmates in the Time of Charles I.*
    1903.
SKIPTON, H. P. K.: *The Life and Times of Nicholas Ferrar.* 1907.
MAYCOCK, A. L.: *Nicholas Ferrar of Little Gidding.* 1938.
BLACKSTONE, B.: *The Ferrar Papers.* Cambridge Press, 1938.

CHAPTER IV.   RICHARD CRASHAW (1612/13–49)

WORKS

Epigrammatum Sacrorum Liber . . . Cantabrigia. 1634.
Steps to the Temple, Sacred Poems, with Other Delights of the Muses. 1646.
Steps to the Temple, Sacred Poems, with Other Delights of the Muses.
    Second edition. Wherein are added divers pieces not before
    extant. 1648.
Carmen Deo Nostro. Paris, 1652.
P(EREGRINE) P(HILIPS): *R. Crashaw's pœtry, with some Account of the
    Author.* 1787.
GILFILLAN, GEORGE: *The Poetical Works of Richard Crashaw and
    Quarles' Emblems.* With Memoirs and Critical Dissertation by.
    1857.
TURNBULL, W. B.: *The Complete Works of Richard Crashaw.* Edited
    by. 1858.

GROSART, A. B.: *The Poems of Richard Crashaw.* Edited by. 2 vols. 1872–73. Fuller Worthies Library.

TUTIN, J. R.: *Carmen Deo Nostro—Sacred Poems.* Edited and with an Introduction by. 1897.

The Delight of the Muses—Secular Poems. Edited by. 1900.

English Poems. Edited and with an Introduction by. 2 vols. 1900.

Poems of Richard Crashaw. Edited by J. R. Tutin, with an Introduction by Canon Beeching. The Muses Library, 1905.

HUTTON, EDWARD: *The English Poems of Richard Crashaw.* Edited and with an Introduction by. The Little Library, 1901.

WALLER, A. R.: *Steps to the Temple, Delight of Muses and other Poems.* The text edited by. Cambridge English Classics, 1904.

SHEPHERD, R. A. ERIC (Editor): *Religious Poems.* The Catholic Library, 1914. St. Louis, Missouri, Herder.

MARTIN, L. C.: *The Poems, English, Latin and Greek, by Richard Crashaw.* Oxford, Clarendon, 1927.

CRASHAW, RICHARD: *Musicks Duell, from the Delights of the Muses and other Poems written on Several Occasions.* 1646. London, E. Walters, 1935.

POPE, A.: *Works.* Edited by W. Elwin, vol. vi, 1871. (Letter to H. Cromwell, 17th December 1710.)

CRITICISM

McCARTHY, D. F.: "Crashaw and Shelley," *Notes and Queries*, 5th June 1858.

BARGRAVE, JOHN (1610–80): *Alexander VII and the College of Cardinals.* Camden Society, 1867.

THOMPSON, F.: *Academy*, 20th November 1897.

Works, vol. iii. 1913.

GOSSE, E.: *Seventeenth-century Studies.* 1883.

COURTHOPE, J. W.: *The History of English Poetry*, vol. iii, 1897–1904.

SKIPTON, H. P. K.: *The Life and Times of Nicholas Ferrar.* 1907.

SHARLAND, E. C.: "Richard Crashaw and Mary Collet," *Church Quarterly Review*, 1912.

MARTIN, L. C.: "Adonais: Crashaw and Shelley Parallel," *Mod. Lang. Review*, 1916.

"A Hitherto Unpublished Poem by Richard Crashaw," *London Mercury*, 1923.

OSMOND, PERCY H.: *Mystical Poets of the English Church.* New York, Macmillan, 1919.

SPENDER, C.: "The Life and Work of Richard Crashaw," *Contemporary Review*, 1919.

GRIERSON, H. J. C.: *The Metaphysical Lyrics and Poems of the 17th Century*, Introduction. Oxford, Clarendon, 1921.
  The Cross Currents in Seventeenth-century Literature. London, Chatto & Windus, 1929.
CONFREY, BURTON: "A Note on Richard Crashaw," *Mod. Lang. Review*, 1922.
BARKER, F. E.: "Religious Poems of Richard Crashaw," *Church Quarterly Review*, 1923.
  "Crashaw and Andrewes," *Times Literary Supplement*, 21st August 1937.
FALLS, CYRIL: "The Divine Poet," *Nineteenth Century*, 1923.
LOUDON, M. K.: *Two Mystic Poets, and other Essays.* Oxford, Blackwell, 1923.
CHALMERS, LORD: *Richard Crashaw, Poet and Saint.* Cambridge University Press, 1924.
PRAZ, MARIO: *Scentismo e Marinismo in Inghilterra.* Florence, 1925.
  Unromantic Spain.
  Studies in Seventeenth-century Imagery. The Warburg Institute, 1939.
ELIOT, T. S.: "A Note on Richard Crashaw." For *Lancelot Andrewes.* London, Faber & Gwyer, 1928.
HUTCHINSON, REV. F. E.: *Cambridge Hist. Eng. Lit.*, vol. vii.
  Church Quarterly Review, cvi, 1928.
WILLIAMSON, GEORGE: *The Donne Tradition.* Oxford University Press, 1930.
WARREN, AUSTIN: "Crashaw and Peterhouse," *Times Literary Supplement*, 13th August 1931.
  "Crashaw and Saint Teresa," *Times Literary Supplement*, 25th August 1932.
  "Crashaw's Residence at Peterhouse," *Times Literary Supplement*, 3rd November 1932.
  "Crashaw's Paintings at Cambridge," *Mod. Lang. Notes*, 1933.
  "The Mysticism of Richard Crashaw," *Church Quarterly Review*, 1933.
  "The Reputation of Crashaw in the Seventeenth and Eighteenth Centuries," *Studies in Philology*, 1934.
  "Crashaw's Epigrammata Sacra," *Journal of English and Germanic Philology*, 1934.
  "Richard Crashaw, Catechist and Curate," *Modern Philology*, 1935.
  "Crashaw's Reputation in the Seventeenth Century," *Mod. Language Association Publications*, 1936.
  Richard Crashaw (A Study in Baroque Sensibility). Louisiana State University Press, 1940.
WATKIN, E. I.: *The English Way.* Ed. by M. Ward. 1933.
BENNET, JOAN: *Four Metaphysical Poets: Donne, Herbert, Vaughan and Crashaw.* Cambridge University Press, 1934.

BEACHCROFT, T. O.: "Crashaw and the Baroque Style," *Criterion*, 1934.

WALLERSTEIN, RUTH: "Richard Crashaw: A Study in Style and Poetic Development," *University of Wisconsin Studies in Language and Literature*, 1935.

NEWDIGATE, B. A.: "An Overlooked Poem by Richard Crashaw," *London Mercury*, 1935.

WHITE, HELEN C.: *The Metaphysical Poets: a Study in Religious Experience.* New York, Macmillan, 1936.

COLVILLE, K. N.: "Crashaw and Andrewes," *Times Literary Supplement*, 28th August 1937.

"Crashaw, Poet and Saint," *Times Literary Supplement*, 1st June 1946.

"*Bibliography* of Criticism" (1912–38): *Studies in Metaphysical Poetry*, by T. Spencer and M. Van Doren. Columbia University Press, 1939.

For general Bibliography on Spanish Translations (including St. Teresa) see:

PANE, R. U.: *English Translations from the Spanish, 1484–1943.* A Bibliography. Rutgers, 1944.

CHAPTER V. HENRY VAUGHAN (1621/2–95)

WORKS

Poems, with the tenth Satyre of Juvenal Englished. 1646.

Silex Scintillans: or Sacred Poems and Private Ejaculations, by Henry Vaughan, Silurist. 1650. This volume was reprinted in 1655 with the addition of new introductory material and the second part of *Silex Scintillans*.

Olor Iscanus. A Collection of some Select Poems, and Translations. Formerly written by Mr. Henry Vaughan, Silurist. Published by a Friend, 1651, 1679.

The Mount of Olives: or Solitary Devotions, with an Excellent Discourse of the Blessed State of Man in Glory. Written by . . . Anselm . . . now done into English, 1652.

Flores Solitudinis. 1654.

Hermetical Physick. By Henry Nollius. Englished, 1655.

Thalia Rediviva. 1678.

The Sacred Poems and Private Ejaculations of Henry Vaughan, with a Memoir by the Rev. H. F. Lyte, 1847. Boston, 1856, 1858, 1883. (Issued in Bohn's Popular Library: New York, Macmillan; London, Bell.)

The Works in Verse and Prose complete of Henry Vaughan, Silurist. For the first time collected, and edited by the Rev. A. B. Grosart. 4 vols. 1871. Fuller Worthies Library.

Secular Poems, with notes and bibliography by J. R. Tutin. 1893.

The Poems of Henry Vaughan, Silurist. Edited by E. K. Chambers, with an Introduction by H. C. Beeching. 2 vols. London, 1896, 1905. Muses Library.

Poems. Edited by Sir I. Gollancz. 1900.

The Mount of Olives, Man in Darkness, and Life of Paulinus. Edited by L. I. Guiney. 1902.

Poems. Edited by E. Hutton. 1904.

Silex Scintillans. Introduction by W. A. Lewis Bettany. 1905.

The Works of Henry Vaughan. Edited by L. C. Martin. 2 vols. Oxford, Clarendon, 1914.

MEYNELL, FRANCIS (Editor): *The Best of Both Worlds. A choice taken from the Poems of Andrew Marvell and Henry Vaughan.* London, Allen & Unwin, 1918.

Poems, and Essays from the Mount of Olives, and Two Letters. Ed. F(rancis) M(eynell), 1924.

VAUGHAN, HENRY: *Poems of Henry Vaughan; an essay from "The Mount of Olives"; and Two Letters from manuscripts in the Bodleian Library.* Limited edition. London, Nonesuch, 1924.

> *Poems.* Edited by Ernest Rhys. The Gregynog Press, Newtown, 1924.
>
> *Three Poems: "Peace," "The Retreat," "Into The World of Light."* Washington, St. Albans Press, 1928.

CRITICISM

"Vaughan's Olor Iscanus," *Retrospective Review*, vol. iii, 1821.

BROWN, JOHN: *Horæ Subsecivæ.* Series I, 1858.

SHAIRP, J. C.: *Sketches in History and Poetry.* 1887.

"Henry Vaughan," *Macmillan's Magazine*, lxiii, 1890.

GUINEY, L. I.: *A Little English Gallery.* 1894.

PALGRAVE, F. T.: *Landscape in Poetry.* 1897.

DOWDEN, E.: *Anglican and Puritan Studies.* 1900.

ELLIS, R.: *Letters of Oxford Welshmen.* Ed. by. Oxford, 1903.

SICHEL, EDITH: "Henry Vaughan, Silurist," *Monthly Review*, April 1903.

SPENS, JANET: *Two Periods of Disillusion.* 1909.

"Henry Vaughan, Silurist," *Nineteenth Century*, vol. lxvii, 1910.

JOHNSON, LIONEL: "Henry Vaughan," reprinted in *Post Liminium*, 1911.

GUINEY, LOUIS I.: "Henry Vaughan the Silurist," *Atlantic Review*, 1894.

> "Lovelace and Vaughan: a Speculation," *Catholic World*, 1912.
>
> "Cromwell and Henry Vaughan," *Athenæum*, 1902.
>
> "Milton and Vaughan," *Quarterly Review*, 1914.
>
> "Unpublished Letters, with a Commentary," *Nation*, New York, 1915.

MORE, PAUL ELMER: "Some Parallels in Henry Vaughan," *Nation*, New York, 1915.
   "Henry Vaughan," *Nation*, New York, 1916.
   "Henry Vaughan," *The Demon of the Absolute*, pp. 143–164. New Shelbourne Essays, vol. i. London, Milford, 1928.
   "The Poetry of Henry Vaughan," *Living Age*, 1915.
   "The Poetry of Henry Vaughan," *Times Literary Supplement*, 15th July 1915.
   "Vaughan and Herrick," *Athenæum*, 12th June 1915.
LYTTLETON, E.: "Henry Vaughan and Optimism," *Contemporary Review*, 1916.
BRETT-SMITH, H. F. B.: "Vaughan and D'Avenant," *Mod. Lang. Review*, 1916.
BENSLY, EDWARD: "Notes on Henry Vaughan," *Mod. Lang. Review*, 1919.
CLUTTON-BROCK, ARTHUR: "Henry Vaughan," *More Essays on Books*. London, Methuen, 1921.
MERRILL, L. R.: "Vaughan's Influence upon Wordsworth's Poetry," *Modern Language Notes*, 1922.
   "The Tercentenary of Henry Vaughan," *Times Literary Supplement*, 20th April 1922.
WELLS, HENRY W.: *The Tercentenary of Henry Vaughan*. New York, Hudson Press, 1922.
LOUDON, M. K.: *Two Mystic Poets and Other Essays*. Oxford, Blackwell, 1923.
SENCOURT, ROBERT: "Henry Vaughan the Silurist," in *Outflying Philosophy*. London, 1925.
MARTIN, L. C.: "A Forgotten Poet of the Seventeenth Century," *Essays and Studies of English Association*, 1925.
   "Vaughan and Cowper," *Mod. Lang. Review*, 1927.
   "Henry Vaughan and the Theme of Infancy," *Seventeenth-century Studies presented to Sir Herbert Grierson*. Oxford, Clarendon, 1938.
   (For Martin's essay on "Henry Vaughan's relation to Hermetic Philosophy" see *Review of English Studies* (1942).
BLUNDEN, EDMUND: "On the Poems of Henry Vaughan," *London Mercury*, 1926.
   On the Poems of Henry Vaughan: Characteristics and Intimations. With his principal Latin poems translated into English verse. London, Cobden-Sanderson, 1927.
JUDSON, A. C.: "Cornelius Agrippa and Henry Vaughan," *Modern Language Notes*, 1926.
   "Henry Vaughan as a Nature Poet," *Modern Language Association Publications*, 1927.
   "The Source of Henry Vaughan's Ideas Concerning God in Nature," *Studies in Philosophy*, 1927.
ELIOT, T. S.: "The Silurist," *Dial.*, 83, 259–263, 1927.

EMPSON, WILLIAM: "Henry Vaughan, Early Romantic," *Cambridge Review*, 1929.

WILLIAMSON, GEORGE: "Henry Vaughan," in *The Donne Tradition*. Oxford University Press, 1930.

HOLMES, ELIZABETH: *Henry Vaughan and the Hermetic Philosophy*. Oxford, Blackwell, 1932.
(For other articles on the influence of Hermetic thought on Henry Vaughan see the Bibliography on Thomas Vaughan.)

MORGAN, GWELLIAN E. F.: "Henry Vaughan, Oxford Silurist," *Times Literary Supplement*, 2nd November 1932.

CHAPIN, C.: "Henry Vaughan and the Modern Spirit," *Nineteenth Century*, 1933.

WINTERBOTTOM, K. M.: "Certain Affinities to Wordsworth in the Poetry of Vaughan and Traherne." (Unpublished dissertation, University of Pittsburgh, 1933.)

BENNET, JOAN: *Four Metaphysical Poets: Donne, Herbert, Vaughan and Crashaw*. Cambridge University Press, 1934.

LEISHMAN, JAMES B.: *The Metaphysical Poets: Donne, Herbert, Vaughan, Traherne*. Oxford, Clarendon, 1934.

MACMASTER, HELEN: "Wordsworth's Copy of Vaughan," *Times Literary Supplement*, 12th April 1934.
"Vaughan and Wordsworth," *Review of English Studies*, 1935.

WHITE, HELEN C.: *The Metaphysical Poets. A Study in Religious Experience*. New York, Macmillan, 1936.

VAUGHAN, HENRY: *A Few Lines by a Welsh Doctor*. New York, Oliver, 1937.

ASHTON, HELEN: *The Swan of Usk*. 1940. (An historical novel.) Vaughan is the hero of this novel.

HUGHES, M. Y.: "The Theme of Pre-existence and Infancy in *The Retreate*," *Renaissance Studies in Honor of Hardin Craig*. Stanford, 1941.

MARILLA, E. L.: "Henry Vaughan and the Civil War," *Journal of English and German Philosophy*, 1942.
For her study of the Secular Verse of Henry Vaughan see: *Ohio State University Abstract of Dissertations*, 1941.

ALLEN, DON CAMERON: "Henry Vaughan's 'The Ass,'" *Modern Language Notes*, 1943.

SIMPSON, PERCY: "Henry Vaughan's Epitaph," *Notes and Queries* 28th August 1943.

CHILDE, WINIFRED R.: "Henry Vaughan," *Essays by Divers Hands*. Royal Society of Literature, Oxford University Press, 1945.

BIBLIOGRAPHY

Studies in Metaphysical Poetry, by Theodore Spencer and Mark Van Doren. Columbia University Press, New York, 1939.

CHAPTER VI

THOMAS VAUGHAN, *pseudonym* EUGENIUS PHILALETHES,
1621/2–1666

WORKS

Anthroposophia Theomagica, by Eugenius Philalethes. 1650.
Magia Adamica, by Eugenius Philalethes. 1650.
Anima Magica Abscondita, by Eugenius Philalethes. 1650.
*The Man-Mouse taken in a Trap and Tortured to Death for Gnawing the
Margins of Eugenius Philalethes.* 1650.
The Second Washer for Moore scour'd once more. 1651.
(The last two tracts deal with the controversy between Thomas
Vaughan and Henry More, the Cambridge Platonists.)
Lumen de Lumine, by Eugenius Philalethes. 1651. Ed. E. A. Waite,
1910.
The Fame and Confession of the Fraternity of the Rosie Cross. 1652.
Ed. F. N. Pryce, 1923.
Euphrates; or the Waters of the East. 1655.
The Chymists Key; or the True Doctrine of Corruption and Generation.
1657.
*Thalia Rediviva (by Henry Vaughan), with some learned Remains of the
Eminent Eugenius Philalethes.* 1678.
The Works in Verse and Prose complete of Henry Vaughan. Edited by
A. B. Grosart. 4 vols. 1871. (Contains the *Poems* of Thomas
Vaughan.)
The Magical Writings of Thomas Vaughan. The reprint of the first
four treatises, with a biographical preface by A. E. Waite, 1888.
Selected Poems (with those of Norris and Thomas Traherne). Edited
by J. R. Tutin, 1905.
The Works of Thomas Vaughan. Edited by A. E. Waite, 1919.

CRITICISM

WOOD, ANTHONY A.: *Athenae Oxonienses.* 2 vols. 1691–92. En-
larged edition, including the *Fasti*, 1721.
MORLEY, H.: *Life of H. C. Agrippa.* London, 1856.
WAITE, A. E.: Biographical Preface to *Magical Writings.* 1888.
The Hermetic and Alchemical Writings of Paracelsus. Edited by.
1894.
"Henry and Thomas Vaughan," *Bookman*, London, 63, 240,
1923.
STODDART, M.: *The Life of Paracelsus.* 1915.
MARTIN, E.: "Thomas Vaughan," *Fortnightly Review*, March 1924.
SENCOURT, ROBERT: *Outflying Philosophy.* London, 1925.

COLLARD, LORNA; "Henry Vaughan and the Region Elenore,"
Occult Review, 1930.
HOLMES, ELIZABETH: *Henry Vaughan and the Hermetic Philosophy.*
Blackwell, 1932.
CLOUGH, W. O.: "Henry Vaughan and the Hermetic Philosophy,"
Modern Language Association Publications, 1933.
SMITH, ARTHUR J. M.: "Some Relations between Henry Vaughan
and Thomas Vaughan," *Papers of the Michigan Academy of
Sciences, Arts, and Letters*, 1933.
WARDLE, RALPH M.: "Thomas Vaughan's Influence upon
the Poetry of Henry Vaughan," *Modern Language Association
Publications*, 1936.
THOMA, H. F.: "The Hermetic Strain in Seventeenth-century
English Mysticism." (Unpublished thesis, 1941, Harvard.)
MARILLA, E. L.: "Henry Vaughan and Thomas Vaughan," *Mod.
Lang. Review*, 1944.

MAGIC AND WITCHCRAFT
(Modern Books)

MOORE, G. H.: *Bibliographical Notes on Witchcraft.* 1888.
JAGGARD, G. H.: *Folklore, Superstition and Witchcraft in Shakespeare.
A Bibliography.* 1896.
NOTESTEIN, W.: *A History of Witchcraft in England from 1558 to 1871.*
American Hist. Association, 1911.
MURRAY, M. A.: *The Witch Cult in Western Europe.* Oxford, 1921.
SUMMERS, M.: *The History of Witchcraft and Demonology.* 1926.
    The Geography of Witchcraft. 1927.
KITTREDGE, G. L.: *Witchcraft in Old and New England.* Cambridge,
U.S.A., 1929.
HOWLAND, A. C.: *Materials Toward a History of Witchcraft.* 3 vols.
University of Pennsylvania, 1939.
WILLIAMS, CHARLES: *Witchcraft.* 1941.

CHAPTER VII. THOMAS TRAHERNE (1637/9–74)
WORKS

Roman Forgeries. By a faithful son of the Church of England.
(Anon.) 1673.
*Christian Ethicks, or divine morality opening the way to Blessedness by the
Rules of Vertue and Reason.* 1675. (Contains 8 poems.) Two
chapters—"Of Magnanimity and Charity"—have been edited
by J. R. Slater, Columbia University, 1942.

A Serious and Pathetical Contemplation of the Mercies of God. (Anon.)
1699. (Identified by Dobell; contains 3 rhymed poems.)
This has been recently edited by R. Daniells, University of
Toronto Press and Oxford University Press, 1941.
The Poetical Works of Thomas Traherne. Now first published from
the original manuscripts. Edited and with a memoir by B.
Dobell, 1903 and 1906.
Selected Poems by Thomas Traherne, Thomas Vaughan and J. Norris.
Edited by J. R. Tutin, 1905.
Centuries of Meditations by Thomas Traherne. Now first printed from
the author's manuscript. Edited by Bertram Dobell, 1908 and
1928. Revised edition.
Traherne's Poems of Felicity. Edited from the MS. by H. I. Bell, 1910.
(The MS. mentioned here (B.M. Burney 392) was prepared for
the press probably by the poet's brother, Philip. In this MS.
there are 39 poems which are not in Dobell's volumes, and
there are considerable variations in the 23 poems which are
common to both MS. collections.)
The Poetical Works of Thomas Traherne (including the *Poems of Felicity*).
Edited by G. I. Wade, 1932. (Contains the poems from the
Burney MS.)
Felicities of Thomas Traherne. Ed. Sir A. T. Quiller-Couch, 1935.
A Book of Private Devotions and Prayer (Dobell MS. still unpublished).

Criticism

WOOD, ANTHONY A (1632–95): *Athenæ Oxonienses.* 2 vols. 1691–92.
AUBREY, JOHN (1626–97): *Brief Lives.* Edited by Andrew Clark.
2 vols. 1898.
DOBELL, B.: "An Unknown Seventeenth-century Poet," *Athenæum,*
7, 14, April 1900. (Dobell's first announcement of his discovery
of the MSS. of Traherne.)
JONES, W. L.:"Traherne and the Religious Poetry of the Seventeenth
Century," *Quarterly Review,* October 1904.
QUILLER-COUCH, SIR A. T.: *From a Cornish Window.* Cambridge,
1906.
WILLCOX, L. E.: "A Joyous Mystic," *North American Review,*
June 1911.
SPURGEON, C. F. E.: *Mysticism in English Literature.* 1913.
FLEMING, W. K.: *Mysticism in Christianity.* 1913.
LOCK, W.: "An English Mystic," *Constructive Quarterly,* i, 826–836,
1913.
JONES, RUFUS M.: "Thomas Traherne and the Spiritual Poets of
the Seventeenth Century," *Spiritual Reformers in the 16th and 17th
Centuries,* pp. 320–335. London, Macmillan, 1914.
HUTTON, REV. W. H.: *Camb. Hist. English Lit.,* vol. ii, cap. vi.

HERMAN, E.: *The Meaning and Value of Mysticism.* 1916.

PROUD, J. W.: "Traherne and Theophilus Gale," *Friend's Quarterly Examiner*, April 1916.
> "Thomas Traherne: A Divine Philosopher," *Friend's Quarterly Examiner*, 1917.

QUILLER-COUCH, SIR A.: *Studies in Literature.* 1918.

SHERER, G. R.: "More and Traherne," *Mod. Lang. Notes*, 1919.

WILLET, GLADYS E.: *Traherne: an Essay.* Cambridge, Heffer, 1919.
> "Traherne," *Spectator*, 124, 84–85, 1920.

TOWERS, F.: "Thomas Traherne: His Outlook on Life," *Nineteenth Century*, 1920.

PARKER, S. T. H.: "The Riches of Thomas Traherne," *Living Age*, 1922.

PAYNE, ARTHUR: "A Prose Poet. Thomas Traherne," *Educational Times*, 1922.

DAWSON, M. L.: "Thomas Traherne," *Times Literary Supplement*, 29th September 1927.

HOPKINSON, A. W.: "Thomas Traherne," *Times Literary Supplement*, 6th October 1927.

PRICE, C.: "Thomas Traherne," *Times Literary Supplement*, 27th October 1927.

WATKINS, ALFRED: "Thomas Traherne," *Times Literary Supplement*, 20th October 1927.

NAYLOR, E. W.: "Three Seventeenth-century Poet-Parsons (Thomas Traherne, George Herbert, Robert Herrick) and Music," *Proceedings of Musical Association*, London, 1928.

THOMPSON, ELBERT N. S.: "The Philosophy of Thomas Traherne," *Philological Quarterly*, 1929.

BEACHCROFT, T. O.: "Traherne and the Cambridge Platonists," *Dublin Review*, 186, 278–290, 1930.
> "Traherne and the Doctrine of Felicity," *Criterion*, 1930.

WADE, GLADYS I.: "The Manuscripts of the Poems of Thomas Traherne," *Modern Language Review*, 1931.
> "Traherne and the Spiritual Value of Nature Study," *London Quarterly Review*, 1934.
> "Thomas Traherne as Divine Philosopher," *Hibbert Journal*, 32, 400–408, 1934.
> "Mrs. Susanna Hopton," *English Review*, 1936.
> *Thomas Traherne, a Critical Biography with a Selected Bibliography of Criticism by R. A. Parker.* Princeton and Oxford University Presses, 1944.

MACAULAY, ROSE: *Some Religious Elements in English Literature.* 1932.

GRIGSON, G.: "The Transports of Thomas Traherne," *Bookman*, London, 1932.
> "Thomas Traherne," *Contemporary Review*, 1932.

WINTERBOTTOM, K. M.: "Certain Affinities to Wordsworth in the Poetry of Vaughan and Traherne." Unpublished dissertation, University of Pittsburgh, 1933.

LEISHMAN, JAMES B.: *The Metaphysical Poets: Donne, Herbert, Vaughan, Traherne.* Oxford, Clarendon, 1934.

IREDALE, Q.: *Thomas Traherne.* Oxford, Blackwell, 1935.

HOBHOUSE, S.: "A Poet's Resurrection," *Spectator*, 1936.

INDEX